ELECTRONIC COMMERCE

ON-LINE ORDERING AND DIGITAL MONEY

THIRD EDITION

Pete Loshin / John Vacca / Paul Murphy

CHARLES RIVER MEDIA, INC.
Hingham, Massachusetts

Production: Publishers' Design and Production Services
Cover Design: The Printed Image
Printer: InterCity Press, Rockland, MA.

CHARLES RIVER MEDIA, INC.
20 Downer Avenue
Suite 3
Hingham, MA 02043
781-740-0400
781-740-8816 (FAX)
www.charlesriver.com

This book is printed on acid-free paper.

Electronic Commerce, 3/E
Pete Loshin, John Vaccca, and Paul Murphy
ISBN: 1-58450-030-1
Printed in the U.S.A.

All brand names and product names mentioned in this book are trademarks or
service marks of their respective companies. Any omission or misuse (of any
kind) of service marks or trademarks should not be regarded as intent to
infringe on the property of others. The publisher recognizes and respects all
marks used by companies, manufacturers, and developers as a means to
distinguish their products.

Printed in the United States of America
01 7 6 5 4 3 2 First Edition

CHARLES RIVER MEDIA titles are available for site license or bulk purchase by
institutions, user groups, corporations, etc. For additional information,
please contact the Special Sales Department at 781-740-0400.

Requests for replacement of a defective CD must be accompanied by the
original disc, your mailing address, telephone number, date of purchase and
purchase price. Please state the nature of the problem, and send the information to
CHARLES RIVER MEDIA, INC., 20 Downer Avenue, Suite 3, Hingham, MA 02043. CRM's
sole obligation to the purchaser is to replace the disc, based on defective materials or faulty
workmanship, but not on the operation or functionality of the product.

Dedication

In memory of Giacchi and Agrippina.

Contents

Preface

On January 24, 1848, gold was discovered near the confluence of the American and Sacramento rivers in Northern California. As news of wild fortunes spread, people from all over the world descended on the previously unknown corner of America, creating the gold rush of the 1840s.

Today, a gold rush is also under way. However, instead of picks, shovels, and sifting pans, the tools are computers, electronic switches, routers, telephone lines, and programmers. Things are happening, not at the confluence of the American and Sacramento rivers, but on your desktop.

Despite the obvious tangible differences between the California gold rush of the 1840s and today's electronic commerce opportunities, both events have one thing in common: an undeniable level of excitement. A spirit of opportunity.

Today, merchants, software companies, and financial institutions are racing to provide the products and services that will make online purchasing as common and convenient as ordering by telephone or fax. Finding the best electronic commerce solution for your business or personal online shopping needs will be guided by several factors. Despite the daily flow of new products and alliances, services, and several years of hard work already behind us, it is still too early to announce the winners in the race to provide an electronic online marketplace. In addition to the search for more efficient and secure applications, there are still questions about what type of networks will be used. Many companies—and technologies—are still in their first few years of operation.

No matter whose products and services will be used, though, the foundation of the digital marketplace has already been laid. Logistics dictates that, in these early years, electronic commerce will be heavily oriented toward products that can be ordered and delivered through Internet connections (anything that can be digitized, from music to news to software to pictures), while the realities of the market require ease of use for both merchant and consumer. The continued perception of a lack of security and reliability inherent in the Internet's network architecture calls for the creation of commercial transaction methods and software that add both, for peace of mind all around.

This book introduces the issues involved in bringing business to the Internet—the obstacles to online commerce, as well as the advantages. Once the issues are laid out, we explain how advances in cryptography make it possible to reliably and securely transmit business information across unreliable and unsecure networks. Once the general concepts are presented, different current commercial schemes and systems are discussed in their proper perspective. After the various schemes are examined, other relevant and related issues can be discussed, including digital currencies, techniques for marketing on the Internet, and related services available to the online merchant.

Appendices include an Internet and networking glossary, a guide to locating the most current and complete electronic commerce resources on the Internet, a list of EDI codes, a guide to the companion CD-ROM, and a complete listing of the major e-commerce conferences and tradeshows.

CHAPTER 1: INTRODUCTION AND CONCEPTS

The idea of doing business electronically over networks is not new. We think nothing of ordering products from catalogs or TV by telephone, requesting information by fax, or using ATMs for banking. The promise of the Internet is to allow business to be transacted directly between consumer and merchant with instant response, no intermediaries, and virtually no overhead costs. The issues raised by electronic commerce include transaction security, authentication and certification of orders, and fulfillment. This chapter introduces the Internet and presents the benefits that can accrue from using the Internet for commerce, as well as the problems that must be resolved before such commerce is possible.

CHAPTER 2: SECURITY TECHNOLOGIES

Online commerce is impossible without working on the security and reliability problems. While some are attacking the problem by taking sensitive material offline, many others are using public key cryptography to encrypt sensitive information, to digitally *sign* orders and responses, and to make sure that messages have been transmitted unmodified.

This chapter explains why the Internet is inherently unsecure and unreliable, as well as why that does not necessarily keep transmissions from being secure and reliable. It also introduces the concepts behind public key cryptography, and explains how public key applications are implemented within the Internet to produce frameworks for secure commerce.

CHAPTER 3: ELECTRONIC PAYMENT METHODS

There are many approaches to the problem of transferring money from one individual to another. They range from using existing methods such as bank draft authorization and credit cards, to indirect use of existing methods (such as registering your payment information with a third party who processes all transactions, or registering it with the vendor outside of the public network and using an account number online), all the way to the use of digital currencies that permit the digital movement of cash endorsed by digital signatures.

This chapter examines the different general methods for processing electronic transactions. A brief discussion of the (apparently) more mundane methods of exchange, such as cash, check, and credit card, will highlight some of the obvious and not-so-obvious advantages and disadvantages. Electronic transaction options will then be examined, including the following.

- Encryption of payment information transmitted from buyer to seller.
- Use of an intermediary to handle transaction settlement and keep consumer payment private, even from merchants.
- Electronic checking, using digital signatures to authenticate the exchange of value between two individuals as if a check were used.
- Electronic currencies, using digital signature technology to authenticate the exchange of value between individuals with no intermediaries at all (allowing truly private exchange of money).

This chapter examines these alternatives in the context of actual systems and schemes that use them. Chapter 5 introduces a more comprehensive listing of industry players, and Chapters 6 through 8 highlight some of these companies and products in greater detail.

CHAPTER 4: PROTOCOLS FOR THE PUBLIC TRANSPORT OF PRIVATE INFORMATION

A universal medium of exchange is necessary to make electronic commerce work. Like a standard currency, a standard for transactions makes it possible for everyone to participate. Transactions are most often made through the World Wide Web, and add-on protocols that define the exchange of sensitive information across the Web have been defined and implemented. The Secure Sockets Layer (SSL) is a solution offered by Netscape Communications Corporation for use in its own secure Web products. The Secure Hypertext Transport Protocol (S-HTTP) is an extension of the Web's basic protocols that also allows the transmission of sensitive information.

There are other solutions and other protocols; many of the organizations offering electronic commerce solutions also offer their own protocols for moving transaction information among the buyer, the seller, and interested third parties such as banks and credit card authorizers. Some of these are discussed, primarily to highlight how they differ from each other. We also outline the basics of the still-developing Secure Electronic Transaction, or SET, protocol currently being developed by MasterCard and Visa.

CHAPTER 5: ELECTRONIC COMMERCE PROVIDERS

Billions of dollars are at stake in this industry, and there are many organizations looking for at least part of the bounty. Ranging from financial heavyweights such as Visa, MasterCard, and Wells Fargo Bank, to software giant Microsoft, to newcomers such as DigiCash and Netscape, the players today may not be the winners tomorrow—but that's the way to bet.

This chapter introduces a selection of the companies now offering electronic commerce products and services. Company contact information, product profiles, corporate background, and other pertinent information are included.

CHAPTER 6: ELECTRONIC PAYMENT SYSTEMS

Anything that makes it possible for a consumer to spend money online can be construed as an electronic payment system. As discussed earlier, these can be electronic checking systems, third-party systems (a third party handles the payment information, collecting money from the consumer through a credit card or checking account and then paying money to the merchant), or digital currency systems that allow direct interchange of values. These systems all share the requirement of some type of prior action on the part of all participants, both merchant and consumer. Profiled in this chapter are representative payment systems, all in current use.

CHAPTER 7: ONLINE COMMERCE ENVIRONMENTS

Online commerce environments, unlike payment systems, tend not to make assumptions about customers, nor do they necessarily require the consumer to take any specific prior action to be able to use them. The simplest example would be a secure Web server that encrypts the customer's credit card information prior to transmitting it to the merchant across the Internet. Though a credit card is required, no special preparation is necessary prior to placing an order, and the merchant handles the rest—possibly processing the process by hand through a *traditional* credit card authorization process.

More commonly, though, secure server vendors will be seeking to maximize the benefits of electronic commerce by automating payment authorization, order fulfillment, account management, and other functions. Commerce environments can also coexist with payment systems by facilitating their use; just as traditional merchants now accept payment by various credit and charge cards, checks, and cash, electronic merchants will be able to accept payment through a variety of different payment systems. Like the preceding and following chapters, this one examines in more detail a sampling of currently available electronic commerce software.

CHAPTER 8: DIGITAL CURRENCIES

Digital currencies can be considered a special case of the electronic payment system, though they are not necessarily limited to the World Wide Web, the Internet, or even networks in general. Government agencies around the world are keeping especially close watch on these systems, since they could enable the virtually instantaneous and anonymous transfer of unlimited funds, making a mockery of tax and currency-transfer statutes. This chapter examines a widely available prototype for digital cash, and discusses in greater detail how digital cash works.

CHAPTER 9: STRATEGIES, TECHNIQUES, AND TOOLS

There has been a flood of books discussing strategic marketing on the Internet; however, given that Internet marketing is in its infancy, there are no time-proven strategies yet available. This chapter discusses some of the options open to consumers and merchants, as well as ways to safely and happily transact business across Internet connections.

CHAPTER 10: DESIGNING AND BUILDING E-COMMERCE WEB SITES: HANDS-ON

Like the recent *real TV* show *Survivor*, survival strategies can take many forms. In this chapter, the crucial business objectives (building the right team, merchandising, listening to customers, etc.) and several survival strategies for the site itself are described.

CHAPTER 11: E-COMMERCE ENVIRONMENTS AND FUTURE DIRECTIONS

The growth of business-to-business (B2B) electronic commerce is being driven by lower purchasing costs, reductions in inventories, shorter cycle times, more efficient and effective customer service, lower sales and marketing costs, and new sales opportunities. This final chapter does not attempt to size the current market or predict the size of the future market. Instead, it describes the underlying drivers of growth of business-to-business electronic commerce, using specific company and industry examples as illustrations. The chapter also focuses on three specific areas of business-to-business e-commerce: electronic data interchange (EDI), supply-chain management (SCM), and the outlook for electronic commerce.

APPENDIX A: INTERNET GLOSSARY AND ABBREVIATIONS

The Internet's history as a research project done largely for the U.S. military may have something to do with its propensity for often opaque acronyms, and as a new technology it comes with its own unique terminology. This appendix should help both the technical and non-technical reader to decipher some of these terms and acronyms.

APPENDIX B: ELECTRONIC COMMERCE ONLINE RESOURCES

Information about the Internet has always been some of the most easily obtained material on the Internet. There is a wealth of information about transacting business through Internet connections, as well as pointers to participating organizations. This appendix should be useful to anyone who wants to locate the latest news.

APPENDIX C: GUIDE TO THE CD-ROM

This appendix offers a brief guide to the contents of the companion CD-ROM, as well as instructions for using it.

APPENDIX D: ELECTRONIC DATA INTERCHANGE CODES

ANSI X12 transaction sets can be grouped together by business functionality. This appendix lists all of the EDI ANSI X12 transaction set codes.

APPENDIX E: LISTING OF E-COMMERCE CONFERENCES

This appendix lists the major e-commerce conferences and trade shows, including contact information regarding upcoming conference dates and locations.

APPENDIX F: PDG SHOPPING CART

This appendix examines the PDG Shopping Cart (PDG Software's core product that serves as a complete e-commerce solution), which is included in CD-ROM as a free, 30-day trial version for both Microsoft Windows NT and multiple UNIX platforms. Some of PDG Shopping Cart's most notable features are also examined.

Acknowledgments

There are many people whose efforts on this book have contributed to its successful completion. I owe each a debt of gratitude and want to take this opportunity to offer my sincere thanks.

A very special thanks to my publisher, David Pallai, without whose initial interest and support would not have made this book possible; and for his guidance and encouragement over and above the business of being a publisher. Thanks to my copyeditor, Beth A. Roberts, whose fine editorial work has been invaluable. Thanks also to my marketing manager, whose efforts are greatly appreciated. And, a special thanks to Michael Erbschloe who wrote the Foreword. Finally, thanks to all of the other people at Charles River Media whose many talents and skills are essential to a finished book.

Thanks to my wife, Bee Vacca, for her love, her help, and her understanding of my long work hours.

Finally, I wish to thank the organizations and individuals who granted me permission to use the research material and information necessary for the completion of this book.

Foreword

The ways in which companies can benefit from using the Internet are increasing every day. There are new marketplaces. There are new marketing, sales, and customer service methods. The worlds of business and consumers have rapidly become the wired and connected world. It is truly an exciting time to be business.

However, *dotcom* funerals have become as frequent and as regular as rain in the tropics. Has something gone wrong? Was the dream of e-commerce a false and deceptive fantasy? No, the Internet is still real, and there is still a world of new opportunity opening up for both businesses and consumers.

Something did go wrong, however. As companies attempted to move part or all of their business practices and operations to the Internet, many were not prudent and did not have a good basic understanding of Internet business opportunities and limitations. Too many companies tried to move too fast into a future that was not yet a reality. They had hopes and dreams, but failed to recognize real opportunity because they were lost in buzzwords and jargon and blinded by greed.

To win on the Internet, you must understand where the opportunity is today and how to prepare for tomorrow. This book is a guide to reality. It shows you where there is opportunity. It also shows you how to benefit from using the Internet as a practical business tool, and how to reap benefits quickly and permanently. This book shows you how to succeed where others have failed.

There are many building blocks in the world of electronic commerce. This book explains Internet business models, business applications that can be supported on the Internet, and how companies can benefit from using new models and new tools. Don't deceive yourself. Don't think you know it all already. The dead dotcoms thought they knew how to do it, but they didn't. You need a good grasp on the models and the potential applications, and this book provides you with that understanding.

You need to know the building blocks, but you also need to know how to put those blocks together in a winning combination to build a good foundation for your business to grow and thrive in the world of electronic commerce. The blocks are just like parts to a puzzle. They will not work unless you properly combine tools and methods, and know how to exploit opportunity. This book explains how to mix the essential building blocks into a working and winning combination that can help drive your business in new directions.

After you learn about the parts and how to put them together to supercharge your company, you will also need to know how and where to drive your new business machine. Other how-to-do-business-on-the-Internet books will leave you high and dry. This book shows you how to drive your business like a race car, how to steer through uncertainty, and how to grip the road so you do not end up in a dotcom graveyard.

However, you need to understand more than just the gas pedal if you are going to succeed in electronic commerce. Entering the world of e-commerce is like going on a safari or expedition into unexplored lands. You need to be able to navigate your business into uncharted territory. You will need balance, intuition, and considerable daring if you are going to maximize the tools of the Internet. You need to know where the edge of the cliff is and how to not fall off, like so many of those who came before you. That is the big pay-off of this book.

This book provides you with a good foundation, the ability to understand and assemble parts into a functioning whole, how to steer through rough terrain, how to navigate through uncertainty, and how to live to tell about it. Before you go down the path of electronic commerce, read this book. If you are already on the electronic highway and you are concerned about stability and your future, read this book. If you are stuck somewhere on the Internet and do not know where to turn, read this book. Don't be afraid to move ahead, to move to the Net—just know where you want to go and how to get there. Read this book!

Michael Erbschloe
Vice President of Research
Computer Economics
Carlsbad, California

1 ⁝ Introduction and Concepts

"We are an all-IBM shop, but thanks for calling."

—A TYPICAL END TO A TELEPHONE CONVERSATION FROM A SALES REPRESENTATIVE
OFFERING NON-IBM HARDWARE AND SOFTWARE TO A LARGE CORPORATION.

There are thousands of definitions used to describe the Internet. One of the most popular is the concept of a *standard*. For years, the major forces in the computer (personal, midrange, and mainframe) industry were building proprietary systems, and customers were committing to one-vendor solutions. This practice slowed the ability to share information.

At the most fundamental level, the Internet is a series of standards for three basic tasks:

- Sharing a file with one or more parties
- Sharing e-mail with one or more parties
- Allowing the user of one computer system to log on to another computer system

From these three functions, Internet applications like the World Wide Web, file transfer, telnet, and others are created.

The growth of the Internet is accredited to the widespread acceptance and implementation of the Internet standards. After all, if everyone is using the same basic method to send and receive e-mail, files, etc., it does not matter what systems are used.

In the business world, although we have different currencies, we already have existing standards for exchanging money. Chances are that you used a credit card or check to pay for this book.

The focus of this book is to shed light on the collision of these two industries/standards. The ultimate goal for the electronic commerce industry is to make conducting business with your computer as pain- and worry-free as using your credit cards or checkbook.

But, what do we mean by electronic commerce (e-commerce)?

WHAT IS ELECTRONIC COMMERCE?

The term *electronic commerce* has evolved from its meager notion of electronic shopping to mean all aspects of business and market processes enabled by the Internet and the World Wide Web technologies.

Electronic Commerce as Online Selling

Narrowly defined, electronic commerce means doing business online, or selling and buying products and services through Web storefronts. Products being traded may be physical products such as used cars or services (arranging trips, online medical consultation, and remote education). Increasingly, they include digital products such as news, audio and video, database, software and all types of knowledge-based products. It appears then that electronic commerce is similar to catalog shopping or home shopping on cable TV.

Electronic Commerce as a Market

Electronic commerce is not limited to buying and selling products online. For example, a neighborhood store can open a Web store and find the world at its doorstep. Along with customers, it will also find its suppliers, accountants, payment services, government agencies, and competitors online. These online or digital partners demand changes in the way we do business from production to consumption, and they will affect companies that might think they are not part of electronic commerce. Along with online selling, electronic commerce will lead to significant changes in the way products are customized, distributed and exchanged, and the way consumers search and bargain for products and services.

In short, the electronic commerce revolution has had an effect on processes—a process-oriented effect. The process-oriented definition of electronic commerce offers a broader view of what electronic commerce is. Within-business processes (manufacturing, inventorying, corporate financial management, operation), business-to-business processes (supply-chain management, bidding) are affected by the same technology and network as are business-to-consumer processes. Even government functions, education, and social and political processes undergo changes. So why should one care about e-commerce? Let's take a look.

Why Care about E-Commerce?

Participants in the electronic marketplace (See the sidebar, "What Is the Electronic Marketplace?") are not limited to so-called digital product companies such as those in publishing, software, entertainment, and information industries. The Digital Age and the digital revolution affect all of us by virtue of their process innovations. At the least, through WebTV and digital television, the way we watch TV news and entertainment programs will change. Changes in telecommunication will affect the way we receive information, product announcements, orders, etc. As telephones, fax machines, copiers, PCs, and printers are essential ingredients in doing business, so will be e-mail, Web sites, and integrated digital communications and computing.

While today's office business machines are not integrated (faxed orders have to be typed on computers), the much talked-about convergence will drive all this equipment into one digital platform. The digital platform could be a computer connected to the Internet and intranets, or a new device capable of interacting with other devices—because that device will prove to be more efficient and productive.

 Will platforms or devices be easier to use? That depends on how developers and industry leaders promote interoperability and standardization.

Even seemingly mundane bookstores face different challenges in the electronic marketplace by virtue of having digital processes in their business operations. The recent case of Amazon.com versus Barnes & Noble shows that the very definition of stores has to be reevaluated. This also touches upon the issue of taxable nexus and sales tax collection on the Internet.

Distributing books requires numerous local outlets (local bookstores) to provide convenient access to customers. At the same time, various book clubs have used mail order distribution for many decades. Taking this direction into the Internet, Amazon.com has become the leading online bookstore, billing itself as the largest bookstore on earth, not by opening

What Is the Electronic Marketplace?

Electronic markets ordinarily refer to online trading and auctions; for example, online stock trading markets, and online auctions for computers and other goods. The *electronic marketplace* refers to the emerging market economy where producers, intermediaries, and consumers interact electronically or digitally in some way. The electronic marketplace is a virtual representative of physical markets. The economic activities undertaken by this electronic marketplace collectively represent the digital economy. Electronic commerce, broadly defined, is concerned with the electronic marketplace.

The electronic marketplace resembles physical markets (the ones we know) in many aspects. As in physical markets, components of the digital economy include:

- Players (market agents such as firms, suppliers, brokers, shops, and consumers)
- Products (goods and services)
- Processes (supply, production, marketing, competition, distribution, consumption, etc.)

The difference is that, in the electronic marketplace, at least some of these components are electronic, digital, virtual, or online (whichever term you may prefer). For example, a digital player is someone with e-mail or a Web page. Purely physical sellers may be selling a digital product (digital CD-ROM). One that sells physical products at a physical store may offer product information online (thereby allowing consumers to search online), while production, ordering, payment, and delivery are done conventionally. Currently, the emphasis is on the core of the electronic marketplace where everything (all value chains or business activities) is online. If any aspect of your business or consumption dwells upon the digital process, you are already part of the electronic marketplace. That is, almost all of us are already players in the electronic marketplace!

How Is the Electronic Marketplace Different from Physical Markets?

Business strategies must be based on a sound understanding of the market dynamics, for which we rely on standard economics. So, is the electronic marketplace a perfect, frictionless market? Will transaction costs become zero? Will the market be perfectly competitive, yielding lowest possible prices? Should the market be left alone to march toward those predictions?

On the surface, the electronic marketplace appears to be something of a perfect market, where there are numerous worldwide sellers and buyers, who in turn have bountiful information about the market and products, and where no intermediaries are necessary. Such a market is very competitive and efficient (with no need to regulate or intervene arbitrarily).

However, a closer look indicates that consumer searches are not very efficient (due to the cost of having a complete, easily searchable database, and because sellers may not provide all information necessary). Although wholesalers and retail outlets may not be needed, other types of intermediaries appear to be essential for the electronic market to function adequately (certification authorities, electronic malls that guarantee product quality, mediators for bargaining and conflict resolution, etc.). All these brokers add transaction costs.

Will prices be lower? Digital products are highly customizable due to their transmutability (easy to revise, reorganize, and edit). With information about consumer tastes, products will be differentiated or customized (custom news). The number of potential sellers may be low, or even only one, in a highly differentiated and segmented market; and the price will tend to approach the maximum price the buyer is willing to pay.

NOTE: *In economic terms, sellers practice first-degree or perfect-price discrimination, which is the exact opposite of the result we get in a perfectly competitive market.*

How about the often heard zero marginal cost argument that digital products will be priced at zero (given out free) because their reproduction costs will be minimal? The price will approach zero only if:

1. The marginal cost is really approaching zero.
2. There is effective competition among sellers.

In short, the marginal cost of a digital product may be substantial. Even when it is close to zero, prices in a noncompetitive market will be determined more by demand (or the buyer's willingness to pay) than by marginal cost. Unless we think all information and digital products are of no value, they will never be priced at zero by sellers with market power.

NOTE: *Giving out free products today does not mean that sellers are doing it because the costs are zero nor that they will continue to do so when they monopolize the market.*[1]

numerous branch stores but via the Internet. The biggest bookstore Barnes & Noble, with a towering share of revenues and physical book stores, has been forced to respond to Amazon.com's challenge by opening its own Web store and by bringing a law suit against its challenger. What are the competitive strategies of these two bookstores? Will any business selling physical products face a similar competition? Probably so!

Types of Electronic Commerce Technology

There are many types of e-commerce technologies, and it is beyond the scope of this chapter and book to cover them all. However, we will discuss the most important. With that in mind, we will briefly examine the following technologies:

- Business-to-Business Electronic Commerce
- Customer Relationship Management
- Data Warehousing Solutions
- Distributed Training for the Modern Enterprise
- Electronic Mail
- Enterprise Resource Planning Solutions
- Sales Force Automation: Remote Networking Solutions Increase the Productivity of Mobile Sales Professionals
- The Call Center Revolution: Converged Networks Enable Integrated Customer Service Solutions
- Managed Network Services[2]
- Business-to-Business Electronic Commerce

Electronic business (e-business) is a technology-enabled application environment to facilitate the exchange of business information and automate commercial transactions. E-business encompasses the exchange of many kinds of information, including online commercial transactions, commonly referred to as *e-commerce*. Thus, online marketing to consumers via the Internet, known as business-to-consumer (B2C) e-commerce, is only one of several fronts on the e-business landscape. E-business is also driving deep and profound changes in the structure and business practices of organizations and the interactions between businesses. Business-to-business (B2B) e-commerce includes a variety of applications and networking technologies designed to automate and optimize interactions between business partners. This technology is discussed in greater detail in Chapter 11, "E-Commerce Environments and Future Directions."

Customer Relationship Management

In today's business climate, marketing programs must focus on value-oriented differentiation to be successful. Increasingly, businesses are seeking to leverage the customer relationship to win and maintain customer loyalty. Customer relationship management (CRM) fosters a single, enterprise view of the customer for the purpose of cultivating high-quality relationships that lead to improved loyalty and profits. In addition to helping to identify and retain customers with a high-profitability profile, CRM is emerging as a critical success factor in both electronic commerce and supply chain management initiatives. See Chapter 3, "Electronic Payment Methods," for more information on this e-commerce technology.

DATA WAREHOUSING SOLUTIONS

A data warehouse is an integrated, multi-subject repository containing highly detailed historical data. It accepts and processes queries for a group of end users. It also is a complex system that requires a distinct architecture to successfully deliver sophisticated support for business decisions. See Chapter 11 for more information on this e-commerce technology.

DISTRIBUTED TRAINING FOR THE MODERN ENTERPRISE

Today's business environment rewards companies whose employees can rapidly acquire new skills and information, and companies that can quickly train customers to use new technologies as they become available. There is a great need for distributed training, also known as *distance learning*, in today's enterprise. It consists of three classic applications: professional development of corporate employees, sales force training, and customer and reseller training. It also provides recommendations for network infrastructure designs to support each of the three. See Chapter 11 for more information on this e-commerce technology.

ELECTRONIC MAIL

Electronic mail enables networked collaboration among key members of a business team, allowing faster and more intelligent decision-making. In the past several years, e-mail has evolved far beyond the exchange of simple text messages into a universal messaging framework that delivers rich multimedia content in support of complex business processes such as calendaring and workflow management.

E-mail has attracted interest among business executives and IT staff alike who understand that communication among employees plays a critical role in competitive success. Unlike more specialized applications that are targeted to specific user groups, e-mail reaches virtually everyone in the organization. However, while it extends to every corner of the enterprise, few people have recognized the demands that e-mail can place on the enterprise's IT infrastructure. The fact is that effective support for today's e-mail environment requires nothing less than consistent, high-performance network services for the entire enterprise. See Chapter 10. "Designing and Building E-Commerce Web Sites: Hands-On," for more information on this e-commerce technology.

ENTERPRISE RESOURCE PLANNING SOLUTIONS

Enterprise resource planning (ERP) application suites help corporations maintain a competitive advantage by providing a software architecture that automates and integrates a wide range of business processes. ERP helps companies to be more responsive to changing markets and to deliver better service at a lower cost. However, implementing ERP solutions involves significant architectural and organizational challenges as well. For large companies, ERP applications often force organizations to completely rethink IT strategies. Network performance and availability become paramount, while package customization replaces traditional application development. These shifts start with applications developers and drive changes throughout an organization. See Chapter 11 for more information on this e-commerce technology.

SALES FORCE AUTOMATION: REMOTE NETWORKING SOLUTIONS INCREASE THE PRODUCTIVITY OF MOBILE SALES PROFESSIONALS

A growing number of enterprises are implementing applications to provide their sales professionals with access to customer information and other valuable business data from the road. The potential return on investment (ROI) of such applications is very compelling. By automating various functions such as scheduling presentations, tracking issues, managing customer information, and coordinating customer care, corporations can reduce their overall cost of sales and enable sales teaming to increase the efficiency of each sales individual. This prospect has led many organizations to purchase laptops equipped with basic applications for their salespeople. However, application capabilities and features have typically been rudimentary and very inconsistent from individual to individual. As a result, the cost of maintaining a networked sales force has been high and the ROI has not generally been realized. See Chapter 11 for more information on this e-commerce technology.

THE CALL CENTER REVOLUTION: CONVERGED NETWORKS ENABLE INTEGRATED CUSTOMER SERVICE SOLUTIONS

Customer service centers have become profit centers for many businesses. According to the Direct Marketing Association, direct sales and marketing via call centers accounted for $466 billion, or 47 percent, of total business-to-business sales in 1998.[3]

The fact is that call centers have become essential to the survival of a growing number of businesses. What financial services institution could compete today without a call center? Companies of every size and type are beginning to realize that investing in state-of-the-art call center capabilities can be their single best competitive differentiator. A well-designed call center can enable the organization to (see Chapter 10 for more information on this e-commerce technology):

- Improve customer intimacy and retention
- Increase competitiveness by taking advantage of emerging technologies
- Increase revenue through broader opportunities to sell
- Increase employee productivity by streamlining business processes[4]

MANAGED NETWORK SERVICES

Every business organization today needs an IT infrastructure that can extend globally to all prospective customers, employees, suppliers, and partners; and that can enable innovative and efficient business processes. However, few organizations have the internal resources to ensure the stable operation of such an e-business-ready network infrastructure.

This situation creates a tremendous opportunity for service providers to offer value-added managed network services (MNS), including voice/data integration services, virtual private network (VPN) services, business-to-business extranets, guaranteed service levels, and application outsourcing. Analysts estimate that the market for such services is as much as $48 billion per year. See Chapters 2, 3, 4, 5, and 11 for more information on this e-commerce technology.

NETWORKS AND COMMERCIAL TRANSACTIONS

The idea of doing business electronically over networks is nothing new: We think nothing of ordering the products we've seen advertised on television or in printed catalogs with a phone call or a fax, and ATMs are always within reach for quick, easy, and automatic banking. Corporations advertise through broadcasting networks, and consumers flock to local outlets of national and international franchise networks. As the world becomes increasingly interconnected, particularly through the Internet with its open protocols, forward-looking businesses will be able to make their products available to a global market, the largest possible market, without having to create and maintain their own private networks for sales, delivery, and customer support.

Although the techniques for attracting consumer attention, describing products, and delivering them electronically will all be of interest to those who wish to participate in this new market, this book simply explains how business transactions can be executed across an unreliable and unsecure medium like the Internet, and discusses some of the methods currently being planned and implemented; in other words, how you will be buying and selling in the future, and how it will work.

The number of businesses devoted to promoting commerce on the Internet has been growing exponentially since the end of 1997, but they all share the goal of making commercial transactions over the Internet safe, simple, and secure—and earning a profit in the process. The methods employed to achieve these ends are somewhat more various, but can be categorized as either creating secure and reliable channels to carry transactions across Internet connections (which are inherently unsecure and unreliable), or using more traditional channels to carry sensitive information.

Electronic merchants need to feel confident that they can safely market and deliver their products, get paid for all products purchased, and not lose any product to theft. Electronic consumers need to feel confident that they can safely select and take delivery of products, pay for them, and not be concerned about compromise of payment information (such as credit card or bank account numbers). Everyone wants to feel confident that the individuals they deal with across the Internet are who they say they are, to avoid losses to fraud.

THE INTERNET AND OTHER NOVELTIES

The apparent overnight success of the Internet blindsided many people. In fact, the Internet has its roots in internetworking research that began in 1969 (the same year people first walked on the moon), and it has been steadily doubling in size roughly every year. Consider some of the other technologies introduced since 1969 that have become ubiquitous: the videocassette recorder (VCR), cable access television (CATV), automatic teller machine (ATM), compact disc (CD), personal computer (PC), and cellular telephone, to name just a few.

The Internet functions as a medium for data transmission in much the same way that the international telephone network functions as a medium for voice (and other signal) transmissions. The telephone system consists of connections (and the required supporting hardware and cabling) to people, organizations, and devices (answering and fax machines, computers, and others), but does not include those things—nor does it include the signals being sent over it. Similarly, one can say that the Internet consists of the connections (and the required supporting hardware and cabling) between networks, but not the data stored on and made accessible from those networks.

As shown in Figure 1.1, the standard representation of the Internet is as a cloud, to stress the fact that there is something going on between systems communicating across the Internet. That something encompasses any number of intermediate computers and networks (discussed in slightly more detail in Chapter 2, "Security Technologies"), but it is not necessary to know exactly what it is to be able to use it.

There are no worldwide organizations "running" the Internet, any more than there are such organizations "running" the global telecommunications network. Instead, there are standard bodies for both networks who define the rules (or protocols) to be used by anyone connecting to those networks. If the rules are properly implemented, then the telephone, fax, or computer will be able to pass signals to and from the network. In other words, if your telephone company conforms to the Consultative

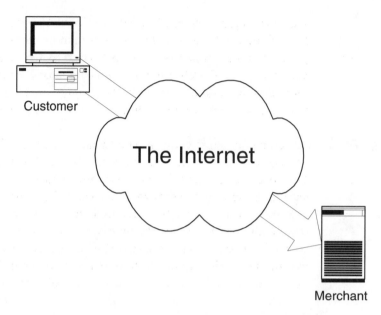

Customer

The Internet

Merchant

FIGURE 1.1 Consumers can gain access to an Internet merchant's system across the Internet without having to know anything about the intervening networks.

Committee for International Telephone & Telegraph (CCITT)—Comite Consultatif International de Telegraphique et Telephonique (International Telegraph and Telephone Consultative Committee)—now known as the International Telecommunication Union-Telecommunication (ITU-T)—a standards organization for telecommunications) protocols, you can talk to anyone connected to the global telephone network, as long as their telephone company also conforms to those protocols. If you subscribe to a telephone service that has implemented its own proprietary protocols, however, you may find yourself limited in who you can connect to (or at least in how you can make a connection).

The same goes for the Internet: The Internet Architecture Board (IAB) provides oversight to the Internet Engineering Task Force (IETF), which is responsible for evaluating and defining Internet protocols. If you are using a computer connected to a network that conforms to the Internet protocols and is connected to the global Internet, you can exchange data with any other computer connected to the global Internet, as long as that computer also conforms to the Internet protocols. If you connect to some other type of internetwork, you may have problems connecting to the Internet.

NOTE *The Internet protocols are also known as TCP/IP, for the two most central protocols defining internetwork transmissions: the Transmission Control Protocol (TCP) and the Internet Protocol (IP). These protocols, and the many others included in the TCP/IP suite, define how Internet traffic is passed between computers and between networks; how information is passed between communicating systems; and how the Internet functions as a network of networks.*

Using the right protocols won't guarantee connectivity, though, unless you actually have some point of connection to the desired large network. Your organization could have a telephone and a computer on every desk, with both connected to the organizational switchboard and network. However, without a connection between the organization and the outside world, you could use those facilities only for internal communication. As shown in Figure 1.2, an organizational internetwork has to be connected to the Internet for it to be accessible outside the organization using the Internet protocols.

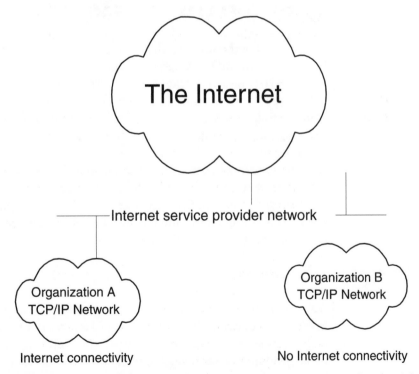

FIGURE 1.2 You can connect to the Internet as long as you are using the right protocols AND are connected to the Internet.

NETWORKS AND ELECTRONIC TRANSACTIONS TODAY

When considering online commerce, it is important to maintain a perspective and define a context. Broadcasting networks, particularly television networks, have a long history of being used to market products, although viewers cannot use that same medium to place orders. With widespread use of credit cards, consumers and merchants have been happily transacting business over the telephone network for many years. Highly sensitive banking transactions have been routinely processed through Asynchronous Transfer Mode (ATM) networks since the late 1970s.

Once participants in the electronic marketplace understand the mechanisms set up for transacting business across the Internet, buying and selling online will be at least as simple and trusted a method as buying by telephone or in person.

A MODEL FOR COMMERCIAL TRANSACTIONS

Understanding the ways in which commercial transactions take place online, across the Internet, requires understanding the way in which any commercial transaction takes place. There will be differences between different types of transactions. Although the way a large corporation buys raw materials in bulk from its supplier is different from the way the schoolchild buys candy at the corner drugstore, both transactions share certain characteristics.

Let us examine some of the issues involved in electronic commerce by looking at what happens in the course of any commercial transaction. We'll focus on the issues involved in simple retail transactions, since virtually everyone is familiar and comfortable with this type of transaction.

ESTABLISHING TRUST

Before any purchase can be made from a retail store, a customer must enter it. Most shops are open to the public, so all it takes is for a customer to walk in. However, this is not always the case: The merchant may control access to the goods it offers in several different ways. It can sell to any and all comers through an open storefront, or it can restrict its sales to a certain clientele (wholesalers may sell only to resellers; exclusive merchants may do business only with referred customers). The merchant can decide which customers to give access to its merchandise, and how that access is provided.

The consumer also makes choices prior to entering a store. The consumer must determine, often by just looking in a display window, whether the establishment carries the product being sought and whether the establishment is a reliable place to do business. To entice customers, the merchant may display brand names of the products carried, stickers on the door indicating payment methods accepted, and sample products. Additional customer acceptance can also be gained through use of a well-known company name, by being a branch or a franchise holder of a nationally known company.

The degree to which the merchant will restrict access to its products will vary, depending on the type of business. An automobile dealer will require a driver's license before permitting a test drive; although most bookstores don't mind strangers browsing through their books, some encourage it with tables and comfortable chairs for browsers. Likewise, buyers may be more careful about selecting vendors of products that can affect their health or well-being (such as prescription drugs or safety items) or are expensive (such as automobiles or computers) than they are about buying products that are relatively benign (household items or musical recordings) or inexpensive (newspapers or chewing gum).

The merchant and the consumer establish a level of trust in the other. The merchant trusts that the consumer is a potential purchaser, capable of selecting and paying for some product offered; the consumer trusts that the merchant may be offering the desired product and will be capable of delivering (and servicing, if necessary) that product if needed. As we will see later, if the two parties actually come to an agreement, a higher level of trust may be required.

There are other identity issues that both buyer and seller are concerned with when first initiating contact. Many products have distribution limits. For example:

- Prescription drugs may not be dispensed to anyone without a legitimate prescription.
- Alcoholic beverages may not be sold to minors, and may be subject to other sales restrictions (may not be sold on Sundays, for example) depending on the locality.
- Firearms and ammunition are subject to a wide range of restrictions, varying by locality.

■   Tobacco products may not be sold to minors.
■   "Adult" entertainment products may be subject to local restrictions on sales to minors.

Establishing trust between parties in a commercial transaction that takes place across a public network is difficult. While the merchant can use judgment during in-person transactions (the white-haired customer does not have to show ID to buy a six-pack of beer), online transactions offer no opportunity to exercise judgment because it is difficult to correlate identities on the Internet with actual individuals. Electronic merchants cannot afford to trust everyone—or even to trust anyone.

The same goes for the consumer. There is no way to tell how long a Web page has been in existence, or whether it will be there tomorrow. Constructing a counterfeit Web page, representing itself as part of a large corporation, is much easier than constructing a counterfeit retail outlet, restaurant, or supermarket, and potentially more lucrative.

Online transactions require mechanisms for establishing trust between prospective buyers and sellers.

NEGOTIATING A DEAL

Determining the item to be purchased, and the price to be charged, are trivial matters in most retail stores. The buyer selects the desired item, and the price is usually clearly marked either on the item itself or near its display area. In most cases, this is all that is necessary.

However, when the desired item is not immediately available (the desired color, size, flavor, version is not in stock), the retailer may have to order the product or offer an alternative deal, perhaps selling a similar item for a similar price or extending a special price to be applied at a later time (like rain checks offered by supermarkets on products that are on special but out of stock).

The validity of the merchant's offering price, as well as the exact identity of the item desired by the consumer, is easy to determine in a retail store. Electronic transactions sometimes require special mechanisms to ensure that the buyer did, in fact, place an order, and that the seller did, in fact, offer the product for the specified price.

Such mechanisms are a requirement if electronic transactions are to be kept free of fraud. When you select an item from a store's shelf, pay for it, and walk away with it, there is no question about what was bought and at what price. When you order products by telephone from a catalog, you can refer to the price in the catalog (but you still make a leap of faith that the order-taker accurately records your purchase order and will not abscond with your credit card number). Ordering products over the Internet does not offer an explicit method to reference the offering price, nor does it offer an explicit method to reference the original order.

Neither the buyer nor the seller should be able to repudiate the offered price or the products ordered; mechanisms to accomplish this are available for electronic commerce.

PAYMENT AND SETTLEMENT

At the heart of any transaction is the exchange of values, generally some standardized currency traded for some product or service. Probably because we are so accustomed to purchasing items in person, the process seems to be straightforward: The buyer gives cash, a check, or a credit card, and receives in return the product being purchased and a receipt.

Translating these actions into electronic form takes some doing. Many participants will want the entire process to be private; after all, most consumers would not announce their credit card numbers out loud in a crowded store—and some would prefer to purchase certain items or services anonymously. There are mechanisms that allow payment information to be kept private, by encrypting it, by keeping it entirely offline, or by using third parties to settle transactions.

In the store, the transaction is completed as soon as the buyer pays for an item; the buyer can then walk away with the purchase. Over the Internet, unless the product being purchased is available digitally (information, pictures, software, or other information-based products), the buyer must trust the seller to deliver the goods. One way the consumer can avoid problems is by patronizing trusted Internet vendors; another way is to use a major credit card company that will back up the consumer in the event of a problem with a vendor.

The vendor takes a smaller risk when selling online, since credit cards can be authenticated through automated connections to settlement companies. This is similar to the authentication done in person when a clerk uses a credit card authorization terminal ("swipe box") to verify a credit card. Both parties to an online transaction can benefit from the use of *digital signatures*, which are discussed in Chapter 2.

PAYMENT VEHICLES AND CURRENCIES

A great deal of attention is focused on consummation of the online transaction—, as it should be, since this is the point at which values are exchanged. The offline buyer has many options for transacting exchanges, of which the most common is cash, universally accepted and totally anonymous; personal check, providing an audit trail and a paper record of the transaction; and credit, charge, or ATM card, offering audit trails, guarantees for recourse through the sponsoring credit card company, and no-questions-asked credit extension.

When presented in person, all these payment methods are subject to some degree of scrutiny. Merchants may examine large-denomination bills for counterfeits (or refuse to accept large bills); may accept personal checks only if the customer offers sufficient personal identification (or cash checks only for frequent customers); and may verify identity and signature when accepting credit cards (as well as getting payment authorizations through settlement companies).

Similar mechanisms for using electronic currencies, personal checks, and credit cards are available for electronic transactions. Digital currencies are being developed to allow anonymous transactions across public networks such as the Internet. Digital signature technologies permit the authentication and certification of digitally transmitted documents like personal checks. These transactions, including credit card transactions, can all use special encryption methods to ensure reliability and privacy.

Finally, digital currencies need not be limited to digital representation of actual currencies. Other units of exchange may be used, whether they are barter units, airline frequent flier miles, or some other unit of exchange. Likewise, since there is no reason to limit currencies to a single "real" currency, international currency exchanges and transfers could become virtually instantaneous and untraceable: a prospect that many governments would prefer not to have to contend with.

PRODUCTS AND DELIVERY

You can't stuff a food processor or football or even a computer down a wire, so merchants selling products with a physical presence electronically still have to physically deliver them to the customer. Merchants who wish to sell physical items need to inspire a greater level of trust in their customers; after all, those customers must wait for a delivery, and they may not be convinced the product will arrive until it arrives. Merchants may allay some of these fears by giving the buyer detailed delivery information (when the product will be packed and shipped, how the product is to be shipped, approximate delivery date or time).

Digital products, however, that can be delivered electronically increasingly are being sold electronically. Figure 1.3 shows the relation between online accessibility and scale of various digital products. Information products such as news articles, information from databases, and other traditional text or data items can all be delivered immediately after purchase over a network connection.

It isn't always practical to sell information products this way, though. The text of a 600-page book may only consist of about a megabyte of data, and transferring that amount of data across a typical 56-Kbps (thousand bits per second) dial-up connection would take at least three minutes or so. However, graphical elements such as photographs, drawings, and tables can add significantly to the amount of data to be transmitted. In either

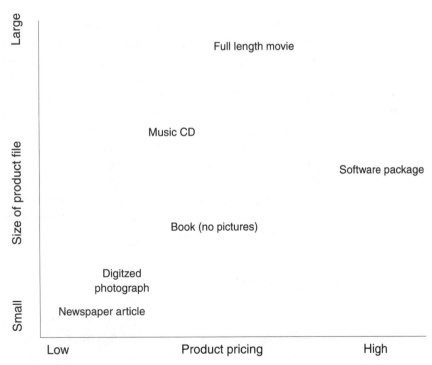

FIGURE 1.3 Opportunities for online selling of digital products will depend on price as well as the completeness of the product purchased when compared to traditional retail outlets.

case, book readers still find it preferable to read the printed page rather than on screen. Whether selling books electronically is or is not a good thing, it is not yet entirely practical.

Photographs and other images can be digitized and sold electronically. Small black-and-white snapshots may take only a few seconds to transfer across the typical modem connection; larger photos scanned at higher resolutions and in color may take up to a minute or more. There is already a brisk trade in images across the Internet, particularly those with an erotic content.

There are many more information products than books and images, however. Recorded music and movies, now sold mainly on compact disc and videotapes, could be sold digitally. Downloading the contents of a CD, which contains up to 600 megabytes, is impractical even with a very fast network connection. On-demand sales of single-play video or audio is a more promising application, though not yet practical.

Finally, software itself is an excellent example of a digitizable product. Despite the fact that software vendors go to great lengths to give a physical presence to their products—by putting them in boxes, adding manuals, folders, quick reference cards, and other collateral materials—the software could just as easily be sold on a single CD-ROM, complete with online manuals, licenses, and special offers. There are a number of options, including distributing the software directly across the network (as is now done with many shareware programs), or freely distributing the actual software on CD-ROM and selling "keys" online to unlock the software for installation.

Delivery of digital products online raises issues that parallel those raised by online transactions. Some vendors may want to ensure that a third party cannot eavesdrop on the product transmission and gain use of the material being sold without paying for it. Buyers want to ensure that they are getting the material they requested, from the source from which they requested it. Everyone wants to ensure that the material received by the consumer has not been altered in any way by any third parties. These issues can be resolved with the same tools that make secure and reliable transactions possible online.

TYPES OF BUSINESS MODELS AND MARKETS

Business plans should precede e-commerce. Without planning and deciding on a revenue model beforehand, companies can over invest in their sites and not achieve a return. By making a more modest, long-term investment, companies can achieve a winning e-commerce strategy.

ONLINE BUSINESS MODELS

E-commerce gives rise to various models for conducting business, although most of these models are not new. Typically, they have been used in other contexts, but are innovative for the markets in which they are currently being used. For example, many software applications can now be test-driven. Prospective customers can download fully functional trial versions of software, use the software for a period of time, and then purchase it if it meets their needs. Previously, purchasing software had been a gamble in which one relied on word-of-mouth recommendations or reviews in the trade press. While automobile test drives are short, software test drives last much longer, typically 25 to 80 days. In late 1994 and early 1995, Netscape was credited with bringing this model into widespread use. Netscape's giveaway strategy enabled the company's browser market share to reach 75 percent in a matter of months.

THE ELECTRONIC COMMERCE MODEL

Commerce, whether conducted through traditional means or electronically, relies on the conveyance of information. In traditional commerce, the information may be conveyed by the purchaser going in person to a store, it may be conveyed by the purchaser using the telephone system, or it may be conveyed by the purchaser using the postal system to purchase an item. For a more complicated purchase, the purchaser may type a purchase order and send it through the postal system, or deliver the order in person. Commerce activities need not be restricted to business activities either; in some cases, the conveyance of information is itself the end objective. Mail exchanges, electronic or through the postal system, are typical examples of this type of activity. In each of these activities, information, properly conveyed, is crucial for the success of the transaction.

Properly conveyed information is also crucial for the success of electronic commerce transactions, but the means of conveyance differs from that used in traditional commerce. In electronic commerce, a communications network is typically employed for conveying information. Electronic commerce also differs from traditional commerce in the means used for processing information. Whereas, traditionally human intervention has been required to process and act on information accompanying a business transaction, in electronic commerce, human intervention is minimized. This is achieved by automating procedures, and eliminating the use of paper, wherever possible.

The characteristics, then, of electronic commerce that distinguish it from traditional commerce are the means used for conveying information and the methods used for processing it. To effect changes in the way information is conveyed and processed, two support services are clearly needed: communications and data management. In addition, for realistic use of electronic commerce applications in an operational setting, security is also essential.

To have a clearer understanding of this environment, today's e-commerce model should include the following components:

- Business requirements for the big e-commerce boom
- The e-commerce relationship between customer, vendor, and financial institution

Java Solutions to E-Commerce Problems and Security Issues

Of course, the application must also be part of the e-commerce model. Notably, the model includes a user interface element that has seemingly not been included in any of the preceding discussion. This is because the user interface and the application are typically coupled so tightly that they often exist as a single entity that cannot be separated. Nevertheless, separation of these components is useful for discussing functionally. Each component is discussed briefly in this chapter and elaborated on in later chapters.

Before discussing these components, it is worth noting their relationship with electronic commerce. The major task in effecting electronic commerce is not in enhancing or developing new technologies; rather, it is in integrating existing technologies. That is, the focus of electronic commerce is on incorporating the support services into a cohesive environment that provides a framework for supporting electronic commerce applications. Of course, an examination of each of these areas is necessary to accomplish this.

A few additional comments are warranted before discussing the e-commerce model's components. Neither operating systems nor hardware has been included in the model. This is certainly not due to their lack of importance. As has already been mentioned earlier in the chapter, advances in hardware technology are a major facilitating factor in promoting electronic commerce. Operating systems that take advantage of these advances and provide users and applications with the corresponding benefits are equally important. They are left out of the model primarily because they are taken for granted (their presence is implicitly clear), and because they do not present any major issues that directly bear on the development of an infrastructure for electronic commerce.

BUSINESS REQUIREMENTS FOR THE BIG E-COMMERCE BOOM

E-commerce patterns are commonly shared and widely reused e-business infrastructure sets that match common business requirements via the Infrastructure Pattern Matching (IPM). IPM's goals are to:

- Assist in translating business requirements into infrastructure requirements
- Focus infrastructure professionals on business requirements that have the most impact on infrastructure requirements
- Establish a set of the most commonly repeated/reused infrastructure patterns that business requirements can be mapped onto again and again

Furthermore, business continuity plans will become paramount for e-business initiatives. IT organizations must look at all potential causes of downtime, and map business requirements with availability guarantees while focusing on application architectures and inter-enterprise application integration. Also, after an e-commerce initiative has been segmented into new service creation and existing service integration, a process is needed to ensure that these services are coordinated and that various technology components (operating system, server, storage, network) can support e-business requirements.

In addition, fast-changing business requirements compel IT groups to shift from function-centered to process-oriented organizational structures derived from center-of-excellence models. Organizations should reform the operational processes that matter most, assessing incurred costs, risks, and paybacks.

Finally, help desk organizations must move beyond a tactical, dispatch orientation to being full-service providers, with offerings tailored to specific line-of-business requirements. This will enable increased levels of service and tighter business-unit and IT integration.

THE E-COMMERCE RELATIONSHIP BETWEEN CUSTOMER, VENDOR, AND FINANCIAL INSTITUTION

Today's financial industry is still in a good position to be both technology and financial provider for electronic commerce. Its existing expertise in payment systems is still unduplicated in the software industry. This expertise is critical to making large systems efficient and competitive. Financial institutions (banks) are developing their own capacity for software development as well. Perhaps most critical is that banks already control the current payments system.

Already Online

Any vendor desiring to offer financial proxy services must have some relationship with its customer. Vendors without such relationships will need either to develop them or to buy them. Financial institutions have an existing customer relationship, but they've been unsuccessful in moving that relationship online until recently. The existing online-service providers have an enormously valuable asset here. America Online, Prodigy, MSN, and CompuServe have large customer bases that see their providers as gateways to the outside world. Adding a financial component to that conduit has been a straightforward extension of customer perception.

Home banking didn't succeed because its price was too high for a single-purpose online service. The advantage AOL, say, enjoys is that one online connection provides access to many different services, at a price comparable to home banking. A bank developing a comparable technical communications infrastructure is not going to do so as efficiently as leveraging the existing online services or the Internet.

Remember that a digital signature more authenticates a relationship than an identity. The online services are in a good position to provide a transfer of that authenticated relationship to potential merchants and other sellers. A bank trying to leverage its existing relationship for authentication will require a digital channel to its customer which, again, a bank may obtain more efficiently by using an existing service.

A multiparty cooperation between America Online, Prodigy, MSN, and CompuServe is necessary for a successful payment system. Monopolistic attitudes won't go over well in the banking world. Look at what happened to Microsoft recently: It wasn't able to create arbitrary standards in payments and as expected, other people couldn't follow them. Whether Microsoft is able to function well in an environment where they're not in charge is still an open and interesting question. Should Microsoft become able to work with financial institutions and other vendors instead of against them, they would be in a good position to prosper in that market. On the other hand, Microsoft could have another failure similar to handing the networking market to Novell and remain a niche player in payments.

JAVA SOLUTIONS TO E-COMMERCE PROBLEMS AND SECURITY ISSUES

The exponential growth of the Web has offered new opportunities for doing commerce on the Web. However, commerce on the Web has been held hostage due to security concerns. This part of the chapter reviews Java solutions to e-commerce problems and security issues; specifically, the Java Electronic Commerce Framework that uses a security model based on digital signatures to enable application programming interfaces to authenticate their caller.[5]

Why Credit Card Purchasing Isn't Secure

If you have been surfing on the Web long enough, you have come across some Web sites that try to do business on the Internet. In order to purchase something over the Internet, you would have to submit, usually by filling a form, your credit card number to those sites. Your credit card number might be seen by a third party if the underlying protocol is not encrypting the messages before conducting the transfer. On the other hand, there are sites that give you instant access to their information once you submit your credit card number. However, since the algorithm for validating credit card numbers is widely known, it is possible to easily generate valid credit card numbers that could be used to get access to information from such Web sites.

THE JAVA ELECTRONIC COMMERCE FRAMEWORK—JECF?

As commercial use of the Internet grows, the need for a secure mechanism for conducting commercial transactions becomes greater. Java creates ways to enhance electronic commerce beyond credit card purchasing. Java adds components to support emerging technologies of sophisticated payment instruments such as smart cards, electronic cash, and electronic checks. The Java Electronic Commerce Framework (JECF), a secure, extensible framework for creating financial applications on the Internet, is Java's solution for the growing need for a secure mechanism for conducting transactions on the Internet. Using JECF, a transaction goes into five phases as follows:

Phase 1: *A shopper selects items for purchase.* An online shopper using a Java-enabled browser (Netscape) downloads a Web page containing a shopping cart applet. The shopper selects the items he or she wants to purchase. Once all the items are placed in the shopping cart, he or she clicks a button to initiate the payment processing using JECF.

Phase 2: *A shopper's private database is opened.* After pressing the button at the end of Phase 1, the shopper's identity is identified, and his or her private transaction database is opened. The software that performs the payment on the shopper's machine is called a *cassette.* Cassettes are similar to applets, in that they are downloaded from servers to client machines. However, unlike applets, cassettes are retained on the customer's system when the user quits the browser. Cassettes store information in a database provided by JECF, and provide long-term relationships between the customer and the financial institution. Examples of cassettes include brokerage account and home banking.

Phase 3: *The seller payment page with three applets is opened.* The seller payment page has three applets: one is the identity applet of the seller; a second is the tally applet that contains information about the goods and services being purchased and the total price; and the third helps the user in the selection of a payment instrument accepted by the seller.

Phase 4: *A confirmation page appears.* This page appears after the shopper reviews all the information in the payment window and clicks the button that dismisses that page. The confirmation page is displayed by the JEFC to ensure that the amount of $$ seen by the JEFC matches the amount on the tally applet on the seller's page. The shopper at this point has the opportunity to confirm the transaction. Once he or she does that, the cassette will perform the actual payment by transmitting its data to the appropriate server. While the cassette is performing the actual payment, information about the purchase is saved in the pending transaction list. This information can be used to back out of a transaction in the case of systems crash during transactions.

Phase 5: *A Verification page appears*. Once the transaction has been completed successfully, a verification page is displayed to the shopper indicating so, and information about the purchase is removed from the pending transaction list and saved in a permanent transaction register that allows the user to view his or her past purchases.

The JEFC framework supports payment instruments such as smart cards, electronic checks, coupons, credit cards using the Secure Electronic Transaction (SET) protocol, and others. Since JEFC is an extensible framework, it can be extended to provide other types of financial services, such as accounting, tax reporting, and so forth.

The JEFC framework sounds like a great step forward toward secure electronic commerce. Hopefully, it will increase the volume of commercial transactions on the Internet. All that is needed is a very high-speed network to handle all the transactions.

There is so much information about the Java Electronic Commerce Framework, that it is beyond the scope of this chapter to cover it all. See Chapters 2 and 10 for further information on this topic.

BUSINESS MODELS FOR SELLING CONTENT AND SERVICES

Online business models vary depending on what is being sold and the perceived value of the resource. Business models for selling online goods such as information, database access, or entertainment differ considerably from those used for selling traditional hard goods. Four models for selling content are available:

- Selling by the item (pay-per-view)
- Supporting content giveaways by advertising
- Giving away products to encourage either future sales or sales of related products
- Selling by subscription

The subscription business model, which is typically used for magazines and cable television, has been the main model used by commercial online services. It has also been used on the Web with varying degrees of success.

SELLING SUBSCRIPTIONS: ONLINE SERVICES

AOL, CompuServe, Prodigy, and the Microsoft Network (MSN) share something in common: A pricing mode that allows subscribers to access the service for a set monthly subscription fee. Because Internet Service Providers (ISPs) offer flat rates for consumer Internet access, online services now follow their lead, allowing unlimited access to the Internet and to their proprietary value-added content for a flat monthly fee. The flat-fee subscription is a change from the hourly charges that characterized online services until mid 1997.

As a subscription-based service, online services can be very effective. Their predictable revenue model is attractive to premium content providers such as traditional magazine publishers as compared with the unknown returns on the Web at large. Because an online service then has exclusive rights to carry the online version of certain magazines, newspapers, or other resources, the place to read articles from *Consumer Reports Online*, for example, becomes AOL. Online services make excellent content aggregators. When individual online periodicals require passwords for each visit, it becomes difficult to find time to visit the sites, and to remember the passwords. Online services provide users with a convenient gateway to a variety of premium resources.

Another value-added service of online services is a supportive atmosphere for new users. Online services provide help desks, both online and by telephone, who are generally more tolerant of new users and their questions than are busy ISP support staffs. This support for new users, along with competitive pricing, may ensure the continued existence of online services even in the face of the increased content and popularity of the Web.

Because online services run over proprietary networks, their security can be more robust than that of the Internet at large. Banks such as Bank of America and Union Bank of California offer their services on the Internet. Subscribers to online services initially provide their credit card numbers and are more comfortable shopping in the online services environment.

Additional security services are provided by online services; for example, software made available for downloading is scanned for viruses.

Proprietary networks also have their disadvantages. Rapid growth has made outages on AOL's network infamous and has caused businesses to move to alternate providers to ensure reliable e-mail service. Local ISPs are generally faster than online services for downloading Web pages, for example.

Because of the growing popularity of the Web, investor confidence in the continued viability of online services continues to decline. However, the fact that such services are indispensable for a certain class of users makes their demise unlikely, at least in the short term. Because of aggressive marketing (AOL trial disks can be found everywhere—software packaging, cereal boxes, mailboxes, airline snack packages, and the list continues), their subscription base continues to grow. Adding to their charm, most computers sold to consumers in the United States come with trial subscriptions and are preloaded with software to access online services. Table 1.1 summarizes characteristics of the major online services.[6]

TABLE 1.1   Online Services

Service	Members	Market
America Online	16.5 million	Primarily home users
CompuServe	14.1 million	Business and advanced users
MSN	4.8 million	Windows 2000 users
Prodigy	4.2 million	Consumers

SELLING SUBSCRIPTIONS TO ONLINE PUBLICATIONS

Selling subscriptions on the Web is proving more difficult (particularly for online publishers) because the subscriptions are not bundled with Internet access. The proliferation of Web sites provides users with many alternatives to paying for content. As a result, the predominant business model for periodicals is advertising.

In 1996, a number of sites, including *USA Today* and *Wired* magazine, attempted to charge subscriptions to their sites. These periodicals and others later made their content available for free as visits to the sites plummeted. In 1997, sites that charge subscriptions typically provide a combination of free content and subscriber-only access areas.

Subscriptions are reemerging, however. In August 1998, the *Wall Street Journal* began charging its 760,000 trial subscribers $60 per year for access to the site. National newspaper *USA Today* has reintroduced subscription fees for those who access the site's searchable archives. Other sites combining free and subscriber-only content include Time-Warner's Pathfinder, AT&T Personal Online Services, and ESPN Sport Zone.

Subscriptions to more specialized resources are meeting with more success. Professional databases have always charged for access, and researchers seem more willing to pay these charges, whether they are available on the Web or elsewhere. Forrester Research, for example, provides access to its reports online to large corporate subscribers willing to pay the hefty subscription fee.

Are subscriptions a successful model for selling mainstream content online? Research and experience both indicate they are not. Given the tendency toward information overload and the hectic pace most professionals keep, it is difficult to read all the publications that arrive by mail (an example of information push), let alone pay to pull information from the Web. Users are reluctant to pay for content because similar content is available for free elsewhere, and users fear that they may not use the subscription enough to justify the cost because time to visit Web sites is limited.

Web users in general are price-sensitive. The *Encyclopedia Britannica* offers individual subscriptions for $260 per year, a price far too high for most consumers who will likely balk at the *Wall Street Journal*'s $60 annual subscription fee. Even subscriptions as low as $3 to $6 per month may be resisted if information of comparable quality is available on other sites.

However, targeted subscriptions are selling online. ESPN Sport Zone combines free content with subscription-only premium content. Subscribers can attend exclusive online interviews with famous athletes. Sport Zone also raises revenues by selling stakes in high-ticket contests, where users pay $39.95 to enter dream football sweepstakes, for example.

SELLING SUBSCRIPTIONS TO ONLINE ENTERTAINMENT

One area that will undoubtedly be successful with the subscription model is online games. 3D0 charges $10.95 per month for access to its popular

Medieval game, Meridian 59. Games are also a likely candidate for paying per use or by the hour.

By the year 2003, Jupiter Communications expects that 70 percent of all Web users will pay for subscriptions. Despite this prediction, subscriptions will not amount to much in relation to advertising, bringing in only about $543 million in revenues compared with conventional advertising's predicted $7.8 billion within the same time period.

SELLING BY THE ITEM: PAY-PER-VIEW

An attractive alternative to paying for online subscriptions is to pay for certain necessary information by the piece. Depending on a customer's needs, the customer can elect to purchase an article, a chapter from a book, or a page from a reference work. A single database query can be purchased. Pay-per-play games will also be commonplace.

Pay-per-view is an emerging business model. What hinders this model? Customers need to know in advance that the information in question is worth paying for. Second, vendors need a transaction method that cost-effectively handles such payments. Vendors cannot afford credit card fees on very small transactions. Micropayments provide the ability to purchase small bits of information online such as a magazine article or an online video game. As the ability to conveniently purchase a coin's worth of information increases, the pay-per-view model can be more thoroughly tested.

One marketplace where information is currently bought and sold is First Virtual's InfoHaus, an online mall where customers can purchase information using First Virtual's Internet Payment System. In this model, customers download information, and then decide if it is of sufficient value to pay for. The vendor incurs some risk in the process, but First Virtual's FAQ points out that vendors have little to lose given the fact that the cost of production of another copy is close to zero. Further, First Virtual's internal controls enable it to close accounts of customers who abuse the system by repeatedly downloading information and refusing to pay for it. For participating in its mall, First Virtual charges 9.9 percent of the sale price on top of the typical transaction charges for using the Internet Payment Service.

Content vendors are concerned about intellectual property rights and fear that customers who obtain information may redistribute it or resell it.

Technology vendors are developing content protection technologies that address this issue. The Cadillac of content protection technologies is IBM's Cryptolope Live!, which provides an encrypted envelope that triggers payment to the content provider when opened. To address fear of redistribution of copyrighted materials, cryptolopes are designed to give users who resell information a commission on the sale, creating an incentive to redistribute information legitimately.

Cryptolopes are used in IBM's information mall, InfoMarket. AOL users can gateway to the service and have transactions added to their monthly bill. Other users can have InfoMarket aggregate charges for them. IBM charges vendors 40 to 50 percent of each transaction.

Some content protection systems only enforce paying for the original content. Metering systems such as those from InfoSafe Systems, Inc. and CD-MAX, Inc. enable users to unlock paragraphs using a key. Once the content is unlocked, it can be redistributed at will.

Micropayments create another difficulty: Keeping track of many small payments. Clickshare Service Corp. of Williamstown, Massachusetts provides an aggregation service. By opening a Clickshare account, customers can peruse and purchase information at the site of any Clickshare vendor. Publishers that currently sell content through Clickshare include *The Christian Science Monitor*, *The American Reporter*, and *Studio Briefing*.

More traditional entertainment pay-per-view events are also being considered by companies such as MediaCast, which broadcasts events on the Internet. To date, however, cybercasts and online celebrity interviews have been free on the Web, although these events are rarer on the Web than on online services that provide such premium content regularly. MediaCast has charity events that benefit such organizations as the Electronic Frontier Foundation, a not-for-profit organization that lobbies for favorable legislation for the Internet.

SUPPORTING CONTENT GIVEAWAYS BY ADVERTISING

The most successful business model for content sales is advertising. When content location services Yahoo! and Lycos moved from educational sites to corporate entities, advertisers were recruited to cover the costs of providing the service. Because navigational services are essential to finding relevant information on the Web, advertisers were willing to pay for *banners*, clickable advertisements that enable interested users to go to the site in question.

According to Jupiter Communications, total advertising revenues on the Web reached $14.6 billion in 1998. Considering that advertisements on the Web did not exist in 1994, it is obvious that this market has considerable momentum. In 1999, Web advertising brought in an estimated $102 billion. By the year 2003, total Web-based advertising revenues are expected to reach from $545 billion, depending on whose projections one believes. While long-term projections vary greatly, one thing is certain: Advertising is growing quickly. Although advertising on the Web comprises only 17 percent of the total $600 billion spent on advertising by U.S. corporations, its accelerated growth should enable it to surpass revenues from radio advertisements by the end of 2001.

Advertising revenues support most online periodicals, search engines, and other sites providing valuable services. Table 1.2 lists the top 10 Web sites by advertising revenue.[7]

These top 10 sites garner approximately 25.8 percent of all advertising revenues on the Web. Note that the top five are all primarily navigational sites, rather than content-providing sites. The overwhelming popularity of Netscape's site, whose advertising revenues comprise 75 percent of the company's total revenues, arises from the fact that the Netscape browser includes navigational buttons that take users to Netscape's own search, directory, and News&Cool pages, which accept advertising.

To gain advertisers, however, sites must provide objective measurements of their success. Typically, rates are based on the cost per thousand

TABLE 1.2 Top 10 Web Sites for Advertising Revenue

Rank	Web Site	Third Quarter 1999 (billions)	Year-to-Date (billions)
1	Netscape	2.8	6.1
2	Yahoo!	1.9	3.8
3	GO.COM	1.7	3.7
4	Excite	1.	2.4
5	Lycos	1.1	2.3
6	CINET	1.0	2.1
7	WebCrawler	1.0	1.7
8	ZDnet	.7	1.8
9	Magellan	.6	1.0
10	ESPNet Sports Zone	.5	1.4

times an advertisement is viewed (known as *impressions*). While the going rate for a general audience Web site is $40 to $50 cost per 1000 impressions, those with a targeted market can bring in higher rates. ZDnet, owned by computer publisher Ziff-Davis, commands rates of $200 cost per thousand (CPM) because the site's audience is comprised of computer professionals. A few sites deliberately target advertisements based on keywords users enter. GO.COM (formerly InfoSeek) charges $60 CPM per keyword. Another example of targeting is Newspage, where users obtain content tailored to their profiles. Newspage charges the most for advertising of the companies outlined in this section at $386 CPM. According to AdSpend, a tracking service of Jupiter Communications, targeted sites and high traffic sites attract the most advertising dollars.

A few advertisers, including Procter & Gamble, are insisting on paying not by the number of times their advertisements are seen, but by the number of times users click on them, known as the *clickthrough rate*. Only about 2 percent of online advertisements are clicked in this manner, providing a low-clickthrough rate, although research shows that animating advertisements increases this clickthrough rate.

Because most sales on the Web relate to computers, telecommunications, or the Internet itself, it is not surprising to discover that the top 10 advertisers are all in these industries (see Table 1.3).[8] The advertising base is diversifying over time, however. Toyota USA and Procter & Gamble,

TABLE 1.3 Top Web Advertisers

Rank	Advertiser	Third Quarter 1999 (in millions)	Year-to-Date (in billions)
1	Microsoft	994.7	2.0
2	AT&T	720.3	1.3
3	Netscape	651.7	1.4
4	Excite	514.5	1.2
5	GO.COM	514.5	1.1
6	IBM	514.5	1.2
7	McKinley Group, Inc.	80.2	1.0
8	Lycos	445.8	.9
9	Yahoo!	411.6	.9
10	BigYellow	411.6	1.0

which were among the top 25 Web advertisers in the first half of 1999, were joined in the third quarter of 1999 by Ford and General Motors.

Advertising is the revenue mainstay for content-related sites. Despite the advertising rush, the content market as a whole (whether supported by subscription, pay-per-view or advertising) is a difficult one in which to achieve profitability. Research indicates that content sites lose money for approximately three years before becoming profitable.

GO.COM's site, while ranked third in advertising revenue (see Table 1.2), is not yet profitable. Time-Warner's Pathfinder lost $11 million in 1998. Even the popular online version of *Wired* magazine, *HotWired*, does not expect to turn a profit until 2001. While an online presence is important for many publishers (particularly periodical publishers), it is by no means a quick way to realize return on investment (ROI). At present, most content Web sites are recouping only 20 to 30 percent of costs.

While retail sites may achieve short-term profitability depending on the size of the investment, content sites take longer to show a profit. Unlike stores, which can continue to offer the same products for a period of time, content sites must refresh their offerings regularly, even daily, to continue to draw an audience. The investment required to create and post fresh content further challenges publishers in their attempt to achieve a return on investment.

GIVING AWAY PRODUCTS TO ENCOURAGE EITHER FUTURE SALES OR SALES OF RELATED PRODUCTS

The most nontraditional business model the Web has spawned is that of giving away products. Netscape, among others, pioneered this model by giving away its browser in hopes of bolstering Web server sales. In this model, many companies give away product A in hopes that others will buy product B. Another example is RealAudio's player, the first software to offer real-time audio from the Web. RealAudio gave away thousands of copies of its player in hopes of encouraging content developers to include RealAudio clips on their sites, which required the content developers to purchase RealAudio's software. Similarly, Adobe provides its Acrobat viewer for free as an incentive for content developers to purchase Adobe software for online publishing in Acrobat's portable document format (PDF).

A few years ago, few suspected that Microsoft would engage in the strategy of software giveaways to gain market share. Indeed, the company has surpassed Netscape in its use of this model, giving away its browser, Internet Explorer, and its Web server, Internet Information Server (IIS). In part, Microsoft hopes to gain market share in this way. However, examined more closely, the tie-in of the browser and the server to other Microsoft products makes users more likely to choose Microsoft solutions in other areas such as using Exchange for E-mail services or structured query language (SQL) servers for back-ending interactive Web sites.

A twist on the giveaway model is try, then buy. Users can evaluate hundreds of software packages before purchasing them by downloading trial copies from Web sites. Software buyers traditionally relied on reviews and word-of-mouth recommendations for selecting software. Now, they download and try it for a period of 60 days to 90 days, and then decide whether to license the software. This can be an effective ploy; a common result is that users download the trial version too early, lack time to evaluate it, and purchase it because a need for it arises even before it can be fully evaluated.

Companies introducing new products or new versions of software typically make the beta version available for free. Doing so not only gains market share, but also provides them with a larger testing group. When the final version is released, users can then purchase the product and may be offered discounts for participating in the beta testing.

Software companies are not alone in the try and then buy model. The *Wall Street Journal*, most online services, and other publications offer a free-trial period. The *Wall Street Journal* essentially beta tested its site using its 650,000 registered readers. A portion of these then became paying customers.

Netscape changes its client software frequently enough to charge for software subscriptions rather than have its customers purchase a particular version. Users who want or need the latest version do well to pay the marginal difference between the license price and the annual subscription rate.

The Internet has become a proving ground for software sales techniques. While products in the marketplace ultimately stand or fall by their quality, the Internet has made it possible for smaller software companies to gain an entry into the market more quickly than was traditionally possible. Certainly, software buyers with Internet access are more reticent to purchase shrink-wrapped software that they know nothing about than software that can be freely evaluated.

MULTITIERED WEB ARCHITECTURE

As challenging as it may seem, developing a Web application from scratch is kid's stuff when compared to the complexity of moving a legacy business application to the Web. You can't do it on the fly. Success depends on understanding and addressing all the critical issues up front in the multitiered Web architectural design phase. You need to know early on what the issues are. What technologies have to play together? How will they communicate? What is the lifecycle of a business transaction? How will security work? How will the new application integrate with your existing support systems and infrastructure?

COMPONENTS OF A WEB APPLICATION SYSTEM

The following are some of the components that make the design of today's Web application system more complex than the factors that originally influenced the design of your multitiered Web architecture:

- Number of users is an order of magnitude higher; users may be disconnected.
- Security is more important than ever; it must be designed in versus bolted on.
- Most Web-application technologies are designed to work with relational database systems, but still require access to data in legacy systems. Moving data is risky and expensive.
- Information is moved in small to medium-sized data sets.
- User requirements versus system performance requirements drive the application design.[9]

COMPLEX TRANSACTION MODELS AND BATCH PROCESSING

Web users expect to transact business on the Web any time of day, and they have little tolerance for delays in processing their requests. Legacy systems are typically set up to deal with transactions in batch processing windows. They can't handle the operational impact on the production systems when you open them up to the dynamic processing model used by most Web applications. Doing so would overload the legacy system resources.

So, a major issue to resolve in moving legacy applications to the Web is to design a multitiered architectural model for processing business transactions that allows Web-based users to connect, do their business, be done, and still work with the batch transaction-processing model used by your legacy system.

One way to solve the problem is to design your transaction processing lifecycle in two parts: one focused on user-dependent processing, and the other focused on back-end processing. In the user-dependent part of the lifecycle, you need to collect all the information required to complete the transaction and qualify the input by applying editing and validation rules while the user is still engaged. The state of the transaction is carried downstream to the back-end processor, where the transaction can be completed within the batch-processing window defined by the legacy system. Because the completion of the transaction lifecycle is completed after the user has exited the picture, the success of the transaction depends on the quality of the front-end data collection and validation process.

GETTING WEB APPLICATION SERVERS TO TALK TO LEGACY SYSTEMS

To implement communication between today's Web application servers and older legacy systems, there are three basic approaches to consider: remote procedure calls, message-oriented middleware, and the old standby, dump and load data. Depending on your architectural constraints and the transactional requirements of your application, you may need to use one, two, or even all three of these approaches to accomplish the task at hand. In designing widely distributed heterogeneous systems, the thing to remember is that there is no such thing as a silver bullet—no single technology will meet all of your requirements.

Other Issues to Consider

Accessing legacy data is hard. Because of the complexity involved in accessing legacy data through the legacy system interface, developers are often tempted to access that data directly, which bypasses all the business rules and processing constraints that are typically embedded in the legacy system front end. Going in the back door (accessing legacy data directly) poses significant risks to the security and integrity of your data.

Another consideration, and one of the most overlooked areas in building multitiered Web systems that use the Internet, is support. Working with an application through a 56K modem is very different from having a direct connection through a T-1 line. Whom does the user call if he or she has a problem? Support is critical to the user experience, and support should come in many forms.

In any Web application system, optimizing system performance and scalability are critical. If, during the development on your local area network, performance is slow to your browser, then it will be much worse for the end user at home sitting at his or her computer.

Addressing the issues of multitiered Web architecture-to-legacy integration starts and succeeds with design and planning. Because of the different technologies and complexity that systems integration poses, today's application systems cannot be simply bolted together. There is no one tool or technology that solves all your problems, so look for technologies and architectures that play well together in a reliable, robust manner. Understand the characteristics of the problem you are trying to solve, the technologies and architecture you plan to use, and most importantly, build an infrastructure to support your system.

BUSINESS MODELS FOR SELLING HARD GOODS

What about selling goods and services on the Internet that may be ordered online, but are delivered through traditional means? Shopping on the Internet is producing significant revenue. It is typical for online vendors to receive orders from other parts of the world, providing them with a reach far beyond that provided by traditional storefronts or even mail order. An innovative product such as the topless sandals called BareSoles receives $50,000 in orders from South Africa, Malaysia, and Japan. A Japanese customer who orders food products from U.S.-based Salami.com pays a shipping charge equal to the cost of the product. However, the customer is satisfied because obtaining such products locally is even more expensive. Table 1.4 shows shopping revenue by market segment.[10]

Reach is not the only advantage of selling online. Virtual stores need fewer employees and can be run from a warehouse. In some cases, the stores order directly from distributors, eliminating the need for a warehouse. In addition, specialty shops that offer unique products do particularly well online. A shop with elephant-related products sold $80,000 worth

TABLE 1.4 Online Shopping Revenue by Market Segment

Market Segment	1999 (billions)	2000 (billions)	2001 (billions)	2002 (billions)	2003 (billions)
Computer products	1.228	2.105	3.608	6.184	10.600
Travel	.961	1.579	2.594	4.262	7.003
Entertainment	.733	1.250	2.132	3.636	6.201
Apparel	.234	.322	.443	.610	.839
Gifts and flowers	.386	.658	1.122	1.913	3.262
Food and drink	.227	.336	.497	.736	1.089
Other	.221	.329	.490	.730	1.087
Total	3.990	6.579	10.886	18.071	30.081

of merchandise online in only two months. In most locations, the number of customers interested in a particular type of specialty item is relatively limited. On the Internet, with a much wider population and virtual communities that group together by their interests, niche products can be more successful. Another type of product that sells well online is known quantities. Books, CDs, and brand-name computer merchandise can be ordered from anywhere.

There are significant barriers to conducting business online, however. The Web is so large that getting noticed is a problem for small to medium-sized enterprises. In addition, storefronts that handle online ordering are relatively expensive to develop, requiring a larger investment.

Retail stores typically come in one of two forms: as independent storefronts or as part of an online mall. Typically, ISPs who help create independent storefronts give home-page access to member sites, creating a kind of shopping mall. In general, independent stores such as WINE.COM, CDnow, and Amazon.com are currently doing the most business on the Web.

More online malls are thriving than a few years ago. However, InternetMCI Marketplace has closed its doors. Others such as the Internet Shopping Network (ISN) have kept their focus narrow. ISN remains a very successful computer store. Attempts by its parent, the Home Shopping Channel, to diversify its product lines (which would create a type of virtual mall), have also been very successful.

COMBINING THE MODELS

Most businesses on the Web do not choose a single model on which to run their business. Businesses adopt a combination of models over time.

GolfWeb, a site with 68,000 pages of information on golf, has a varied strategy, intending to derive 40 percent of revenues from subscription and service fees, 35 percent from advertisements, and 25 percent from retail proceeds from the site's ProShop. GolfWeb's advertising revenue currently stands at $137,200,000. The site has attracted advertisers such as Bank of America, Lexus, AT&T, and Buick, just to name a few. The ProShop alone recently brought in $34,000,000 in revenue.

Some retail outlets on the Web draw advertisements simply because of their popularity. CDnow runs advertisements from Lands' End and Microsoft. In a real-world music store, such cross-advertisement is uncommon. It is more common for a store to have advertisements for products it carries, although charging for such advertisements can be difficult in real stores. On the ISN, which generates $4 million monthly in sales, advertisers of computer products pay to advertise on the site.

If a site's primary revenue model has been defined, consider the possibilities derived from varying the models. A travel site charges passengers for any travel bookings. It also offers discount prices to subscribers and accepts advertising from resorts, airlines, hotels, and tourism promotion agencies. Bookstores not only sell books online, but offer a book-of-the-month club subscription and accept cross-advertising from other retailers in other segments. On the Web, experimentation with secondary revenue models can result in additional income.

BECOMING PROFITABLE

Few businesses show a profit in the first year. Not surprisingly, most online businesses also do not become profitable immediately. Currently on the Web, for every one company showing a profit, there are two that are not. According to recent research by ActivMedia, 42 percent of the Web-based businesses surveyed were profitable, and another 39 percent expected to show a profit in the next two years.[11] The combined revenue of the companies ActivMedia surveyed was $44.6 billion. These companies are more representative of mainstream Internet businesses than are well-known and highly profitable sites such as CDnow or Amazon.com. ActivMedia focused its research on small to medium-sized Internet businesses.

Profit largely depends on investment. Sites that provide compelling content to gain advertising must make a large initial and ongoing investment in their sites. As a result, these sites take approximately four years to become profitable.

AN OVERVIEW OF SELECTED MARKETS

Interestingly, the travel, investment, and banking markets recognized the opportunity for doing business online early. Investment brokerages delivered software to their computer-literate customers who wanted to conduct online trading. American Airlines created easySabre, a means for users to book flights from their PCs. Online banking, however, largely failed in its attempt to gain a foothold among consumers—a failure that is viewed only in the context of the total consumer market. If the same users who wanted to book their own flights and trade stocks online were asked if they would like bank statements delivered to their PC, this wired market would probably welcome the service.

ONLINE BANKING

Today, between 90 and 95 percent of all banking transactions occur electronically. By volume, however, only 8 to 13 percent are handled in this way. By bringing online banking to the mass market, banks hope to increase the number of electronic transactions and thereby reduce costs by a substantial degree. Processing a paper check costs between $1.02 and $1.60. Handling the same transaction electronically costs about $.18.

Electronic transactions have become as widespread as automatic teller machines (ATMs), and electronic funds transfers (EFTs) have become more common. Debit cards are accepted as easily as checks in many stores in the United States. In countries where the telecommunications infrastructure for point of sale (POS) systems is more expensive or unavailable, stored value smart cards are taking hold more quickly.

What is inciting banks to move toward online banking? Reduced cost is part of the answer, but customer requests play an even larger role.

According to Ernst & Young, 96 percent of banks plan to offer online banking by 2001.[12] Of course, naysayers are quick to point out that consumer-oriented online banking has been tried in the past and has met with meager success. Yet, with the advent of the Web, the momentum toward online banking is increasing. Many banks offer personal finance software such as Managing Your Money or Quicken to interface with bank statements. More than 50 banks offer services on proprietary online services such as AOL. Approximately 90 percent of U.S. banks currently have a Web site and offer advanced services.

For many banks, the first step toward full online banking is accepting credit card and loan applications online. First Union Bank of Charlotte, North Carolina receives credit card applications from about 4 percent of all users who visit their online form. Considering that the rate for direct mail is 5 percent, First Union is gaining new customers without the expense of mailing forms to prospects. Bayshore Bank and Trust of Toronto accepts consumer loans and mortgage applications online.

Some banks provide full-service banking on the Internet. Banks such as Wells Fargo of San Francisco, Banco Brandesco of Brazil, and Merita of Finland provide a variety of services to customers online, from bill payment, account access, and online transactions such as EFT, to loan processing and approval. Although Banco Brandesco offers online banking during limited hours, the prolific 1100-page site receives 400,000 visits per day, 87 percent of which come from Latin America.

Merita of Finland, under its Solo program, offers EFT over the Internet. Customers fill in forms online and clerks later arrange with the receiving party to complete the transaction. Merita also offers electronic cash (E-cash) to its customers, provided by EUNet NV using technology developed by DigiCash. Forty-four vendors accept E-cash, and more are interested in doing so. These services are currently limited to transacting business with others living in Finland because of international banking laws.

Security First Network Bank (SFNB—based in Atlanta, Georgia) is one of the first completely virtual banks, with no physical branches. Most other banks, even those with strong online presence such as Wells Fargo and Toronto Dominion, are online outlets for real-world banks. As a result of being completely virtual, SFNB can offer lower prices and attractive rates to its customers. Its security is, of course, of paramount importance. The bank uses a secure OS from SecureWare, recently acquired by Hewlett-Packard (HP) and incorporated into the company's HP Virtual Vault technology.

Bill payment services are an emerging category for most banks. Check-Free Corporation is the largest provider of bill-payment services, and many banks ally with it.[13] CheckFree currently has captured 68 percent of the market, which is electronic, although not Internet-based. CheckFree's services are used on CompuServe, AOL, and by Cellular One. In 1999, the company processed $40 billion in payments with only $17,000 in bad debt. Other players moving to enter this market include IBM, which won a bid from the Internet Banking Consortium to handle payment of utility and credit card bills over its Global Network. The Internet Banking Consortium includes institutions such as BankAmerica, NationsBank, and the Fleet Financial Group.

Banks are also expanding into Internet-related services. NationsBank negotiates automobile loans for online car sales from AutoConnect (http://www.autoconnect.com/). First Union Bank of Charlotte, North Carolina has a mall attached to the bank where it generates a lot of online retail business.

WARNING! URLs are subject to change without notice.

Wells Fargo Bank introduced a service targeted at small business owners. The New Jersey Business Gateway Service, which addresses the security concerns of small businesses and can be accessed with a Web browser, runs over a private Internet protocol (IP) network established by Wells Fargo. Businesses pay a one-time fee of $17.95 for the software to dial up. The monthly service charge of $8.00 includes unlimited transactions.

Recognizing the difficulty many banks have in offering online banking to their customers, Block Financial, a subsidiary of H&R Block, offers a service that banks can offer to their customers. Block Financial handles all the transactions, and consumers can use the bill payment service. The service interfaces with bank office software from Jack Henry and Associates, software that is installed in 4583 U.S. banks.[14] Block Financial Corporation has enlisted 400 to 500 banks for the service to date.[15] Although customers will interact with their accounts over the Internet, the connection between H&R Block and member banks will run over leased lines.

The rush to move online is somewhat surprising from the typically conservative financial industry, but the lure of cost reduction is strong. In addition, banks fear that other types of companies may offer banking services online if they delay. While banks once held 73 percent of all financial assets, today they hold only 27 percent. By 2001, analysts predict that online access to bank accounts will be routine for everyone. Nevertheless, while banks are not known for cutting-edge technology, the investments market has used online forums for some time, use that is now burgeoning and spawning online investment sites that employ the leading-edge interactive Web technology.

INVESTMENTS ONLINE

Trading stocks online gained an early foothold among PC users. For example, about 85 percent of all CompuServe subscribers own some stock. The movement of investment advice and stock trading to the Web follows naturally for this community.

Part of the motivation is cost. Traditional brokers charge between $130 and $1,400 commission on sales. As a result, discount brokerages emerged, reducing the commission charges. The discount division of Fidelity Investments, for example, charges between $85 and $300 per trade. However, one private investor claims to have saved more than $4,000 in commissions in three months by trading online with Ameritrade.

TRADITIONAL BROKERAGES

Among traditional, established brokerages, Charles Schwab & Company is the recognized leader on the Web.[16] Twenty-seven percent of Schwab's income comes from PC-based services, which include trades from its own online software, its presence on online services, and its Web site. Online commissions stand at $6.9 billion, and the company processes an average of 5,316,500 online trades per day. Approximately 70 percent of all trades on the Web come from Schwab.

As a traditional brokerage house, Schwab offers both advice and expertise. For those who want to trade online only, e-Schwab software handles trades at $9.95, a 67-percent discount on its usual prices. E-Schwab users are restricted to online resources, however, and cannot tap the expertise of Schwab's staff.

At PrudentialSecurities.Com, Inc.'s Web site, customers can gain online access to their accounts.[17] Some companies, including Ferris, Baker, Watts, Inc. of Baltimore, Maryland use the Web site primarily to refer users to agents.

DISCOUNT BROKERAGES

Discount brokerages handle trades at a lower fee than do traditional brokerages, and were among the first to appear on the Web. E*Trade Securities, Inc. of Palo Alto, California, gets 1.1 percent of its total sales from its Web site. In February 1999, Web-based trades amounted to $185 million of $17 billion. Over time, E*Trade's price has decreased from $15 per trade to $8 per trade.

Lombard Brokerage, Inc.'s site is frequently mentioned as one of the favorite investment sites on the Web.[18] The site, which receives more than one million hits per day, uses leading-edge technology such as Sun's Java programming language. Small, embedded applications called *applets* add interactivity such as drawing graphs of a particular stock's performance to a company's site. Currently, 18 percent of Lombard's annual revenue of $8 billion comes from the site. Lombard expects the share earned from the Web site to increase to 70 percent over the course of two years.

Portfolio Accounting World Wide (PAWWS) Financial Network is a conglomeration of brokerage sites rather than a single site.[19] PAWWS, includes investment houses such as Jack White & Co. of San Diego, National Discount Brokers, and Net Investor, a discount division of Howe Barnes Investments of Chicago, just to name a few. The companies involved in PAWWS need not develop their Web sites independently; the consortium serves as an online investment mall.

PAWWS offers portfolio management and databases of information about companies. As of June 1999, 2.8 million investors participated in PAWWS, a figure that is growing monthly at about 10 percent.

BEYOND DISCOUNT BROKERAGES: NO BROKERAGE

Some companies on the Web are attempting to completely eliminate brokerage fees by creating a virtual trading environment on the Internet. The most well-known of these sites is New York-based Wit Capital (WITC). The site matches buyers and sellers. Trading does not take place on the site. After stocks are matched and the transaction is agreed upon by both parties, it is shipped to the New York Stock Exchange (NYSE) and the National Association of Securities Dealers Automated Quotations (NASDAQ) to complete the sale. Wit Capital derives its income from the percentage of initial public offerings (IPOs) that occur at the site, and does not charge investors for the stock matching service. This type of environment obscures the line between a brokerage and a virtual online marketplace.

PAYING FOR INVESTMENT ADVICE

The Motley Fool is an example of a business that grew up on AOL. The forum, which receives 508,000 visitors per month, provides anonymous investment information and has been expanded into a Web site and a successful book. The Motley Fool makes $1.7 billion annually through these venues.

Quote.com provides a subscription service to information. Free trials and free delayed quotes are available. Real-time quotes are available only to subscribers. News services from respected sources such as Reuters, BusinessWire, and the S&P MarketScope are also available at Quote.com, to name a few.

DRAWBACKS TO ONLINE INVESTING

Investing online, while safe in many cases, is being watched carefully by regulatory agencies. The possibility for fraud exists, and the line between sharing advice and insider trading in online forums or e-mail could be easily crossed. Additionally, information online that appears to be up to date could in fact be old, misleading investors who rely on it. Advice received and acted upon could be misguiding. Few, if any, of these pitfalls are new to experienced investors, but the Internet intensifies the problem to broader dimensions. Agencies watching Internet investments carefully include the National Association of Securities Dealers Regulation, Inc. (NASDR); the Securities and Exchange Commission (SEC); and, the National Fraud Information Center (http://www.fraud.org welcome.htm) run by the National Consumers League.[20]

Travel

Many believe conducting business on the Internet will eliminate intermediaries of all types; one often-cited example is the elimination of travel agents. Airlines are particularly interested in doing business online, thereby reducing the fees they pay to travel agents for booking flights. Telephoning a travel agent is more convenient than booking travel on the Internet, however, and such agencies are unlikely to be eliminated, although demand may be somewhat reduced.

Airlines

Allowing customers to book flights online substantially reduces an airline's costs, and legacy systems are being used in the process. Most sites that enable customers to book flights translate between the Web's HTML interface and the proprietary reservation system that creates the tickets.

PCTRAVEL, was one of the first travel sites on the Web, and interfaces with the Apollo reservation system.[21] Designed to appeal to business travelers, some 1.4 million people use the site on a regular basis, about 50 percent of whom book their travel on that site.

Travelocity.com, a site designed by American Airlines but offers travel on a number of carriers, interfaces with American's Sabre system. In addition to selling airline tickets, the site features travel accessories. American Airlines is by no means a newcomer to the online travel world. Its PC-based EasySabre software has been in use for over 15 years. In 1999, 343 million bookings were placed using EasySabre.

Some carriers are currently selling tickets on their Web sites, including American Airlines. Continental Airlines, whose Web site also interfaces with the Sabre system, is also selling tickets on their Web site.

Booking flights online may also lead to some new revenue models for airlines willing to try the models. Cathay Pacific Airlines pioneered auctioning unsold seats on the Internet when it offered 500 unsold Hong Kong to Los Angeles tickets. Some 24,000 bidders contested for the 500 tickets, which sold at about half their normal price. If U.S. carriers were to adopt the auction paradigm to increase occupancy during slow periods, it could transform a stagnant market. Prices would go down overall by 58 percent, while the occupancy rate, which today stands at 78 percent, would rise to almost 100 percent. Had this been done in 1999, for example, profits could have increased more than threefold from $18.2 billion to $58.1 billion. Despite the potential, auctioning unsold tickets is not a widespread practice, although American Airlines has begun offering periodic ticket auctions.

Hotels

The hotel industry is also interested in reducing the cost of reservations. While 69 percent of hotel reservations are not handled by travel agents, the percentage that is, is nonetheless costly when compared with doing business on the Web. Having an operator take a telephone reservation costs approximately $13; using a service such as TravelWeb reduces this cost to about $5.

TravelWeb, run by The Hotel Industry Switch Company (Thisco) of Dallas, Texas, is a consortium of 23 hotel companies, and has 9000 sites online. It charges hotels $4.75 per online booking. TravelWeb has added airline, car rental, restaurant, and golf course reservations to its site. It has already expanded the site to include features such as five-day weather forecasts and maps.

While TravelWeb aggregates access to properties from many companies, each major hotel chain has its own Web site. Sites often include pictures of rooms, the view from the room, and information on rates and locations. Some hotels offer reduced rates to Internet users.

Despite the relative ease of booking hotel rooms online, online reservations are expected to account for less than 50 percent of all bookings in 2001. While the Web remains a rich information source for people researching areas they plan to visit (creating an indirect effect of bringing tourism to areas promoted online), completing travel reservations online is a market still evolving.

Finally, companies moving their businesses to cyberspace or creating new online ventures should carefully consider which business models are most advantageous. Success depends not only on choosing effective models, but also on the usefulness and attractiveness of the site.

THE INTERNET ENVIRONMENT

As mentioned earlier, electronic commerce is not an entirely new idea; nor is the online transaction. Dial-up computer services, such as those provided by CompuServe since 1980, usually include services and products that can be ordered online. Electronic funds transfer (EFT) is another relatively mature field that is only now reaching a mass market as ATMs, gas stations, and supermarkets increasingly accept credit, debit, and charge cards.

In 1993, when the World Wide Web protocols were first being proposed as Internet standards, few people outside the research and academic world had even heard of the Internet, let alone used it. Today, the Internet and the World Wide Web are such a part of daily life that major mainstream publications no longer define Internet-related terms like Web site, home page, or news posting.

BUILDING OUT THE INTERNET

Where advances in telecommunications and computing largely occurred side by side in the past, today they converge on the Internet. Soon, virtually all information technology investment will be part of interlinked communications systems, whether internal to a business, between businesses, between individuals and businesses, or individual to individual. However measured, the Internet is expanding at a very rapid pace as shown in Table 1.5.[22]

TABLE 1.5 Growth of Internet Hosts and Domain Names

Date	Number of Hosts	Number of Domains
July 93	1,776,000	26,000
July 94	3,212,000	46,000
July 95	6,642,000	120,000
July 96	12,881,000	488,000
July 97	19,540,000	1,301,000
July 98	29,642,000	3,469,000
July 99	44,966,000	9,250,000

NOTE

Internet host *refers to a computer that is connected to the Internet that has a unique Internet Protocol (IP) address. A domain name represents a record within the Domain Name System.*

For instance, the number of Americans using the Internet grew from fewer than 5 million in 1993 to as many as 143 million by 1999.[23] Unix-To-Unix Network (UUNET), one of the largest Internet backbone providers, estimates that Internet traffic doubles every 100 days.[24]

The number of names registered in the Domain Name System grew from 26,000 in July 1993 to 9.3 million in six years. Over the same period, the number of hosts connected to the Internet expanded from under 1.8 million to nearly 45 million (see Table 1.5).

In January 1995, just over 27,000 top-level commercial (.com) domain names were assigned. Most businesses used them for little more than posting product and company descriptions, store locations, annual reports, and information about how to contact corporate headquarters. Five years later, commercial domain names number 2,037,186.[25] Static brochures and bulletin boards are giving way to full-fledged businesses offering financial services, news and information, manufactured goods, and travel and entertainment to individuals and businesses. To meet this increased demand, consumer electronics companies, media giants, telephone companies, computer companies, software firms, satellite builders, cellular telephone businesses, Internet service providers, television cable companies, and, in a few cases, electric utilities, are aggressively investing to build out the Internet.

Hundreds of new firms are starting up around the country to help businesses use the World Wide Web effectively. They design Web sites and advertising banners, create Web-based catalogs, build security tools, create and track direct marketing campaigns, provide consulting services, and, develop technology to speed the flow of data and information across the network. Venture capitalists gave just under $14 billion to hundreds of information technology start-ups in 1998 and 1999.[26]

MAKING THE INTERNET FASTER AND MORE ACCESSIBLE

Households typically connect to the Internet through a PC and a telephone line. This method of access means that most households without PCs (just under 63 percent of all U.S. households) do not have Internet access.[27] It also means that most Internet connections from the home are slow.[28] To illustrate the importance of speed, it takes 23 minutes to download a 3.5-minute video using a 56- Kbps (thousand bits per second) modem, the modem most commonly used by households today (see Table 1.6).[29]

Telephone companies, satellite companies, cable service providers, and others are working to create faster Internet connections and expand the means by which users can access the Internet. New technologies such as Asynchronous Digital Subscriber Line (ADSL) enable copper telephone lines to send data at speeds up to 8 million bits per second (mbps). At this speed, that same 3.5-minute video takes 10 seconds to download.[30]

PC manufacturers and software developers are also taking steps to make home computers cheaper and easier to use.[31] Some PCs can now be purchased for less than $700 apiece. New network computers are expected

TABLE 1.6   Time to Download 3.5-Minute Video Clip Using Different Technologies

Technology	Transfer Time
56-Kbps modem	23 minutes
128-Kbps ISDN	10 minutes
4-Mbps cable modem	20 seconds
8-Mbps ADSL	10 seconds
10-Mbps cable modem	8 seconds

to be introduced at prices of a few hundred dollars apiece. At the same time, new and enhanced software programs (for instance, better graphical user interfaces, search tools, and voice recognition technology) will make the PC and the Internet easier to use and thereby able to reach a broader community of consumers.

Many Americans are now using their televisions to access the Internet. Present in nearly every household, TVs are easy to operate and require little or no maintenance. Digital broadcasting services (high-definition television, or HDTV) are available in the top 10 markets, and broadcasters are expected to make the transition to digital broadcasting by 2006.[32] With digital broadcasting, TV viewers will be able to interact with their televisions and surf the Web, pay bills, plan a weekend trip, or make dinner reservations.

Already, satellite dishes and signals carried over cable television lines enable consumers to receive data from the Internet through their TVs and television programming through their personal computers. At speeds of 10 million bits per second, a household connected to the Internet via a cable modem can download a 3.5-minute video in 8 seconds.[33] In most cases today, however, the outgoing communication (the speed at which the Internet receives the commands by the user) is still limited to the fastest modem speeds that copper telephone wires will support.

Two-way cable traffic would be much faster, but only 12 percent of the 136 million cable subscribers in the United States and Canada (16 million homes) live in zones where two-way cable connectivity exists. In addition, only a small number of them (444,000) have actually subscribed to the service. By 2003, analysts estimate that two-way cable connectivity will be available to 67 million households, of which 4.9 million are expected to subscribe to the service.[34] Cable operators are planning to make significant investments in the next few years to upgrade their systems to carry two-way Internet traffic.

The wait for broadband Internet access to households is measured in years, not decades. Within the next five to ten years, the vast majority of Americans should be able to interact with the Internet from their television sets, watch television on their PCs, and make telephone calls from both devices. These combined services will be brought to homes by satellite, wireless, microwave, television cable, and telephone lines, all interconnected in one overall system (see the sidebar, "The Race to Build Out the Communications Infrastructure of the Internet").

People will also access the Internet away from their homes or offices. Cellular telephones and Personal Digital Assistants (PDAs) have become

The Race to Build Out the Communications Infrastructure of the Internet

During the 19th and 20th centuries, governments played a key role in helping build or actively regulate much of the country's transportation, communication, and energy infrastructure powering the Industrial Revolution. Although the Internet originated in U.S. Defense Department research, private sector investments will largely drive its future expansion.

Telecommunications

Manufacturers and software companies have been developing new technologies to allow higher-bandwidth communications across the existing copper network infrastructure, including DSL technologies, compression, and faster electronic switches. Communications carriers around the world are building out fiber optic networks. Technological advancements including optical amplification and new photonic switches make these high-speed networks more powerful and more efficient.

Satellite

Satellite, telecommunications, electronics, and aerospace companies plan to spend close to $50 billion to build out a global broadband network in the sky between 2001–2005 to reach most of the 2 billion people who live in areas around the world where telephone service is unavailable.

Cable

Thick cable wires pass more than 90 percent of U.S. households, piping in TV programming at speeds much faster than telephone copper carries voice traffic. Seven years ago, many cable companies began to prepare the cable network for two-way Internet traffic, investing in fiber optic cable and set-top boxes to decipher voice, video, and data sent in digital form.

Wireless

Over time, wireless networks will be integrated with the Internet. Investments in satellites and repeater stations are now being made at a rapid rate to accomplish this. Cellular telephones, pagers, and hand-held computers will be able to transmit and receive voice, data, and Internet traffic.

Electric Utilities

A number of utility companies around the country are beginning to lay thousands of miles of new fiber cable for Internet access at speeds 10 times faster than today's high-speed telephone connections.

very sophisticated devices capable of sending faxes, receiving e-mail and electronic pages, video (now in Japan; in 2003 in the United States), and, now, accessing the Internet. Industry experts predict that users of cellular telephones and digital personal communications devices (on a global scale) will more than increase sevenfold in 1997 from 77 million to 584 million by 2002.[35]

Technology already exists to enable many appliances and consumer electronics devices to transmit and receive data. The first products to link home appliances with PCs are already available. Entering a simple message into a computer on a desk will turn off the television or pre-heat the oven for dinner (the networked home). Automobiles with video monitors are already receiving data from overhead satellites to warn about traffic jams, give directions to the nearest gas station, and deliver the latest news and information.

The U.S. Government's FY 2000 budget calls for $961 million to be invested in high-performance computing and communications. As part of this effort, the budget provides $220 million for the Next Generation Internet Initiative, which will create a research network that is 100 to 1000 times faster than today's Internet, and invests in R&D for smarter, faster networks that support new applications such as telemedicine, distance learning, and real-time collaboration.

As the number of Internet users grows, accessing the Internet becomes faster and easier to do. In addition, as the number of Internet-enabled devices multiplies, the IT industry's share of the economy can be expected to continue to expand rapidly.

THE INTERNET ADVANTAGE

Despite the Internet's long existence as a noncommercial research network, its commercialization owes its apparent success to several factors:

- The Internet is an open system.
- The Internet itself does not belong to anyone.
- The World Wide Web is the Internet's "killer app."
- The Internet is open.

All the Internet protocols are open and public, and anyone can use them to write software implementations that can interoperate with other computers and networks running the Internet protocols. Most of the competition between vendors of Internet and TCP/IP software is based on performance, ease of use, and compatibility. None of these vendors is foolhardy enough to announce a new version of their software that provides even the most attractive of new features at the cost of compatibility with other TCP/IP implementations.

LAN (local area network) operating system vendors such as Novell and Microsoft have traditionally kept their product specifications private and incompatible, but have lost the benefits of having an entire community of researchers and developers working on interoperable implementations, as has happened with the Internet protocols.

Because of this openness, a wide range of implementations are available, from freeware and shareware versions of Internet application and networking software, to high-performance, high-function versions of Internet software sold by companies like Graphics Plus Printing and Sun Microsystems. The result of this competition is lower cost barriers to small companies and individuals who previously could not afford to connect to the Internet.

THE INTERNET DOES NOT BELONG TO ANYONE

Part of the openness of the Internet is derived from the fact that you do not have to belong to any special group, pay any special fees, or become anyone's customer to access any Internet content. True, there are fees to be paid to the Internet Service Provider (ISP) for initiating service, charges for connect time, and perhaps other value-added services such as e-mail accounts, but the ISP functions in the same way as a telephone company, providing access and connectivity only.

In contrast, the more traditional online services (like America Online, CompuServe, and Prodigy) still charge users fees for connect time, as well as to access certain value-added content and activities. More important is the limitation on the participation in any AOL, CompuServe, Microsoft Network (MSN), or Prodigy forums. For example, only CompuServe members can read or submit to CompuServe forums. The same is true for AOL and Prodigy members.

Connectivity through the Internet allows any connected individual to browse any freely available content, without regard to memberships. At least as important is that anyone with a dedicated Internet connection and a computer can be not just an information consumer, but also an information provider. In addition, instead of communicating with an online service population, people with Internet connectivity can potentially communicate with anyone else connected to the Internet: 60, 70, or 80 million people or more, depending on when you read this.

The online services have recognized that, when given the choice, users prefer full Internet access to more limited online service access. To meet this need, the online services are also offering true Internet service.

For new computer users going online for the first time, the traditional online services offered by AOL, CompuServe, and Prodigy are very attractive, as they offer hand-holding and support for the online "freshman." Eventually, the majority of users will migrate to full Internet access. However, the flow of new online users is not likely to slow in the near future, and many people do stay with the traditional online services for one reason or another. Building a successful electronic commerce application will require implementing the needs of these users and the proprietary functions of the online services they use.

WORLD WIDE WEB, KILLER APP OF THE INTERNET!

Most Internet applications were developed by computer scientists more often concerned with performance and extensibility than with usability. Applications such as telnet (for running terminal sessions on remote computers) and ftp (the File Transfer Protocol application, for transferring files between two computers) required from the user a high level of awareness about the operating systems of the local and remote computers. While not entirely unusable by the less technically sophisticated, these applications nevertheless had a sufficiently high cost of entry (long learning times) to turn off many potential users.

Even before 1993, there were enough different information providers on the Internet to make it a complicated matter to find a desired resource. Various applications were developed to make searching the Internet simpler, but none was sufficiently compelling to users. One application, Gopher, held promise. Gopher servers simply made various Internet resources available through a common interface, using menus instead of requiring entry of explicit commands. The resources could be file repositories or remote computers allowing guest logins, or they could use any other allowable Internet application; Gopher simply provided a simple character-based system, with a menu-based front end to those resources.

No serious contender for a killer application appeared until the World Wide Web began and graphical browsers became available. It had always been a hassle to track down sources of information on the Internet, connect to the server, and attempt to locate the desired data. The World Wide Web offers improvements both to the end user, who can point and click to navigate the Web and locate interesting or necessary information, and to the information providers, who can offer access to their own data as well as other related providers to a much wider audience. Even more attractive is the ease with which regular users can create and publish their documents for Internet consumption.

The result was an application that appealed to a huge potential user base: those wanting access to free or cheap information and entertainment, but without the hassles of figuring out how to work all the different computers and programs.

THE NEW KILLER APP OF THE INTERNET: VOICE!

In an age of emerging technologies, mobile computing, and thus mobile e-commerce, is rapidly moving to the forefront as the need to service customers—anytime, anywhere becomes the ultimate goal for global e-businesses. So, what is the equivalent killer app on wireless telephones? Voice!

Until recently, the killer app on Personal Digital Assistants (PDAs) was believed to be the Personal Information Manager (PIM), but since the advent of Vindigo (the ultimate city guide that's caught on like wildfire for Palm Pilot users), all bets are off. So what if wireless telephone shoppers could use the GPS (global positioning system) built into their telephones in conjunction with something like Vindigo to find the nearest theater showing *Mission Impossible II* with a show starting in the next 25–55 minutes? Definitely cooler than voice and the self-destructing sunglasses on MI 2.

Eventually, though, there will be profitable and acceptable models of advertising to wireless telephones that wouldn't annoy the owners. Engage is doing testing right now to find them![36]

Among the general youth (Gen-Y) population of users, the wireless telephone facilitates community and communications among a group (not commerce, career advancement, or entertainment), and that's what they care about. If that's true, then one wonders whether that's the result of Gen-Y being less materialistic than everyone else is. Or, it could be that by virtue of their youth, Gen-Y users are less likely to be married with families and houses—the things that make the rest of us such voracious consumers.

According to Forrester Research, traditional demographic categories such as age, income, sex, etc., do not predict the likelihood to be online and shop online to any degree, but their categorization does.[37] However, Forrester's data is all about PC-based access to the Internet. It will be interesting to see whether they have any plans to re-run the study based on people's motivations to be online via alternate devices, and if they do, what the results are.

Thus, the killer app for commerce on wireless devices (both telephones and PDAs) may be online aggregators that allow you to pull up the best price for a product while you're standing in Circuit City looking at the item with the salesperson. Of course, an aggregator isn't an app.

So, is voice the killer app for wireless devices? Until the answer is clear, merchants should make sure they support voice as a backup to Web shopping, that their Web sites are reengineered (not just translated) into a wireless-friendly format, and that the telephone support they offer doesn't require long hold times, since wireless telephones do not lend themselves to waiting on hold comfortably.

THE WORLD WIDE WEB

In 1989, the World Wide Web began to take shape as the ultimate networked hypertext document. The idea was to use a markup language to create documents, relying on *tags* (function-oriented labels that define how a part of a document behaves) rather than using traditional word-processing formatting options to control the way the document is displayed. The result is that parts of each marked-up document behave the way they are supposed to, no matter how they are being displayed. For example, if a line is tagged as a title, it can be printed out in a specified font and size appropriate for hard copy, but when it is displayed on a monitor, it may appear in a different specified font, size, and color appropriate for that particular video display monitor.

This is a very dry and technical way of saying that Web documents can be created in such a way that a person using virtually any kind of computer (with a character-based or graphical user interface) can access virtually any information, resource, or device connected to a World Wide Web server. The user starts up client software and connects to a home page, and then can surf to other Web documents by traversing links on the home page and other connected pages. The result is a worldwide web of connections between information services on the Internet.

Connected services are often provided directly through Web documents, but the protocols allow any type of Internet application to be accessed, including more traditional file transfer servers and terminal sessions on larger host systems.

Although backward compatibility with existing services and systems is important, the Web owes its success to an extraordinarily simple user interface. Rather than requiring an explicit search for Internet resources using arcane tools, all the services are available in a graphic format and the user simply points and clicks to access them. As it becomes trivially easy for increasing numbers to access a Web site, it also becomes an especially attractive avenue for companies looking for new ways to market their products.

World Wide Web document development, server maintenance, specifications, and standards are all important topics, but are also mostly beyond the scope of this book. Some pointers for more information about the World Wide Web standards and protocols are provided in Appendix B, "Electronic Commerce Online Resources."

WORLD WIDE WEB STANDARDS

The World Wide Web is defined by a handful of protocol specifications. Software developers use those specifications to implement the Web browser and Web server programs. The interaction between browser and server is defined by the Hypertext Transfer Protocol (HTTP). Web browsers send messages conforming to this protocol to Web servers; these, in turn, return the requested information.

Traditional Internet addressing conventions are for locating computers attached to specific network interfaces. Special Internet host names and addresses are used, but these are sufficient only to locate a computer—locating a specific resource on a computer can be equally complicated, requiring the user to search through (sometimes unfamiliar) operating system directories, folders, and files. The Uniform Resource Locator (URL) protocol specifies how individual resources (files, documents, or even a specific section of a document) are to be identified within the World Wide Web. Web browsers use these URLs in HTTP requests to remote servers. They identify to the server exactly what resource is being requested.

Information transmitted from servers to browsers comes from Web documents stored on the server that have been specially tagged using Hypertext Markup Language (HTML) tags, which define the different functional pieces of each document. As mentioned earlier, tags allow different parts of a document to behave differently; most important are the abilities of text and graphics to behave as pointers to other parts of a document, other documents and resources, and especially resources on other Web servers. HTML documents consist of plain text (ASCII) files and may point to graphics files, other types of multimedia files (for example, sound or full-motion video files) stored in standard formats, or other network resources (URLs).

It isn't possible to put all the information that a person browsing the Web would like from your site into HTML-formatted files. Large databases, in particular, work better when they stay in their original formats. The Common Gateway Interface (CGI) specifies mechanisms for passing information from the person browsing your Web server to other resources available through that server, in particular by collecting information from the remote user in Web forms and then passing that information along to the other resource.

This type of interchange is vital to allow the remote user to access resources such as databases, but it is equally critical to collecting information (and then using it correctly and automatically) for the purposes of transacting business through the World Wide Web. Designing forms to collect orders through a Web site is not enough; there must be some mechanism outside the server to handle that information. The user's order needs to be processed: If a physical product has been ordered inventory and shipping information must be handled, and billing information must always be processed. CGI provides the link between the Web server and the rest of the commercial process. Tools such as CGI are discussed in Chapter 3.

Finally, the security protocols relevant to the World Wide Web include Secure Sockets Layer (SSL) and Secure Hypertext Transfer Protocol (S-HTTP). These are discussed in greater detail in Chapter 4, "Protocols for the Public Transport of Private Information," but very simply, they add security to existing protocols between the browsers and servers that support them.

BROWSERS AND SERVERS

Web browsers (or clients) must be able to send HTTP requests and receive HTTP replies from servers. The most popular browsers are fully graphical, although nongraphical browsers are a necessity for character-based operating systems. Browsers range from spartan text-only implementations like

Lynx for UNIX and other operating systems, to full-featured commercial products like Netscape Navigator and Microsoft Internet Explorer. Browser functions can also be integrated into more complete network or communications packages (like Netcom's Netcruiser or Attachmate's (formerly Wollongong) Emissary), or even into operating systems (like IBM's OS/2 Warp).

There is no shortage of Web browsers for any taste or budget. All should provide access to any Web-connected resource, although some will offer extra functions or features such as integration with other Internet tools (e-mail, network news), options for saving or copying retrieved data to files, and display-customization options. Performance enhancements, like the ability to "cache" or save documents already retrieved, can also differentiate browsers.

Just as Web browsers are available for virtually every computer and operating system, Web server software is also widely available. To offer Web services, a computer must be connected to the Internet, be running a Web server program, and have Web documents available. Web servers can contain highly graphical content without being able to display that content locally: The server system need only be able to run the server software and store the hypertext documents and files.

Although a basic PC with a full-time dial-up telephone link to the Internet is sufficient to act as a Web server, it would not be sufficient to serve very many simultaneous users. More often, Web servers are set up on higher-performance systems with higher-performance connections to the Internet (i.e., T-1). Individuals and organizations wishing to provide Web services have the option of setting up (and managing and maintaining) their own system, or paying an Internet presence provider to run their Web sites for them. Secured or commercial-grade servers for the World Wide Web are discussed in Chapter 7, "Online Commerce Environments."

SELLING ON THE WORLD WIDE WEB

With its easy-to-use and graphical interface, the World Wide Web seems an ideal medium for commerce. The biggest obstacle to commercialization of the Internet, its funding by government agencies for research purposes only, disappeared rapidly in the early 1990s as those subsidies expired and were not renewed. Obstacles such as a lack of market penetration and lack of mechanisms for secure transactions are rapidly disappearing, as consumers and businesses are flocking to the Internet and developers are turning their attentions to the problem of securing the Internet for commerce.

Keeping in mind the previous discussion of commercial transactions, selling on the World Wide Web parallels selling in the real world. Very simply, the customer enters the merchant's Web site and views product and company information. If the merchant successfully sells a product and fosters sufficient trust in the customer to generate an order, the customer will place an order.

The merchant's overall presentation, online and offline, determines the consumer's level of trust. The Web page presentation content—products, descriptions, pricing, and delivery—will help the consumer to make a decision. The rest of the transaction is carried on across the World Wide Web, but may require additional mechanisms connected to it. For example, the purchase of a digital product such as the text of an article can be carried on entirely through the Web page: The buyer selects the desired article and enters a credit card account number, and the Web server transmits the article. Assuming that some security mechanism is in place to keep the credit card account number private, no other network mechanisms are required (remember, of course, that the vendor in this instance would have to collect the sale information and process the credit card transaction manually).

Commerce over the World Wide Web requires more than transaction security; it requires mechanisms for processing sales as well. Those mechanisms cover the process from the point at which the sale information has been captured through the Web, moving information to the appropriate systems within the merchant's organization as well as outside, to companies that provide services like credit card authorization, to banks providing electronic banking services, and to other organizations involved in electronic transfers of value.

Chapter 2 discusses the actual mechanisms behind secure transactions, while Chapter 4 examines how these mechanisms are applied to protocols defining secure applications for use over the Internet.

OTHER INTERNET SALES VENUES

For many years before anyone even imagined the World Wide Web, electronic mail and network news existed. In addition, for many years before Internet access providers started selling dial-up access, people were doing business with each other by e-mail and network news.

Acceptable Use Policies (AUPs) prohibited commercial use of those parts of the Internet supported with government funds until the government moved out of the Internet business, but in practice this was interpreted to mean activities engaged in purely for profit. Personal possessions were routinely advertised in the appropriate news forums, although trying to sell magazine subscriptions or aluminum siding in lists devoted to computer operating systems was highly inadvisable. Used cars, computers, memory, and telephone answering machines were routinely sold online, generally through postings on lists devoted to personal items for sale.

Setting aside some of the "religious" discussions that "for sale" posts often incited (Is it appropriate to advertise a used network hub for sale on a network discussion group? Is puppy farming a hobby or a business?), the problems of transacting business across an unsecure, unreliable, and public medium became glaringly obvious.

First was the problem of fraud. Negotiating prices and delivery options by e-mail is quite easy; making sure that payment and delivery both occur is hard. Unless the parties were able to meet physically, there was no satisfactory solution to this problem. With no control over online identities, it is difficult or impossible to determine exactly who has sent an e-mail message, and unscrupulous individuals have taken advantage of this fact. Buyers often found that they had sent a check or money order off to a post office box, but never received the disk drive or monitor they thought they bought. Sellers often shipped their used equipment off to a remote address and then never got the check that was forever in the mail.

Obviously, there were enough honest individuals buying and selling to make it worthwhile, and there were ways to check up on uncertain quantities: One was to get telephone numbers, addresses, and references for faraway buyers and sellers—but this added significant costs in time and money. Another option was to limit all sales to cash, in-person transactions, which also limited the number of potential buyers, but eliminated the problems of nonpayment and nondelivery.

Credit card sales, though far from common, did happen. Some individuals had set up as corporations for the sale of specialized books, software, music CDs, and other products; when buying from these people, it was possible to send a credit card account number by e-mail. Despite it being transmitted in clear text between any number of different hosts through the Internet, we are not aware of any instance of a credit card number being intercepted on the Internet and misused. Either no one is willing to admit having sent credit card numbers by e-mail (it is widely considered to be pure folly to do so), or thieves looking for credit card numbers have easier ways to steal them than by attempting to put a packet sniffer on an Internet backbone and digging them out of the gigabytes of e-mail, news posts, and World Wide Web graphics image downloads.

Commerce by e-mail is becoming more viable an option for those without World Wide Web access as more security and authentication products become available. These are discussed at greater length throughout this book; they are generally equally applicable to the World Wide Web and any other Internet application, including e-mail.

ONLINE COMMERCE SOLUTIONS

As the previous sections make clear, commercial transactions over the Internet are not only possible, they are easy—as long as the proper tools are used. The rest of this book addresses these solutions, describing their general terms and providing overviews of some of the specific implementations announced and currently being delivered.

Beyond the basic issues of security (as manifested in authentication of offers, authorization of buyers and sellers, and verification of content), merchants and consumers also need to understand how these methods (as well as the use of digital currencies) can all be fitted into a commercial environment for the processing of orders.

PUBLIC KEY CRYPTOGRAPHY

Development of public key cryptography has paralleled the development of the Internet over the past 25 years or so. This should not be surprising, because improvements in the average computer's processing power have been rapid, constant, and remarkable—and both internetworking and cryptography require lots of computer power.

Cryptography is, literally, "secret writing" and refers to the arts and sciences of codes and secrets. Traditional cryptography relied on the use of keys and coding algorithms (procedures used to process text). The algorithm, which was generally kept secret, manipulated the message to be coded in a repeatable way; the key, also kept secret, provided a starting point for encoding and decoding texts. For example, a simple algorithm uses replacement. To encode, replace each plain-text letter with the letter a certain number farther down the alphabet (wrapping around to the start of the alphabet after the letter "z"). There are 25 distinct and usable keys for this algorithm. If the key selected is "1," then the word

rabbit

would be rendered as

sbccju

This code has been implemented as a cereal-box giveaway, and it becomes trivially easy to break when the message is more than a very few words: The letter distribution and patterns are sufficient for rapid solution of this type of puzzle.

Private key codes like this may depend on the algorithm as well as the key remaining unknown. Much more sophisticated codes have been developed as computing equipment has been increasingly relied upon for cryptographic purposes. Developments have included methods that make distribution and pattern solutions (without the code-breaker having any knowledge of the algorithms or keys used), but all codes are breakable with sufficient time and resources.

Public key methods, which are discussed in greater detail in Chapter 2, rely on schemes that employ two separate keys—one private and the other public—employed in a well-known algorithm. All the information needed to break the code is available to any code-breaker, as long as the code-breaker has the time and computer resources required. Depending on the way the code has been implemented, this could keep today's most advanced supercomputer occupied for many, many years. Since most encrypted information loses its value to code-breakers rather quickly, this approach to security works quite well.

Public key methods are useful beyond encryption: They make it possible for an individual to digitally sign a digital document, and they make it possible to verify that a digital transmission has been completed unmodified from the original. All these functions are vitally important to electronic commerce, and are discussed in greater detail in Chapter 2.

SECURITY STANDARDS

As mentioned earlier, the Secure Sockets Layer (SSL), originally proposed by Netscape Communications Corp., and the Secure HTTP (S-HTTP) specification add significant security functions to the World Wide Web.

These and other proposed standards (like that announced by Visa/Master-Card in late 1995) generally incorporate the public key cryptographic tools described earlier and in Chapter 2 to provide security. SSL and S-HTTP are described in greater detail in Chapter 4.

COMMERCE MODELS AND ENVIRONMENTS

The movement of money between buyer and seller is rarely simple even in the traditional storefront. Credit cards, debit cards, and charge cards all represent different payment methods; add to the mix cash, personal and third-party checks, traveler's checks, and money orders, and it is no longer simple to figure out where the money is and where it is going.

Electronic commerce systems include many of the same options as nonelectronic commerce, but add different methods of transmission. Electronic payments can be as simple as the unencrypted transmission of a credit card account number, or as complex as the encrypted transmission of a digitally signed electronic check. Third-party payment processors and electronic currencies add to the complexity. Chapter 3 introduces the various options for implementing electronic transfer of values, and it builds a conceptual foundation for the reader to better understand the vendors and products described in Chapters 5–8 and how they interact with each other. Chapter 9, "Strategies, Techniques, and Tools," discusses some tools, services, and products related to the implementation and support of electronic commerce. Chapter 10 shows you how to design and build e-commerce Web sites. Finally, Chapter 11 examines the future directions for e-commerce environments.

END NOTES

[1] Center for Research in Electronic Commerce, Department of MSIS, CBA 5.202, The University of Texas at Austin, Austin, TX 78712, 2000.

[2] 3Com, Santa Clara Site, 5400 Bayfront Plaza, Santa Clara, CA 95052, 2000.

[3] WEFA Group, Economic Impact: U.S. Direct Marketing Today: A Landmark Comprehensive Study, 1999.

[4] Ibid.

[5] Sun Microsystems, Inc., 901 San Antonio Road, Palo Alto, CA 94303 USA., 2000.

[6] U.S. Department of Commerce, Herbert C. Hoover Building, 14th and 15th Streets on Constitution Avenue in northwest Washington, DC., 2000.

[7] Ibid.

[8] Ibid.

[9] ONTOS, Inc., CrossPoint, 900 Chelmsford Street, Lowell, MA 01851-8107, 2000.

[10] U.S. Department of Commerce, 2000.

[11] ActivMedia Research LLC, 46 Concord Street, Peterborough, NH 03458, 2000.

[12] Ernst & Young, Laguna Niguel, CA., 2000.

[13] CheckFree Corporation, Corporate Headquarters, 4411 East Jones Bridge Road, Norcross, GA 30092, 2000.

[14] Jack Henry & Associates, Inc., 4135 S. Stream Blvd. 3rd Floor, Charlotte, NC 28217, 2000.

[15] Block Financial Corporation, Kansas City, MO, 2000.

[16] Charles Schwab, NY Operations Center, P.O. Box 179, Newark, NJ 07101-9671, 2000.

[17] Prudential Securities Incorporated, New York, NY, 2000.

[18] Lombard Brokerage Inc., 333 Market Street, 25th Floor, San Francisco, CA 94105-3407, 2000.

[19] PAWWS Financial Network, 101 Hudson Street, Jersey City, NJ 07302, 2000.

[20] National Consumers League, 1701 K Street, N.W., Suite 1201, Washington, D.C. 20006, 2000.

[21] TradeWave, Headquarters: Digital Signature Trust Co., Gateway Tower East, 11th Floor, One South Main Street, Salt Lake City, UT 84111, 2000.

[22] U.S. Department of Commerce, 2000.

[23] Ibid.

[24] Ibid.

[25] Ibid.

[26] Ibid.

[27] Ibid.

[28] Ibid.

[29] Ibid.

[30] Ibid.

[31] Ibid.

[32] Ibid.

[33] Ibid.

[34] Ibid.

[35] Ibid.

[36] Engage, 100 Brickstone Square, Andover, MA 01810, 2000.

[37] Forrester Research, Inc., 400 Technology Square, Cambridge, MA 02139, USA, 2000.

2 Security Technologies

Three may keep a secret, if two of them are dead.

—BENJAMIN FRANKLIN, *POOR RICHARD'S ALMANAC* (1733)

Secrets have always been hard to keep, and we have more secrets today than ever, what with Social Security numbers, credit card accounts, and Personal Identification Numbers (PINs) for accessing practically everything. With computers to keep records and collect data, the informed person is examining what information is solicited, what is shared, and what is kept private. The Internet is open, meaning that transmissions can be overheard, intercepted, and forged. However, some simple tools can eliminate (for all intents and purposes) the risks inherent in communicating over an open link. This chapter explains why the Internet is unsecure and examines the tools used to secure it. Internetworking protocols and cryptography don't make for easy reading, but they do build a base for understanding the issues of online commerce.

WHY THE INTERNET IS UNSECURE

The Internet is simply an implementation of protocols, rules of operation, or standards that define the way in which connected computers communicate with each other. When every connected system follows these rules, they can all communicate with each other, even if they use different hardware, software, or operating systems. Connected systems can even be connected to different types of networks, but as long as they all run the Internet protocols, they will be able to interoperate.

The people upon whose work the Internet is based intended to prove the feasibility of internetworking, not to produce a commercial product for internetworking. As a result, the things consumers of commercial computer products look for, such as easy-to-use interfaces and secure operations, have long been missing from Internet Protocol suite implementations.

In the early days of the Internet, the overwhelming majority of people connected to it were academics or researchers, and Internet traffic was restricted to not-for-profit uses. Users then, as now, were advised not to trust any sensitive information to the Internet. Most computers connected to the Internet were UNIX boxes, with the remainder being large, multiuser systems—all of which had their own security implementations. One of the most important functions fulfilled by Internet newsgroups was dissemination of security information and warnings about risks uncovered in different operating systems and Transmission Control Protocol/Internet Protocol (TCP/IP) implementations. The prudent network manager used heavily monitored Internet firewalls to strictly filter data being sent in to and out of the organizational network; this is still highly recommended today, and is discussed later in the chapter.

Securing personal computers on a network is considerably more difficult than securing UNIX workstations and mainframes: There are as many points of entry to the network as there are personal computers, PC security tools range from nonexistent to barely adequate, and the PC users themselves are notoriously lax in their security practices.

In any case, the Internet is definitely an open network. Once data is transmitted beyond the organizational network, it may be handled by any number of different intermediate computers (called *routers*) that make sure the data is delivered to its intended destination. Data is also likely to travel across Internet backbone networks, which move vast quantities of data over large distances. Information is vulnerable at many points, including the originating computer (which may have been tampered with at some point to subvert it), the local or organizational network (local traffic is almost trivially easy to listen to and requires little more than a connection to the same network), and some intermediate system or network out on the Internet—and the same risks exist for the networks and systems on the receiving end. Figure 2.1 shows the type of route that data may take between two hosts on the Internet.

Smart network managers and administrators take great care before connecting any corporate system to the Internet, implementing elaborate and extensive filtering systems and firewalls. Another growing issue for many companies is the creation and enforcement of a security policy and

Tracing route to openmarket.com [199.170.183.2] over a maximum of 30 hops:
 1 486 ms 212 ms 166 ms dial2.primary.net [205.242.92.16] 2 151 ms 168 ms 133 ms
bigrtr.primary.net [205.242.92.254] 3 149 ms 140 ms 140 ms ATM1-0-STL.dmnd.net
[206.114.210.7] 4 210 ms 308 ms 179 ms 902.Hssi3-0.GW1.STL1.ALTER.NET [137.39.168.5]
5 270 ms 360 ms 469 ms 127.Hssi5-0.CR1.CHI1.Alter.Net [137.39.69.45] 6 594 ms 401
ms 394 ms 106.Hssi4-0.CR1.BOS1.Alter.Net [137.39.30.57] 7 195 ms 215 ms 320 ms
Fddi0-0.GW2.BOS1.Alter.Net [137.39.35.7] 8 284 ms 189 ms 249 ms
OpenMarket1-gw.customer.ALTER.NET [137.39.207.226] 9 298 ms 397 ms 212 ms
screen1.openmarket.com [204.254.94.3] 10 373 ms 535 ms 703 ms bb-router-2.openmarket.com
[204.254.94.126] 11 406 ms 381 ms 252 ms openmarket.com [199.170.183.2]
Trace complete

FIGURE 2.1 Once data is transmitted past the organizational network, it can pass across many different computers and networks, where eavesdroppers may be able to intercept it. To demonstrate this, the following is the result of a trace route (tracert.exe) from the computer used to write this book to Open Market, Inc.

acceptable use policy. Before one dismisses this attitude as overly paranoid, it must be put in the context of other information risks:

- Long-distance telephone calling card accounts (along with Personal Identification Numbers, PINs) are routinely looted by watchers (some using binoculars) at airports and train stations.
- Intruders routinely take advantage of unprotected systems not just to search for valuable or interesting information, but as steppingstones to further attacks on other systems.
- More than 65,000 credit card numbers stored on a computer at an Internet Service Provider (ISP) were compromised by an intruder in early 2000.
- Credit card skimming is an e-commerce scam that is running rampant, and can affect even the most careful and security-conscience consumers (see the sidebar, "Credit Card Skimming").

The service provider had not implemented sufficient security to prevent the attack, which apparently had not taken advantage of any inherent Internet weakness, but exploited security weaknesses in the actual computer. The point is that property must be protected, whether it is information or has a physical existence, because immoral people will try to steal it if they possibly can. Those apparently paranoid network managers realize that any corporate resource exposed on the Internet is at risk, and the solution is eternal vigilance.

Credit Card Skimming

The Secret Service is currently investigating a national credit card fraud scheme that involves copying information (swiping/scanning the card on a miniaturized scanner) from customers' charge cards while they are being used for legitimate purchases.

The scheme, called *skimming*, involves the use of credit card scanners to surreptitiously copy the electronic information from the magnetic stripe on credit cards. The data then is used to manufacture counterfeit cards.

According to the Secret Service, the scheme is run out of legitimate businesses, and 11,000 people so far have been targeted by it. The information stolen from one customer's card was used to make at least $20,000 of unauthorized purchases. The illegal purchases were made around the world, from Virginia, West Virginia, Ohio, and Maryland to Hong Kong.

The suspects in the cases were employees of a local business usually patronized by the victims. The suspects usually worked there a short time before leaving on good terms, but sometimes on bad terms. Management had no knowledge that the skimming was going on in most of the cases.

Scanners are now made as small as a pager. The perpetrators can scan your card right in front of you, and you won't even realize it.

Why is the Secret Service involved instead of the FBI or ATF? In addition to protecting the President, the Secret Service is charged with combating monetary crimes such as credit card fraud and currency counterfeiting.

All but 100 of the 11,000 victims learned of the unauthorized charges from their credit card companies, while the others spotted them on billing statements. The card information apparently was stolen during the first half of 2000, and most of the unauthorized charges discovered so far were made between the second week of April and the end of June.

According to the Secret Service, skimming is *the most significant financial problem facing the credit card industry today and for the near future*. Card readers that attach to a laptop or personal computer can be bought for less than $200, and portable readers that fit in a person's palm sell for $900 and up.

The portable readers can store information from up to 100 cards at a time. With commercially available software and equipment, criminals can use the data to create their own magnetic strips for counterfeit cards. One company that retails credit card scanners has stopped selling them to individuals because of the problem with fraud.

It's the Protocols

The Internet protocol, TCP/IP, is a layered protocol with seven layers. In many circles, these are referred to as the seven layers of Open Systems Interconnection (OSI). The seven layers are formed in a hierarchy with the lowest level, level one, focusing on the raw physical connection between two devices. The highest level of the protocol works with the actual application such as the Web, Internet mail, or file transfer protocol.

For the purposes of this discussion, we will discuss four of the levels, as shown in Figure 2.2. Understanding a little about the way information moves around the Internet will help explain why the Internet itself is unreliable and unsecure, but can still allow reliable and secure messages to be sent and received.

The different layers represent different kinds of interactions. They are useful in the design of internetworks because they separate and distribute important functions in an efficient way. The specific type of network cable my computer is connected to is a vital part of Internet traffic, but only as it concerns moving that traffic from my ISP to my actual computer. Likewise,

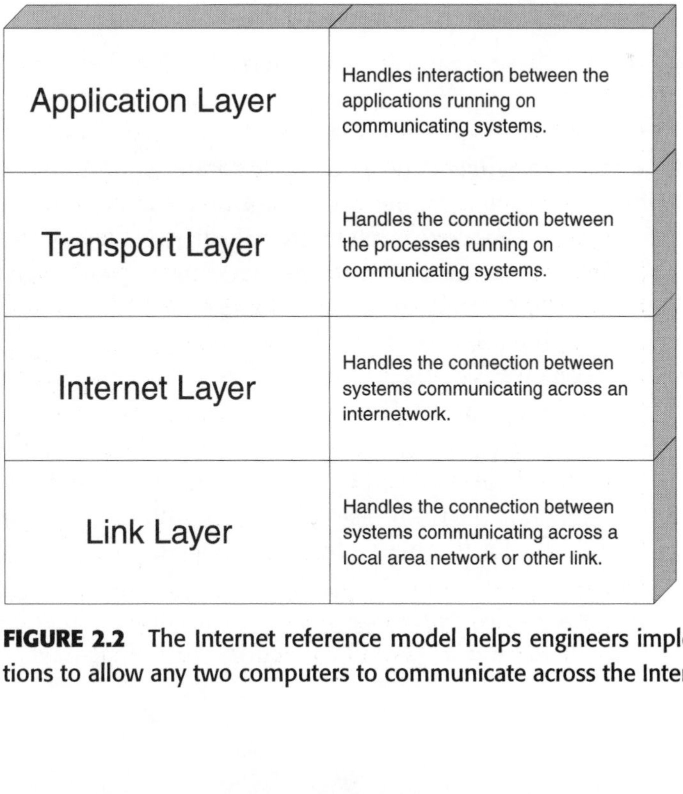

Application Layer	Handles interaction between the applications running on communicating systems.
Transport Layer	Handles the connection between the processes running on communicating systems.
Internet Layer	Handles the connection between systems communicating across an internetwork.
Link Layer	Handles the connection between systems communicating across a local area network or other link.

FIGURE 2.2 The Internet reference model helps engineers implement applications to allow any two computers to communicate across the Internet.

my computer operating system and version of e-mail software is important, but only as it relates to the display of e-mail that I receive from the Internet.

Link Layer

The lowest level at which the Internet functions involves connections across the local area network (between the network connections of computers physically linked together); in other words, actual signals that pass along a wire (or wireless) link. Because the Internet is actually a network of networks, this layer operates only at the local level between computers connected to the same wire.

Called the Link or Network layer, this level may be an Ethernet cable LAN installed in a corporate office, or a telephone link between a home PC user and an ISP. In theory, the Link layer can control just about any communication medium (one April Fool's Internet specification describes IP as implemented with carrier pigeons), but is largely irrelevant to Internet security. Any security mechanisms that might be in place on a local network or telephone connection work only as long as the data remains on that local area network or phone link. As soon as the data is forwarded to another network, it has to be made accessible to systems on that network.

Internet Layer

The next layer is the Internet layer. This is where connections between computers are handled, using the Internet Protocol. Internet addresses uniquely identify each and every connected computer on the Internet and are used to deliver data. The source computer addresses its information to the destination computer. If the destination system isn't on the same physical wire as the source system, intermediate router computers (which have connections to more than one network) pass the information on until it arrives at the destination system's home network.

The Internet Protocol is known as a "best effort" protocol: There are no mechanisms defined through IP to guarantee delivery of any particular piece of information. That type of mechanism would require any recipient system to notify the origination system in the event that it received the data, but also in the event that expected data was not received. That type of transaction is relatively easy when the communicating systems are sitting on the same local network; however, when data has to be passed across any number of different networks by routers, it becomes burdensome to offer any type of delivery guarantees. As a result, the Internet Protocol leaves delivery guarantees (as well as security) to a higher layer.

Transport Layer

The Transport layer is next, handling the connection between the actual programs running on the source and destination systems. This is important because each computer can have more than one active link to another computer, so there must be a way for each individual session to be differentiated. Because there are different types of network application programs that need to be run on the Internet, there are two different protocols defining the way the programs can interact: the User Datagram Protocol (UDP) and the Transport Control Protocol (TCP).

These two protocols carry two different types of Internet traffic. TCP is the workhorse of the Internet: Applications that require a "virtual circuit" (the functional equivalent of a direct connection between two computers) use TCP to ensure that information being sent has been received by the remote system. TCP supplies reliability for Internet applications that require it; any application that offers users some degree of interaction with remote network resources. For example, interactive terminal sessions (telnet) and file transfers using the File Transfer Protocol (FTP) both use TCP, as do World Wide Web protocols (usually).

The User Datagram Protocol, like the Internet Protocol, is an unreliable, best-effort protocol. Most often used by applications that don't support direct interaction or don't require every single message to get through, UDP is a much more efficient protocol: It takes less programming to implement it, and it uses far fewer network resources to communicate between programs using it. Neither of the Internet's transport protocols currently implements security features—those are left for a higher layer.

Application Layer

The highest layer is defined by the interaction between end user and network resource. Called the Application layer, its relevant protocols define the different applications available to users on the Internet. For instance, the World Wide Web application is defined by the Hypertext Transport Protocol (HTTP), and the most common method for file transfer is defined by the File Transfer Protocol (FTP). Each Internet application is defined by its application protocol, which prescribes how commands are passed from the user to the remote system, and how requested information is passed back to the user.

Security and reliability may both be built into the Application layer, if desired. Doing so means that no intermediate routers need to worry about the reliability or security of the data they transfer from network to network (which would mean additional computations for verifications)—they just make sure it arrives at its destination. Once the data reaches its destination, the target computer can then make sure the data it receives is reliable and secure.

By using several different layers, data can move efficiently across the Internet. The program at the Application layer collects information (from the end user or the network resource), wraps it up (encapsulates it), addresses it to the destination resource, and passes it down to the Transport layer. The Transport layer wraps the data up, addresses it to the target program on the destination system, and then passes it on down to the Internet layer. The Internet layer program wraps the data up, addresses it to a particular computer on a particular network, and then passes it down to the Network layer. If the destination computer is on the same network as the source computer, the software at the Network layer simply sends the data directly to the destination; if not (as is usually the case), the data gets sent to an appropriate router, to be forwarded to the destination network and host.

The software operating at any given layer is concerned only with moving data chunks to its destination at the same layer. Network layer software moves chunks of data between connections on the same physical wire; Internet layer software moves chunks of data between two specific computers connected to the Internet; Transport layer software moves chunks of data between two programs; and Application layer software moves data between a user and a resource. When Network layer software receives a chunk of data, it unwraps it and passes it up to the next layer; this process continues until the actual application data is unwrapped and passed to the user or network resource.

This is a much-abbreviated summary of how the Internet protocols work, but it is enough to show how data moves around the Internet, as well as where some of the security risks lie.

Where the Risks Are

It should be stressed from the very start that the greatest threat to security in any organization almost invariably comes from within. Insiders have the access, they know what is valuable, and they know what is most damaging. The same goes for the Internet, at least for now: The hacker who stole 65,000 credit card numbers did not exploit any weakness in the Internet protocols; he exploited the weakness in the security of the computer where those numbers were stored.

What the Risks Are

In any case, there are still some serious risks that you take on when you transmit data across the Internet:

- Interception by a third party (someone other than the intended recipient reads mail you send)
- Forgery (someone sends mail and signs your name)
- Modification (someone intercepts your mail, changes it, and sends it on to its final destination)

Interception of your network traffic is only a problem if you are sending sensitive information, like credit card numbers or electronic cash. However, most traffic is largely pretty boring or irrelevant except to the parties involved. One sure way to keep eavesdroppers in the dark is to not speak publicly about private matters: This works as well on the Internet as it does in a restaurant.

Forgery can be a much more serious risk. The nature of the e-mail protocols makes it a relatively simple matter for someone to send a message that appears to be coming from someone else. The possibilities for mischief (at least) are infinite, from sending poison pen letters to someone's boss to ordering a dozen pizzas electronically in someone else's name. With no physical evidence, e-mail forgery is relatively easy to get away with, which eliminates one restraining factor that might keep someone with insufficient moral compass from doing it.

Another insidious threat is that someone will intercept transmissions, modify them, and send them on to their destinations. For instance, a criminal could intercept a message from a vendor and change the payment instructions, directing payment to the criminal's account. Again, the devious mind can come up with any number of other options for mischief.

Internet Security Holes

Once you've secured your own computer system—using access codes or passwords, physically restricting access to it, and making sure that it is not left unattended while connected to any remote services—you can start to worry about the risks from your Internet connection.

The first place your data goes when it leaves your computer is a router connected to the Internet. If you are linked through an organizational Internet connection, your own system may actually be visible to anyone else connected to the Internet; more likely, though, your organizational

Internet connection will sit on the other side of a firewall system. Firewall gateways function by hiding organizational systems from the rest of the Internet, while still providing access for approved applications to send and receive data. Organizations that use firewalls also usually put their public access systems, such as World Wide Web servers, just outside their firewalls and keep sensitive material off those servers.

What if you don't have a corporate connection, but rather use a dial-up connection (Serial Line Internet Protocol (SLIP) or Point-to-Point Protocol (PPP)) to an ISP across a telephone line? In theory, your computer is vulnerable to attacks any time you are connected. Your system at those times can act as a server, but only if you are running a server program.

The larger issue is what happens to your Internet transmissions when they leave (or before they arrive at) your computer. Anyone with access to the router through which you receive your Internet traffic (or the network to which it is connected) has the ability to eavesdrop on your sessions. Security depends on the integrity of participating network and system managers, as well as on their ability to keep out intruders.

As someone who has been entrusted with access to sensitive systems like these, I would like to believe that anyone who has been given that kind of access is an upstanding, moral person. But, although the vast majority of people are upright, there will always be a few bad apples who will betray their trust for money, for power, for ego, or just for fun.

This security risk exists at every interconnection, so if you purchase your Internet service from a local reseller, chances are that your transmissions are passed from the local company to a regional company, who passes them on to Internet backbones. There may be quite a few intermediate networks and systems between your computer and the computers you communicate with, each with its own support staff that must be trusted to be capable of running both a secure network (to keep outside intruders out) and a moral one (to keep insiders from selling out).

A Bigger Risk

Security methods that use digital signatures and encryption can, in general, be considered secure, for all practical purposes. The cost of a brute-force attack against this type of mechanism would be astronomical, far in excess of any conceivable potential benefit to the attacker.

However, whenever the user must provide his or her own password, attacks on individual accounts are possible, just as they are in any system that uses passwords for access. This means that customers must take as much care in protecting the passwords to their secure commerce services as they would in protecting their own wallets:

- The password should not be easy to guess (like a name or birth date).
- The password should not be written down near the computer from which it will be used.
- The user should not give out the password to anyone, ever.
- The user should not leave an active session running on an unattended, unprotected system.
- Passwords should be changed periodically.

As long as precautions are taken, and passwords protected properly, they will keep the system secure. If the passwords are not protected, however, the only thing they provide is a false sense of security. It should also be noted that requiring users to maintain (and remember) a separate user ID and password for every commercial site they connect to makes it increasingly difficult for users to actually follow basic security principles and more likely that they will fail to do so.

Fighting Back

Despite the ominous description of the Internet and firewalls, there are steps you can take to recover some peace of mind in connecting a corporate network to the Internet. The firewall software market is evolving on a daily basis. There is tremendous competition in this field, yielding great results for end users.

One great product of the development is virtual private networking or VPN, often referred to as *tunneling*. Fundamentally, VPN gives the network/firewall administrators of two firewalls the ability to create a virtual encrypted path between the two firewalls. Assuming each firewall is equipped with the VPN feature, the two administrators enter the IP address of the other firewall into their home firewalls. The two firewalls exchange messages and create a special encryption algorithm or code. When data is sent from one firewall to the other, the originating firewall will detect that the data (packets) are headed to a participating firewall and use the previously arranged encryption algorithm to encrypt the data. Upon arrival at the destination firewall, the data will be recognized and the shared algorithm will be used to decode the data once inside the firewall. And, of course, while the data passed over the Internet, the data was encrypted, and the only device on earth that could quickly decode the information was the destination firewall.

The first installations of VPN were limited to firewalls from the same manufacturer. However, to promote interoperability, the IP Security (IPSEC) standard has been created and is being implemented by leading firewall vendors.

VPN is only practical for business-to-business transactions such as one between a railroad and an auto manufacturer. However, the functionality will be applicable as more servers managing electronic commerce transactions automatically communicate with banks and similar high-security sites. VPN also holds opportunities for mid-sized and large companies looking to create secure wide area networks over the Internet. See the sidebar, "Everyone's VPN" for the latest VPN security solution.

VPNs and firewalls are good first lines of defense. But, how do you really fight back effectively to eliminate Internet security risks or threats? Let's take a look!

Really Fighting Back

The FBI, the Justice Department, the Federal CIO Council, the Critical Infrastructure Assurance Office (CIAO), the Computer Emergency Response Team/Coordination Center (CERT/CC), and a bunch of others have joined with the System Administration, Networking, and Security (SANS) Institute in releasing a new SANS study identifying the 10 top security vulnerabilities on the Internet. They are joining in a worldwide campaign to fix the flaws because these 10 clusters account for a surprisingly large percent of all successful break-ins.

The SANS (System Administration, Networking, and Security) Institute is a cooperative research and education organization through which more than 96,000 system administrators, security professionals, and network administrators share the lessons they are learning and find solutions for challenges they face. SANS was founded in 1989.

The following study has both the vulnerabilities and the fixes.[1] That way, when your bosses ask you whether you know about the 10 vulnerabilities, you can tell them that you already have detailed fixes in hand and are planning how to scan all the machines to be certain where the fixes are required.

Everyone's VPN

The case for running IP VPNs in sites with dynamic, meshed connectivity requirements got another shot in the arm recently. Services that could challenge frame relay in some scenarios have gone live from a start-up called OpenReach, a Wakefield, Massachusetts company determined to let you point-and-click your way to setting up secure intranet/extranet connections on the fly.

The services are new, so the usual proof-in-the-pudding disclaimer applies. But OpenReach has a pretty interesting idea. For organizations whose WAN connectivity needs happen to change a lot, sites that don't have staff steeped in the intricacies of IP Security (IPSec) or temporary work teams such as construction sites, the concept of setting up a secure business-class connection in minutes by clicking a mouse at least begs some investigation.

Points of particular interest about OpenReach's TrueSpan service are:

- It doesn't matter what access network you use (DSL, cable, whatever), and the service can span the networks of multiple ISPs.
- The price of the service starts at less than $100 a month per site, for a 384K bit/sec link.
- The only equipment you need at each site to build a VPN is an Intel-based PC.
- To build your network, you register at OpenReach's Web site, download some software onto a floppy disk (no charge), and run it on the PC. The PC boots as a network server, connects to the OpenReach service, downloads routing tables, and is ready to automatically connect to the locations you specify.
- The service automatically invokes Triple-DES encryption, IPSec tunnels, and digital certificates for security. OpenReach acts as the certificate authority, using a patent-pending process that does not let even OpenReach see bearer traffic.

All this said, let's reiterate that the frame relay we know and love isn't going away anytime soon. Among the reasons are:

- Frame is still a solid choice, price-wise, security-wise, and reliability-wise, for hub-and-spoke networks, particularly those whose configurations do not change much.
- If you need to support Layer 3 protocols other than IP, IP VPNs obviously aren't an option.
- If it ain't broke, why fix it?

How to Eliminate the Ten Most Critical Internet Security Threats

The majority of successful attacks on computer systems via the Internet can be traced to exploitation of one of a small number of security flaws. Most of the systems compromised in the Solar Sunrise Pentagon hacking incident were attacked through a single vulnerability. A related flaw was exploited to break into many of the computers later used in massive distributed denial-of-service attacks. Recent compromises of Windows NT-based Web servers are typically traced to entry via a well-known vulnerability. Another vulnerability is widely thought to be the means used to compromise more than 40,000 Linux systems.

A few software vulnerabilities account for the majority of successful attacks because attackers are opportunistic—taking the easiest and most convenient route. They exploit the best-known flaws with the most effective and widely available attack tools. They count on organizations not fixing the problems, and they often attack indiscriminately, by scanning the Internet for vulnerable systems.

System administrators report that they have not corrected these flaws because they simply do not know which of over 600 potential problems are the ones that are most dangerous, and they are too busy to correct them all.

The information security community is meeting this problem head-on by identifying the most critical Internet security problem areas—the clusters of vulnerabilities that system administrators need to eliminate immediately. This consensus Top Ten list represents an unprecedented example of active cooperation among industry, government, and academia. The participants came together from the most security-conscious federal agencies; from the leading security software vendors and consulting firms; from the top university-based security programs; and from CERT/CC and the SANS Institute. Here is the experts' list of the Ten Most Often Exploited Internet Security Flaws, along with the actions needed to rid your systems of these vulnerabilities:

1. BIND weaknesses: *nxt, qinv,* and *in.named* allow immediate root compromise.
2. Vulnerable CGI programs and application extensions (ColdFusion) installed on Web servers.
3. Remote Procedure Call (RPC) weaknesses in *rpc.ttdbserverd* (ToolTalk), *rpc.cmsd* (Calendar Manager), and *rpc.statd* that allow immediate root compromise.
4. RDS security hole in the Microsoft Internet Information Server (IIS).

5. Sendmail buffer overflow weaknesses, pipe attacks, and MIMEbo that allow immediate root compromise.
6. *sadmind* and *mountd*.
7. Global file sharing and inappropriate information sharing via NFS and Windows NT ports 135->139 (445 in Windows2000) or UNIX NFS exports on port 2049. Also, AppleTalk over IP with Macintosh file sharing enabled.
8. User IDs, especially root/administrator with no passwords or weak passwords.
9. IMAP and POP buffer overflow vulnerabilities or incorrect configuration.
10. Default SNMP community strings set to "public" and "private."

BIND Weaknesses

The Berkeley Internet Name Domain (BIND) package is the most widely used implementation of Domain Name Service (DNS)—the critical means by which we all locate systems on the Internet by name without having to know specific IP addresses—and this makes it a favorite target for attack. Sadly, according to a mid-1999 survey, about 50 percent of all DNS servers connected to the Internet are running vulnerable versions of BIND. In a typical example of a BIND attack, intruders erased the system logs, and installed tools to gain administrative access. They then compiled and installed Internet Relay Chat (IRC) utilities and network scanning tools, which they used to scan more than a dozen class-B networks in search of additional systems running vulnerable versions of BIND. In a matter of minutes, they had used the compromised system to attack hundreds of remote systems abroad, resulting in many additional successful compromises. This illustrates the chaos that can result from a single vulnerability in the software for ubiquitous Internet services such as DNS.

The systems affected consisted of Multiple UNIX and Linux. As of this writing, any version earlier than BIND v.8.2.2 patch level 5 is vulnerable. The following advice is given on correcting the problem:

1. Disable the BIND name daemon (named) on all systems that are not authorized to be DNS servers. Some experts recommend you also remove the DNS software.
2. On machines that are authorized DNS servers, update to the latest version and patch level (as of this writing, the latest version is 8.2.2 patch level 5).

3. Run BIND as a nonprivileged user for protection in the event of future remote-compromise attacks. However, only processes running as root can be configured to use ports below 1024—a requirement for DNS. Therefore, you must configure BIND to change the user-id after binding to the port.
4. Run BIND in a *chroot( )ed* directory structure for protection in the event of future remote-compromise attacks.[2]

Vulnerable CGI Programs and Application Extensions Installed on Web Servers

Most Web servers support Common Gateway Interface (CGI) programs to provide interactivity in Web pages, such as data collection and verification. Many Web servers come with sample CGI programs installed by default. Unfortunately, many CGI programmers fail to consider ways in which their programs may be misused or subverted to execute malicious commands. Vulnerable CGI programs present a particularly attractive target to intruders because they are relatively easy to locate, and they operate with the privileges and power of the Web server software itself. Intruders are known to have exploited vulnerable CGI programs to vandalize Web pages, steal credit card information, and set up back doors to enable future intrusions, even if the CGI programs are secured. When Janet Reno's picture was replaced by that of Adolph Hitler at the Department of Justice Web site, an in-depth assessment concluded that a CGI hole was the most probable avenue of compromise. Allaire's ColdFusion is a Web server application package that includes vulnerable sample programs when installed. As a general rule, sample programs should always be removed from production systems.

The systems affected consisted of all Web servers. The following advice is given on correcting the problem:

1. Do not run Web servers as root.
2. Get rid of CGI script interpreters in bin directories.
3. Remove unsafe CGI scripts.
4. Write safer CGI programs.
5. Don't configure CGI support on Web servers that don't need it.
6. Run your Web server in a *chroot( )ed* environment to protect the machine against yet to be discovered exploits.[3]

RPC Weaknesses that Allow Immediate Root Compromise

Remote procedure calls (RPC) allow programs on one computer to execute programs on a second computer. They are widely used to access network services such as shared files in NFS. Multiple vulnerabilities caused by flaws in RPC are being actively exploited. There is compelling evidence that the vast majority of the distributed denial-of-service attacks launched during 1999 and early 2000 were executed by systems that had been victimized because they had the RPC vulnerabilities. The broadly successful attack on U.S. military systems during the Solar Sunrise incident also exploited an RPC flaw found on hundreds of Department of Defense systems.

The systems affected consisted of Multiple UNIX and Linux. The following advice is given on correcting the problem:

1. Wherever possible, turn off and/or remove these services on machines directly accessible from the Internet.
2. Where you must run them, install the latest patches.[4]

RDS Security Hole in the Microsoft Internet Information Server (IIS)

Microsoft's Internet Information Server (IIS) is the Web server software found on most Web sites deployed on Microsoft Windows NT and Windows 2000 servers. Programming flaws in IIS's Remote Data Services (RDS) are being employed by malicious users to run remote commands with administrator privileges. Some participants who developed the *Top Ten* list believe that exploits of other IIS flaws, such as.*HTR* files, are at least as common as exploits of RDS. Prudence dictates that organizations using IIS install patches or upgrades to correct all known IIS security flaws when they install patches or upgrades to fix the RDS flaw.

The systems affected consisted of Microsoft Windows NT systems using Internet Information Server. The following advice is given on correcting the problem:

1. Implement custom handlers AND delete the references to VBBusObj at HKEY_LOCAL_MACHINE/System/CurrentControlSet/ Services/W3SVC/Parameters/ ADCLaunch/VbBusObj.VbBusObjCls.
2. Use the information posted by Microsoft to disable the service, or correct the RDS vulnerability and all other security flaws in IIS.

Sendmail Buffer Overflow Weaknesses, Pipe Attacks, and MIMEbo that Allow Immediate Root Compromise

Sendmail is the program that sends, receives, and forwards most electronic mail processed on UNIX and Linux computers. Sendmail's widespread use on the Internet makes it a prime target of attackers. Several flaws have been found over the years. The very first advisory issued by CERT/CC in 1988 made reference to an exploitable weakness in sendmail. In one of the most common exploits, the attacker sends a crafted mail message to the machine running Sendmail, and Sendmail reads the message as instructions requiring the victim machine to send its password file to the attacker's machine (or to another victim) where the passwords can be cracked.

The systems affected consisted of Multiple UNIX and Linux. The following advice is given on correcting the problem:

1. Implement patches for sendmail.
2. Do not run Sendmail in daemon mode (turn off the *-bd* switch) on machines that are neither mail servers nor mail relays.
3. Consider running an alternate Mail Transfer Agent such as Postfix, QMail, or Exim.[5]

The preceding programs are not transparent replacements, and may have weaknesses of their own that have yet to be discovered.

Sadmind and Mountd

Sadmind allows remote administration access to Solaris systems, providing graphical access to system administration functions. Mountd controls and arbitrates access to NFS mounts on UNIX hosts. Buffer overflows in these applications can be exploited, allowing attackers to gain control with root access.

The systems affected consisted of Multiple UNIX and Linux. The following advice is given on correcting the problem:

1. Wherever possible, turn off and/or remove these services on machines directly accessible from the Internet.
2. Install the latest patches.[6]

Global File Sharing and Inappropriate Information Sharing

These services allow file sharing over networks. When improperly configured, they can expose critical system files or give full file system access to any hostile party connected to the network. Many computer owners and administrators use these services to make their file systems readable and writeable in an effort to improve the convenience of data access. Administrators of a government computer site used for software development for mission planning made their files world readable so people at a different government facility could get easy access. Within two days, other people had discovered the open file shares and stole the mission planning software.

When file sharing is enabled on Windows machines, they become vulnerable to both information theft and certain types of quick-moving viruses. A recently released virus called the 911 Worm uses file shares on Windows 95 and 98 systems to propagate, and causes the victim's computer to dial 911 on its modem. Macintosh computers are also vulnerable to file sharing exploits.

The same NetBIOS mechanisms that permit Windows file sharing may also be used to enumerate sensitive system information from NT systems. User and group information (usernames, last logon dates, password policy, RAS information), system information, and certain Registry keys may be accessed via a *null session* connection to the NetBIOS Session Service. This information is typically used to mount a password-guessing or brute-force password attack against the NT target.

The systems affected consisted of UNIX, Windows, and Macintosh. The following advice is given on correcting the problem:

1. When sharing mounted drives, ensure that only required directories are shared.
2. For added security, allow sharing only to specific IP addresses because DNS names can be spoofed.
3. For Windows systems, ensure that all shares are protected with strong passwords.
4. For Windows NT systems, prevent anonymous enumeration of users, groups, system configuration, and Registry keys via the *null session* connection. Block inbound connections to the NetBIOS Session Service (tcp 139) at the router or the NT host. Consider implementing the RestrictAnonymous Registry key for Internet-connected hosts in standalone or nontrusted domain environments.
5. For Macintosh systems, disable file sharing and Web sharing extensions unless absolutely required. If file sharing must be enabled, ensure strong passwords for access, and stop file sharing during periods in which it is not required.[7]

User IDs

Some systems come with *demo* or *guest* accounts with no passwords or with widely known default passwords. Service workers often leave maintenance accounts with no passwords, and some database management systems install administration accounts with default passwords. In addition, busy system administrators often select system passwords that are easily guessable (*love, money, wizard* are common) or just use a blank password. Default passwords provide effortless access for attackers. Many attackers try default passwords and then try to guess passwords before resorting to more sophisticated methods. Compromised user accounts get the attackers inside the firewall and inside the target machine. Once inside, most attackers can use widely accessible exploits to gain root or administrator access.

All systems are affected. The following advice is given on correcting the problem:

1. Create an acceptable password policy, including assigned responsibility and frequency for verifying password quality. Ensure that senior executives are not exempted. Also include in the policy a requirement to change all default passwords before attaching computers to the Internet, with substantial penalties for noncompliance.
2. *Very Important!* Obtain written authority to test passwords. Test passwords with password-cracking programs.
3. Implement utilities that check passwords when created.
4. Force passwords to expire periodically (at a frequency established in your security policy).
5. Maintain password histories so users cannot recycle old passwords.[8]

IMAP and POP Buffer Overflow Vulnerabilities or Incorrect Configuration

Internet Message Access Protocol (IMAP) and Post Office Protocol (POP) are popular remote access mail protocols, allowing users to access their e-mail accounts from internal and external networks. The *open access* nature of these services makes them especially vulnerable to exploitation because openings are frequently left in firewalls to allow for external e-mail access. Attackers who exploit flaws in IMAP or POP often gain instant root-level control.

The systems affected consisted of Multiple UNIX and Linux. The following advice is given on correcting the problem:

1. Disable these services on machines that are not e-mail servers.
2. Use the latest patches and versions.
3. Some of the experts also recommend controlling access to these services using TCP wrappers and encrypted channels such as Secure Shell (SSH) and Secure Sockets Layer (SSL) to protect passwords.[9]

Default SNMP Community Strings Set to Public and Private

The Simple Network Management Protocol (SNMP) is widely used by network administrators to monitor and administer all types of network-connected devices ranging from routers to printers to computers. SNMP uses an unencrypted *community string* as its only authentication mechanism. Lack of encryption is bad enough, but the default community string used by the vast majority of SNMP devices is *public*, with a few *clever* network equipment vendors changing the string to *private*. Attackers can use this vulnerability in SNMP to reconfigure or shut down devices remotely. Sniffed SNMP traffic can reveal a great deal about the structure of your network, as well as the systems and devices attached to it. Intruders use such information to pick targets and plan attacks.

The systems affected consisted of all system and network devices. The following advice is given on correcting the problem:

1. If you do not absolutely require SNMP, disable it.
2. If you are using SNMP, use the same policy for community names as used for passwords described in Vulnerability Cluster.
3. Validate and check community names using snmpwalk.
4. Where possible, make MIBs read only.[10]

Various Scripting Holes in Internet Explorer and Office2000

Recent virus attacks have illustrated how macro and script code could spread easily through e-mail attachments, and people were admonished to avoid opening potentially dangerous attachments. However, Windows users can also spread malicious viruses without opening attachments. Microsoft Outlook and Outlook Express will execute HTML and script code in an e-mail in their default installations. In addition, several so-called ActiveX components are incorrectly executable from an e-mail containing HTML and script code. Some of the vulnerable controls include the Scriplet.*typlib* (ships with IE 4.x and 5.x) and the UA control (Office 2000). Other vulnerabilities arising from the use of Active Scripting are that an e-mail could be used to install new software on a user's computer.

A relatively benign virus known as the *kak* worm is already spreading through these mechanisms. A malicious version of *kak* can be anticipated at any time. It is recommended that all users and administrators set Outlook and Outlook Express to read e-mail in the *Restricted Sites Zone*, and then further disable all Active Scripting and ActiveX-related settings in that zone. This is done in the Options dialog's Security tab, but can be automated using System Policies. Microsoft has made patches available for the individual problems and is readying a patch that will set the security settings in Outlook, but apparently has no plans to fix Outlook Express.

The systems affected consisted of all Windows systems with Internet Explorer 4.x and 5.x (even if it is not used) or Office 2000. Windows 2000 is not affected by some of the IE issues. The following advice is given on correcting the problem:

1. Set your Security Zone to restricted sites, and then disable all active content in that zone.
2. Apply the patch to Outlook as soon as it becomes available.
3. Updating your virus detection software, while important, is not a complete solution for this problem. You must also correct the flaws in Microsoft's software.

Perimeter Protection for an Added Layer of Defense In Depth

In this part of the chapter, ports are listed that are commonly probed and attacked. Blocking these ports is a minimum requirement for perimeter security, not a comprehensive firewall specification list. A far better rule is to block all unused ports, and even if you believe these ports are blocked, you should still actively monitor them to detect intrusion attempts. A warning is also in order: Blocking some of the ports in the following list may disable needed services. Please consider the potential effects of these recommendations before implementing them:

1. **Block *spoofed* addresses**–Packets coming from outside your company sourced from internal addresses or private (RFC1918 and network 127) addresses. Also block source routed packets.
2. **Login services**–Telnet (23/tcp), SSH (22/tcp), FTP (21/tcp), NetBIOS (139/tcp), rlogin et al (512/tcp through 514/tcp).
3. **RPC and NFS**–Portmap/rpcbind (111/tcp and 111/udp), NFS (2049/tcp and 2049/udp), lockd (4045/tcp and 4045/udp).
4. **NetBIOS in Windows NT**–135 (tcp and udp), 137 (udp), 138 (udp), 139 (tcp). Windows 2000—earlier ports plus 445(tcp and udp).
5. **X Windows**–6000/tcp through 6255/tcp.
6. **Naming services**–DNS (53/udp) to all machines that are not DNS servers, DNS zone transfers (53/tcp) except from external secondaries, Lightweight Directory Access Protocol (LDAP (389/tcp and 389/udp)).

7. **Mail**–Simple Mail Transfer Protocol (SMTP (25/tcp)) to all machines that are not external mail relays, POP (109/tcp and 110/tcp), IMAP (143/tcp).

8. **Web**–HTTP (80/tcp) and SSL (443/tcp) except to external Web servers; may also want to block common high-order HTTP port choices (8000/tcp, 8080/tcp, 8888/tcp, etc.).

9. **Small Services**–Ports below 20/tcp and 20/udp, time (37/tcp and 37/udp).

10. **Miscellaneous**–Trivial File Transfer Protocol (TFTP (69/udp)), finger (79/tcp), Network News Transfer Protocol (NNTP (119/tcp)), Network Time Protocol (NTP (123/tcp)), Link Problem Determination (LPD (515/tcp)), syslog (514/udp), Simple Network Management Protocol (SNMP (161/tcp and 161/udp, 162/tcp and 162/udp)), Border Gateway Protocol (BGP (179/tcp)), and Windows Sockets (SOCKS (Winsock) (1080/tcp)).

11. **Internet Control Message Protocol (ICMP)**–Block incoming echo request (ping and Windows traceroute), block outgoing echo replies, time exceeded, and unreachable messages.[11]

What It All Means

The bottom line is that the Internet is a public network, and anyone concerned with transmission security needs to approach the Internet in the same way one would approach communicating by any other public means. Internet communications are functionally equivalent (at least as far as security goes) to communicating in a public hall. Conversations between you and your neighbor can be overheard by anyone who wants to eavesdrop; if you want to talk to someone at the opposite end of the hall, you've got to rely on intermediaries to carry the message between you.

Now let's examine in detail some of the security technologies that were previously mentioned in the *Top Ten Internet SecurityThreats*—and some that weren't. This part of the chapter will briefly examine routers, firewalls, Public Key Infrastructure (PKI), Intrusion Detection Systems (IDSs), authentication and encryption that protect network and system vulnerabilities on systems attached to the Internet, as well as for private networks.

TYPES OF SECURITY TECHNOLOGIES

Corporate networks are built assuming certain levels of trust in how the information passing through them is accessed and used. When they're hooked into public networks, like the Internet, a safer and more intelligent route leads security administrators to trust no one on the outside.

To help answer any questions you may have about where security technologies are needed and used, this part of the chapter briefly explains how these technologies are used to defend against attacks initiated from both within and outside of an organization. This part of the chapter also examines the pieces of the security puzzle to see how to best fit them together for effective defenses and coverage. It also explores several security methods that are used wherever the Internet and corporate networks intersect. These include the uses of the most favored security technologies:

- Routers
- Internet firewalls
- Intrusion Detection Systems (IDSs)
- PKI
- Authentication
- Encryption

Routers

A *router* is a network traffic-managing device that sits in between subnetworks and routes traffic intended for, or emanating from, the segments to which it's attached as shown in Figure 2.3.[12] Naturally, this makes them sensible places to implement packet-filtering rules, based on your security polices that you've already developed for the routing of network traffic.

Internet Firewalls

While the phenomenal growth of Internet connections has understandably focused attention on Internet firewalls, modern business practices continue to underscore the importance of internal firewalls. Mergers, acquisitions, reorganizations, joint ventures, and strategic partnerships all place additional strains on security as the scope of the network's reach expands. Someone outside the organization may suddenly need access to some, but not all, internal information. Multiple networks designed by different people, according to different rules, must somehow trust each other. In these circumstances, firewalls play an important role in enforcing access-control policies between networks and protecting trusted networks from those that are untrusted.

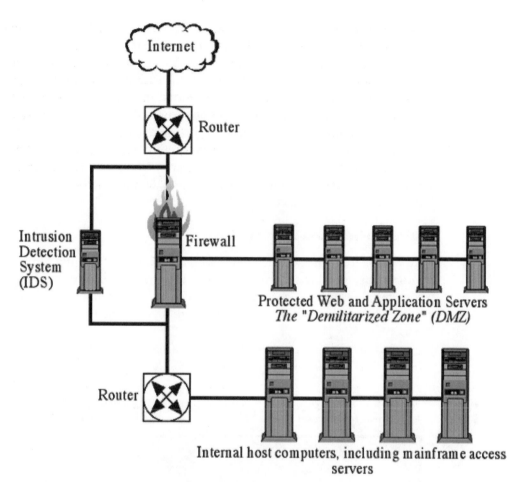

FIGURE 2.3 A basic network security model.

Consider a manufacturing company that has, over time, developed separate networks within the sales, marketing, payroll, accounting, and production departments. Although users in one department may wish to access certain other networks, it is probably unnecessary and undesirable for all users to have access to all networks. Consequently, when connecting the networks, the organization may choose to limit the connection, either with packet-filtering routers or with a more complex firewall.

In a WAN that must offer any-to-any connectivity, other forms of application-level security can protect sensitive data. However, segregating the networks by means of firewalls greatly reduces many of the risks involved; in particular, firewalls can reduce the threat of internal hacking—that is, unauthorized access by authorized users, a problem that consistently outranks external hacking in information-security surveys. By adding encryption to the services performed by the firewall, a site can create very secure firewall-to-firewall connections as shown in Figure 2.4.[13] This even enables wide area networking between remote locations over the Internet. By using authentication mechanisms on the firewall, it is possible to gain a higher level of confidence that persons outside the firewall who request data from inside the firewall (for example, salespersons on the road needing access to an inventory database) are indeed who they claim to be.

Intrusion Detection Systems (IDSs)

An *intrusion* is somebody (A.K.A. *hacker* or *cracker*) attempting to break into or misuse your system. The word *misuse* is broad, and can reflect something as severe as stealing confidential data to something as minor as misusing your e-mail system for spam (although for many of us, that is a major issue!).

An *Intrusion Detection System (IDS)* is a system for detecting such intrusions. IDS can be broken down into the following categories:

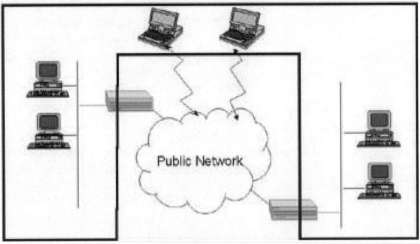

Extending the Perimeter

Public Network

FIGURE 2.4 Firewall-to-firewall encryption.

- Network intrusion detection systems (NIDS)
- System integrity verifiers (SIV)
- Log file monitors (LFM)
- Deception systems[14]

Network Intrusion Detection Systems (NIDS)

Network intrusion detection systems (NIDS) monitors packets on the network wire and attempt to discover if a hacker/cracker is attempting to break into a system (or cause a denial-of-service attack). A typical example is a system that watches for a large number of TCP connection requests (SYN) to many different ports on a target machine, thus discovering if someone is attempting a TCP port scan. A NIDS may run either on the target machine that watches its own traffic (usually integrated with the stack and services themselves), or on an independent machine promiscuously watching all network traffic (hub, router, probe).

A network IDS monitors many machines, whereas the others monitor only a single machine (the one on which they are installed).

System Integrity Verifiers (SIV)

System integrity verifiers (SIV) monitor system files to find when a intruder changes them (thereby leaving behind a backdoor). The most famous of such systems is *Tripwire*. A SIV may watch other components as well, such as the Windows Registry and chron configuration, in order to find well-known signatures. It may also detect when a normal user somehow acquires root/administrator level privileges. Many existing products in this area should be considered as *tools* rather than complete *systems*: Something like *Tripwire* detects changes in critical system components, but doesn't generate real-time alerts upon an intrusion.

Log File Monitors (LFM)

Log file monitors (LFM) monitor log files generated by network services. In a similar manner to NIDS, these systems look for patterns in the log files that suggest an intruder is attacking. A typical example would be a parser for HTTP server log files that is looking for intruders who try well-known security holes, such as the *phf* attack (or swatch).

Deception Systems

Deception systems (A.K.A. decoys, lures, fly-traps, honeypots) contain pseudo-services whose goal is to emulate well-known holes in order to entrap hackers. They also use simple tricks, like renaming an *administrator* account on NT, and then setting up a dummy account with no rights.

PKI

Public Key Infrastructure (PKI) has emerged as the de facto standard to integrate security for e-business digital content and processes as well as e-documents and files. It lets businesses take advantage of the speed of the Internet while protecting their business-critical information from interception, tampering, and unauthorized access. A PKI enables users of a basically nonsecure public network such as the Internet to securely and privately exchange data through the use of a public and a private cryptographic key pair that is obtained and shared through a trusted authority.

PKI is a set of standards, technologies, and procedures employed for user authentication and transfer of data. Using public and private digital keys to encrypt and decrypt data, as well as digital certificates that contain a user's credentials and public keys, which validate a user's identity, PKI allows for the secure transmission of electronic data.

PKI uses asymmetric cryptography, which is based on the use of key pairs, one of which is made public and is accessible to anyone. The other remains private and is kept with the user. Public keys are distributed by a trusted third party known as a *Certificate Authority* (CA).

When two parties want to communicate with each other, the sender of the information will use the recipient's public key to encrypt the information and then send it. The recipient will then use his or her private key to decrypt the information in order to read it. Since this key is private and not accessible to anyone else, only the person for whom the information was intended can read it.

If the sender wants the recipient to be able to verify that the information sent originated from him or her, he or she signs that information, using his or her private key. The recipient can then verify the signature using the sender's public key, thereby establishing the origin of the information and the integrity of that information.

The bottom line here is that PKI is gaining wider acceptance, moving from pilot testing into the real world of intercompany e-commerce. For example, RSA's Keon® is a family of interoperable, standards-based PKI products for managing digital certificates and providing an environment for authenticated, private, and legally binding electronic communications and transactions.[15] The RSA Keon family (from a robust CA to developer components and turnkey enterprise solutions) provides a common foundation for securing Internet and e-business applications.

Authentication

Authentication provides for centrally managed, strong, two-factor user authentication services for enterprise networks, operating systems, e-commerce Web sites, and other IT infrastructure, ensuring that only authorized users access data, applications, and communications. Two-factor authentication solutions create a virtually impenetrable barrier against unauthorized access, protecting network and data resources from potentially devastating accidental or malicious intrusion.

Encryption

As previously explained, *encryption* is the transformation of data into a form that is virtually impossible to read without the appropriate knowledge (a key). Its purpose is to ensure privacy by keeping information hidden from anyone for whom it is not intended; even those who have access to the encrypted data. *Decryption* is the reverse of encryption: It is the transformation of encrypted data back into an intelligible form. More information on encryption is coming up next!

A BRIEF INTRODUCTION TO CRYPTOGRAPHY

Modern cryptography offers solutions to the problems of an open network. This section introduces some of the basic concepts of modern cryptography, on which most online commerce schemes depend. This section simply raises some of the pertinent cryptographic issues as they relate to passing commercial transactions across an open channel; discussion of the actual algorithms, implementations, and the mathematical basis for private and public key cryptography are all far beyond the scope of this book, but the interested reader will find some excellent references in Appendix B, "Electronic Commerce Online Resources."

Cryptography

As an individual, if you've got something "sensitive" to say to someone, chances are you can find a way to do this without resorting to secret codes:

A whisper in the right person's ear, a confidential chat in a bar, or a discreet letter are all reliable ways to share a secret (keeping the secret later is another story). You've got control over who is listening, and you need not worry about anyone trying to read your mail (unless you are a criminal kingpin, revolutionary leader, or subject of some other investigation).

If you did want to protect your sensitive communications, chances are you'd try to use some kind of code or cipher, replacing the "real" words with "code" words, or shifting characters to hide the real meaning of your messages.

Chances are that some form of cryptography first came about shortly after the invention of writing, although the earliest surviving ciphers date from the time of Julius Caesar.

Governments and military organizations have always needed to protect their communications (lives depend on it). And since the stakes are so much higher, there is more risk that the messages will fall into the wrong hands—so there is greater incentive to hide the meaning of the message. If there were a method of passing messages that could not be detected by anyone but the intended recipient, then cryptography would be unnecessary. As it is, with radio transmissions being highly public, cryptography has become indispensable.

By offering reliable and secure communications methods like a (relatively) sacrosanct postal service and (usually) bug-free telephone service, governments argued that their law-abiding citizens had no need for cryptographic services: Only the government had the power to read your mail and listen to your telephone conversations, so that was OK. In an increasingly digital world, though, there are more opportunities for practically anyone to listen in—and those opportunities are more lucrative.

A criminal would much rather discover your credit card number than find out how your vacation went or what subjects your children are flunking. Making a purchase across the Internet may put your credit at risk, but using cryptography can help protect it. It should be noted that the individual consumer in the United States is liable for no more than $50 when a credit card is compromised, so the greatest risk is taken on by the credit card companies and the merchants. While individual credit card accounts may be susceptible to hijacking when transmitted over the Internet, there is far greater risk of theft from concentration points, like the computers where the account numbers are stored. And while criminal hackers may be responsible for some thefts, insiders familiar with those systems are more likely to exploit them.

The Objective of Cryptography

The whole point of cryptography is to keep information out of the hands of anyone but its intended recipient. Even if the message is intercepted, the meaning won't be apparent to the interceptor—unless the interceptor is able to decipher it.

Cryptography as we know it uses encryption to transform plain texts into encrypted texts. Ideally, encoding or decoding them should not require too much effort, but decoding without the keys should be hard enough to discourage anyone from trying to do so. The fact is that encryption schemes can always be broken, if you have enough time and resources. The idea behind modern encryption methods is to make it so costly in time and resources for an interceptor to interpret a message that it is not practical to even attempt it—while keeping it easy for an authorized recipient to read.

The strength of the encryption scheme needed is determined by how long you want to keep your secret. For example, if you're planning a surprise birthday party in two weeks, you might trust a scheme that required a month of continuous effort to break; a corporation would want a stronger method to protect long-term plans or trade secrets.

Codes and Ciphers

The terms *code*, *cipher*, *encryption*, and *decipher* all have quite specific meanings. Strictly speaking, a code actually uses some method of interchanging vocabularies so that each code word represents some other noncode word. Codes require special code books that act like dictionaries; if the code book is lost, encoded text cannot be interpreted—and anyone with the code book can read encoded text.

Ciphers are the basis of encryption schemes. Ciphers act on each character of a message, transforming it according to some repeatable rule, or algorithm. Keys are special numbers that help initialize the algorithm; different keys used with the same algorithm will produce different versions of encrypted texts.

At this point, keep in mind the objective of cryptography: keeping secrets secret. As was mentioned earlier, encryption is used when you cannot guarantee that a message will not fall into the wrong hands. Ideally, you want to keep the plain text of the message secret, but you know that is not always possible. If you encrypt it, you prefer that the algorithm you are using not become known to the bad guys, because that would mean they could try every possible key to break your cipher. However, really good algorithms don't grow on trees, and there are plenty of ways to figure out which one is being used (this is discussed in the next section). So, you'll settle for a key that can be kept secure, and an algorithm that's tough to break even if you know which one it is.

Traditional ciphers use a single key, which the sender and the recipient share (and try to keep secret from anyone else). The sender runs the algorithm using the key to turn the plain-text message into an encrypted message, and the recipient runs the same algorithm in reverse (using the same key) to decrypt the message. This is known as *symmetric cryptography*.

Breaking Encryption Schemes

Encryption schemes are vulnerable on several fronts: You can analyze encrypted text for things like word and character frequencies, or trick someone into sending some particular message and then figure out what was done to that message, or find out what the encryption algorithm is and do a brute-force attack on it by trying every single possible key. The last method is a completely reliable way to break any encryption scheme—as long as you have enough time.

Cryptographers accept that all ciphers are vulnerable to brute-force attacks, and they design ciphers with this in mind. The key to security is usually the cipher key size. A cipher key can be compared to a combination lock: If you have the correct key, you can unlock the message. The three-digit combination locks often found on luggage offer minimal protection, since there are only 1000 different options. Sometimes you'll hit on the right combination in only a few tries (for example, if the combination was "007"), and sometimes the combination will be more elusive (for example, "999"); on average, though, you'll break the lock after trying half the total possibilities. At about a second per combination, this means I can open your briefcase, on average, in about eight minutes (and it shouldn't take more than about 17 minutes).

This level of security may be acceptable for keeping your coworkers away from the doughnuts in your briefcase, but not for much else. Adding another digit to the lock increases the number of possible combinations by a factor of 10; doubling the number of digits to six increases the number of possible combinations to 1 million. A brute-force attack on a six-digit combination lock, at a second per combination, takes an average of almost six days (and could take as long as 11.5 days). Add another two digits, and you'd need over a year and a half, on average, to break in.

Of course, with computers in the picture, you can use much larger numbers, and much more complicated algorithms. Adding to the length of the key you use doesn't necessarily make encrypting or decrypting messages more difficult if you know the key, but does make it much less practical to apply brute-force techniques. I may want to steal your credit card number, but if it would take me a century using 10 of the biggest supercomputers in the world running at full tilt to do it, I won't bother (since the account will undoubtedly have expired by then).

Another risk is that computing technology will continue improving sufficiently to make practical brute-force attacks on currently adequate encryption schemes. Increasing the size of the key makes it more secure over a longer period of time, but it also makes it harder to implement right now. The bottom line is that a good encryption scheme must represent a compromise between security and practicality.

Encryption schemes are also vulnerable to non-brute-force attacks. Although it is possible to prove that a cipher can be broken through some application of analysis or a smart search for keys, there is no way to unalterably and conclusively prove that an algorithm is secure from attack. However, making details of the algorithm public, as discussed in the next section, can help improve the odds that it's secure.

Securing Algorithms

Keeping your algorithm a secret may be a tempting way to keep the algorithm secure, but it turns out that is not the case. If your algorithm is to be used in a commercial product, it doesn't take long for it to be reverse-engineered. Someone buys the product, runs sample texts through it, and figures out what your algorithm does. Security through obscurity seldom works, particularly in commercial products: Software vendors had their copy-protection schemes defeated almost immediately after they introduced them; cable operators lost revenues when their inadequate encryption was broken and illegal cable boxes were widely distributed; early cordless-telephone security features were trivially easy to defeat.

More recently, cryptographers have made their algorithms public either by publishing them in academic journals or by patenting them; in either case, one objective is to subject them to trials by fire. Mathematicians earn bragging rights, among other things, for breaking algorithms that were thought to be secure; getting credit for creating a strong encryption scheme is a major incentive for publishing. Algorithms that can withstand direct attacks are much stronger (and more elegant) than those that fall apart as soon as you know how they work. As indicated earlier, the less you have to keep secret, the easier it is to maintain security.

Distributing Keys and Keeping Them Secret

Up to now we have been considering secret key algorithms: If you have the key, you can read any encrypted messages. One major weakness with this approach is that you need to have a dependable way to pass keys around to the people who need them. You have to treat the key with at least as much care as you do the messages; losing a single message may be harmful, but losing the key means losing all messages. Another weakness is that if you want to send a secure message to a group, you've either got to rely on everyone involved keeping a single key secure among them, or you've got to assign a separate key to each individual and use it for all communications.

While the simplest answer is to hand-deliver all keys, and have a single key for each pair of people who want to exchange secure messages, it soon becomes clear that this solution doesn't scale up well at all. You and I can communicate securely with a single key; add my brother to the mix, and I need one key to talk to him, one to talk to you. You need another key to talk to him; each of us now has two keys, and there are three keys in all. Adding new participants in our little secret circle adds more keys; if we were running a company and wanted to assign secret keys to our customers, we'd soon be in the business of assigning and distributing keys.

Online commerce requires that you be able to securely exchange messages with anyone, whether you know that person or not. Private key solutions are available, but by and large they require some degree of trust either in the parties exchanging messages, or in some intermediary agency with access to both parties' secret keys. As it happens, public key cryptographic techniques make this unnecessary.

Data Encryption Standard

One widely distributed secret key solution is the Data Encryption Standard, or DES. The United States National Bureau of Standards published DES in the late 1970s for commercial uses. For instance, Automatic Teller Machine networks use DES to encrypt consumers' PINs (Personal Identification Numbers) when they are transmitted through shared networks and data communications lines.

DES is considered safe against all but brute-force attacks, which are considered to be impractical against DES for all but the very largest and most determined organizations (like major governments, for example). More to the point, DES can be implemented reasonably efficiently for bulk encryption like that required by electronic commerce applications.

While there are software implementations, the DES standard specifies that only hardware-only implementations comply with the standard.

The Public Key Solution

Public key cryptography relies on the fact that it is relatively easy to perform modular arithmetic, even on large numbers, and that it is relatively difficult to find the factors of very large numbers. This means that you can use a very, very large number that has only two factors as the basis of an encryption scheme, where you encrypt using one of those factors, and you can decrypt the resulting ciphertext only using the other factor. Decrypting the text using the same key it was encrypted with does not reverse the process.

Modular Arithmetic

Modular arithmetic is similar to regular arithmetic, but it adds division by some number and is concerned only with the remainder resulting from that division. For instance, the expression

$8+17$

is equal to 25; calculating this value modulo (or mod) another number (called the modulus) simply produces a remainder:

$25 \bmod 10 = 5$

because 10 goes into 25 two times, with a remainder of 5;

$25 \bmod 15 = 10$

because 15 goes into 25 once, with 10 left over.

Any regular arithmetic expression can also be calculated modulo some other number, including raising to powers. For example:

$5^2 \bmod 10 = 5$

This turns out to be extremely useful because you can represent a piece of data as a number, encrypt it by raising it to a certain power, and then find the remainder when dividing the result by another number. For the moment, it's enough to know that doing modular arithmetic on very large numbers can be a lot easier than evaluating the underlying expressions themselves. For instance, the numbers in the expression:

some large number$^{\text{some other large number}}$

don't have to be very large before they begin to tax the capacities of most computers to evaluate. The expression:

$$1000^{1000}$$

is easy to evaluate, but would take up a couple of pages in this book. Change the expression to:

$$1013^{967}$$

and all of a sudden this is a very difficult number to figure out, even with a computer.

However, if the number used as the exponent is chosen carefully, calculating the remainder after dividing by a carefully chosen modulus will actually prove fairly simple.

Factoring and Large Numbers

Although doing modular arithmetic on powers of large numbers can be relatively easy (certainly well within the capacities of the average desktop personal computer), factoring large numbers is not easy. Factoring, or determining what numbers can be evenly divided into another number, is hard to do and becomes harder to do reliably as the number to be factored becomes larger. Some factors are easy: If the number in question ends in a zero, one of its factors is 10 (and two more are 2 and 5); all even numbers are divisible by 2, and all numbers ending in 5 are divisible by 5.

There is no way to look at a large number and quickly determine whether it is prime, or whether it has factors. The brute-force solution to factoring is to try dividing the number in question by every smaller number. If a number is the product of two prime numbers, especially if those two prime numbers are already big numbers, the number of divisions needed to find the correct factors becomes astronomical, even though the numbers in question remain relatively easy to work with.

Public Key Encryption

By choosing two large prime numbers and properly manipulating them, you can extract two keys; multiply them to get the number to evaluate the modular expressions. You can now encrypt a message by chopping it up into small chunks, converting those chunks to numbers, raising those numbers to the power of one of the keys, and calculating the result modulo the sum of the two original primes.

As a result of the nature of modular exponentiation, the two keys work together to create an encryption algorithm. You can encrypt a message with one of the keys, but you must use the other key to decrypt it, doing the same process on the encrypted text. That means that this is an asymmetric encryption scheme: Encrypting with one key cannot be reversed without the other key, as shown in Figure 2.5. In practice, one of the keys is called a *public* key and can be safely distributed publicly; the other key is called a *private* or *secret* key and is not for distribution.

This is, very simply, the idea behind the dominant public key encryption scheme. Named for its inventors, Ron Rivest, Adi Shamir, and Len Adleman, RSA was patented, and it is now owned by RSA Data Security, Inc. (RSADSI). Because it has held up against attacks by cryptographers, mathematicians, computer scientists, and amateurs over the nearly 23 years since it was first published, it is widely held to be a secure encryption method.

How It Works

Very simply, once you have your public and private keys, you can communicate securely and reliably. Individuals with public keys often add those keys to the bottom of any document or e-mail they distribute; companies using public keys can include those keys in network application software like security-equipped Web browsers.

Although public key encryption is practical on personal computers, it still requires a lot of computing power. As a result, it is often implemented

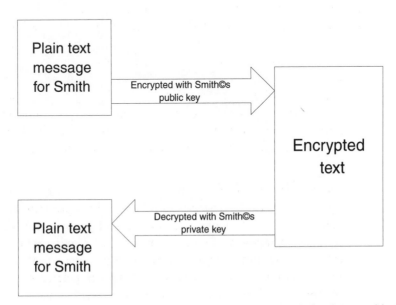

FIGURE 2.5 Text encrypted with a public key can only be decrypted by the private key, and vice versa.

as a method of exchanging a single-session, traditional secret key between participants, rather than encrypting the entire transmission with a public key. Encryption of that key is done with the recipient's public key; only the recipient is able to decrypt that transmission. Once both parties have the secret key, each is able to encrypt and decrypt the communication (much more efficiently, too, since symmetric cryptography is easier to do on the fly than public key or asymmetric cryptography).

Encryption solves the security problem, but authentication of content and sender are also solved with RSA. Let's say that you and your sweetheart are separated geographically and can only converse by e-mail. If you were to send a proposal of marriage by e-mail, your partner might want you to digitally sign it, just to be sure it's you (you might have a malevolent hacker as a rival). Doing so is a simple matter of using a digest function to summarize the contents of your message mathematically, and then encrypting the result using your own private key. The result can be decrypted by anyone using your public key; your paramour simply runs the same digest function on the signed message and decrypts the signature. If the result matches, it proves that no one but you could have sent the message; if they don't match, your friend will know that the message sent was not the same as the message received.

Of course, a consumer can verify the validity of a product offering made across the World Wide Web just as easily, and vendors can also confirm and authenticate electronic orders made by their known customers.

It should be noted that the RSA method is not perfect; public keys may be made public, but only work reliably if there is a reliable way to guarantee that the public key someone advertises actually is their own. There are also some reasonably well-known weaknesses that can be eliminated by taking certain precautions. However, RSA public key techniques are stronger and more secure than many easier methods.

Why It Works

If the numbers you select as keys are too small, someone could intercept your encrypted messages and apply a brute-force attack with some chance of success. However, by choosing numbers sufficiently large (100 digits and up), solving the cipher (essentially, finding the factors of the modulus) requires factoring a huge number—which, while theoretically possible, approaches impracticality as the size of the numbers used goes up.

As new techniques are devised for factoring large numbers, RSA loses its effectiveness. In addition, computing power has already increased sufficiently since RSA was first formulated to make brute-force attempts against smaller key sizes possible. One group in 1994 factored an RSA modulus that was 129 digits long (using hundreds of workstations over a period of about eight months); the same group would have needed about 200 years to break a 150-digit public key. The implication, of course, is that it won't take very many years for the computer industry to produce much cheaper workstations capable of much faster computing—at which point the public keys will have to be much bigger numbers to continue to be secure against a concerted effort.

Legal Issues

The United States government classifies cryptographic devices as munitions and restricts their export. RSA represents a very strong method of keeping secrets, and the government would prefer that it not fall into the wrong hands. Unfortunately, the RSA algorithm has been globally disseminated in professional journals, and the cat is out of the bag—pretty much anyone who wants it can have it.

Reality, however, does not get in the government's way, so any software or hardware that implements strong encryption methods has to be approved for export from the United States. Vendors of such products have few options: move their operations off-shore and import the products into the United States; go through the process of getting proper certification of the products for export; or weaken the product to make it acceptable for more general export and get proper certification.

Noncompliance with the export law is not usually seen as an option, since the penalties range up to 20 years in federal prison and fines of up to $2,000,000. The government's position is that our enemies, terrorists, drug lords, and other organized criminals can use strong encryption techniques to hatch plots against the United States, and we will have put the tools in their hands and be powerless against them. Given the reality of the situation, that it's too late to keep the technology out of the wrong hands, and the fact that limiting distribution of this type of tool hampers domestic and foreign online trade, easing of these restrictions may be on the horizon.

Key Distribution and Certification

The preceding discussion about private and public key cryptography has avoided the issue of how to manage key distribution. As with all the other aspects of cryptography, there are well-known problems pertaining to secure and reliable key distribution. To illustrate, a simple scenario:

- Bob and Alice are two acquaintances who communicate by e-mail on occasion.
- Evil Robert, impersonating Bob, sends a forged piece of e-mail to Alice, requesting a secure communication channel using public key encryption.
- Included in this forged message is Evil Robert's public key (which he represents as Bob's public key).
- Alice receives the message and encrypts a reply using what she believes to be Bob's public key (but which is actually Evil Robert's public key).
- Evil Robert receives the message, decrypts it with Alice's own secret key, and is able to communicate with Alice while pretending to be Bob.

Of course, this scenario can be easily defeated if Jones (the Security Administrator) or Alice herself could somehow verify that the public key matches the person who sends it.

Trusted Key Distribution and Verification

With the wider application of public key cryptography for the purpose of commerce, mechanisms for the trusted publication and distribution of public keys are necessary. Simply having a merchant (or customer) send a copy of a public key will not do, since a forger could send her own public key while pretending to be someone else.

One solution is for some (respected) organization to offer key-publishing services. Those who wish to can report their keys and their identities, and anyone else can find a key by looking for a person's name. To add further trust, people can have other people certify their public keys. In other words, one person (or organization) can vouch for another one by adding his or her own name and public key to the listing. The greater the resulting "pedigree" to your public key, the greater amount of trust others can put in your digital signature.

THREE CRYPTOGRAPHIC APPLICATIONS

As may already be obvious, cryptography, and public key cryptography in particular, plays a vital role in making online commerce a secure option. Three applications of cryptography are almost constantly mentioned throughout this book (and elsewhere), so these are explicitly defined and summarized here.

Encryption

As previously explained, requiring the use of a key to "unlock" data is called *encryption*. The key can be a secret key, used symmetrically, or it can be one of a public key pair, used asymmetrically. The longer the key, the less likely it is that a brute-force attack on the encrypted data will be successful (assuming that the encryption algorithm is not susceptible to other types of attack).

Public key pairs include a private key and a public key. When sending a public-key-encrypted message, the sender encrypts the message with the recipient's public key. The resulting message can now only be decrypted using the recipient's private key.

In practice, public key cryptography is very secure, but very costly in terms of computer resources. As a result, it is often combined with secret key cryptography. For example, a sender can use public key encryption to encrypt a secret key to be used for bulk encryption purposes. Both participants could use a single secret key, or they could use a single key to generate some other set of keys to use for their communication. The exchange of the secret key uses the very secure public key encryption, while the bulk encryption of the remainder of the communication would use some other encryption method.

An eavesdropper could capture the encrypted communication, and thereby attempt to break the encryption. However, by using very long secret keys, using them only for one communication session, and not reusing them, this method can be made quite secure.

Digital Signature

If the sender encrypted data using the sender's own private key, the resulting message could be decrypted by anyone who had the sender's public key. This process can't be considered a way to protect the message from anyone, since anyone with access to the sender's public key can decrypt it. However, it does offer a method of signing a document digitally.

Encrypting a message in this way will ensure that it can only have come from the person whose public key will decrypt it; however, it also ensures that every such message must be decrypted. As has been mentioned, since public key encryption uses lots of resources, this becomes impractical. Also, there is the problem of keeping track of and certifying public keys.

A better option for digital signatures is to use a *digest function* to summarize the contents of a particular message in a smaller, more manageable chunk of data. This chunk can then be encrypted using the sender's private key, and appended to the message. The recipient can then use the same digest function on the received message and use the sender's public key to decrypt the digest included by the sender. If the two digest results match, then the message has been certified as signed. If the results don't match, then the message cannot be certified as signed.

Nonrepudiation and Message Integrity

There are two by-products of the use of digital signatures. *Nonrepudiation* is a cryptographic term describing the situation when the originator of a message cannot deny having sent it. Normal electronic mail is deniable, since it is (relatively) easily forged and easily modified. Electronic mail that has been digitally signed, however, is nonrepudiable. If the digital signature checks out properly, the owner of the signature is the only entity capable of having signed the message.

The other important by-product of digital signatures is a guarantee of message integrity. If a message has been digitally signed and transmitted, verifying the signature also verifies that the message has been received unchanged from the source. A signed message that has been intercepted, modified, and forwarded on to its original destination will not produce a verified signature.

The ability to verify a digital signature also confirms that the signed message was delivered intact and unchanged. Furthermore, the person signing the message cannot later deny having sent it.

Now, let's take at a brief high-level look at the development and evolution of Java™ security. Java is a maturing technology that has evolved from its commercial origins as a browser-based scripting tool. This part of the chapter reviews the various deployment environments in which Java is being targeted; some of its run-time characteristics; the security features in the current releases of the base technology; new Java Development Kit (JDK™) 1.3 and higher policy-based security model; limitations of stack-based authorization security models; general security requirements; Java Cryptography Extensions (JCE); and, future directions that Java security might take.

EXPLOITING JAVA SECURITY

The software industry is focused on providing support for developing and deploying mission-critical applications written in Java. The Java environment encompasses a broad spectrum from enterprise servers to embedded devices. A range of Java-based systems, including JavaOS, EmbeddedJava, and PersonalJava, among others, is now available, providing potentially different levels of underlying services. This situation results in requirements for varying levels of security strength.

The initial focus of Java security has been in the support of downloaded *applets* (small programs) within World Wide Web browsers. To a large extent, the security features in Java reflect this heritage. As Java matures, it will increasingly support additional security features to address the needs of the target application environments. Included is the addition of security features generally found in large-scale server applications.

We have seen examples of how e-business (business conducted electronically via the Web) increases a customer's reach by orders of magnitude. As the customer base increases, the absolute magnitude of losses from malicious behavior can become great enough to warrant improved security products deployed in information technology systems. However, should a security exposure become widely publicized, a customer's reputation can become tarnished. Customers demand systems implementations that are nearly flawless and that address the needs of their enterprise. They look to vendors to ensure that risks are known and to respond quickly with action when exposures are uncovered.

Realistic expectations are important: no system is 100 percent secure. However, it is crucial to recognize three things about Java security:

1. Java enables a function that was never before commercially deployed on a broad scale: dynamic loading of code from a source outside the system. This important feature aggravates a significant *Trojan horse* security problem. However, it also provides an extremely valuable function.

2. Java security was not designed to solve the same problems as security software functions in traditional enterprise security technologies. The security for Java is designed to protect the user's workstation and resources from hostile code.

3. Other traditional enterprise security technologies work well because they assume (and their environments provide) strong operating system integrity as a foundation. Java also assumes this integrity; however, the predominant desktop operating systems do not provide it sufficiently.[16]

Security technologies are needed to prevent or mitigate the following types of threats:

- **Unauthorized resource usage**, including theft of software or CPU usage, corruption of data and software, disclosure of information, and unaccountable action.
- **Abuse of privilege**, including misrepresentation of identity, affiliation, value of items exchanged, and entitlement of services; impersonation; fraud; and extortion.
- **Malicious code**, including protection from viruses, worms, Trojan horses, and logic bombs.
- **Wiretapping**, including active and passive measures.
- **Denial of service**, including destruction of resources, saturation of services, and interruptions of communications.[17]

Trojan horse and spoofing attacks have been the most common Java security threats publicized to date. Once identified, it has been relatively easy to provide fixes as the majority of attacks have occurred due to implementation errors in browsers or in Java rather than fundamental design flaws.

Java Security Foundation and Evolution

Since initial commercial deployments of Java were in Web browsers, much of the focus of Java security has been in providing features for protecting against hostile applets; that is, against hostile code downloaded from Web sites on the Internet. Java security builds upon three fundamental aspects of the Java run-time environment: the *ByteCode Verifier*, the *Security Manager*, and the *ClassLoader*.

The ByteCode Verifier ensures that downloaded code is properly formatted; that bytecodes (Java Virtual Machine instructions) do not violate the safety restrictions of the language or virtual machine (no illegal data conversions); that pointer addressing is not performed; that internal stacks cannot overflow or underflow; and that bytecode instructions will have the correct typed parameters.

The Security Manager initiates run-time access controls on attempts to perform file I/O and network I/O; create new ClassLoaders; manipulate threads or thread groups; start processes on the underlying platform (operating system); terminate the Java Virtual Machine (JVM); load non-Java libraries (native code) into the JVM; perform certain types of windowing system operations; and load certain types of classes into the JVM. For example, the Java applet sandbox severely constrains downloaded applets to a limited set of functions that are considered relatively safe.

The ClassLoader determines how and when applets can load code, and ensures that applets do not replace system-level components within the run-time environment. In addition, a number of features in the Java programming language and run-time environment, including automatic memory management and strong data type safety, facilitate writing safe code.

Through the use of digital signature services provided in JDK 1.3 and higher, trusted applets can be treated in a manner similar to applications written in Java. That is, these trusted applets have much greater access to JVM resources than applets that run in the restricted Java sandbox. Improved and much more flexible access control features are the major security addition in JDK 1.3. Today's computing environments have a number of security weak points that are addressed by features available in Java prior to JDK 1.3:

- **Strong memory protection**–Java removes the possibility of either maliciously or inadvertently reading or corrupting memory locations outside boundaries of the program. As a result, Java applications or applets cannot gain unauthorized memory access to read or change contents.
- **Encryption and digital signatures**–Java supports the use of powerful encryption technology to verify that an applet came from an identifiable source and has not been modified.
- **Rules enforcement**–Java is completely object-based. By using Java objects and classes to represent corporate information entities, it is possible to explicitly state the rules governing the use of such objects.[18]

Java Run-Time Environment

Java, as an object-oriented language, can be used to develop applications in much the same way as C and C++ are used to improve programmer productivity. In contrast to many other programming languages, Java provides a standard set of libraries, including a broad range of communications and security capabilities, thus simplifying construction and deployment of client/server and distributed systems applications. It also provides data type safety and performs bytecode verification when the code is loaded into the JVM run-time environment. This catches bugs that arise from programming errors, especially with pointer arithmetic and array out-of-bounds indexing errors. Additionally, Java-based support environments exist for the following:

- **Applets**–Downloadable code with restricted access, usually coupled with a browser.
- **Aglets**–Code pushed to the end device rather than the pull model of applets.
- **Servlets**–Java code on the server.
- **Orblets**–Code utilizing object request broker communication mechanisms.[19]

Any of these environments may use a component model for reusability, such as JavaBeans and Enterprise JavaBeans. Java is evolving to support a multitude of system configurations:

- Embedded systems destined to be found in many consumer devices in the home and elsewhere
- Java-based smart cards
- Personal management devices such as pagers and PDAs (Personal Digital Assistants)
- Network computers—thin and flat clients
- Mobile systems
- Highly scalable enterprise servers[20]

To support this range of configurations, a family of products (including JavaOS, PersonalJava, Enterprise Java, and JVMs hosted in application builder environments) is evolving to meet the unique needs found in the respective environments. Security requirements vary depending on the unique characteristics of these substantially different environments. Initial work indicates that a common security model is likely, and that the environmental differences can be supported by providing extensions rather than deploying significantly different security models. The use of a common security model will simplify and reduce the cost of application and library development and deployment.

Java and Browser-Based Security Models

Browsers and other Internet technologies were in the marketplace prior to the broad introduction of Java. Consequently, it is not surprising that mismatches exist in the security models provided by the rapidly evolving Java-related technologies. Major progress toward synchronization can occur if agreement can be reached on selected parts of the models in an orderly fashion. The mismatches result primarily from the early limitations of Java security and the desire to fill these voids to meet customer requirements. One such area where there is a concerted effort in model alignment is in the access control model.

This part of the chapter provides a high-level view of the capability classes of a representative browser with comparable features found in the Java 1.3 or higher security architecture. Both use a stack-based approach to authorization. However, they employ significantly different access control models and authorization mechanisms. The browser's proposal is more ambitious, but the added functionality may be more difficult to manage.

It should be recognized that mismatches also exist among browser security models as they expand support to cover the hosting of HyperText Markup Language (HTML) pages, scripts, and applets. In some environments, signed Java applets will have reduced access to some Java elements because the containing page or script calling the applet is not signed. Only the Java access control mechanisms of the browser are highlighted in the following discussion.

Alternative Access Control Model

A commercially available Web browser's Java Virtual Machine implementation that uses an alternative access control model based on targets and explicit activation or deactivation of permissions was examined. A target is a mapping of a principal to an operation on an object (roughly a traditional permission representation). Whether a permission can be enabled depends on a three-valued logic for *enabling* policy. Essentially, if at least one principal (user, systems administrator, target class definer) permits the target and no principal forbids the target, the target can be enabled. Java developers can enable such targets at run time. Also, developers can disable (forbid) or revert (undo enabling of) targets at run time. This model enables the policy of multiple principals to be combined and less than maximal rights to be granted to an applet. It is up to the applet code to manage this subset of enabled permissions.

At run time, targets are activated by `enablePrivilege()`, prohibited by `disablePrivilege()`, and deactivated by `revertPrivilege()`. Reverting only affects the calling stack frame, so targets enabled in previous stack frames are still active and supersede the reversion. Therefore, it is not possible for a descendant method to remove a privilege, possibly enabling security exposures.

The browser authorization mechanism checks the stack for an enabled privilege for the request. If one is found, the operation is permitted regardless of the trust of the classes in the thread's stack (the method's callers). Therefore, explicit prohibition or proper permission reversion of rights is necessary to prevent an unauthorized principal from using another's *enabled* privilege.

There may be other methods that enable the permission higher in the thread stack.

If a method in the Java core classes (the basic Java run time) requires the addition of access controls to close a security hole, the browser model described in this part of the chapter will cause trouble for existing code. It is straightforward to add a permission to allow the code to enable the permission. However, the code does not already contain code to enable the permission, since the permission was not required when the code was originally written. The same would be true for library and bean writers who discover in subsequent versions of their software that they need to add access controls. The implication is that application writers would have to update their code to support (enable) any new permissions added to the base Java classes or libraries and beans they employ. This results in severe version management problems. This problem does not exist with the JDK 1.3 or higher access control model. In JDK 1.3 or higher, only an update to the policy database is required. Thus, the browser model provides more functionality than the Java model, but this functionality places more responsibility on programmers to track granted and retracted rights, and to be aware of browser, JVM, or library/bean version differences.

Stack-Based Authorization

The current access control mechanisms in Java are based on *stack introspection*, or logically walking the stack frames of the thread to see whether the calling methods or classes have sufficient permissions to perform a requested operation. Given the coarse granularity of the current permission structure, the performance of stack-based authorization appears to be acceptable. However, since all security issues cannot be reduced to stack introspection, it is possible for one object to pass rights to another object and obtain information that it could not otherwise directly obtain. For example, it may be possible to induce another object to pass a right (a file descriptor) to an unauthorized object. The unauthorized object was not on the stack when the file descriptor was created, yet it still received the object reference (*off-the-stack* spoofing). This style of security attack is inherent to stack-based authorization techniques because the technique does not track all unsafe interactions between objects.

In environments such as those with stringent communication requirements (requiring hierarchical, lattice-like communication protocols regarding information flow), the Java security model may not be adequate. However, for most of the envisioned uses of Java, stack introspection-based access control features are adequate for implementing mission-critical applications.

SECURITY REQUIREMENTS—A HIGH-LEVEL VIEW

The following requirements address needs identified beyond the level of function delivered in JDK 1.3 and higher. Discussions are underway with JavaSoft on many of them, and some are addressed by JDK 1.3 or will be in follow-on JDK releases. These are representative categories and examples of requirements within each category, not necessarily a complete compilation of known requirements within each category.

- Java Virtual Machine high-integrity computing environment
- Policy-driven Java security model and security services
- Simple security programming models
- Standards for secure deployment of applications
- Standardized programming models
- Native security services support
- Standards for development and deployment of (cryptographic) service providers
- Maintainability, scalability, and interoperability
- Removal of security as an impediment to performance

Java Virtual Machine High-Integrity Computing Environment

The requirement is to support concurrent applet or servlet execution with multiple sets of security credentials. Because authentication and credentials requirements vary between systems, and sometimes between subsystems, it is necessary for the applets or servlets within a JVM to support handling multiple sets of security credentials. Simplified APIs (application programming interfaces) will make it easier for application writers to exploit these security features. Satisfaction of this requirement should enable secure interactions between clients and servers and between server subsystems as is needed for e-commerce applications.

Policy-Driven Java Security Model and Security Services

Customers should be able to define and deploy a security policy. The underlying systems (Java) should have sufficient mechanisms to implement and enforce that policy. Mechanisms for enforcing policy need to include support for access control; cryptographic and quality of protection; trust; secure delivery of policy statements to the JVM; policy administration; and JVM support of a policy engine. Satisfaction of this requirement may reduce the total cost of ownership through simpler configuration and policy administration by making the JVM a single point of policy enforcement for all Java applications.

Simple Security Programming Models

Require simple high-level APIs for quality of protection (privacy, integrity, and nonrepudiation) to allow security-unaware applications to obtain default security protection for such functions as secure communications, secure documents or mail, secure streams, and secure remote method invocation (RMI) and Internet Inter-Orb Protocol (IIOP). This requirement may simplify the programming model, making security permissions readily available to any application and reducing potential mistakes made by security-naive programmers.

Standards for Secure Deployment of Applications

A manifest format and single signature standards (such as W3C) for applet and application delivery are needed. This requirement should establish a single and low-cost way of ensuring the delivery of applications both to the server and client systems.

Standardized Programming Models

Create standards for establishing trust and integrity of applications consisting of multiple applets embedded in HTML or XML (Extensible Markup Language) documents. This requirement may provide a single model for the allocation of access control or other policy to an application that may consist of a number of componentized elements.

Native Security Services Support

Utilize the security features of the underlying platform. This requirement should maximize platform security functionality, improve performance, and allow for consistency.

Standards for Development and Deployment of (Cryptographic) Service Providers

Cryptographic service providers should be signed and provide enumerated descriptions of the services within the provider. This requirement should ensure that international deployment requirements are met, and needed information is accessible to applications requiring these services. Cryptographic services can be deployed internationally with control of the strength of cryptographic operations (key length, signature length, algorithm strengths, etc.).

Maintainability, Scalability, and Interoperability

Provide centralized administration and the ability to react to changes, the ability to interoperate and utilize non-Java security capabilities, and the ability to support full security functionality in a distributed manner as needed between clients and servers. This requirement should allow for the controlled deployment of Java, and improve performance and migration.

Removal of Security as an Impediment to Performance

Allow hardware-supported or native-supported implementations of algorithms to be used during validation of class files, and allow policy to define where a combination of trusted signer and usage of a trusted compiler will permit the override of dynamic bytecode verification at class load time. Many security functions are highly performance-intensive (hashing, key generation). Improvements are needed to approach performance found in non-Java environments.

Java does not run in isolation; it runs in the context of the operating system platform on top of which it has been implemented. In addition, Java is frequently embedded inside another application, such as a Web browser or Web server. Each of these operating systems and subsystems has an impact on the JVM and Java run-time vulnerability to security attacks. When deploying Java programs, care should be taken in configuring the JVM and application

files to minimize vulnerability to security attacks; this discussion is outside the scope of this chapter.

JAVA CRYPTOGRAPHY EXTENSIONS

The Java Cryptography Extensions (JCE) enable developers to encrypt applets and applications, which can also be digitally signed and transmitted via secure streams. The secure streams capability will let encrypted Java objects and applications cross platforms and protocols.

The crypto tool kit, which is written in Java, is useable with the JDK 1.3 and higher. According to Sun Microsystems, one of the most substantial improvements to the Java security model is the use of permissions-based access to Java applets and applications. This enables different users or servers to access objects according to rules, such as domain or time of day.

Support of digital signatures as a way to verify the source of a Java object has been available since the JDK 1.1. That version of Java improved upon the *sandbox* security model by enabling applets, digitally signed by trusted sources, to read and write files. JDK 1.3 and higher takes this further, allowing for *finer grained* access controls, according to Sun.

The JCE is offered separate from the JDK because it offers encryption levels that are not freely exportable outside of the United States and Canada. The system is based on the Diffie-Hellman key sharing technology, and Data Encryption Standard (DES) and 3DES encryption technology.

Meanwhile, some analysts question how important Java applet security will be in the short term, given the fact that few business-critical applications on the public Internet today (where security is the chief concern) rely on Java objects. For more information on Java security, Java applets, and Java wallet, see Chapter 10 "Designing and Building E-Commerce Web Sites: Hands-On."

Future Directions for Java Security

With continued strong support from the software industry, many enhancements required to bring the Java environment in line with the most stringent needs generally provided in the non-Java environment today are possible. These features include stronger encryption, sophisticated access control, and the ability to provide centralized security policy management. Some of these capabilities are likely to become available beginning in mid-2001 and throughout 2002. Much work is also underway to provide more Java extensions for accessing existing industrial-strength security mechanisms, thus improving system integrity, performance, and functionality. In the future, we will also see more high-level e-commerce and other types of applications migrate from individually provided security capabilities to utilize the capabilities in the latest release of the JDK. By late 2000 or early 2001, very significant initial security functionality should be expected in all Java environments.

IMPLEMENTING ELECTRONIC COMMERCE SECURITY

Security is the cornerstone of e-commerce. Although most people associate transaction security with e-commerce, it is even more critical to protect the corporate network and the e-commerce Web server from illegal access, from both inside and outside the corporation. To secure the Internet connection and leave internal systems vulnerable is no security at all. Under e-commerce, many transactions will ultimately be processed without human intervention to question their legitimacy. Therefore, the internal network must be trustworthy.

Security is not a simple *on* or *off* switch. One cannot purchase a single product (even a firewall) and have a secure network. Secure networks require a layered approach that considers many security aspects, including:

- Host security
- OS security
- Web server security
- Network security
- Firewalls
- Antivirus tools
- A security policy, coupled with education

Security is only as strong as its weakest link. In most cases, that link is end users. Many relatively secure sites are put at risk when intruders ask questions of employees, who in the course of being helpful, provide information that helps the intruder gain access to corporate systems. The importance of a written security policy, coupled with education, cannot be overemphasized. Because security is a large and complex issue, many feel intimidated and want to implement a comprehensive plan before beginning to write a policy. Even a brief policy and a lunch hour training session on selecting secure passwords is an effective step toward increasing corporate awareness of security issues. Security efforts must not end with simple measures, however, because the risks that corporations face in e-commerce are very real indeed.

What Are the Risks?

As mentioned earlier in this chapter, an awareness of the substantial risks that companies face when putting Web servers on the Internet may cause managers to pay additional attention to the security issues and network configuration that could potentially put the corporate network at risk. When the Computer Security Institute[21] of San Francisco asked 539 information security managers whether their systems had been subject to unauthorized use during the last year, 53 percent of them said yes. A slightly smaller group (26 percent) said no, and about 21 percent admitted that they did not know if unauthorized use had taken place.

Military sites are known for their security. However, the Pentagon found some disturbing vulnerabilities when it had its computer professionals attempt to break in to 60,000 of its own computers. More than two-thirds of the computers, 76 percent, could be breached. At the sites where break-ins occurred, 97 percent failed to detect the intrusion. Of the 3 percent that detected the intrusion, only one in five sites reported it.

Internet security incidents provide great content for front-page headlines. These stories are not simply overblown media hype of a random problem (if anything, given that most incidents are undetected and those that are discovered are underreported, one must conclude that the problem is worse than statistics indicate).

Facing the risks enables IT managers to make convincing arguments for putting security in the budget. E-commerce can result in substantial cost savings to the organization. A portion of these savings must be invested in security systems and personnel.

Outsourcing Web servers to a security-conscious and aware ISP offers a partial solution. Responsibility for the security of the corporate Web server then becomes the responsibility of another. However, if the organization has an Internet connection, security issues must still be dealt with in-house; when using an outside IT, one should be aware of the security issues in question to successfully evaluate the outsourcer's qualifications.

Risks of Intrusion

As mentioned earlier in the chapter, an organization faces several risks when putting a Web server on the Internet. If the Web server is breached, intruders may perpetrate a variety of crimes. They may steal corporate information, vandalize the Web pages, or use the server as a home base for criminal activities. Alternatively, the intruder may attempt to shut down the Web server by flooding it with requests.

Stealing Corporate Information

Information has value. A company's profits depend on its customers, its knowledge base, and its strategic advantages. Competitors, in particular, stand to gain by obtaining this information. For this reason, it is prudent to exercise caution when choosing the information to be put on a Web site. Anyone who can view a site with a browser can save information in a file or print the page. Putting up a price list, for example, enables customers to comparison shop, but it also advertises the current pricing structure to competitors. Web servers, unless secured by passwords, are forums for public information.

Depending on how the Web server is configured and secured, intruders may be able to access files on the Web server that are not intended for the public. For example, one company taking orders online left its credit card files in a supposedly secure area of the Web server. A journalist found these files exposed in a public area of the server instead. Keeping sensitive files on the e-commerce Web server is foolish, given the dangers of errors and accidental misconfiguration.

Corporate espionage is a growing problem. If no sensitive files are on the Web server, intruders may burrow further into the corporate network to explore the intranet for information to put them at a competitive advantage. The growing trend of opening the intranet to third parties, while eminently useful, must be done with sufficient security measures for both the Internet connection and the internal network. For example, common devices such as modems provide a means to circumvent firewalls.

When considering the value of corporate data, reflect on the potential beneficiary of the proprietary information (whether competitors, suppliers, and the like). According to the U.S. federal government, the annual cost of data theft in the United States alone is estimated at $40 billion. In addition to corporate espionage where intruders enter from the outside, employees and other personnel such as consultants with close connections within the company have committed the bulk of security incidents. When the Boston-based Yankee Group[22] surveyed 700 security professionals, they discovered that 55 percent had experienced a security breach perpetrated by someone inside their organization, compared with only 25 percent reporting an intrusion from outsiders. Companies must secure e-commerce Web servers and intranets from unauthorized access, whether such access comes from the Internet or from within its own ranks.

Guarding Against Web Server Vandalism

The corporate home page projects an image of the company to the world at large. For many, the home page *is* the company. By tampering with this image, intruders wreak havoc on companies. Takeover rumors and false press releases posted to the corporate Web site by third parties could have severe repercussions in the marketplace. Protecting the content of Web pages is, by far, the most difficult security problem.

Launch Point for Criminal Activities

For small- to medium-sized enterprises not engaged in a competitive marketplace, it may seem unlikely that intruders would bother to attack the Web site. However, unsecured Internet-connected systems are valuable to intruders who can store stolen files on them or use them as a launching point for attacking other, more valuable sites. No system should have a dedicated Internet connection without adequate security, just as no abandoned building should be left unlocked for criminals to use at will.

A Different Malicious Tactic: Denial-of-Service Attacks

Another type of attack that has made recent headlines (which is in fact relatively difficult to prevent) is the attempt to shut down a server by flooding it with requests. The server is then either busy (and unable to respond to legitimate requests from customers) or shut down altogether by the volume of requests.

Denial-of-service attacks underscore the need for all organizations that rely on the Internet to consider alternatives in case of an interruption in service. It is wise to secure a redundant connection for emergencies, even if that connection is of a relatively low speed.

Strategies for Protecting Electronic Commerce Systems

As more and more business deals are closed online, the need for security increases. How does a company protect against these threats?

No strategy can stand alone; rather, a layered approach to security is necessary. As discussed earlier in the chapter, firewalls, if correctly configured, can greatly reduce the likelihood of unauthorized access from the outside, but cannot, for example, protect the corporate network against computer viruses.

Firewalls: Protecting Proprietary Information

Again, as discussed earlier in the chapter, an important component of protecting Internet sites is firewalls—computers or routers that filter traffic to and from the Internet based on predefined rules. Firewalls are prevalent. According to research from the Computer Security Institute,[23] 80 percent of the organizations surveyed already have a firewall. Of the remaining organizations, 73 percent plan to install one. So great is the demand for firewalls that the market is expected to reach nearly $3.4 billion by 2001.

Firewalls come in two basic types: *packet filters*, which are router-based, and *application gateways*, which run on a dedicated or specially secured computer. Packet filters examine each incoming and outgoing data packet to ensure that it is allowed to enter or exit the network based on predefined rules. Application gateways, which also perform packet filtering, have proxies for each implemented application and translate requests so addresses of internal systems are hidden from the Internet. All requests appear to come from the firewall, which in turn disperses information to internal systems. The overall price range for firewalls is between $40,000 and $80,000, a wide range that indicates the diversity of functions such as reporting and intrusion alerts.

Secure Network Configurations

When securing the corporate Web server, several network configurations are possible. The sacrificial lamb configuration places the Web server, which contains only information widely available to the public, outside the corporate firewall. Because this configuration leaves the Web server vulnerable, it is not suitable for taking orders online.

Depending on the firewall purchased, some highly secure firewalls allow the user to run the Web server on the firewall and include a Web server with the firewall. However, the server may or may not include the advanced features needed for e-commerce, so evaluate it on that basis. It is not recommended that typical commercial or freeware Web servers run on the firewall system.

To allow secure access to corporate databases, it is recommended that you use a configuration with two firewalls. The Web server sits between firewalls, and a portion of the data on that server is replicated from the corporate intranet. Using passwords, authorized customers and business partners can access secured portions of this Web server.

The most conservative approach to intranet access is to have a Web server that is completely unconnected from the corporate network by either using a second Internet connection or an ISP host. It is further recommended that you use a standalone, secure computer whose OS has been stripped of all functions except those essential to running the Web server.

Operating System Security

Why do secure operating systems strip out all but the essential features? Because the more complex and flexible an OS is, the more services it offers. More services can result in an increase in possible errors in the OS programming and additional potential backdoors that enable intruders to take over the machine.

UNIX

On UNIX systems, the system administrator is called the *root* or *superuser*. This highly privileged account essentially has free reign on the system. Most UNIX-related security alerts sent by CERT concern a flaw in a version of UNIX that enables unauthorized users to gain root access to the machine and, in effect, gain control.

The best defense against such problems is awareness. Additionally, timely application of the patches supplied by OS vendors reduces the amount of potential break-ins.

Running a version of UNIX that has had some of the more vulnerable services and functionality removed is a sound option. For example, the UNIX sendmail program has been responsible for any number of system break-ins, including Robert Morris' 1988 Internet worm incident, which shut down systems across the Internet. Security increases if sendmail is replaced with a less complex and more secure program. In general, any unnecessary services should be disabled, particularly Internet-related services such as File Transfer Protocol (FTP), Telnet, and finger (a program that provides information about users).

Windows NT

Windows NT has an account similar to root on UNIX systems. The administrative user account has access privileges similar to that used with the

UNIX root account and can modify the Registry, which includes all passwords for the system. It is recommended that you rename the administrative user or disable the account.

Windows NT has safeguarding features, but administrators must enable them. For example, NT offers account lockout and auditing features in addition to a virtual *burglar alarm* to detect intruders. Turning on these features makes it possible to monitor Windows NT more effectively.

OS bugs are only one category of flaws that might allow unrestricted access to the system. Problems in Web server software, a common gateway interface (CGI) form that enables users to overflow the input buffer; and guessing the root password are other means by which intruders can gain root access to the machine.

Security Scanners

A security measure less well known than firewalls is the use of *security scanners*. These are programs that scan the current network configuration and OS for vulnerabilities and suggest ways to address them. For example, RealSecure, from Internet Security Systems,[24] monitors network connections for attacks and other unusual network activity, such as the SYN flooding that occurs during a SYN attack. Network managers select options to determine how such situations should be handled, whether by logging the session for later review, alerting the administrator, or terminating the connection. While firewalls filter traffic according to predefined rules, RealSecure is an intrusion detection tool that specifically monitors for network attacks.

Web Server Security

Web server software provides varying security features. Most servers provide the ability to password-protect documents. Many now also support Secure Sockets Layer (SSL), Netscape's standard for encrypting browser-to-server communications. The Web security FAQ, maintained by Lincoln Stein, is a reliable source of information about securing Web servers, and can be found at http://www-genome.wi.mit.edu/WWW/faqs/www-security-faq.html.

URLs may be subject to change without notice.

Most Web servers now feature forms in which users can enter information. To create these forms, developers may write a CGI script that reads the input from these forms and performs an action such as sending e-mail to the Webmaster or processing an order. The scripts should check for illegal characters and for overly long input that can enable an intruder to break out of the Web server program and arrive at an OS prompt. Despite the fact that these problems have been frequently reported in the trade press, many break-ins are still occurring from poorly designed scripts. Web developers must not assume that scripts provided with Web servers or available on the Internet perform the necessary checks.

Policies and Procedures: Keys to Secure Systems

Security technology enforces security policies. As a result, companies must develop a policy before implementing a protection component such as a firewall. Corporations that implement a written policy placed on the intranet for easy access, followed with security audits and employee education, have the edge in conducting secure business. Model policies from the Internet can be modified to reflect corporate needs. By creating and enforcing a security policy and by investing adequate resources in security technology that enforces this policy, companies can glean the benefits of doing business online without exposing themselves to unnecessary risk. Companies that do not have the needed expertise in-house can hire a security consultant or an information security administrator. Security is too complex and important an issue to place on already burdened IS staff.

CGI scripts are commonly used and have the vulnerability described here. Other methods for creating Web forms such as through software applications should be examined carefully to determine if the same vulnerabilities exist. Some Web development software automatically generates CGI scripts. Such scripts, whether found in commercial software or on the Internet, should be evaluated to see if they expose the Web server to risks such as those described here.

This part of the chapter has provided a broad overview about implementing e-commerce security. Now, let's look at secure transaction technology, the primary enabling technology that underlies online security.

TRANSACTION SECURITY

Before e-commerce can reach its potential, transaction security must be in place to give consumers and businesses confidence that their transactions are safely handled on the public Internet. Transaction security is the single most important enabling technology for e-commerce.

E-commerce offers immediate transaction clearing, without the *float* period built-in to transactions such as checks. Electronic purchasing reduces costs, and also speeds transactions and orders across wires without the delays entailed by mail- and paper-based transactions.

Although encryption knowledge is important in understanding how transaction security works, the complex details are generally transparent to the user in well-implemented systems. While an understanding of the details may build consumer confidence, transaction security should be implemented in such a way that users need not understand public key encryption to make purchases.

Securing Your Storefront

As discussed earlier in the chapter, encryption protects information by scrambling it so that only the information owners can read it. Putting messages in secret code was once the province of espionage, but encryption technology is becoming increasingly common as more business is conducted electronically.

Why do companies and individuals need encryption? The answer is because information is invaluable. A wide variety of information must remain confidential. Health care records, legal files, financial transactions, and research and development (R&D) plans must all be safeguarded. Once these records are computerized, the danger of the information falling into the wrong hands is very real. By encrypting the data, only authorized users can access it.

Restrictions on Encryption Technology

However, the United States and many other nations, including Russia, France, Iran, Iraq, and Israel, regulate encryption based on its military use in espionage and counter-espionage. Currently in the United States, the International Traffic in Arms Regulation (ITAR) classifies encryption technology as munitions, and there are strict rules about exporting strong encryption as a result. Because encryption is increasingly a requirement in software systems and because so much software is developed in the United States, these restrictions put U.S. companies at a disadvantage in the global market. Various industry alliances—including the Computer Systems Policy Project (CSPP),[25] the Alliance to Promote Software Innovation, and the Business Software Alliance (BSA)[26]—are attempting to change U.S. policy, so far with little result. In addition, given that strong encryption is available throughout the world from vendors outside the United States, ITAR does little except cripple U.S. companies that would like to implement strong encryption in exportable versions of their software. However, ITAR supporters see the regulation as a deterrent to crime, as criminals might well use encryption technology to cover their tracks.

ITAR does allow for certain exceptions to their expert prohibition. U.S. citizens traveling internationally with laptop computers can carry secure software on it if they sign papers that state the software is for their personal use only. Stronger encryption can be used for subsidiaries of U.S.-based companies. Another significant policy for e-commerce: Stronger encryption can be used if only the financial portion of a transaction is encrypted rather than encrypting the entire transaction.

Despite the exceptions, ITAR's greatest negative impact is on U.S. software manufacturers who cannot effectively compete in the global market. Increasing awareness of this restrictive regulation and heightened lobbying efforts may ultimately bring about changes in U.S. policy.

How Encryption Is Used

Encryption technology makes any electronic transmission more secure. The recipient of the encrypted transmission must be capable of decrypting the message; therefore, strict adherence to encryption algorithms is extremely important. One cannot assume interoperability between encryption products as a result, unless the underlying encryption is supplied by a single vendor. Most encryption in fact does come from the market leader for encryption, RSA Data Security of Redwood City, California. RSA's encryption technology is currently included in at least 108 million copies of software products, with 61 million copies in Netscape products alone.

Encryption can be implemented at a number of levels: transmission, session, application, and file.

Although any one type of encryption is generally sufficient, multiple levels of encryption can be used simultaneously. For example, under SET, a financial transaction over the Web is encrypted at the application level. Netscape's SSL can be used in addition to encrypting the communications between the Web browser and the Web server, adding a second layer of protection.

Symmetric Key versus Public Key Encryption

Encryption includes both symmetric key and public key encryption, different technologies with various strengths. To understand how financial transactions are secured and how such technology as digital signatures is implemented, the details of how these encryption schemes work must be discussed.

In both types of encryption, keys are used to mathematically encrypt or *lock* a message, and to later decrypt or *unlock* a message. In symmetric key cryptography, the same key is used to encrypt and decrypt the message. The encryption key must somehow be kept secret, which leads to a complex problem with no apparent solution. To send the encryption key, one needs a secure channel. But if one had a secure channel, encryption itself would probably be unnecessary. In practical terms, any cryptographer could decrypt the message if the key is intercepted.

Symmetric key encryption is sometimes referred to as private key encryption *or* secret key encryption. Symmetric *is the more descriptive term; private and secret key encryption are rather misleading because the terms sound more secure than public key encryption. Public key encryption is in fact the more secure of the two methods.*

This deficiency in symmetric key cryptography led Whitfield Diffie and Martin Hellman to develop public key cryptography in 1976. In public key cryptography, each individual has a public key and a private key. Public keys are widely available and can be published rather like telephone numbers in a telephone directory. Anyone who wants to send an encrypted message to a person can use the recipient's widely available public key to encrypt it. Because the public key fits together mathematically with the private key, which is known only to the recipient, only the recipient can decrypt the message. Public key encryption, then, provides a greater degree of security than symmetric key encryption, which relies on a single key used by both parties. If private keys are carefully guarded, only the intended recipient can decrypt the message.

Diffie and Hellman's original plan called for new private and public keys to be generated for each session. While this provides optimal security, it makes communicating with others more difficult if the keys change with each session. Imagine how difficult telephone calls would be if telephone numbers changed with each call. Rivest, Shamir, and Adleman, whose initials comprise RSA's name, recognized the practicality of using the same set of public and private keys for a period of time.

The primary patent holder for public key cryptography is RSA Data Security. Interestingly, RSA's patent hinges on the ability to patent an algorithm, which is possible only in the United States. Companies using RSA technology license it from the vendor. Its patent expired in the year 2000, at which point it entered the public domain. For this reason, among others, RSA chose to be purchased by another firm, Security Dynamics. The decision to be purchased rather than to undergo an IPO was encouraged by investors.

RSA's prevalence in cryptography may change over time. RSA's algorithm relies on factoring very large numbers. Other mathematical techniques can be used to arrive at public keys; for example, Certicom Corp. of Toronto has developed a public key technology that uses elliptical curves to derive public keys.

Combining Public and Symmetric Key Encryption

Public key encryption is both more effective and more computationally intensive than symmetric key encryption. Because it takes longer to encrypt and decrypt information by this method, public key encryption is slower and delays software response time. To circumvent this problem, the most common encryption software combines symmetric key encryption with public key encryption.

The weakness of symmetric key encryption is that the key must be sent securely, a requirement necessitating a secure channel or another method to ensure that the key is only readable by the recipient. Public key encryption provides another method. A typical public key encryption scheme first encrypts the message with a symmetric key, and then encrypts the symmetric key with the recipient's public key. The recipient uses his or her private key to decrypt the symmetric key, and then uses the symmetric key to decrypt the message.

In this discussion, the terms *sender* and *recipient* were used to simplify the encryption method description. In practice, the sender and recipient could be a software application or a network firewall as well as an individual. Software automatically handles most of the details of the encryption process. When encryption is optional, a person may select an option to encrypt a message, but the process itself would typically be transparent to the user.

Digital Signatures

Digital signatures, another technology enabled by public key encryption, allow people to sign documents and transactions in such a way that the recipient can verify the identity of the sender. Digital signatures consist of a unique mathematical fingerprint of the current message (referred to as a *one-way hash*) encrypted with the sender's private key. The recipient's computer runs the same algorithm on the message, decrypts the signature using the sender's public key, and compares the results. If the fingerprints are identical, the recipient can be assured of two things: the sender's identity and the message's *integrity*, which guarantees that it has not been tampered with in transit.

Digital signatures, then, are unique to each message. At first glance, one might think that a digital signature could easily be forged. In fact, because of the algorithms involved and because digital signatures are unique to each transaction or message, they are more secure than physical signatures.

Providing Greater Proof of Identity: Certification Authorities

In most cases, a simple physical signature is not enough to complete a financial transaction. A signature, after all, can be easily forged. A second piece of ID such as a passport or driver's license must be provided. This ID is issued by an established organization and often has both a photograph and the bearer's signature.

Digital signatures also need additional proof; alone, they only indicate that the person who has the associated private key sent the message. The additional proof is the electronic equivalent of a passport. This electronic ID card, referred to as a *digital certificate*, is issued by a certification authority (CA) and contains information about the person and a copy of his or her public key. It also has an expiration date. ISO standard X.509 defines what information digital certificates should contain. Software that uses certificates typically mentions that its certificates comply with this standard.

Secure transactions can occur online using a valid certificate and public key encryption. Additionally, documents that typically require a signature can be digitally signed, making it convenient to file tax returns, sign contracts, and conduct business over the Internet.

Players in the Certification Authority Market

Being able to positively identify business partners is of paramount importance in e-commerce. For this reason, establishing certification authorities (CAs) is critical.

The most widely known participant in the CA market is VeriSign, a joint venture of RSA Data Security, Ameritech, and Visa International. VeriSign[27] issues certificates called *digital IDs*. The company's first digital

ID was issued to Netscape. There is an initial $600 charge for a site license for corporations using VeriSign's services, and a subsequent charge of $108 per server to renew. For individuals, the charge is between $9 and $21 annually.

VeriSign and Coordinate.com, an Internet-focused subsidiary of ePresence[28] (formerly Banyan Systems), are jointly developing an initiative called Switchboard,[29] where users can look up public keys for others and send them encrypted messages, similar to the function of a telephone switchboard. The software provides secure access and gives users control over the content of the information listed about them. They can update information and can decide what information is publicly available. An additional feature called Knock Knock enables users to see who is looking up information about them. Currently, Switchboard lists names, addresses, and public keys.

When doing business online, the potential pool of customers and business partners becomes much larger—global, in fact. As a result, CAs must interoperate. Whether the customer is in Singapore or Sweden, the certificate must be found quickly to complete the transaction. The configuration and connection of CAs into a coherent interoperable network is referred to as a *public key infrastructure* (PKI).

In Canada, Northern Telecom Ltd. of Ottawa has built a PKI (discussed earlier in the chapter) for its government with plans to support 60 million users by 2001. The infrastructure was built primarily to allow the public to securely access government information relevant to them and to allow various government entities to share information.

Of course, the most likely participants in the CA field will be banks and similar institutions that can positively identify customers and verify their ability to pay. MasterCard and Visa, among others, have set up a certificate infrastructure as needed for the SET standard and have become major players in certification.

Other participants include BBN, and GTE's CyberTrust.[30] CyberTrust issues certifications that comply with SET. SETsign provides certificate management for card issuers, and CYBERsign is a CA service for businesses.

NOTE

Baltimore Technologies[31] has acquired GTE CyberTrust to consolidate its position in e-security. Baltimore Technologies provides e|security, offering a full range of products, technologies, and services, enabling security for e-business.

Some companies that write certification software also offer certification management services; Salt Lake City, Utah-based TradeWave is one such example. In other cases, companies may choose to manage their own certificates apart from a certification authority. Microsoft's Certificate Server enables companies to enforce whatever certificate management policy they choose. Some groups use informal key signing parties where identities are verified in person (known as the *web of trust* model).

Certification is a controversial area. Clearly, VeriSign and other major players would incur significant liability if their security system was breached and digital signatures misused. As an early and prominent entrant into this market, VeriSign's potential for financial success is equally great. CAs are an essential element of the emerging digital economy. Full-scale e-commerce requires CAs that provide strong, reliable IDs of those users involved in transacting business over the Internet.

Legal Stature of Digital Signatures

Many nations and smaller jurisdictions are evaluating laws that permit documents to be signed electronically. Digital signatures must meet certain standards to hold up in court, including being backed by a CA. Without digital signatures, evidence such as e-mail, which is simple to forge under most systems, would quickly be refuted by anyone knowledgeable of the workings of e-mail systems. Without digital signatures, perpetrating electronic forgery is far easier than paper forgery. For digital signatures to be accepted by most legal entities, they must:

- Be authentic (the signature could only come from the signer).
- Be deliberate (the process cannot be so transparent to the user that he or she is unaware that he or she has signed a document, a fact that many software systems today fail to consider).
- Apply only to a single document (they cannot be reusable).
- Render the document incapable of subsequent tampering.
- Be verified in real time in case a certificate has expired or has been revoked (in the case of employee dismissal or death, for example).

In the United States, Utah and Wyoming have established digital signature statutes, and most other states are considering them. Utah's law endorses digital signatures for signing government documents, but not commercial documents. The American Bar Association's (ABA's) Digital Signature Guidelines present proposed model legislation to ease the process of regulating this emerging area and to avoid having each state pass a different law concerning digital signatures.

Utah's law limits pecuniary actions against CAs who comply with its regulations. However, the statute is currently so strict that no organization complies. Digital signatures are an emerging area, both in technology and in hardware and software implementation. See the sidebar, "Electronic Digital Signature Act," for more information on the latest pending digital signature legislation.

Session-Based Security

To date, session-based encryption, which encrypts communications between browsers and servers, has been the foundation for secure online ordering. Session-based security methods include Netscape's SSL, EIT's Secure HTTP (SHTTP), and Microsoft's private communications technology (PCT). Of these methods, SSL dominates.

Netscape's Secure Sockets Layer

Netscape's SSL is in widespread use today, and is often the only secure payment tool used. Far from being *owned* by Netscape, SSL is widely supported by browser and server vendors and has become an ad-hoc standard. In essence, SSL negotiates encryption between the browser and the server. For example, one can browse in a catalog-based Web site such as the bookstore Amazon.com. After adding books to the shopping basket and selecting the option to buy, Amazon.com provides an option to switch to the secure server. At the Amazon.com site, the broken key at the bottom left corner of a screen indicates that SSL is not currently encrypting the transmissions. When one chooses the option to select the secure server, the typically broken key in the lower left corner of the display becomes solid. Additionally, the server changes the URL to read *https://amazon.com* instead of *http://*. The prefix "https" indicates that SSL is being used.

After entering secure mode, all transmissions are encrypted between the browser and the server. Once these transmissions reach the server, a program must decrypt the information and create an order from it. A disadvantage to session-based security is that credit card numbers are often stored on the merchant's system, leaving them potentially vulnerable to hackers or to merchant-based fraud. SSL includes interfaces to VeriSign's digital certificates and Palo Alto, California-based VeriFone's credit card validation network. See Chapter 4, "Protocols for the Public Transport of Private Information," for additional information about the SSL protocol.

Electronic Digital Signature Act

Following long negotiations, on June 9, 2000, the House and Senate reached a compromise on electronic signature legislation and molded H.B. 1714 and S. 761 into a single version (S. 761) that went into effect on October 1, 2000. A week later, the Bill was validated by House as well as the Senate. The final version requires a consumer to agree to electronically signed contracts and consent to receiving records over the Internet. Companies must verify that customers have an operating e-mail address and other technical means to receive information. Some notices, such as evictions, health insurance lapses, or electricity lapses, must still come in paper form. The legislation, which consolidates the many state laws on e-signatures, does not prescribe the technology that must be used to verify an electronic signature. Security protocols can be as simple as a password, or can use fast-emerging new technologies such as thumbprint scanners.

In any event, President Clinton ushered in a new stage in the Digital Age where the electronic signature and Internet-conveyed record have the same legal standing as a pen-and-paper document. The President has strongly backed the electronic signature legislation that cleared the Senate by an 87 to 0 vote, saying "it will marry the old value of consumer protection with the newest technologies, so we can achieve the full measure of the benefits that e-commerce has to offer."

The bill, which the House passed earlier by 426 to 4, sets a national framework for giving online signatures legal status. With that, consumers who shop online for a new car or a home mortgage will also be able to seal the deal over their computers.

It could also provide big savings in money and time for businesses that now must use paper and the postal service to conclude transactions or transmit documents. It is a bottom-line issue for the high-tech industry, hastening the day when commerce online is as common as it is offline. This bill literally supplies the pavement for the e-commerce lane of the information superhighway.

Both the House and the Senate passed e-signature bills in 1999, but it took months of negotiations between Congress and the administration to work out a compromise that protected consumers from abuses without overly burdening businesses with new regulations. The final version of the bill finds a constructive balance. It advances electronic commerce without terminating or mangling the basic rights of consumers.

SHTTP from Enterprise Integration Technologies

Secure Hypertext Transfer Protocol (SHTTP) takes a modular approach to security; any document can be signed, encrypted, authenticated, or any combination of these measures can be employed, including using no security at all. The protocol can negotiate the encryption method, transaction mode, and any certificates. It can also timestamp transactions. SHTTP is based on privacy-enhanced mail (PEM), an Internet standard for secure mail. See Chapter 4 for additional information about the SHTTP protocol.

Microsoft's Private Communications Technology

Microsoft's session-level security protocol, PCT runs over the Transfer Control Protocol/Internet Protocol (TCP/IP). It forms an intermediary security layer between TCP and specific application protocols such as HTTP, FTP, and the like. Like SHTTP, it negotiates the encryption method and a symmetric key.

Microsoft continues to support the more established SSL protocol while including PCT in its Internet Security Framework. Interestingly, the online documentation for Microsoft's free Windows NT Web server, IIS, refers only to SSL. Internet Explorer supports both Netscape SSL and PCT.

Transaction Security Systems

While session-based protocols provide a channel over which an order can be securely delivered, the continued processing of that order is in the merchant's hands. Protecting financial data in transit is a critical concern. Data is in transit only briefly, however. More complex systems are needed to secure the entire transaction process.

A few years ago, orders received at the Seattle-based Amazon.com online bookstore were stored on diskette and taken to a DOS-based PC equipped with credit card processing software. In many cases, more manual processing was necessary because personnel had to validate credit cards by reading numbers from a screen into a telephone or retyping them into other systems. Clearly, this was not seamless e-commerce. Transaction security standards have been implemented to automate this portion of the processing.

Payment is not limited to credit cards; digital cash, electronic checks, and smart cards are among the methods being explored for use on the Internet. Credit cards and their standards and implementation currently predominate.

Credit Card-Based Transaction Technology

Credit cards account for 93 percent of all transactions currently handled on the Internet. The transition to Internet commerce has been natural as an infrastructure is already in place to handle any cases of fraud. Further, consumers are accustomed to *cardless* transactions involving credit cards, either over the telephone or by mail.

Indeed, credit card use in cyberspace is in many ways more secure than their use in the real world. Carbons for credit card slips can be easily retrieved from a restaurant or retail store trash can. Merchants see the numbers in any case, enabling unscrupulous employees to defraud customers. Tapping a telephone line to listen in for credit card numbers is far easier than capturing and decrypting transactions over the Internet.

However, consumers on the whole want more assurance. Businesses want to verify an account's status before agreeing to ship an order. Automating the clearing of credit card payments over the Internet in a way that would be standard among merchants, banks, and credit card companies is clearly the only way for e-commerce to move forward. This standardization is now in place.

Secure Electronic Transactions

The proposed SET standard, jointly developed by MasterCard and Visa, promises to bring more credit card sales to the Internet. The combined customer base of MasterCard and Visa numbers more than 1 billion worldwide. Bringing secure transactions to this many consumers can clearly make an important difference, resulting in lower transaction costs for banks and credit card companies. In addition, American Express has stated that it will also implement SET.

Such joint cooperation is a relatively new development. Originally, MasterCard teamed with Netscape and IBM to develop an SSL-based transaction security system called *secure encryption payment protocol* (SEPP). Rivals Visa and Microsoft countered with a different standard, *secure transaction technology* (STT). Pressure from the banking industry eventually brought about a convergence and the joint development and publication of the SET standard.

SET implementation by computer companies, networking companies, banks, and credit card companies has now taken place. While SET was designed to be transport-independent, meaning that it would work with any IP, including unadorned TCP/IP, HTTP, and SMTP, vendors developing SET products requested transport definitions to ensure interoperability.

Although necessary, the enhancements have delayed the widespread availability of SET-compliant products.

How safe is the SET standard? The encryption in SET is better than that used in military launch codes. A combination of the data encryption standard (DES), RSA, SSL, and SHTTP provide multiple layers of encryption for each transaction. To enable SET to pass U.S. encryption restrictions on export, only the financial portion of the transaction uses strong encryption. Weaker, exportable encryption is used on the remaining portions of the transaction.

What Secure Electronic Transaction Does

SET provides assurance that:

- **The order sent is the order received, referred to as *integrity*.** A one-way hash or message digest, stored in the digital signature, represents the unique digital fingerprint of the order.
- **The order is confidential.** By encrypting ordering information and payment information, the order remains confidential.
- **The cardholder is who he or she claims to be.** This is called *authentication*. Using X.509 certificates, SET confirms to the merchant that this person has the account number indicated. The merchant, although he or she does not know the customer's credit card number, is given assurance that the transaction will clear.
- **The merchant is who he she claims to be and can accept SET payments.** The merchant's X.509 certificate and its endorsement by a third party (the bank) provide proof of the merchant's identity.

Interoperability is part of SET's design. Fortunately, because many implementations currently exist, the interoperability of the standard is a design success.

Before Using Secure Electronic Transaction

Before a SET transaction can occur, both parties must have accounts with an institution that uses SET, and have software that is SET-enabled. For example, this could be a Web browser with SET support for the customer, and a Web server with SET support for the merchant.

SET can handle cases in which customers have a credit card, but do not have a certificate with public keys. An extra measure of symmetric encryption is used in this case.

When the customer sets up an account with the bank, he or she receives a certificate and two pairs of public and private keys. One pair is used for encrypting and digitally signing orders, and the other is used for authentication and payment information. Two key pairs are used, resulting from the fact that stronger encryption can be legally used for the authentication and financial portions of the transaction than is possible for ordering information.

For example, a bank could issue both the customer and the merchant a certificate in the form of a computer file, not a paper certificate. Copies of the certificates are exchanged during each order, enabling the merchant to encrypt information so only the customer can read it, and vice versa.

How SET Transactions Work

To the user, SET is transparent. The user simply confirms the order being placed with a merchant. Although the terms *customer* and *merchant* are used to describe the actions taken on behalf of each party, software automatically performs these functions.

After the user selects an item and places an order, the merchant replies with a copy of its certificate. The customer then verifies the identity of the merchant. The customer encrypts the order with a symmetric key, and then encrypts the key with the merchant's public key. In this way, only the merchant can unlock the key that enables him or her to decrypt the order. The financial portion of the order, a credit card number, is encrypted in the same way, this time with the bank's public key (the merchant never sees the credit card number). The third part of the order is a message digest, a unique fingerprint of this message that provides a guarantee to the merchant that the order is intact and is exactly what the customer intended.

The merchant uses his or her private key to decrypt the symmetric key, and then decrypts the order. He or she forwards payment information to the bank along with a copy of the order. He or she relies on the bank to authorize the transaction.

The bank verifies the merchant's identity and the message's integrity. It opens the payment information and verifies that the payment is for this merchant and for this order. The bank checks the customer's credit limit to make sure the transaction will clear, and then authorizes the merchant to proceed with the transaction. The merchant can then ship the order to the customer, whether online or through traditional shipping methods.

SET Limitations

Finally, SET's main advantage over other systems is that it is designed to be interoperable. Most payment systems today require that both parties have a relationship with the same company or implement the same software. SET also has limitations.

For example, SET only accepts credit cards and related debit cards that do not require a Personal Identification Number (PIN). Most SET-based transactions will be processed via credit card. Typical debit cards and forms of digital cash may be added in later versions of the protocol. SET is limited in the type of transactions it can process; straightforward purchases, returns, and voids can be handled, but not more complex payment scenarios such as installment payments. See Chapter 4 for additional information about the SET protocol.

Well, it's certainly an exciting time for e-business. However, businesses need to pay close attention to the changing landscape in order to provide adequate security for customers, partners, suppliers, and employees. Security will become more important than ever as e-business continues to expand.

END NOTES

[1] SANS Institute, 5401 Westbard Ave., Suite 1501, Bethesda, MD 20816, 2000.

[2] Ibid.

[3] Ibid.

[4] Ibid.

[5] Ibid.

[6] Ibid.

[7] Ibid.

[8] Ibid.

[9] Ibid.

[10] Ibid.

[11] Ibid.

[12] Young-Seock Cha, "E-Commerce Security Technologies: Fire Wall," 2000.

[13] Ibid.

[14] Robert Graham, Network ICE Corporate Headquarters, 2121 S. El Camino Real, Suite 1100, San Mateo, CA 94403, 2000.

[15] RSA Security Corporate Headquarters, 20 Crosby Drive, Bedford, MA 01730, 2000.

[16] International Business Machines Corporation, New Orchard Road, Armonk, NY 10504, 2000.

[17] Ibid.

[18] Ibid.

[19] Ibid.

[20] Ibid.

[21] Computer Security Institute, 600 Harrison Street, San Francisco, CA 94107, 2000.

[22] The Yankee Group, 31 St. James Avenue, Boston, MA 02116-4114, 2000.

[23] Computer Security Institute.

[24] Internet Security Systems, Headquarters, 6600 Peachtree-Dunwoody Road, Building 300, Atlanta, GA 30328 USA, 2000.

[25] Computer Systems Policy Project, 1341 G Street, NW Suite 1100 Washington D.C. 20005, 2000.

[26] BSA United States, 1150 18th Street, N.W., Suite 700, Washington, D.C. 20036, 2000.

[27] VeriSign Worldwide Headquarters, 1350 Charleston Road, Mountain View, CA 94043, 2000.

[28] ePresence, 120 Flanders Road, P.O. Box 5013, Westboro, MA 01581, 2000.

[29] Switchboard, 115 Flanders Road, Westboro, MA 01581, 2000.

[30] GTE Corporation, 1255 Corporate Drive, Irving, TX, 75038, 2000.

[31] Baltimore Technologies, 77 A Street, Needham Heights, MA, 02494, 2000.

3 Electronic Payment Methods

"A New Way to Pay Old Debts"

—Phillip Massinger (play title, 1632)

UPDATING TRADITIONAL TRANSACTIONS

The typical modern consumer uses a handful of different methods to pay for goods and services on a regular basis:

- Cash
- Credit
- Personal check

This list is far from complete, leaving out choices like debit cards, money orders and bank checks, traveler's checks, barter systems, tokens, and other instruments used by consumers. Organizations have their own instruments available, including purchase orders, lines of credit, and others. However, most consumer transactions can be handled by cash, credit cards, or personal checks.

Internet-based electronic commerce methods also focus on secure transmission of credit card information, electronic checking, and digital currencies.

Credit cards like MasterCard, Visa, and Discover allow consumers to extend themselves credit on purchases; charge cards like the American Express card do not extend credit. Debit cards are tied to checking accounts, and the amounts charged are debited immediately from the account. However, for the purposes

of electronic transactions they are used similarly, and for the purposes of this book the term credit card *should be taken to cover all credit-card-like plastic payment tokens (unless otherwise specified).*

ADAPTING EXISTING METHODS

Credit cards are the easiest method of the three to adapt to online transactions, in part because people are already accustomed to using them remotely, whether for telephone transactions or for mail orders. Credit card transactions simply require that the consumer provide a valid credit card number and expiration date (and often a billing address) when placing an order—that information can be, and often has been, provided through standard Internet applications like e-mail. This exposes the credit card to eavesdroppers monitoring for sequences of digits specific to credit cards along the message's route. Although I have not heard of any actual instance of an eavesdropper stealing credit information in this way, it is definitely possible. Securing Internet credit card transactions can be as simple as applying secure encryption (as described in Chapter 2, "Security Technologies").

Adapting cash for use over an open network is considerably harder, in part because most people associate cash with the physical exchange of currency, but doing so makes it possible to spend anonymously. There are other problems to solve in the process of digitizing cash, where actual currency is replaced by digital "coins" represented as chunks of data. These are discussed in greater detail in Chapter 8, "Digital Currencies," but one of the most prominent schemes uses public key encryption as well as digital signatures, deployed within a framework managed by a central bank.

Checking across a network is conceptually simpler to grasp, in part because the check itself is simply a document with very specific information (bank, account number, payee, and dollar amount) and has been signed by the account holder. Turning a hard-copy check into an electronic check requires that the electronic check be transmitted securely and signed digitally. In some ways, the process is similar to digitizing cash, but is simpler because there is no need to even consider the anonymity of the person "writing" the check.

BUILDING A COMMERCIAL ENVIRONMENT

It's one thing to engineer and implement a technique for making purchases electronically, and another to make it useable and accessible. So much commercial activity is centered on the World Wide Web because it seems to provide an easily accessible forum for merchants to display and distribute their products, and an easily accessible environment for consumers to shop and make purchases. Since the World Wide Web was not designed for commerce but for information publishing, making it safe for commerce requires adding security features and protocols, as described in Chapter 4, "Protocols for the Public Transport of Private Information." These techniques only make it possible to transmit information securely; they do not address transmission of payments, nor do they do anything to further the transaction once payment information has been received.

An online commerce environment must go beyond the simple transmission of payment information, but it must start there, usually with an Internet server capable of transmitting data securely. Although the payment information is usually the only portion of the transaction that must actually be transmitted securely, some systems offer methods of guaranteeing information such as shipping instructions, offering prices, and other order information through digital signatures. Security goes beyond encryption of ordering information, however, and it is necessary to guard against criminals who masquerade online as merchants authorized to accept consumer credit card information. Even more important is to secure the merchant's server system where credit information is collected.

As an entire solution, the commerce environment should be as flexible as possible, accepting different payment methods consistent with the market and the business. Next, it should help the merchant collect information about customers (wherever relevant and possible). It should be integrated into the general business environment, generating actions to be taken as a result of the order:

- Product delivery instructions
- Transaction settlement
- Account activity reports
- Confirmations
- Order status reports
- Gathering of marketing information

Some merchants will be able to do business on the Internet simply by purchasing and installing a secure World Wide Web server, and manually processing orders received over the Internet in the same way they process mail or telephone orders. Merchants who do not expect a large volume of orders from the Internet will prefer to operate in this way, since it costs less than the more holistic approaches. However, merchants wishing to maximize the benefit of selling online will invest in a more complete commercial environment. Secure servers and related commerce environment products are discussed in more detail in Chapter 7, "Online Commerce Environments."

OFFLINE AND ONLINE TRANSACTIONS

In general, direct commerce solutions that use the Internet directly to transmit transaction information protect that information with some kind of encryption method. This neutralizes what is perceived to be, but actually isn't, the greatest threat to Internet transactions: the eavesdropper. Data encrypted with a sufficiently strong method is immune to likely threats (the cost of computer resources required to decrypt your credit card number ranges from millions of dollars to many billions of dollars, depending upon whether the decryption must be complete in a matter of decades or faster). There are easier ways to steal credit card numbers.

However, it is not strictly necessary to transmit any sensitive information over open networks when there are much more secure channels that can be used to carry sensitive information. For example, many people feel more comfortable discussing business with associates in person than discussing business over a telephone. Barring the relatively extreme instances of those whose business is under government scrutiny, personal conversations inspire a high level of confidence that no one is listening in— eavesdroppers in most cases would most likely be noticed.

Although telephone conversations have a greater potential for eavesdropping (legal and illegal taps, someone listening in on an extension, cellular and cordless telephone scanners), with a minimum of care a telephone conversation can be relatively secure. The same type of consideration can be applied to fax transmissions, as well as to postal mail and other delivery services. The result is that there are other channels across which sensitive information can be sent. Some Internet commerce solutions take advantage of the relative security of these alternative media to eliminate the need for software security solutions.

These solutions require that the consumer make a telephone call, send a fax, or send a hard copy with sensitive information like credit card numbers, consumer names, and billing and shipping addresses.

SECURE ONLINE TRANSACTION MODELS

It may be simplest to contract with some other company, like an electronic mall operator, Internet Service Provider (ISP), or some other organization, to manage servers, orders, and content. However, that company itself must use some method or methods of accepting and processing orders. As has been mentioned, the simplest method of doing direct business online on the Internet is to set up a secure World Wide Web server, and then create content pages and program forms to take orders.

SECURE WEB SERVERS

The current battle for domination of the secure World Wide Web server and Internet browser markets is between Netscape and Microsoft. However, Web browsers and servers from any vendor are expected to interoperate with the servers and browsers of any other vendor—this is the whole point behind using Internet standards. (The Netscape and Microsoft secure servers and browsers are discussed in greater detail in Chapter 7.)

A secure World Wide Web server must, by definition, support some type of security protocol. At the moment, the two most important of these are the Secure Hypertext Transport Protocol (S-HTTP) and the Secure Sockets Layer (SSL), which was initially developed by Netscape and offered to the Internet community as a proposed standard in 1995. These protocols, as well as some others, are discussed in greater detail later in this chapter and in Chapter 4. However, one of their primary advantages is their relative unobtrusiveness to the consumer using an SSL- or S-HTTP-enabled browser.

Secure Server Purchasing

The resulting browser/server interaction is, to the consumer, very closely mapped to the interaction that occurs when a consumer makes a purchase from a catalog. The consumer browses through graphical and textual descriptions of the merchant's products, selects a purchase, and usually clicks on a button that says something like "BUY NOW" to make a purchase. If the consumer is using a secure browser supported by the secure server, that button will produce a form on the consumer's screen, which the consumer must complete. Delivery and payment information will usually be required, and at some point after this information has been provided, the product will be delivered. If the customer is using a browser that is not secure or that uses a protocol not supported by the server, then some other method must be employed to consummate the transaction (alternative methods are discussed later in this chapter).

Delivery information represents name, address, delivery address, e-mail address, and any other information necessary or desirable to deliver the product. If the product happens to be a physical item, then a physical destination, preferred shipper, and telephone number may be necessary. If the product is a digital item, then it may be transmitted directly to the consumer via the browser, by e-mail, or through some other application such as file transfer.

Secure Server Selling

Merchants want to make it economical, pleasant, and easy for consumers to buy their products, and doing so with a secure Web server is no different. There is a broad spectrum of options to choose from to balance price against a pleasing shopping experience; these issues are beyond the scope of this book, but ease of use is definitely a factor for the consumer using a secure browser.

First, the merchant needs to publish product offerings on the Internet with a secure server. Servers are available that support SSL, S-HTTP, and both. Because the Internet is an open network, based strictly on the proper and widespread implementation of standards, it doesn't make sense for merchants to limit their potential customers by using only one standard. By supporting both SSL and S-HTTP, they support transactions with consumers whose browsers use either of those standards.

However, the merchant must go beyond merely setting up the server. As with mail orders, there must be a mechanism for processing the information contained on an order form. The Internet programming community has created and offers several utilities to manipulate data. One of the first was the Common Gateway Interface (CGI), which uses scripts or lines of code to perform different tasks. More recently, Java and ActiveX have arrived on the market, offering growing levels of sophistication and power in managing data between users and the Web sites they are visiting. World Wide Web forms prompt the consumer for some kind of information, and on receipt of the form, either the data is reported back to a database, or the

Web site massages the data, with CGI, ActiveX, or Java, to take the user through another task.

In the simplest case, the information provided by the consumer might be dumped into a data file to be manually processed later. The merchant would go through this file, processing credit card information and shipping the product off to the indicated delivery address. This may be an acceptable solution for low-volume applications—merchants who do not anticipate a large flow of online transactions, for instance. It is not acceptable where the product sold is digital in nature: If the product is delivered immediately, there is no guarantee for the merchant that the payment information is correct, but waiting to ship the digital product may not be acceptable to the consumer who assumes immediate delivery.

More often, the merchant will use interfaces of some type to automate transactions. For example, banks, credit card clearing organizations, and credit card companies are all increasingly willing to authorize transactions executed over the Internet. Companies selling physical products over the Internet use e-mail confirmations and shipping notices to keep customers up to date on the status of orders, and all merchants can use network applications to notify their internal organization of orders.

REQUIRED FACILITIES

The merchant must understand (and the educated consumer should understand) that purchasing products over the Internet requires a significant investment in software, hardware, and services. Surprisingly, the software and hardware components are probably the smallest part of the investment, while the "services" can be acquired from any number of different providers.

The majority of Internet merchants will be unlikely to set up their own secure servers, because doing so can be complicated for the Internet novice, and also because there are so many companies now offering such services. However, merchants who are aware of what their options are can be smarter consumers of these services, and customers who are aware of how their online orders are processed can be smarter online consumers.

Hardware

Technically, any computer that can run an implementation of TCP/IP (including a World Wide Web server program) and that can be connected to the Internet can be a World Wide Web server. More realistically, the system should have a great deal of processing power to handle many simultaneous or near-simultaneous requests for information. It should have a hard disk sufficiently large to store all the information to be published in the Web server as well as system software. It should have a sufficiently fast Internet connection to support the maximum expected load on the system. And, it should have security features sufficient to protect it from unauthorized access. Perhaps surprisingly, a graphical user interface, or any graphics capability, is not technically necessary on the server—it does not have to display any information locally, but rather sends and receives data across the Internet.

In practice and at a minimum, this translates to a fast, current personal computer capable of running an operating system such as Windows NT (or possibly Windows 2000), using an Ethernet connection to an Internet router. A UNIX workstation or PC-architecture server system is preferred, though. The Internet connection itself should probably be at least a dedicated telephone line running at 56 Kbps (thousands of bits per second). Internet routers are often included in Internet service packages, but they are often simply fast personal workstations with special networking software and hardware.

Some organizations using the Internet may prefer to simply get a server and an Internet connection, and leave their internal networks out of the loop. However, those who do opt to connect their organizational networks to the Internet along with their Web server will almost certainly want to invest in some kind of firewall architecture to protect their network from intruders. This is likely to add to the cost of the hardware required for an Internet connection, but is necessary whether they are running a Web server or not.

There is also a blossoming software industry enabling the presentation of data already existing on an internal computer system in a Web server without reentering the data. This will be very useful for companies looking to offer online order processing of inventories experiencing a high level of turnover.

Total initial cost, depending on the systems selected, can be anywhere from $700 on up. A typical implementation, using a low-end PC server/high-end personal workstation, should cost somewhere between $1,000 and $7,000, including router, network cards, and cable.

Software

As mentioned earlier, a TCP/IP implementation is necessary for the Web server. This may be built in to the operating system, or it may be a part of the Web server package; in any case, it is necessary. Likewise, a Web server package is required. This is the software that responds to requests from browsers on the Internet and sends out the desired information. Security, as mentioned before, should be part of the operating system.

Savvy system administrators make sure that there is no other software on Internet servers. This guarantees that if an intruder should compromise that system, no software is available to the intruder for further mischief. For example, network software installed and configured on a server allowing access to organizational data could be used by an intruder to access, modify, or delete that information.

Services

The raw materials are relatively cheap, but the knowledge of how to put it all together is (at least right now) expensive. There is quite a handful of different things that need to be done to set up a server:

- Obtain Internet service
- Administer Internet link and servers
- Create Web server content
- Process transactions

Obtaining Internet service is simply the process of getting connected to the Internet, and keeping that access up and running. In some ways it is comparable to getting a telephone connection—the ISP simply offers connectivity, not content.

Some ISPs will also manage your link and your server hardware. This should mean that they will keep the systems up and running and manage access to and from those systems. This often includes security and firewall services.

Creating and maintaining Web server content is critical and is a task often farmed out to consultants. While this approach may be effective for getting a Web site online quickly, maintaining and updating content must be an ongoing task. Fortunately, there are many tools available to make Web authoring easy, and these will tend to drive down the cost of managing Web content.

Finally, transactions using credit cards must be settled. Most people will be familiar with the "swipe" machines used in stores where credit cards are accepted. These transmit information about the transaction to a clearing company, which then provides an authorization code indicating whether the transaction will be processed. This same process can be linked to a secure Web server, for a price. This is just one of the services included in online commercial environments, to be discussed later in this chapter and in Chapter 7.

Electronic Malls

Setting up a Web site for buying and selling can be complicated and expensive; it is not for everyone. However, some companies have been setting up electronic, or virtual, or online malls. The shopping mall is a familiar and comfortable model for consumers and merchants, and it is relatively straightforward to simulate using the World Wide Web. Mall operators allow individual merchants to "rent space" on the mall. The financial arrangements may vary, but generally include some type of monthly charge, charges for storage space required, and usually some charge for each transaction.

As with other Internet commerce service providers, digital malls provide a way for individual merchants to sell online without having to assemble all the parts themselves. The parts are still all there, and merchants investigating online commerce options should consider the systems and networking expertise of the service provider as well as the commercial facilities.

ONLINE COMMERCIAL ENVIRONMENTS

As should be apparent from the preceding discussion, simply having a secure World Wide Web server is far from a complete online commerce solution for merchants (although having a secure World Wide Web browser can be a complete solution for the online consumer). There is an entire "back end" infrastructure needed to support electronic sales and fulfillment. This includes links to credit card authorization networks, as well as integrating alternative payment methods into the solution. Merchants maximize their potential sales by making it easy for all customers to buy, and this includes accepting different payment methods.

Companies offering online commerce environments strive to produce an integrated and complete solution for Internet merchants. This may include software tools for creating World Wide Web documents and commercial offerings, secure Web server software, Web site management tools, and links to commercial transaction settlement services for credit cards as well as other digital payment methods.

MERCHANT REQUIREMENTS

As part of the ability to sell products electronically, the online commercial environment should provide at least some of the following abilities:

- Automatically process transactions received through the Internet, and send payment information to credit card authentication services, also via the Internet
- Automatically process responses from the credit card authentication service
- Get digital signatures or other proof of approval of the order from the customer
- Generate necessary transaction tracking information, including electronic receipts, customer statements, and internal documentation of orders
- For nonelectronic material, have a link to the delivery company (e.g., FedEx) for delivery status between the vendor and the customer
- Be able to handle occasional telephone or fax transactions as well as online transactions

Online commerce environment vendors must offer at least some of these functions because they are necessary to transact business online. Many of the functions described in the preceding section (*Required Facilities*) may also be provided in an online commerce environment, but these are offered as a convenience to merchants—the merchant can just as easily supply his or her own facilities, or contract them out to some other vendor.

CUSTOMER REQUIREMENTS

The successful online commerce environment makes no demands at all on the customer, other than requiring the ability to access the online sales facility and the intention to buy something offered. However, the environment should permit the customer to use whatever payment method is desired, consistent with good business practice. In practice, this means major credit cards, as well as an appropriate selection of electronic payment methods.

Customers, like merchants, will want some kind of audit trail or account statements, particularly when purchasing information products.

The ability to provide receipts, monthly billing statements, and account status reports will be important to customers evaluating online business partners.

Chapter 7 discusses an online commercial environment that includes some of these services.

DIGITAL CURRENCIES AND PAYMENT SYSTEMS

While secure commerce servers are intended to protect transaction data being sent over the Internet, digital currencies and other types of digital payment mechanisms are intended to carry value in a protected digital form over the Internet. Digital currencies and payment systems do not necessarily compete against secure Internet servers or commercial environments, but can complement such products by adding another way to exchange values.

Two approaches are taken by companies offering this type of service. One is to link a customer payment method (credit card, checking account, or some other source of funds) to an online identity, managed by the service provider. Merchants selling to a participating customer can then authenticate the payment information through the service provider, who may also provide authorization and clearing services. This type of service may seem to overlap somewhat with commerce environment services. The difference is that the payment system usually requires participants to register in some way with the payment system sponsor, while commerce environments usually permit the customer to use a credit card or a payment system. The payment method may also become merged into the applications themselves as new protocols are introduced that define procedures for transacting business using existing, nondigital payment methods.

The CyberCash payment systems are discussed in greater detail in Chapter 6, "Electronic Payment Systems."

Digital checking can also take advantage of the same techniques, in much the same way that debit cards are used the same way as credit cards—consumers present the card to the merchant, who must get an authorization for the purchase. The charges are paid immediately out of the consumer's checking account, rather than at the end of the monthly billing cycle.

A different approach is used for actual digital currencies, as opposed to payment systems. Usually, anyone can participate by opening an account with a financial institution offering digital currency service. Client software is used to withdraw money from the account, check on balances, and maintain a "digital wallet" that holds the value on the participant's computer. Cash exchanges between a user and the bank use the same types of cryptographic technologies described in Chapter 2. Digital signatures guarantee cash transfers, and transactions may be encrypted.

New technologies for transferring cash without hard currency or a traditional check are also appearing on the market and are discussed in Chapter 8.

OFFLINE SECURE PROCESSING

All of the options discussed so far in this chapter require some type of online security, whether it is a secure channel between the customer and the merchant or encryption of some or all data sent from one application to another. As entrepreneurs and developers investigated the methods for doing business online, it became apparent that there were two general approaches:

- Use cryptographic techniques to secure the channel and enable online, real-time transaction initiation and completion.
- Use alternative, secure channels to transmit sensitive data.

To some developers, the advantages of using cryptography—all related to the securing of a previously unsecure channel—are outweighed by the costs of implementing it. These costs include the following:

- Licensing fee for patented cryptographic tools
- Creation and distribution of new Internet browsers and servers
- Maintenance of public key certification facilities
- Increased computing overhead needed to transact business exchanges
- Difficulty in distributing cryptographic technologies outside of the United States due to export restrictions on strong cryptography

It has been argued that by taking the sensitive data out of the online Internet loop, companies can provide relatively secure commercial services on the Internet without the costs associated with implementing a secure channel or secure payment protocol. Most important is that implementing this type of system independently of the underlying application means that the end user—the customer—does not have to upgrade or buy any special software to support new security protocols. All existing channels are capable of supporting commerce, whether through a World Wide Web server, file transfer or terminal emulation, or even e-mail. In addition, any future application or network can also be supported just as easily, with no need for modification.

In this approach, customers must telephone, fax, or mail (all relatively secure, or at least familiar, methods) their credit card payment and shipping address information to the sponsoring organization. They are then provided with an account ID, which they can use to order goods from participating merchants. The information about an order, including order status, can be transmitted in the clear, while the sensitive information, such as payment information, is kept entirely offline.

Although this approach has some interesting and attractive features, it is not likely to dominate the electronic commerce world. It is likely to continue to be used in certain specialty and niche markets, but some assumptions that motivated this approach are proving wrong. For example, as larger numbers of new Internet users come online, it becomes easier to implement new Internet browsers supporting commercial security features. Also, the United States government is granting export licenses for some electronic commerce applications of varying strength.

PRIVATE DATA NETWORKS

The use of the Internet for the exchange of business data is a growing, unstoppable trend. Internet-based transactions are in the future for most, if not all companies. However, many companies are still reluctant to use the "open" Internet to conduct mission-critical business transactions. A genuine problem faces many companies, as they want to groom existing systems and bring on new applications, but do not want to close out future possibilities. An alternative is available.

A solution for many companies may lie in the use of private data networks to pass Internet data. For example, a large distribution company clearly sees the Internet as a transaction medium in the next few years. They are proceeding with plans to build an online catalog and order processing application, but, at first, will not hook it to the Internet. Instead, they will connect it to a private third-party network.

This is not a new technology. For years, companies such as CompuServe, Advantis, AT&T, and, more recently, BBN Planet have offered private data networks for companies that are looking for a large network, but would like to avoid the cost of building such a network from scratch.

In this scenario, users access the application and information with a standard Internet browser, and the distribution company will employ all of the required security methods, including firewalls, secure browser support, and electronic commerce servers. The only difference is that when the customers connect to the distribution company, they will dial a toll-free number and be connected to a third-party company, which will in turn be connected to the distribution company. The third party will have a network in place that functions exactly like the Internet but will not be accessible to the general public.

In the future, management opinions may change, the nature of the application may change, or new Internet technologies may be deployed, and the company will have the option of connecting the application to the open Internet. Now, let's look at some payment technology issues.

PAYMENT TECHNOLOGY ISSUES

CyberCash, based in Reston, Virginia pioneered many of the concepts found in the SET standard and pledged to be one of the first to implement SET. Many customers and merchants around the world currently use CyberCash's simple Internet payment system (SIPS), described in Internet RFC 1898.

 Internet standards are defined in documents called Request for Comments (RFCs).

Using CyberCash's software has an incentive: In addition to enhanced security, the software is free to both customer and merchant. The cost for using the CyberCash system is absorbed by the credit card processing fee.

CyberCash invented the concept of the client software known as a *wallet*. The wallet analogy is accurate; its name accurately explains its services. As with most real wallets, Visa CyberCash Wallet allows for a variety of payment methods to be used: cash (digital cash), credit cards (most widely used), and checks. The wallet also provides ID for the holder. Each wallet is associated with a *persona*, an online shorthand for the person's public key. The online wallet does not store important financial information about the customer; this information is established with CyberCash when registering the wallet software. This process eliminates the necessity of retransmitting sensitive information over the Internet with each purchase.

Following in the footsteps of the recent MasterCard International/IBM e-wallet announcement, Visa USA is working with CyberCash on a nonexclusive agreement to provide a wallet that can be branded by member issuers.

Merchants need only have an account with a participating bank and incorporate the PAY button into their Web page at the appropriate point in the ordering process. When the customer pushes the PAY button, it invokes the wallet software and begins the interaction to clear the payment. The financial portion of the transaction is encrypted at 768 bits; the order itself is sent without encryption. Because only the financial portion uses strong encryption, CyberCash's technology is exportable and is becoming widely used internationally.

For example, Virtual Vineyards was CyberCash's first online merchant. The company was enthusiastic about no longer needing to maintain customer credit card numbers on its network, thus reducing the likelihood of hacker attacks.

CyberCash's server is an intermediary between the merchant and the payment processing organization, and between the customer and the merchant. The company's software provides the *glue* that holds the secure transaction together.

Both CompuServe and CheckFree Corporation have licensed Cyber-Cash's wallet technology, enabling customers to use their wallet at merchants that accept any of the three types. Another licensee is the Bank of Canada, which uses the system for online banking. In addition to its payment system, CyberCash also offers CyberCoin for micropayments. Electronic checks are also offered.

CyberCash is committed to being one of the first vendors to offer SET-enabled transactions. Because SET essentially replaces the CyberCash protocol (in fact, in its details, SET would seem to have been inspired by the CyberCash protocol, which was created in 1994), CyberCash offers migration to its customers. For the latest information (particularly regarding international banks), check http: //www.cybercash.com and Chapter 6.

URLs are subject to change without notice.

PAYMENTS WITHOUT ENCRYPTION: DIGITAL CASH

Digital cash is the most radical form of e-commerce and is being implemented at a slow pace. As opposed to the simple conversion of an existing monetary transaction into an Internet-based electronic form such as credit card processing or electronic checks, digital cash is a new type of currency. It could make sweeping changes in how money is spent and globally regulated. Digital cash initiatives can be divided into three categories:

- **Anonymous cash**–Cash, as a medium, is anonymous. It can be spent anywhere by anyone with no proof of ID (except for very large purchases such as automobiles and houses). A few companies have devised an E-cash system that preserves the anonymity of real cash online. In most other digital cash initiatives, the transactions are recorded, whether by the bank or third party issuing the digital cash, the merchant, or both.
- **Micropayments**–Micropayments are perhaps the primary use of digital cash. On the Internet and in online services, articles can be purchased, games can be played, and software can be used. For small purchases, credit card processing is impractical. Micropayments enable very small purchases to occur, purchases that would take only coins in the real world. Micropayments make it possible to offer online vending machines for information, games, entertainment, and software usage.
- **Smart cards**–Smart cards are a form of digital cash that are used currently more often in the physical world than they are online. Smart cards can be loaded with cash, and then used at any merchant who accepts the card in question. No online validation is necessary; the cards contain a chip that automatically deducts the purchase from the card and transfers it to the merchant in question. Because processing is quick (no communications with a processing network is necessary), smart cards can be used for small purchases for which cash is traditionally used. Mondex International, a leading vendor of smart cards, points out that about 48 percent of all physical transactions fall within the range of $4.50 to $10.50, making them noncost-effective for credit cards or checks.

Digital cash has its potential dangers. Money laundering is an important concern. According to British Intelligence, money-laundering schemes account for $800 billion annually. Half of the money laundered is from illegal drug trade; the other half is attributable to organized crime and terrorism.

Because of the potential for money laundering and other illegal activities such as online bribes, truly anonymous digital cash is likely to be highly regulated, when it is allowed at all. Because the industry is still in its infancy, policies and laws are just being formed. Governments are likely to watch developments in the area of e-commerce with much interest and step in with regulations sooner than in other areas.

eCASH TECHNOLOGIES, INC.'S E-CASH

eCash Technologies, Inc.'s (formally DigiCash) E-cash technology is one of the only true implementations of digital cash that shares the characteristics of real cash. A key feature of eCash Technologies' system is anonymity, making it possible to spend cash on the Internet like cash is spent at a mall—without anyone having a record of who made the transaction.

E-commerce poses a danger to privacy. If all transactions are online and all transactions can be aggregated into databases, detailed spending profiles on each individual could be constructed and sold to various marketing firms. Although, like encryption, people suspect that anonymity is only for those who have something to hide. In fact, everyone enjoys a certain measure of anonymity. No one wants to be greeted on the telephone by a telemarketer mentioning that the brand of deodorant they have used for the last 15 years is inferior to the brand that they sell. Anonymity, then, is a valid concern, and eCash Technologies' system excels at protecting it.

eCash Technologies' E-cash (a term it has trademarked) is purchased from a bank and assigned serial numbers. As online funds are spent, banks can verify that the serial numbers are valid and that they were used, but a scrambling algorithm keeps the bank from knowing who spent the money. The E-cash is token-based and stored on the customer's hard drive until it is spent. Using eCash Technologies' client software and a password known only to the user, the customer withdraws money from the bank. The E-cash can then be spent at any store that accepts it.

By the end of 1994, people could trade money for an ad-hoc currency called Cyberbucks, eCash Technologies' issued E-cash. At the end of 1995, Mark Twain Bank of St. Louis issued E-cash in dollars, while EUNet of Finland began offering E-cash through Merita of Finland. No facility for exchanging E-cash into a different currency is currently available, nor can it be re-exchanged for cash.

THE EMERGING ROLE OF MICROPAYMENTS

At this point, selling in cyberspace is similar to catalog sales. Customers generally order real goods and have them shipped. Information sales, on-line games, and entertainment are paid for either by advertisers or by a subscription model. Subscriptions can be costly, however; a one-year subscription to access *Encyclopedia Britannica*'s site is $180 and beyond the reach of most people. On the other hand, a person might be quite willing to save a trip to the library and pay $.28 for an article from the encyclopedia. The Internet could become a vending machine of sorts, with people willing to pay literally pennies for information they need or want. This form of sales is known as *micropayment*. Online games are expected to be one booming area for micropayments: Sierra Online and Rocket Science Games both offer games on the Internet. Digital cash, especially if it is targeted toward small transactions, can provide an inexpensive way to sell information at a profit.

Processing small payments by credit card or check is too expensive. Not only do credit card companies charge for transactions, but even the encryption and decryption necessary for safe commerce are too time-consuming to allow companies to process the volume of transactions that would make online vending practical. Several micropayment schemes have been put forward; CyberCash CyberCoin is one of the few currently in operation.

Micropayment Transfer Protocol

Micro Payment Transfer Protocol (MPTP) has been proposed by the payments group of the Web Consortium (W3C), the standards body that oversees the Web's development. MPTP is based on a protocol called PayWord developed by two of the RSA founders—Rivest and Shamir. Like DigiCash's system, it is token-based. It supports multiple currencies, and digital signatures prevent money from being spent twice. MPTP supports both symmetric and public key encryption. In MPTP, a broker acts as an intermediary, and both merchant and customer must share the same broker.

In other words, once the vendor or broker has authenticated a payment authority, an arbitrary payment token may be authenticated by performing successive hash functions and comparing against the root value. MPTP provides protection against double spending through vendor and broker checking of authority identifiers. A broker might choose to guarantee payments up to a certain amount, but require an authorization to guarantee payments for larger amounts.

MPTP supports an option for the broker to transfer this risk to the vendor by refusing a guarantee of payment.

NetBill

Carnegie Mellon University's NetBill project is designed to handle micro-payments over virtually any application, whether a Web session, a SQL query, FTP, or when viewing a file such as a movie. The cost per transaction with NetBill is $.04 out of every $.13.

In other words, NetBill is a payment system using a mixture of symmetric key and key pair cryptography. It is aimed at payment for information-based goods such as library services, journal articles, CPU cycles, etc. The NetBill system itself charges for transactions, and requires the user to have a pre-funded NetBill account from which all payments will be made. The basic protocol is outlined as follows:

1. The merchant sends the goods in an encrypted form to your machine.
2. Software on your machine verifies that the goods were received intact, and sends verification of this to the merchant's software.
3. The merchant sends your verification message, your account information, and the decryption key to the NetBill server.
4. The NetBill server verifies that there is money in your account to pay for the goods. If there is, it transfers the funds, stores the decryption key, and sends a report back to the merchant's software.
5. The merchant then sends you the decryption key, which your software uses to decrypt the goods. Should the merchant's server fail before completing this step, your software can retrieve the key directly from the NetBill server.

The NetBill system itself holds accounts for all the merchants and customers, and these accounts are grounded by accounts in a conventional financial institute. The system continues to be tested on the Carnegie Mellon campus. Table 3.1 shows the properties of the NetBill system.[1]

TABLE 3.1 NetBill Transaction Properties

	Tok	Atom	Cons	Isol	Dur	Eco	Div	Scale	Inter	Conv
NetBill	N	Y	Y	Y	Y	?	—	?	?	Y

Question marks have been placed against the economy and scale entries due to the requirement for extensive network traffic during the transaction. Table 3.2 shows the visibility properties of the system.[2]

As can be seen, this is not an anonymous system. This is not surprising, as it is a check-based rather than a cash-based system. The group at Carnegie Mellon does suggest an alternative system, where transactions are mediated. That system has the following visibility profile as shown in Table 3.3.[3]

This is an improvement from some points of view—the item being bought is completely hidden from outside observers. Buyer and seller are hidden from each other and from eavesdroppers. However, NetBill still has full knowledge of the identities of the parties.

CyberCash's CyberCoin

CyberCash's CyberCoin implementation is a component of the wallet program. CyberCash wallet holders can download money in $20 increments from bank accounts or credit cards into their wallet for use in CyberCoin transactions. The process is conceptually similar to withdrawing a $20 bill

TABLE 3.2   Visibility of NetBill Transactions

	Seller	Buyer	Date	Amount	Item
Seller	Full	Full	Full	Full	Full
Buyer	Full	Full	Full	Full	Full
Bank	Full	Full	Full	Full	Partial
Observer	Partial	Partial	Full	None	None

TABLE 3.3   Visibility of Mediated NetBill Transactions

	Seller	Buyer	Date	Amount	Item
Seller	Full	None	Full	Full	Full
Buyer	None	Full	Full	Full	Full
Bank	Full	Full	Full	Full	None
Observer	None	None	Full	None	None

from an ATM machine and using it to buy a newspaper and other small items. Transactions as small as $.25 can be made with CyberCoin. A growing number of vendors are offering CyberCoin transactions. Netscape plans to offer CyberCoin technology in its LivePayment server.

Clickshare Corporation

Micropayments provide an effective means to purchase small bits of information, but can be a bookkeeping nightmare if payment is deferred. Clickshare Service Corporation of Williamstown, Massachusetts has developed software that aggregates micropayments into a single bill to the customer's credit card at the end of the month (credit card technology is currently used, but other billing methods are also possible with the Clickshare system). Rather than purchasing a subscription to a site, customers can purchase single articles. Furthermore, users need not remember usernames and password combinations for multiple sites supported by Clickshare; the Clickshare token follows them as they shop.

For the Clickshare system to work, customers must sign with a Clickshare service provider. The service provider is the only party who can ever identify the user, whose anonymity is protected as he or she selects content to read. The merchant (mostly publishers) can identify the user's demographic characteristics, however. In this way, Clickshare balances the need for privacy with the need for advertiser-supported sites to provide accurate demographics on their readership.

Clickshare's Publishing Members (the merchants) pay a fee of $2,295 for the software, and $.06 per year for each of the first 40,000 readers. In addition, Clickshare is paid 23 percent of each online transaction.

SMART CARDS

Smart cards represent a form of e-commerce that typically does not involve the Internet. These stored-value cards take ATM cards a step further. While ATM cards provide access to money in bank accounts when verified over a network, smart cards have money stored in them. A running balance is kept on the card, and purchases are deducted from the total. The transfer of funds happens immediately and no third-party verification process is needed, unlike the use of debit cards at retail stores.

These cards provide some of the benefits of cash without the risks. If the card is stolen, it cannot be used because a Personal Identification Number (PIN) opens the card. However, unlike cash but similar to debit card transactions, complete anonymity is not possible. Records are kept of each transaction by both the merchant and the card.

In Europe, smart cards are gaining wide acceptance in the same manner as other innovative financial payment schemes. EFT and online bill payment are relatively commonplace among consumers, while in the United States most people still use paper checks. Single-purpose cards, which are gaining popularity in the United States for uses such as telephone cards, have already been well accepted in Europe where they are used for such things as public transportation.

Smart cards also provide an alternative means of distributing benefits. British Airways provides its cash travel allowance to pilots and stewards using a smart card because it is easier to manage than cash. In addition, employees can easily convert cash from the smart card into the local currency.

Reloadable stored value cards are relatively expensive to manufacture: They cost $10 to $15 compared with $.15 to $.33 for magnetic stripe cards. Despite their high cost to manufacture, stored value cards are gaining ground in the marketplace. To increase consumer acceptance of stored value cards, hybrid cards that have both traditional magnetic stripe technology and stored value capabilities are being offered first in some regions such as Australia, where 3.8 million such cards are currently in use.

While smart cards are currently beginning to be Internet-based, there is nothing to stop their eventual evolution. For example, home PCs with card readers enable customers to download funds over the Internet or pay for purchases online as they do offline. One of the schemes for combining these technologies is from CyberCash, which has a joint venture with Mondex to create smart card-Internet integration.

Mondex Smart Cards

One of the earliest smart card trials was performed by UK-based Mondex, a joint venture of National Westminster Bank, Midland Bank, and British Telecom. Mondex cards can store up to approximately $580 and lock with a PIN. Digital signatures identify whom the cash is for so funds cannot be easily diverted. Records of transactions are kept, despite earlier claims of Mondex being as anonymous as cash. In addition to being able to make purchases in stores, the Mondex card enables individuals to exchange money.

Trials in Swindon, United Kingdom, included merchants such as Boots (a drugstore chain), Safeway (grocery stores), WH Smith (booksellers), and McDonalds. Further trials took place in Canada, San Francisco, New Zealand, and Hong Kong.

Mondex cards are also being offered in Australia by New Zealand Banking Corp., Commonwealth Bank of Australia, National Australian Bank, and Westpac Banking Corp.

MasterCard recently purchased a 54-percent share in Mondex. Although Mondex will remain in the United Kingdom, its alliance with MasterCard will allow its technology to spread more quickly around the world.

ELECTRONIC CHECKS

Credit cards are not the only existing technologies to find a home online. Electronic checks are also making their way onto the Internet, albeit more slowly.

Currently in the United States, 790 million paper checks are processed per year at a cost of $1.12 per check. In some areas, it costs as much as $1.60 to process a check. Check volume is growing 6 percent annually. In 15 states, laws require that paper checks be returned to the consumer if requested. Moving to electronic checks reduces processing costs from $1.12 to about $.22. If all checks were electronic, the industry could save approximately $560 million per year in processing costs in the United States alone.

Electronic checks generally rely on the established infrastructure for clearing payments, thereby making it simpler for checks to transition to the Internet. In the real world, the payer signs a check (online this would be a digital signature), the payee countersigns when cashing the check (a second digital signature), and the check can clear through normal clearinghouse channels. Given this paradigm, secured e-mail becomes a valid method of using checks.

However, not all electronic check proposals rely on traditional clearing methods. Some proposals bypass the banking structure entirely for clearing payments, a procedure that is, if legal, highly questionable.

FAQs at sites that advocate this practice state that the process is legal.

Businesses and consumers must not assume that all electronic check-processing methods are legitimate. In electronic check systems that bypass the traditional banking structure, customers authorize vendors to print checks with their account information and sign them on their behalf. Sites advocating this method of processing checks online include http://www.

checkmaster.com/; http://www.hoffice.com/; http://www.efunds.com/ eFunds/InternetSite/eFundsInternetHome.nsf; http://www.onlinecheck. com/; and, http://www.redi-check.com/.

CyberCash and CheckFree have jointly developed an electronic checking initiative. When delivered, the scheme will transparently handle multiple currencies.

NetChex works with existing bank accounts, and checks clear through traditional banking networks. It can be downloaded from their Web site at http://www. netchex.com.

PAYMENT TECHNOLOGIES

Netscape's payment technology includes both client and server software. Netscape's wallet is included in Navigator 4.7 and higher. The wallet locally stores receipts and transaction information. The wallet software can be either implemented as a Java applet or as a browser plug-in.

On the server side, Netscape's LivePayment 1.x is an extension of SuiteSpot and is integrated with the company's Enterprise Server (formerly called the Commerce Server). The software uses SSL to encrypt the data stream between browser and server, and offers payment validation by First-Data, a company that authenticates 85 percent of all credit card transactions worldwide. Although LivePayment does not currently support SET, the company aims for inclusion of SET at the earliest possible date. When the SET version of LivePayment is available, the product will be exportable. LivePayment currently uses nonexportable encryption. LivePayment costs $3,295 and is currently available for UNIX (Sun Solaris) and Windows NT 3.51 and higher.

Microsoft's Payment Technology

Microsoft's payment system includes its wallet software, scheduled for inclusion in its Internet Explorer browser in version 4.0 and higher. The company has incorporated the wallet into Windows 2000 and provides a means for users to securely move wallets from one computer to another.

For the server side, Microsoft's Merchant System costs $17,995 and an additional $6,495 for each store hosted on it. The software runs on Windows NT Server and requires an object database connectivity (ODBC)-compliant database.

VeriFone's vGATE and vPOS

In the United States, a glance at the point of sale (POS) terminal device used to accept credit and debit cards often reveals the name VeriFone. VeriFone is the leading supplier of POS credit card systems, with 78 percent of the market share. VeriFone, which purchased Enterprise Integration Technologies (EIT), founder of CommerceNet and creator of S-HTTP, in the fall of 1995, is among the first to introduce SET-based systems.

Designed for merchant systems, vPOS verifies credit cards sent over the Internet and is included in Microsoft's Merchant System. vPOS stores credit card numbers and costs $1,800. vGATE, designed for financial institutions, resides on the bank server and also verifies credit card numbers. Because custom implementations are needed, vGATE's price varies. Both SET-based products interoperate with competitor Netscape's LivePayment system. For end users, vWallet is client software that works with VeriFone's solutions.

VeriFone's business model involves selling to financial institutions, which in turn sell to customers such as retailers. Because VeriFone has a preexisting relationship with financial institutions, it can successfully use them as a sales channel. VeriFone's revenue comes from selling and licensing software, not from per-transaction fees.

IBM's Net. Commerce Server

IBM's Net. Commerce server, which incorporates SET, runs on Windows NT and Advanced Interactive Executive (AIX). An early version of the product was used for selling tickets for the 1996 Summer Olympics. Using Net. Commerce Payment for Acquirers, merchants do not know the customer's credit card number, but only whether the transaction will clear. The product works internationally and has a browser plug-in electronic wallet. IBM also has a toolkit available for creating SET-compliant transactions.

AT&T Easy Commerce Services

Rather than payment software, AT&T Easy Commerce Services sets up stores for customers on the Internet. Through the AT&T SecureBuy Services program, which is implemented in Open Market software, companies can put up stores on the Web. With a one-year contract, the service costs $425 per month for AT&T business customers and $525 per month for noncustomers. There is a one-time setup charge of $800. If a month-to-month contract is desired, the charge is $625 per month plus a $1,300 setup charge. Merchants get 800 transactions per month free for one year; beyond that, a per-transaction fee is charged. AT&T reimburses the merchant a four-month fee for any downtime.

With the SecureBuy system, companies can offer their customers assurance that AT&T will pay the $80 in liability charges if credit cards are ever misused or stolen. To provide further incentives, shoppers receive 400 free minutes of AT&T service if they spend $58 at any store using Secure-Buy technology. For additional convenience, customers need only register at one AT&T-hosted store. Within this system, users never have to input credit card numbers again if shopping at AT&T-hosted sites.

PSINet's eCommerce

Another commerce hosting service is PSINet's eCommerce solutions. Established ISP PSI's service uses Mercantec software that can transfer invoices, shipping, and sales tax information to accounting systems. The service, which uses CyberCash payment processing, costs $325 per month.

A MOVE TOWARD INTEROPERABILITY: THE JOINT ELECTRONIC PAYMENTS INITIATIVE

In the discussion of offerings from various vendors, one striking feature appears repeatedly: Everyone is offering a wallet, but no one is saying that their wallets will interoperate with those of others. While actual consumer tolerance for multiple wallets is unknown, one can only surmise that if purchasing in cyberspace is that inconvenient, consumers will visit the nearest mall instead. Fortunately, there is an organization working toward interoperability.

The W3C oversees the Web's development and growth. Tim Berners-Lee, creator of the Web, directs the W3C, which is based in Cambridge, Massachusetts. One of the many areas of W3C effort is that of streamlining payments and providing standards so systems from various vendors can interoperate. The Joint Electronic Payments Initiative (JEPI) is a joint effort of the W3C and CommerceNet, a business-to-business e-commerce think-tank.

JEPI will involve a live marketplace where customers and merchants can be part of the interoperability trials. At this stage, it involves designing protocols that extend the Web's HTTP to handle other functions.

First, JEPI has created a general format that can be used for extending HTTP for a variety of purposes. This protocol, called *protocol extension protocol* (PEP), is included in HTTP 1.2 and higher.

With this framework in place, the specific task of adding functionality relevant to payments can be addressed. To make shopping as easy for the consumer as possible, Web browsers and servers should be able to tell each other what payment mechanisms are in place, and should agree on a method based on that owned by the user and the user's preferences. This extension is called *universal payment preamble* (UPP). Among other advantages, it will enable browsers and servers to communicate information about:

- Payment instrument (such as check, credit card, debit card, E-cash)
- Brand (Visa, MasterCard, American Express)
- Protocol (CyberCash, SET)
- Payment parameters (currency, amount, incentive, account number, and other information relevant to closing the transaction)

Payments are not a simple issue. Special discounts based on the customer's membership in organizations, age, or prior arrangement with the company could be offered. UPP will enable browsers and servers to securely handle all these details in a manner transparent to the user. The specifications developed by JEPI are handed to the IETF, the organization responsible for the finalization of Internet standards.

PUTTING IT INTO PRACTICE: WHO ACCEPTS ELECTRONIC PAYMENTS TODAY?

Industry analysts recently sampled two types of merchants to discover who is accepting payments online and what methods they use. The first group (71 merchants) was selected at random from Open Market's Commercial Sites Index. The second group of 85 represents about 13 percent of the shopping sites from the top 8 percent of all Web sites—a list derived from user recommendations. The sites were asked the payment method they used, and only the most *wired* method was counted using this hierarchy: digital payment scheme such as CyberCash, secure server (using SSL, for example), unsecured server (credit card numbers sent unencrypted), e-mail, toll-free telephone number, fax, and printing out order forms and mailing them. One scenario not well reflected in the survey results was that of a site accepting credit card numbers in the clear, but encouraging customers to call their toll-free number or fax in their order.

Interestingly, of the group selected at random, none were using digital payment schemes such as those offered by CyberCash and others. Such methods were used by 8.0 percent of the top 8 percent of all Web sites. The most common secure commerce method by far is using a secure server with technology such as SSL encrypting communications between the browser and server. Of the randomly selected sites, 19.9 percent used this method. Of the top 8 percent of all Web sites, nearly one-third did so.

The most surprising finding is the number of sites that send credit card numbers in the clear—nearly 43 percent of the random sample and 33 percent of the top 8 percent of all Web sites used this practice. The primary method used by customers may be toll-free telephone orders, despite the fact that the survey reports these percentages. The percentages given must therefore not be interpreted to imply that the bulk of the orders come through these channels.

According to IDC of Framingham, Massachusetts, 83 percent of all Fortune 500 companies have a Web site today, but less than 8 percent of these accept transactions. Online ordering is still clearly a field in its infancy.

STANDARDS

Although a melee of standards currently exists, convergence is already occurring and the window is closing for new players to enter this market. Particularly promising is SET, a standard around which vendors can unite to achieve interoperability between various payment schemes.

Diverse standards and the need for interoperability also exist in the physical world. Referring to the boxes that process credit cards: Today in the merchant world, the protocols of boxes that clear credit card payments are different depending on the bank, the industry, and the country. Those boxes speak 1700 of these variations.

In the meantime, just as the typical customer has a number of payment methods in his or her wallet, customers who do business on the Internet will probably have multiple electronic wallets. Even if they want to place orders, it is unlikely that customers will be willing to download yet another wallet once they have four already online. This duplicity underscores the need for businesses wanting online orders from consumers to accept multiple payment types, as modeled by Virtual Vineyards, among others.

Finally, in addition to the need for developing standards that make business over the Internet simple, it will take time to overcome resistance to the new method of transacting business. This is particularly true for the consumer market, where it took about 10 years for ATMs to gain wide acceptance.

Secure commerce must be made easier for both customers and merchants for more business to be handled online. When SET becomes even more widely adopted, secure commerce will become more commonplace.

In the meantime, one segment of the e-commerce market is already booming: business-to-business e-commerce. The size of this lucrative market, which is an order of magnitude larger than business-to-consumer e-commerce, is examined in Chapter 11, "E-Commerce Environments and Future Directions."

END NOTES

[1] Intertrader Ltd., 5 John's Place, Edinburgh, U.K., EH6 7EW, 2000.
[2] Ibid.
[3] Ibid.

4 Protocols for the Public Transport of Private Information

"Defense, however, is much more consequence than opulence."

—ADAM SMITH, *WEALTH OF NATIONS* (1776)

Abraham Maslow's hierarchy of needs theory suggests that a person's basic needs, such as food and water, must be satisfied if he or she is to be satisfied with something more complex such as a job or family. Never has Maslow's assertion been more appropriate than in the world of electronic commerce. No matter how attractive the shopping venue, it will fail if customers do not have the fundamental confidence in the process to complete the transaction.

The Internet is rapidly becoming the universal medium for exchange of transaction information, but before we can fulfill our Buck Rogers futuristic dreams, the electronic commerce community must take steps to secure transactions *and* educate consumers about security. The electronic commerce community has taken great steps to adopt security protocols and standards, which are necessary to make the traditionally unsecured channels, such as the Internet, attractive to the average consumer.

SECURITY PROTOCOLS

Until very recently, people wishing secure communications over the Internet had to find products implementing security at the application level. In practice, this meant that communications had to be protected explicitly by the user before being sent across the Internet, usually in the form of encrypted e-mail. Although this approach is quite effective when properly used, the consensus of consumers and merchants is that such an approach to security is unacceptable. Only when security is built into Internet applications and requires an absolute minimum of interaction by the user will it become acceptable to a mass market.

As explained in earlier chapters, the Secure Hypertext Transport Protocol (S-HTTP), an extension of the World Wide Web protocol, adds security features just below the Application layer. The Secure Sockets Layer (SSL) protocol was originally proposed and implemented by Netscape Communications and has also been implemented by other Web browser vendors. SSL operates at the Transport layer, which means it can be used for private Internet transmissions between systems and programs supporting it.

MasterCard International and Visa International continue to cooperate in support of secure credit card transactions on the Internet, and companies involved with electronic commerce have generally pledged to comply with the standards they produce.

Figure 4.1 illustrates how these different security solutions fit into the Internet data architecture. The S-HTTP option adds security directly to the application, while SSL adds security to the entire stream of data between server and client because it operates just above the Transport layer. Secure Courier and other transaction-level protocols operate on the transaction data itself, so it can be transmitted between merchants and financial institutions without compromising that data's security or authenticity even while it awaits transmission from intermediate systems (like the merchant's server).

Secure Courier is an SSL-based secure credit card presentation scheme by Netscape. It has been superseded by SET.

There are other mechanisms and protocols devised for transmitting transaction information across the Internet, and there will undoubtedly be more in the months and years to come. However, these protocols should represent the type of standards that will eventually define the way business is done over the Internet.

These protocols will be discussed briefly, mostly to examine how they use the Internet, the World Wide Web, and security technologies to make secure commerce possible over the Internet.

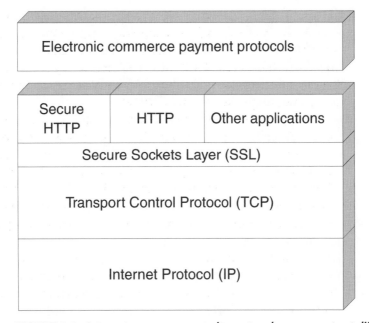

FIGURE 4.1 Internet commerce security protocols can operate at different levels, and thus can all be used together if desired.

SECURE HYPERTEXT TRANSFER PROTOCOL

The Secure Hypertext Transfer Protocol (S-HTTP) is the logical extension of the Hypertext Transfer Protocol (HTTP), which is the basis of the World Wide Web. HTTP defines the interactions between Web browsers and Web servers, determining how Web servers handle requests from browsers (also known as clients). Very simply, a Web browser sends requests for information stored on a Web server, and if that server is connected and the information is available, the server will respond by sending the information back to the browser.

HTTP did not originally include any security features at all, other than those provided by resources accessed through the World Wide Web. For example, HTTP can be used to provide a more user-friendly interface to File Transfer Protocol (FTP) and terminal emulation (Telnet) services, both of which challenge users for user ID and password before providing service. However, the content of Telnet or FTP sessions is transmitted in plain text, and eavesdroppers could intercept the content being sent.

S-HTTP SECURITY FEATURES

S-HTTP was designed to add security at the application level. The objective was to add support for a wide range of security mechanisms on top of the interactions between Web browser and Web server. Protection mechanisms include the following:

- Digital signature
- Message authentication
- Message encryption

These mechanisms are used as negotiated between browser and server. Any one or more of these mechanisms may be used. The protocol also allows unprotected transmissions.

The S-HTTP specification includes support for many cryptographic formats, including private key and public key cryptography, as well as key distribution schemes like Kerberos. S-HTTP supports use of prearranged and predistributed private keys between individuals, public key encryption in one direction (using the server's public key only and not requiring the browser to have a public key), and two-way public key encryption. Each interaction between an S-HTTP browser/server pair is negotiated to determine what protection is available, needed, and capable of being used. Option negotiation can be driven by the requirements of the browser or the server, so either end of the transmission can request protection of some sort for that transmission.

The S-HTTP specification was written to offer the widest latitude in implementing security, with a variety of different cryptographic methods to ensure compatibility across national boundaries (using technologies approved for export from the United States) or between browsers and servers supporting other technologies.

SECURE HTTP DATA TRANSPORT

S-HTTP *encapsulates* the HTTP interactions between browser and server. This means that data being sent from browser to server (or vice versa) is contained within a special S-HTTP chunk of data. Figure 4.2 shows the concept of encapsulation. This chunk uses the same basic format as HTTP (which is also the basis for data sent via e-mail and Usenet news communications), indicating the source and destination systems and other information required by TCP/IP.

Encapsulated data sent across the Internet is comparable to a package that has been wrapped in plain brown paper and addressed for delivery by an express service. The contents of the package are irrelevant, and intermediate handlers do not know (nor do they need to know) exactly what is inside. However, the package will have delivery instructions printed on the outside—*headers* are the parallel structure for Internet data. When a package of data arrives at its destination, the recipient program takes the headers off and interprets the data inside as appropriate.

The typical HTTP session starts out with a user starting up a Web browser. This browser may be pointed to a home page at a remote Web server. On startup, the browser application program sends out an HTTP request to that server for the information on that home page. Assuming the server (and specified home page) is able to respond, it sends back the requested hypertext document (a document created with the Hypertext Markup Language—HTML).

FIGURE 4.2 An S-HTTP message sent from a server to a browser includes data that is "wrapped" by a header with handling and contents information about data.

S-HTTP EXPLAINED

For the details of the S-HTTP implementation, the reader is referred to the appropriate Internet RFC and Internet-Draft documents (see Appendix B, "Electronic Commerce Online Resources," for more details). This section summarizes the extra headers that S-HTTP defines for data connections between servers and browsers on the World Wide Web.

Secure HTTP Header Lines

There are two required header lines for S-HTTP, one identifying the type of content contained within the S-HTTP message ("Content-Type"), and the other identifying the general cryptographic implementation being used ("Content–Privacy–Domain"). Other headers are optional and have the following uses:

- Indicate data representation of enclosed data (what format the enclosed data takes)
- Transmission of session keys and other information relating to the enclosed data
- Message Authenticity Check (MAC) to authenticate and provide an integrity check to the message

The Content–Privacy–Domain header allows the use of digital signatures alone, encryption alone, both signatures and encryption, or neither. Encryption options include use of public key pairs, or encryption with a prearranged key (previously exchanged offline or by some other mechanism).

S-HTTP Message Contents

The message sent by an S-HTTP browser or server can be simple data (a protocol request or response to a request). It can also be HTTP data (a response to an HTTP request for a Web document) or another S-HTTP message (a message that has been digitally signed could actually be an encrypted message). The contents of an S-HTTP message are interpreted by the receiving entity (browser or server) based on how the data package is labeled and what kind of security treatment has been negotiated.

S-HTTP Security Negotiation Headers

S-HTTP adds a set of security negotiation headers used to negotiate security options. Four different issues are negotiated between server and browser:

■ **Property**–What kind of security option is being selected (what kind of cryptographic scheme, such as bulk encryption) to apply to a transfer.

■ **Value**–What specific implementation (which specific algorithm, such as RSA public key encryption) to apply to the transfer.

■ **Direction**–Whether the system negotiating (sending the header) wants the other system to send the specified security-enhanced transmissions, or is willing to receive specified security-enhanced transmissions (in other words, each entity is allowed to indicate the maximum level of security it is capable of sending or receiving).

■ **Strength**–How strongly the system negotiating wants the negotiated option: It can require a security enhancement, make it an option, or refuse to use it.

The negotiating process allows two S-HTTP-compliant participants (a browser and a server) to negotiate secure transmissions using the cryptographic facilities that both support and that both require to transmit sensitive information securely.

RELATED PROTOCOL EXTENSIONS

Data is requested and delivered across the World Wide Web using HTTP and S-HTTP; after all, those are Hypertext Transfer Protocols. However, there are two other important protocols without which the World Wide Web would not exist: the Uniform Resource Locator (URL) protocol, defining the syntax of Web documents and locations; and the Hypertext Markup Language (HTML) protocol, defining the syntax of the documents themselves.

URLs follow a very specific format, usually consisting of three parts: the scheme designation (indicating the protocol used by the underlying document), the Internet host and domain name of the resource hosting system, and the location on that system of the resource document file. Most current World Wide Web resources look something like this:

http://www.mcompany.com/home.html

This example indicates a file named home.html residing on a server named www.mcompany.com using the HTTP protocol. (URLs can now use a protocol designator of S-HTTP to designate a resource using Secure HTTP.)

The Hypertext Markup Language uses tags, as discussed in Chapter 2, "Security Technologies," to indicate the different functional portions of a hypertext document. For example, a paragraph of text is set off by a paragraph tag; a bullet list of items is set off by tags indicating that it is a bullet list.

Security enhancements are not necessary for every piece of data sent from a secure server to a secure browser, so new HTML tags have been defined to mark certain hypertext elements as requiring some kind of security treatment, and to store supporting security information. This information includes the type of security enhancements to use when sending data, cryptographic options to be negotiated, and other options.

SECURE SOCKETS LAYER

In a way, S-HTTP can be considered to be typical of a traditional Internet application solution: It adds security and reliability functions to an application, at the application level. In other words, the browser on one side and the server on the other negotiate their own security independent of the underlying network protocols. The result is that the underlying network protocols need not be reliable or secure to support reliable and secure interaction at the application level, and it is not necessary to make any changes to the basic underlying network implementation.

However, another approach to security is to add a layer on top of the existing network transport protocol and beneath the application. The Secure Sockets Layer (SSL) protocol takes this approach by adding an intermediate step, requiring negotiation of secure transmission options, to the establishment of a network connection. Data flowing between the client and the server on that connection is encrypted before transmission and decrypted before it can be used by the receiving system, as shown in Figure 4.3.

One advantage of this approach is that SSL can be applied to any Internet application, not just the World Wide Web (although it was initially implemented only under HTTP). A second advantage is that once the SSL connection has been negotiated between a server and a client, the resulting data communication channel is private, authenticated, and reliable.

SSL links are initiated with a handshaking exchange between the server and the client, during which the two systems exchange necessary cryptographic information to support the secure channel. After this information has been exchanged, the application programs must subject their trans-

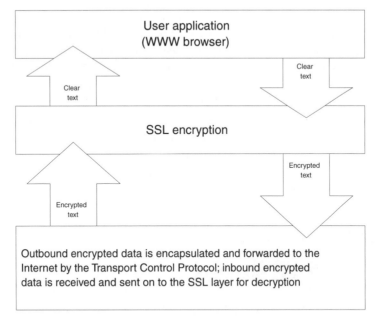

FIGURE 4.3 Data flow and encryption.

missions to the required cryptographic treatment and then send them on to a destination application program—which must then subject that data to the cryptographic treatment necessary to decrypt and authenticate it.

Netscape originally developed SSL as the basis of its secure World Wide Web server. It is implemented in leading browsers that have been distributed widely. Netscape has made the SSL specification publicly available as an Internet draft document to ensure compatibility between its browsers and servers and other vendors' products. Because by definition Internet applications must be able to interoperate with other implementations of the same applications in order to succeed, there is no benefit to Netscape in making SSL proprietary—if it were not widely implemented, there would be no benefit to purchasing servers or browsers from Netscape.

SSL RECORD SPECIFICATION

As with other underlying network protocols (and similar to the way in which S-HTTP encapsulates HTTP data), SSL encapsulates the data transmitted between the client and the server in an SSL record. However, the SSL header is only two or three bytes long, and is primarily used to indicate how much data has been encapsulated and whether that includes *data padding* to fill out the SSL record. Data padding is often necessary to make sure that the "real" data can be properly encrypted with certain types of cipher.

SSL requires a reliable network transport protocol (one that provides some level of confidence that data is being received by the destination host), which means that data is transmitted using the Transmission Control Protocol (TCP) across the Internet. The TCP headers identify the source and destination of the data, while the application headers that have been encapsulated with the rest of the application data (in other words, the HTTP headers and data) remain secure until it reaches its destination.

INITIATING AN SSL SESSION

An SSL session begins after the TCP session is initiated. SSL uses a handshaking protocol, with the client and the software exchanging specific pieces of information in order to build a secure channel for transmitting data. The very first exchange between client and server is in plain text and contains enough information for the two systems to initiate an encrypted and authenticated data stream.

Figure 4.4 shows a typical exchange of SSL information between a client and a server. Because SSL requires the use of TCP, which itself uses a reliable three-way handshake protocol to initiate a connection, the server begins the session by awaiting the opening transmission from the client. This is called a "client-hello" message and includes some *challenge* data (data which is to be used later to authenticate the server) and specifications of supported ciphers.

Upon receipt of this message, the server responds with a random connection ID, its own cipher specifications, and its own digitally signed public key certificate. In response, the client sends off two messages in succession: First, it sends a "client-master-key" message, in which a master key is delivered to the server as the basis for further communication. This master key is encrypted with the server's public key, meaning that it can only be decrypted with the server's private key. The client follows this message with a "client-finish" message, indicating that it is ready to start receiving SSL data. This message includes the connection ID supplied by the server, but encrypted using the client's private key, meaning that it can be

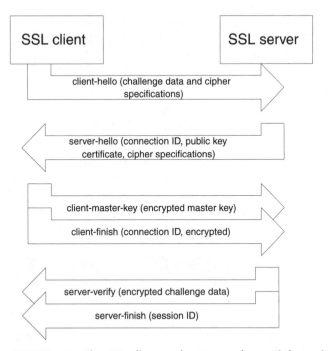

FIGURE 4.4 The SSL client and server exchange information in a connection-opening handshake sequence before opening the secure channel.

decrypted using the client's public key—this authenticates the message as coming from that client.

Completing the handshake, the server responds with a "server-verify" message, followed by a "server-finish" message. The server-verify message functions as the server's digital signature and includes the challenge data mentioned in the client-hello message—but it is encrypted with the server's private key. This message can be decrypted using the server's public key, and this authenticates the server to the client. The server-finish message includes a new session identifier, also encrypted with the server's private key.

OTHER SSL OPTIONS

SSL provides a mechanism for a client and server that have already initiated a connection to reconnect without having to renegotiate encryption options. This process starts with the client sending a client-hello message that refers to a previous session identifier. Both client and server maintain a cache of session identifiers that include encryption options received from the other system. If the server recognizes the client and the specified session ID, the SSL channel can be initiated without the need to re-send any keys.

The connections described so far will authenticate the server to the client, but client authentication is also possible with SSL. The server can request authentication information with a "request-certificate" message after the server-verify message, which includes a different bit of challenge data. The client must encrypt this new data with its own private key, which the server will be able to decrypt using the client's declared public key, thus authenticating the client.

INTEGRATING SECURITY PROTOCOLS INTO THE WEB

Using SSL or S-HTTP is a matter of using special identifiers to indicate World Wide Web documents that require them. For example, a URL indicating a document defined with the Hypertext Transfer Protocol would look something like this:

> http://www.mcompany.com/MAIN.html

The first part of the URL identifies the scheme that must be used to transmit that document. To require S-HTTP to transmit a document, its URL must be defined in the form:

> shttp://www.mcompany.com/SECURE.html

In this case, the scheme, shttp, is defined as Secure HTTP; any browser that supports Secure HTTP will respond appropriately to initiate a connection. Documents requiring the browser to support SSL use a different scheme, https, with a resulting URL that looks like this:

> https://www.mcompany.com/SECURE.html

It should be noted that browsers that have been written to the HTTP specification are supposed to gracefully handle schemes that they don't support. A browser that does not support S-HTTP would not be able to negotiate with the server to access a document defined with S-HTTP—but it should be able to access any HTTP document on the same server. The same goes for SSL, so merchants should be able to maintain secure information and insecure information on the same server.

SET

Several years ago, MasterCard and Visa, traditionally strong rivals, teamed together to create the Secure Electronic Transaction (SET) protocol. The SET protocol aims to provide a uniform standard for secure transactions on the Internet. SET is a complex protocol set that tries to cover all aspects of online commerce, from initial registration of a credit card holder with an on-line SET agency to actual details of payments themselves. Figure 4.5 shows a SET payment transaction. A typical SET purchase scenario is as follows:

1. The customer browses a catalogue and selects items to purchase. The customer then is presented the order details including the total price and selects a payment system (with SET the particular credit card to use).
2. The customer sends the merchant signed order details and payment instructions.
3. The merchant requests payment authorization from the issuer.
4. The merchant sends confirmation of the order to the customer.
5. The merchant ships the goods to the customer.
6. The merchant requests settlement from the issuer via the acquirer.

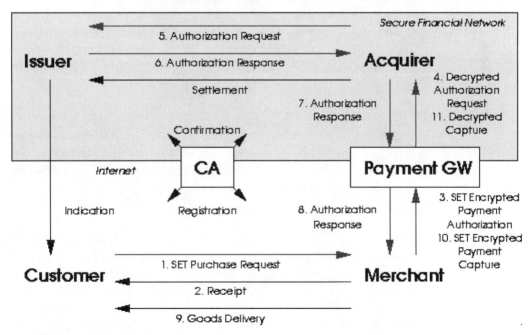

FIGURE 4.5 SET payment transaction.

SET is an open specification for protecting payment card purchases on any type of network (see the sidebar, "SET Profile"). The SET specification incorporates the use of public key cryptography to protect the privacy of personal and financial information over any open network. The specification calls for software to reside in the cardholder's (customer's) personal computer and in the merchant's network computer. In addition, there is technology residing at the acquirer's (the merchant's bank) location to decrypt the financial information, as well as at the certificate authority's location to issue digital certificates.

Although updated just prior to the publication of this book, the SET standard is subject to change over time. You can check for the latest versions of each document by visiting either the MasterCard or the Visa Web site.

http://www.mastercard.com
http://www.visa.com

SET Profile

In early June 1997, SET 1.0 was published by MasterCard, Visa, and a host of business partners including:

- GTE
- IBM
- Microsoft
- RSA
- Netscape
- SAIC
- Terisa Systems
- VeriSign
- Visa

The SET specification is published in three parts:

- Book One: Description
- Programmer's Guide
- Formal Protocol Definition

CREDIT CARD BUSINESS BASICS

Before discussing SET, a few credit card processing feature definitions are in order. These features are used throughout the SET document (see Table 4.1).

It is also important to point out that MasterCard and Visa are associated with banks comprising the membership.

TABLE 4.1 SET Feature Profile

Feature	Definition/Description
Web Resource	VS2000 and MS2000
Name	SET
Origin	Visa, MasterCard, CyberCash, Netscape, IBM, Microsoft, DigiCash, and many others.
Status & Milestones	Active, version 2.0, 2001.
Payment Size	Macropayments.
Money Model	Notational.
Payment Model	Secure credit card presentation.
Validation	Online.
Privacy Control	Confidential, non-anonymous, traceable.
Security Mechanism	RSA, DES, encryption, signatures, passphrases, certificates, chain of trust, dual signatures.
Prerequisites	Wallet software, credit card, maybe later a smart card.
Risk	Customer.
Fees	Most probably none, besides the credit card fees.
Latency/Costs	Fairly high due to online authorization and careful encryption and signing schemes.
User Base	Various electronic commerce systems going to be SET compliant.
Limits	Unknown at this time.
Remarks	Refund from credit card transactions is supported.

(Continues)

TABLE 4.1 (*Continued*)

Feature	Definition/Description
Genealogy	Besides some obsolete payment protocols mentioned below, SET was strongly influenced by CyberCash and iKP (obsolete key payment protocol from IBM).
Customer/Cardholder:	The *customer*, or *cardholder* as it is called in SET, uses a credit card that has been issued by its issuer to buy goods at the merchant.
Issuer:	The *issuer* is a bank that keeps an account for the customer and has issued the credit card. The issuer guarantees payment for authorized transactions.
Merchant:	The *merchant* offers goods and receives SET credit card payments. The merchant has a financial relationship with the acquirer.
Acquirer:	The *acquirer* is a bank that keeps an account for the merchant and processes credit card authorizations and payments.
Payment Gateway (PG):	A *payment gateway* is a device operated by the acquirer or a designated third party that processes merchant payment messages including payment instructions from customers. In CyberCash, this payment gateway is represented by the CyberCash server.
Certification authority (CA)	All customers and merchants are required to register with a SET certification authority before purchasing can commence. All payment gateways, issuers, and acquirers are assumed to be already registered with the certification authority.
Brand:	Visa, MasterCard, Discover, etc.

SET REQUIREMENTS

According the SET Business Description of May 31, 1997 there are seven requirements for SET.

- Provide confidentiality of payment information and enable confidentiality of order information that is transmitted along with the payment information.

- Ensure the integrity of all transmitted data.
- Provide authentication that a cardholder is a legitimate user of a branded payment card account.
- Provide authentication that a merchant can accept branded payment card transactions through its relationship with an acquiring financial institution.
- Ensure the use of the best security practices and system design techniques to protect all legitimate parties in an electronic commerce transaction.
- Create a protocol that neither depends on transport security mechanisms nor prevents their use.
- Facilitate and encourage interoperability among software and network providers.

Table 4.2 shows the requirements profile of SET. SET does not define any particular underlying traditional payment system and could work with debit and credit cards. However, SET demands certain properties of any conforming traditional payment system.

TABLE 4.2   SET Requirements Profile

Requirement/System	*SET*
Token System	No
Transaction	
Atomicity	No
Consistency	Yes
Isolation	No
Durability	Yes
Security	
No Double Spending	N/A
No Counterfeiting	Yes
No Overspending	No
Non-Refutability	Yes
No Unauthorized Use	Yes
Anonymity	No
Untraceability	No

(Continues)

TABLE 4.2 *(Continued)*

Requirement/System	SET
Interoperability	
Divisibility	N/A
Bidirectionality	No
Respendability	No
Acceptability	Yes
Multicurrency Support	Yes
Scalability	
Scalability	Yes, most probably.
Offline Operation	No
Economical Issues	
Operational	Not quite, but many SET compliant electronic commerce solutions under development.
Large User Base	Yes, potentially.
Buyer Risk	Yes, limited by credit card liability limit.
Seller Risk	No
Reliability	Yes
Conservation	Yes
Ease of Use	
Unobtrusiveness	No, looking at the demonstration prototypes, this is unlikely, as they suggest a direct emulation of traditional print through card slip transactions.
Low Latency	**No**
Micropayments	No
Macropayments	Yes
Low Fixed Costs	Unknown. Most probably not exceeding regular credit card costs very far.
HW Independence	Yes, unless they integrate a smart card someday

SET is very careful about authentication and authorization. This makes it unsuitable for micropayments; moreover, if the underlying traditional payment system is a credit card, SET requires four messages between customer and merchant. These four messages involve four digital signatures; four RSA public key encryption and decryption operations; one DES symmetric key encryption and decryption operation; two certificate validations and one payment authorization by the payment gateway (bank) for the merchant that consists of two messages with two digital signatures; three DES symmetric key encryption and decryption operations; five RSA public key encryption and decryption operations; and two certificate verifications. The question of scalability is raised by the need for central servers and online verification.

EARLY SET TRIALS

Visa

On April 29, 1997, the world's first Internet purchases involving a Visa card and Secure Electronic Transaction (SET) technology from multiple vendors began in Singapore. The transactions involved SET technology developed by two different manufacturers. IBM developed the payment gateway linking Citibank to the Internet. VeriSign, using the SET Pilot Root, produced the digital certificates that make it possible for sensitive financial information to be used safely on the Internet.

American Express

At approximately 3:32 A.M. on June 2, 1997, a tiny bit of history was made when an American Express Cardmember purchased a drill press from Wal-Mart's Web site located at http://www.wal-mart.com. This event did not get the attention generated by a man walking on the moon or Alexander Graham Bell making the first telephone call, but it is very significant as the first Internet transaction in which actual goods were purchased using the Secure Electronic Transaction (SET) protocol. This is also the first demonstration of interoperability between different software implementations of the SET protocol. GlobeSet, Inc. provided the SET software used by the American Express Cardmember and Wal-Mart in making the transaction secure, and American Express used its own SET software to receive and authorize the card transaction.

As more trials occur, news will be posted on the respective companies' web sites.

In Chapter 2, "Security Technologies," we discussed the issue of private and public encryption, message authentication, and key certification. These are the building blocks of the SET standard.

An entire book could be dedicated to the entire SET process. However, with the root of the issue being *security*, we use the balance of this chapter to discuss the cryptography methods employed by the SET standard.

SET BUSINESS SPECIFICATIONS DOCUMENT

The following text in the sidebar, "Certificate Issuance," is an excerpt from section 3 of the SET Business Specifications document. The entire SET specification is included on the attached CD-ROM.[1]

CERTIFICATE ISSUANCE

PROTECTION OF SENSITIVE INFORMATION. Cryptography has been used for centuries to protect sensitive information as it is transmitted from one location to another. In a cryptographic system, a message is encrypted using a key. The resulting ciphertext is then transmitted to the recipient where it is decrypted using a key to produce the original message. There are two primary encryption methods in use today: secret-key cryptography and public-key cryptography. SET uses both methods in its encryption process.

SECRET-KEY CRYPTOGRAPHY. SECRET-KEY CRYPTOGRAPHY, also known as symmetric cryptography, uses the same key to encrypt and decrypt the message (see Figure 4.6). Therefore, the sender and the recipient of a message must share a secret, namely the key. A well-known secret-key cryptography algorithm is the Data Encryption Standard (DES), which is used by financial institutions to encrypt PINs (personal identification numbers).

PUBLIC-KEY CRYPTOGRAPHY. Public-key cryptography (see Figure 4.7), also known as asymmetric cryptography, uses two keys: one key to encrypt the message and the other key to decrypt the message. The two keys are mathematically related so that data encrypted with either key can only be decrypted using the other. Each user has two keys: a PUBLIC KEY

FIGURE 4.6   Secret-key cryptography.

and a PRIVATE KEY. The user distributes the public key. Because of the relationship between the two keys, the user and anyone receiving the public key can be assured that data encrypted with the public key and sent to the user can only be decrypted when the user uses the private key. THIS ASSURANCE IS ONLY MAINTAINED IF THE USER ENSURES THAT THE PRIVATE KEY IS NOT DISCLOSED TO ANYONE ELSE, Therefore, the key pair should be generated by the user. The best-known public-key cryptography algorithm is RSA (named after its inventors Rivest, Shamir, and Adleman).

Secret-key cryptography is impractical for exchanging messages with a large group of previously unknown correspondents over a public network. For a merchant to conduct transactions securely with millions of Internet subscribers, each consumer would need a distinct key assigned by that merchant and transmitted over a separate secure channel. On the other hand, by using public-key cryptography, that same merchant could create a public/private key pair and publish the public key, allowing any consumer to send a secure message to that merchant.

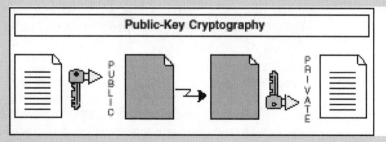

FIGURE 4.7   Public-key cryptography.

ENCRYPTION. Confidentiality is ensured by the use of message encryption.

RELATIONSHIP OF KEYS. When two users want to exchange messages securely, each of them transmits one component of their key pair, designated the public key, to the other and keeps secret the other component, designated the private key Because messages encrypted with the public key can only be decrypted using the private key, these messages can be transmitted over an insecure network without fear that an eavesdropper could use the key to read encrypted transmissions.

For example, Bob can transmit a confidential message to Alice by encrypting the message using Alice's public key. As long as Alice ensures that no one else has access to her private key, both she and Bob will know that only Alice can read the message.

USE OF SYMMETRIC KEY. SET will rely on cryptography to ensure message confidentiality. In SET, message data will be encrypted using a randomly generated symmetric encryption key. This key, in turn, will be encrypted using the message recipient's public key. This is referred to as the "digital envelope" of the message and is sent to the recipient along with the encrypted message itself. After receiving the digital envelope, the recipient decrypts it using his or her private key to obtain the randomly generated symmetric key and then uses the symmetric key to unlock the original message.

NOTE: *To provide the highest degree of protection, it is essential that the programming methods and random number generation algorithms generate keys in a way that ensures that the keys cannot be easily reproduced using information about either the algorithms or the environment in which the keys are generated.*

DIGITAL SIGNATURES. Integrity and authentication are ensured by the use of digital signatures.

RELATIONSHIP OF KEYS. Because of the mathematical relationship between the public and private keys, data encrypted with either key can only be decrypted with the other. This allows the sender of a message to encrypt it using the sender's private key. Any recipient can determine that the message came from the sender by decrypting the message using the sender's public key.

For example, Alice can encrypt a known piece of data, such as her telephone number, with her private key and transmit it to Bob. When Bob decrypts the message using Alice's public key and compares the result to the known data, he can be sure that that the message could only have been encrypted using Alice's private key.

USING MESSAGE DIGESTS. When combined with MESSAGE DIGESTS, encryption using the private key allows users to digitally sign messages. A message digest is a value generated for a message (or document) that is unique to that message.[1] A message digest is generated by passing the message through a one-way cryptographic function; that is, one that cannot be reversed. When the digest of a message is encrypted using the sender's private key and is appended to the original message, the result is known as the digital signature of the message.

The recipient of the digital signature can be sure that the message really came from the sender. And, because changing even one character in the message changes the message digest in an unpredictable way, the recipient can be sure that the message was not changed after the message digest was generated.

EXAMPLE OF THE USE OF A DIGITAL SIGNATURE. For example, Alice computes the message digest of a property description and encrypts it with her private key yielding a digital signature for the message. She transmits both the message and the digital signature to Bob. When Bob receives the message, he computes the message digest of the property description and decrypts the digital signature with Alice's public key. If the two values match, Bob knows that the message was signed using Alice's private key and that it has not changed since it was signed.

Two KEY PAIRS. SET uses a distinct public/private key pair to create the digital signature. Thus, each SET participant will possess two asymmetric key pairs: a "key exchange" pair, which is used in the process of encryption and decryption, and a "signature" pair for the creation and verification of digital signatures. Note that the roles of the public and private keys are reversed in the digital signature process where the private key is used to encrypt (sign) and the public key is used to decrypt (verify the signature).

CERTIFICATES. Authentication is further strengthened by the use of certificates.

NEED FOR AUTHENTICATION. Before two parties use public-key cryptography to conduct business, each wants to be sure that the other party is authenticated. Before Bob accepts a message with Alice's digital signature, he wants to be sure that the public key belongs to Alice and not to someone masquerading as Alice on an open network. One way to be sure that the public key belongs to Alice is to receive it over a secure channel directly from Alice. However, in most circumstances this solution is not practical.

NEED FOR A TRUSTED THIRD PARTY. An alternative to secure transmission of the key is to use a trusted third party to authenticate that the public key belongs to Alice. Such a party is known as a CERTIFICATE AUTHORITY (CA). The Certificate Authority authenticates Alice's claims according to its published policies. For example, a Certificate Authority could supply certificates that offer a high assurance of personal identity, which may be required for conducting business transactions; this Certificate Authority may require Alice to present a driver's license or passport to a notary public before it will issue a certificate. Once Alice has provided proof of her identity, the Certificate Authority creates a message containing Alice's name and her public key. This message, known as a CERTIFICATE, is digitally signed by the Certificate Authority. It contains owner identification information, as well as a copy of one of the owner's public keys ("key exchange" or "signature"). To get the most benefit, the public key of the Certificate Authority should be known to as many people as possible. Thus, by trusting a single key, an entire hierarchy can be established in which one can have a high degree of trust.

Because SET participants have two key pairs, they also have two certificates. Both certificates are created and signed at the same time by the Certificate Authority.

SET AUTHENTICATION. The means that a financial institution uses to authenticate a cardholder or merchant is not defined by this specification. Each payment card brand and financial institution will select an appropriate method.

ENCRYPTION SUMMARY. Figure 4.8 provides an overview of the entire encryption process when Alice wishes to sign, for example, a property description and send it in an encrypted message to Bob. The numbered steps in the diagram are explained on the following pages.

ENCRYPTION. The encryption process in Figure 4.8 consists of the following steps:

1. Alice runs the property description through a one-way algorithm to produce a unique value known as the *message digest*. This is a kind type of digital fingerprint of the property description and will be used later to test the integrity of the message.

2. She then encrypts the message digest with her private signature key to produce the digital signature.

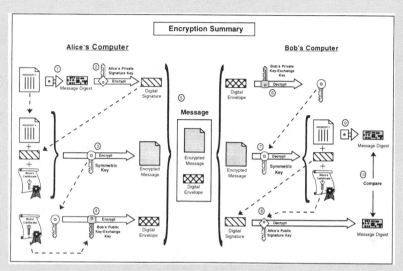

FIGURE 4.8 Encryption overview.

3. Next, she generates a random symmetric key and uses it to encrypt the property description, her signature, and a copy of her certificate, which contains her public signature key. To decrypt the property description, Bob will require a secure copy of this random symmetric key.

4. Bob's certificate, which Alice must have obtained prior to initiating secure communication with him, contains a copy of his public key-exchange key. To ensure secure transmission of the symmetric key, Alice encrypts it using Bob's public key-exchange key. The encrypted key, referred to as the *digital* envelope, is sent to Bob along with the *encrypted* message itself.

5. Alice sends a message to Bob consisting of the following: the symmetrically encrypted property description, signature, and certificate, as well as the asymmetrically encrypted symmetric key (the digitalJ envelope).

DECRYPTION. Likewise, the decryption process consists of the following steps:

6. Bob receives the message from Alice and decrypts the digital envelope with his private key-exchange key to retrieve the symmetric key.

7. He uses the symmetric key to decrypt the property description, Alice's signature, and her certificate.

8. He decrypts Alice's digital signature with her public signature key, which he acquires from her certificate. This recovers the original message digest of the property description.

9. He runs the property description through the same one-way algorithm used by Alice and produces a new message digest of the decrypted property description.

10. Finally, he compares his message digest to the one obtained from Alice's digital signature. If they are exactly the same, he confirms that the message content has not been altered during transmission and that it was signed using Alice's private signature key. If they are not the same, then the message either originated somewhere else or was altered after it was signed. In that case, Bob takes some appropriate action such as notifying Alice or discarding the message.

DUAL SIGNATURE. SET introduces a new application of digital signatures, namely the concept of dual signatures. To understand the need for this new concept, consider the following scenario: Bob wants to send Alice an offer to purchase a piece of property and an authorization to his bank to transfer the money if Alice accepts the offer, but Bob doesn't want the bank to see the terms of the offer nor does he want Alice to see his account information. Further, Bob wants to link the offer to the transfer so that the money is only transferred if Alice accepts his offer. He accomplishes all of this by digitally signing both messages with a single signature operation that creates a dual signature.

GENERATING A DUAL SIGNATURE. A dual signature is generated by creating the message digest of both messages, concatenating the two digests together, computing the message digest of the result and encrypting this digest with the signer's private signature key. The signer must include the message digest of the other message in order for the recipient to verify the dual signature. A recipient of either message can check its authenticity by generating the message digest on his or her copy of the message, concatenating it with the message digest of the other message (as provided by the sender) and computing the message digest of the result. If the newly generated digest matches the decrypted dual signature, the recipient can trust the authenticity of the message.

EXAMPLE. If Alice accepts Bob's offer, she can send a message to the bank indicating her acceptance and including the message digest of the offer. The bank can verify the authenticity of Bob's transfer authorization and ensure that the acceptance is for the same offer by using its digest of the authorization and the message digest presented by

Alice of the offer to validate the dual signature. Thus, the bank can check the authenticity of the offer against the dual signature, but the bank cannot see the terms of the offer.

USE OF DUAL SIGNATURES. Within SET, dual signatures are used to link an order message sent to the merchant with the payment instructions containing account information sent to the Acquirer. When the merchant sends an authorization request to the Acquirer, it includes the payment instructions sent to it by the cardholder and the message digest of the order information. The Acquirer uses the message digest from the merchant and computes the message digest of the payment instructions to check the dual signature.

IMPORT/EXPORT ISSUES. A number of governments have regulations regarding the import or export of cryptography. As a general rule, these governments allow cryptography to be used when:

- The data being encrypted is of a financial nature.
- The content of the data is well defined.
- The length of the data is limited.
- The cryptography cannot easily be used for other purposes.

The SET protocol is limited to the financial portion of shopping, and the content of the SET messages has been carefully reviewed to satisfy the concerns of governments. As long as software vendors can demonstrate that the cryptography used for SET cannot easily be put to other purposes, import and export licenses should be obtainable.

CARDHOLDER CERTIFICATES. Cardholder certificates function as an electronic representation of the payment card. Because they are digitally signed by a financial institution, they cannot be altered by a third party and can only be generated by a financial institution. A cardholder certificate does not contain the account number and expiration date. Instead, the account information and a secret value known only to the cardholder's software are encoded using a one-way hashing algorithm. If the account number, expiration date, and the secret value are known, the link to the certificate can be proven, but the information cannot be derived by looking at the certificate. Within the SET protocol, the cardholder supplies the account information and the secret value to the payment gateway where the link is verified.

A certificate is only issued to the cardholder when the cardholder's issuing financial institution approves it. By requesting a certificate, a cardholder has indicated the intent to perform commerce via electronic means. This certificate is transmitted to merchants with purchase requests and encrypted payment instructions. Upon receipt of the cardholder's certificate, a merchant can be assured, at a minimum, that the account number has been validated by the card-issuing financial institution or its agent.

In this specification, cardholder certificates are optional at the payment card brand's discretion.

MERCHANT CERTIFICATES. Merchant certificates function as an electronic substitute for the payment brand decal that appears in the store window—the decal itself is a representation that the merchant has a relationship with a financial institution allowing it to accept the payment card brand. Because they are digitally signed by the merchant's financial institution, merchant certificates cannot be altered by a third party and can only be generated by a financial institution.

These certificates are approved by the acquiring financial institution and provide assurance that the merchant holds a valid agreement with an Acquirer. A merchant must have at least one pair of certificates to participate in the SET environment, but there may be multiple certificate pairs per merchant. A merchant will have a pair of certificates for each payment card brand that it accepts.

PAYMENT GATEWAY CERTIFICATES. Payment gateway certificates are obtained by Acquirers or their processors for the systems that process authorization and capture messages. The gateway's encryption key, which the cardholder gets from this certificate, is used to protect the cardholder's account information.

Payment gateway certificates are issued to the Acquirer by the payment brand.

ACQUIRER CERTIFICATES. An Acquirer must have certificates in order to operate a Certificate Authority that can accept and process certificate requests directly from merchants over public and private networks. Those Acquirers that choose to have the payment card brand process certificate requests on their behalf will not require certificates because they are not processing SET messages. Acquirers receive their certificates from the payment card brand.

ISSUER CERTIFICATES. An Issuer must have certificates in order to operate a Certificate Authority that can accept and process certificate requests directly from cardholders over public and private networks. Those Issuers that choose to have the payment card brand process certificate requests on their behalf will not require certificates because they are not processing SET messages. Issuers receive their certificates from the payment card brand.

HIERARCHY OF TRUST. SET certificates are verified through a hierarchy of trust. Each certificate is linked to the signature certificate of the entity that digitally signed it. By following the trust tree to a known trusted party, one can be assured that the certificate is valid. For example, a cardholder certificate is linked to the certificate of the Issuer (or the Brand on behalf of the Issuer). The Issuer's certificate is linked back to a root key through the Brand's certificate. The public signature key of the root is known to all SET software and may be used to verify each of the certificates in turn. Figure 4.9 illustrates the hierarchy of trust.

The number of levels shown in Figure 4.9 is illustrative. A payment card brand may not always operate a geopolitical Certificate Authority between itself and the financial institutions.

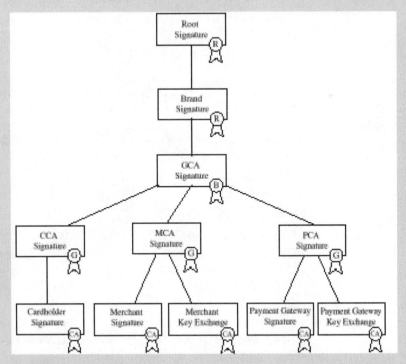

FIGURE 4.9 Hierarchy of trust.

ROOT KEY DISTRIBUTION. The root key will be distributed in a self-signed certificate. This root key certificate will be available to software vendors to include with their software.

ROOT KEY VALIDATION. Software can confirm that it has a valid root key by sending an initiate request to the Certificate Authority that contains the hash of the root certificate. In the event that the software does not have a valid root certificate, the Certificate Authority will send one in the response.

NOTE: *In the extremely unusual case where the software's root key is invalid, the user (cardholder or merchant) will have to enter a string that corresponds to the hash of the certificate. A confirmation hash must be obtained from a reliable source, such as the cardholder's financial institution.*

ROOT KEY REPLACEMENT. When the root key is generated, a replacement key is also generated. The replacement key is stored securely until it is needed.

The self-signed root certificate and the hash of the replacement key are distributed together.

Software will be notified of the replacement through a message that contains a self-signed certificate of the replacement root and the hash of the next replacement root key.

Software validates the replacement root key by calculating its hash and comparing it with the hash of the replacement key contained in the root certificate.

Kinds of Shopping

VARIETY OF EXPERIENCES. Cardholders will shop in many different ways, including the use of online catalogs and electronic catalogs. The SET protocol supports each of these shopping experiences and should support others as they are defined.

ONLINE CATALOGS. The growth of electronic commerce is attributed largely to the popularity of the World Wide Web. Merchants can tap into this popularity by creating virtual storefronts on the Web that contain online catalogs. They can quickly update these catalogs as their product offerings change for seasonal promotions or other reasons.

A cardholder can visit these Web pages and select items to order. When the cardholder finishes shopping and submits a request, the merchant's

Web server can send the cardholder a completed order form to review and approve.

Once the cardholder approves the order and designates a payment card, the SET protocol enables the cardholder to transmit payment instructions by a secure means, while enabling the merchant to obtain authorization and receive payment.

ELECTRONIC CATALOGS. A growing number of merchants are distributing their catalogs via electronic media such as diskette or CD-ROM. This approach allows the cardholder to browse through merchandise offline. With an online catalogue, the merchant has to be concerned about bandwidth and may choose to include fewer graphics or reduce the resolution of the graphics. By providing an offline catalogue, such constraints are significantly reduced.

In addition, the merchant may provide a custom shopping application tailored to the merchandise in the electronic catalogue. Cardholders will shop by browsing through the catalogue and selecting items to include on an order.

Once the cardholder approves the order and chooses to use a payment card, an electronic message using the SET protocol can be sent to the merchant with the order and payment instructions. This message can be delivered online, such as to the merchant's Web page, or sent via a store-and-forward mechanism, such as electronic mail.

Finally, let's look at another very important protocol for the public transport of private information that has rapidly emerged over the last three years. This is our future—WAP technology!

THE WIRELESS APPLICATION PROTOCOL (WAP) AND WAP FORUM

According to The Strategis Group, there will be more than 640 million wireless subscribers by the year 2002. New estimates report that the number of wireless subscribers will break the 2 billion mark by 2005, and a *substantial portion of the telephones sold that year will have multimedia capabilities*. These multimedia capabilities include the ability to retrieve e-mail, and push and pull information from the Internet. In order to guide the development of these exciting new applications, the leaders of the wireless telecommunications industry formed the Wireless Application Protocol Forum (http://www.wapforum.org).

The WAP Forum is the industry association comprising over 600 members that has developed the de-facto world standard for wireless information and telephony services on digital mobile telephones and other wireless terminals. The primary goal of the WAP Forum is to bring together companies from all segments of the wireless industry value chain to ensure product interoperability and growth of the wireless market.

WAP Forum members represent over 91 percent of the global handset market, carriers with more than 200 million subscribers, leading infrastructure providers, software developers, and other organizations providing solutions to the wireless industry. For a current listing of WAP Forum members, please go to http://www.wapforum.org/who/members.htm.

WAP is the de-facto world standard for the presentation and delivery of wireless information and telephony services on mobile telephones and other wireless terminals. In other words, it is an open, global specification that empowers mobile users with wireless devices to easily access and interact with information and services instantly.

As previously stated, handset (handheld digital wireless devices such as mobile telephones, pagers, two-way radios, smartphones, and communicators—from low-end to high-end) manufacturers representing 91 percent of the world market across all technologies have committed to shipping WAP-enabled devices. Carriers representing more than 200 million subscribers worldwide have joined WAP Forum™. This commitment will provide hundreds of millions of WAP browser-enabled products to consumers by the end of 2001. WAP allows carriers to strengthen their service offerings by providing subscribers with the information they want and need while on the move.

WAP enables easy, fast delivery of relevant information and services to mobile users.

Infrastructure vendors will deliver the supporting network equipment. Application developers and content providers delivering the value-added services are contributing to the WAP specification.

Enabling information access from handheld devices requires a deep understanding of both technical and market issues that are unique to the wireless environment. The WAP specification was developed by the industry's best minds to address these issues. Wireless devices represent the ultimate constrained computing device with limited CPU, memory, and battery life, and a simple user interface. Wireless networks are constrained by low bandwidth, high latency, and unpredictable availability and stability. However, most important of all, wireless subscribers have a different set of essential desires and needs than desktop or even laptop Internet users.

WAP-enabled devices are companion products that will deliver timely information and accept transactions and inquiries when the user is moving around. WAP services provide pinpoint information access and delivery when the full-screen environment is either unavailable or unnecessary.

The WAP specification addresses these issues by using the best of existing standards, and developing new extensions where needed. It enables industry participants to develop solutions that are air interface independent, device independent and fully interoperable. The WAP solution leverages the tremendous investment in Web servers, Web development tools, Web programmers, and Web applications while solving the unique problems associated with the wireless domain. The specification further ensures that this solution is fast, reliable, and secure. It enables developers to use existing tools to produce sophisticated applications that have an intuitive user interface. Ultimately, wireless subscribers benefit by gaining the power of information access in the palm of their hand.

The WAP Forum has published a global wireless protocol specification, based on existing Internet standards such as XML and IP, for all wireless networks. The WAP specification is developed and supported by the wireless telecommunication community so that the entire industry—and most importantly, its subscribers—can benefit from a single, open specification.

Wireless service providers are able to offer a new dimension of service that complements the existing features of their networks, while extending subscriber access to the unbounded creativity of the Web. Handset manufacturers can integrate microbrowser functionality at minimal cost, because the WAP specification is open and public. Application developers gain access to a whole new market of information-hungry users, while protecting and leveraging their current investments in Web technology. Subscribers gain real, anytime, anywhere information access with a simple and effective user interface, available on a variety of networks and devices.

WAP is designed to work with most wireless networks such as CDPD, CDMA, GSM, PDC, PHS, TDMA, FLEX, ReFLEX, iDEN, TETRA, DECT, DataTAC, and Mobitex. As you know, WAP is a communications protocol and application environment. It can be built on any operating system including PalmOS, EPOC, Windows CE, FLEXOS, OS/9, JavaOS etc. It provides service interoperability even between different device families.

While the WAP specification solves the transport and content problems of the constrained wireless environment today, the WAP Forum is constantly working to improve the state of wireless access to information. By working to build liaisons with ARIB, CDG, ECMA, ETSI, TIA, and W3C, the WAP Forum will continue to ensure that a single, open standard will be available to meet the wireless information needs of subscribers and industry participants worldwide. The WAP Forum is working with these standards bodies toward a goal of convergence with the XHTML and HTTP standards in order to optimize them for the wireless environment.

NONTECHNICAL CONSIDERATIONS

In addition to the technical considerations when preparing to process online credit card transactions, there are several nontechnical issues. Banks establish deposit accounts for the money collected by the merchant in the form of credit card transactions. As discussed earlier, when a merchant is set up by the bank to accept credit card transactions, the merchant is issued a merchant number. The credit card issuing banks charge merchants a percentage of each credit card transaction. Depending on the merchant's financial profile (length of time in business, assets, etc.) and previous credit card transaction history, the percentage or fee can vary.

The fee is determined by several factors, including raw transaction processing costs, profit for the bank, and risk. Fraud is a huge issue with traditional credit card transactions. Newly established merchants, merchants with a certain business profile, or those with previous fraud experience pay a higher per-transaction fee.

The traditional credit card transaction fee is based on the transaction occurring in-person at the merchant's store or place of business. "MOTO," or mail order and telephone order merchants pay a higher fee in most cases, as the merchant does not see the customer. As a consumer, you may notice this, as many MOTO merchants do not ship to an address different from the billing address on the credit card.

Many startup mail order companies, if they can get a bank to issue them a merchant number, are charged high fees until the merchant builds a good processing track record. This affects the online ordering and processing of credit cards, as the fee for a new business where no one sees or even speaks with the customer at the time of the sale is going to be high—even for companies with a strong credit card processing history. The bottom line is, you can build the most advanced Web site with the greatest graphics and the hottest products, but if you can't get a merchant number, you cannot accept credit card transactions. Additionally, if you do get a merchant number, but do not have a strong credit card processing track record, you will need to consider the impact that processing fees will have on your bottom line.

END NOTES

[1] The algorithm used by SET generates 160-bit message digests. The algorithm is such that changing a single bit in the message will change, on average, half of the bits in the message digest. Roughly, the odds of two messages having the same message digest are one in 1,000,000,000,000, 000,000,000,000,000,000, 000,000,000,000,000,000. It is computationally unfeasible to generate two different messages that have the same message digest.

5 Electronic Commerce Providers

"I have called this principle, by which each slight variation, if useful, is preserved, by the term *Natural Selection*."

—CHARLES DARWIN, *THE ORIGIN OF THE SPECIES*

Over the past few years, a number of companies have been working furiously to crawl up onto dry land by producing acceptable Internet commerce products. Now, an exponential score of firms with "electronic commerce" as their middle name are competing, each with slightly different variations on the major themes spelled out in preceding chapters. Although there is an expectation that some of the largest companies—VISA and MasterCard, for example—will set standards for the electronic commerce field in short order, brash young newcomers can never be counted out.

By looking at a relatively broad cross-section of the products now available, and examining similarities and differences, it becomes possible to better understand the context in which they are being developed and offered to the public. It remains to be seen which technologies will be most successful as they adapt to the Internet business environment. In the long run, of course, only the fittest will survive.

WHAT TO LOOK FOR, WHAT TO LOOK OUT FOR

Attempting to publish an overview of all electronic commerce companies in 2001 is as ludicrous as compiling a directory of all major automobile manufacturers in 1895. Although the dominant players for the short term are already pretty obvious, there is no telling what will happen five years down the road.

ONLINE COMMERCE OPTIONS

Ideally, online consumers should not have to make any choices or any special arrangements to order products electronically. Merchants have a much greater responsibility to implement a specific product or set of products, ranging from the use of secure Web servers to getting set up to accept payment through different payment mechanisms.

Banks are moving quickly to examine and evaluate electronic banking and electronic transactions. Banks and other financial institutions are working with companies like CyberCash, eBay Inc., Netscape, Microsoft, and others in an effort to produce seamless payment systems for consumers and merchants alike.

Consumer Choices

Consumers can opt to do nothing beyond getting a Web browser that supports the secure exchange of transaction information using either the Secure Sockets Layer (SSL) or Secure HTTP (S-HTTP) protocol. Doing so may prove sufficient for many consumer needs: It lets the consumer pay for goods and services by credit card, and it protects the transaction from being intercepted. However, it doesn't protect the consumer from dishonest merchants, who could set up enticing deals on the World Wide Web to trick consumers into sending them their credit card numbers. This possibility can be avoided by educating consumers to exercise the same caution in doing business online that they would use in dealing with telemarketers.

Consumers willing to get more involved have more options, but they can only use these methods with merchants who accept them. As with credit cards, wide acceptance is key: You may like to use your Diners Club or Carte Blanche cards, but you're more likely to find a gas station that accepts MasterCard or VISA. The facts of life dictate that if you only want to use one credit card, you're better off with the card that will be accepted by the most merchants.

Of course, some cards may be accepted at more places, but not at the places you want to shop. If your local gas station only takes its own charge card, a truckload of gold cards will not help you. The same goes for online payment methods—so far, there is no single solution, and it is likely there will always be some degree of choice for the consumer.

Registering with a third-party organization that acts as a go-between for merchants and consumers can provide an extra level of security for consumers. The third party can act on behalf of both the merchant and the consumer, taking the payment information from the consumer and settling transactions for the merchant. This means the consumer does not have to trust the merchant with payment information, because the intermediary company never passes that on to the merchant. This also means that the consumer can make purchases (relatively) anonymously.

For consumers willing to set up special bank accounts, electronic checking or digital cash products may be a good option. These schemes can also work anonymously. A consumer can encrypt payment settlement information and send it to the merchant—who has to pass it along to the consumer's bank, where it is decrypted, and payment is forwarded to the merchant.

Merchant Choices

The Internet merchant must take greater care in setting up to accept electronic payments. The simplest option is to have someone else manage a secure Web server and set up shop there. This could mean setting up a store on an electronic mall or paying an Internet Service Provider (ISP) to manage your Web site for you.

There are many choices at this level. There are literally hundreds of "electronic malls" on the Internet on which a merchant can set up shop. On the other hand, large businesses may be willing to spend a lot to get a commercial environment that securely accepts orders, processes and settles the payment information, and can be integrated into a corporate fulfillment system.

There are other options, too. In addition to secure or commerce servers, which support credit card payment, the merchant can also elect to support some of the less familiar payment methods. Merchants can accept digital cash or electronic checks, or use other systems. Other systems take care of sensitive payment information offline. For example, you can set up as an eBay Inc. merchant if you want to sell a digital product that can be delivered over the Internet.

CHOOSING FUNCTIONS AND FEATURES

For consumers, the most important aspects of an electronic commerce provider will probably be these:

- Reliability
- Security
- Simplicity
- Acceptability

Consumers have come to rely on their credit and charge card companies not just to extend credit, but to extend protection against unscrupulous vendors (providing recourse when improper charges are made), thieves (minimizing liability when a card is lost or stolen), and the vicissitudes of daily life (offering protection plans that replace lost or stolen goods). Likewise, these companies are also relied on to bill correctly, and to credit payments promptly. The same type of reliability will be expected of electronic commerce service providers.

The security issue is one that will never go away. Even if the strongest possible encryption is used to send payment information, there are still many security holes. A security chain is only as strong as its weakest link, and companies engaging in this business can be exposed through any number of non-Internet attacks:

- The disgruntled employee with access to payment information
- Storage of payment information with insufficient security (unlocked file cabinets, unsecured terminals)
- Improper disposal of printed material (thieves could steal unshredded reports)

Although the general reader may suspect me of paranoia, experienced systems and network engineers are likely to come up with half a dozen more possibilities.

Electronic commerce schemes must be simple to achieve widespread appeal. Consumers prefer to use a single, multipurpose credit card such as VISA or MasterCard rather than set up credit accounts with every different retailer they purchase from. Many consumers prefer to pay for groceries by credit card rather than go through the process of getting a check-cashing identification card for a particular supermarket. And if you are in a hurry, cash can't be beat. The same goes for electronic commerce schemes: If they can be made to be simple, painless, and even more easy than transacting business in person, then they will be successful.

Finally, electronic commerce schemes should offer widespread acceptability. A scheme that is accepted by only a few merchants will not be attractive to consumers who don't do business with those merchants; a scheme that few consumers have chosen will be one that few merchants seek out.

WHAT LIES AHEAD

This industry is still in the very earliest phase of its infancy and is undergoing rapid change every day. What is current in the middle of 2001 may not be by the end of the year; however, the fundamental mechanisms are likely to remain in place for longer. This chapter provides overviews of about a dozen companies involved in the Internet commerce arena. Some of them are working together, while others are competing; the only certainty is that things will change.

The descriptions in this chapter and in the rest of this book should be used more as indicators of the way in which electronic commerce works than as exact descriptions of current offerings.

COMPANY PROFILES

The company profiles that follow should not be considered in any way comprehensive or exhaustive, but merely indicative of the types of organizations that are offering tools or products for electronic commerce.

By the time this book gets to the copy editor, not to mention you, the reader, another company will undoubtedly have come to the market with a new electronic commerce product or service. Or, another DOT.COM company may have been bought out or filed for bankruptcy. They're disappearing from—and appearing on—cyberspace as fast as you can say "IPO." Fortunately, the Internet provides a way to stay current with search engines. Chances are you have seen one of the popular search engines listed here:

> http://www.yahoo.com/
> http://www.altavista.digital.com/
> http://www.go.com/
> http://www.lycos.com/
> http://www.webcrawler.com/

CAUTION

All URLs in this chapter and book are subject to change without notice!

AMAZON.COM

P.O. Box 81226
Seattle, WA 98108-1226
E-mail: info@amazon.com
Telephone: 1-800-201-7575
www: http://www.amazon.com/

Amazon.com opened its virtual doors in July 1995 with a mission to use the Internet to sell books online. Today, Amazon.com is the place to find just about anything you want to buy online. They have a customer base of 17 million people in more than 160 countries. They have Earth's Biggest Selection™ of products, including free electronic greeting cards, online auctions, and millions of books, CDs, videos, DVDs, toys and games, and electronics.

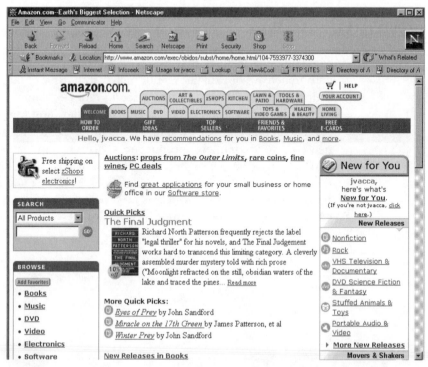

FIGURE 5.1 The amazon.com home page (reprinted with permission from Amazon.com, Inc., © 2000).

BARNES & NOBLE

76 Ninth Avenue
New York, NY 10011
E-mail: corrections@barnesandnoble.com
Telephone: 1-800-843-2665
www: http://www.bn.com

Since launching its online business in March 1997, Barnes&Noble.com (NASDAQ: BNBN) has become one of the world's largest Web sites and the fourth largest e-commerce retailer, according to Media Metrix. The company focuses largely on the sale of books, music, software, magazines, prints, posters, and other related products.

The Barnes&Noble.com Music Store features an online classical music superstore; 16 categories of music with more than 1000 subcategories;

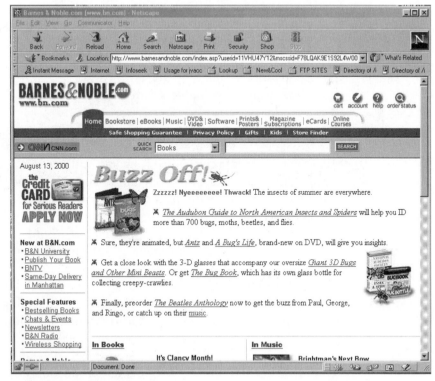

FIGURE 5.2 The Barnes & Noble home page (reprinted with permission from barnesandnoble.com LLC, © 2000).

hundreds of thousands of albums; more than 20,000 artist biographies; and more than 50,000 music reviews and album ratings. Their Music Store was ranked as the second best among "Overall Online Music Stores" by Gomez Advisors, Inc. Other recent additions to the site are the Prints & Posters Gallery, a collection of images that can be produced on demand on museum-quality canvas or high-quality paper, and eCards, a selection of greeting card images that can be personalized and enhanced with animation and music.

Their affiliate network has more than 280,000 members, and they maintain strategic alliances with major Web portals and content sites, such as AOL, Lycos, and MSN. As of September 30, 1999, more than 2.9 million customers in more than 215 countries had purchased books and music from their online store.

BORDERS, INC

Headquarters
100 Phoenix Drive
Ann Arbor, MI 48108-2202
E-mail: CustomerService@Borders.com
Telephone: 1-800-770-7811
www: http://www.borders.com/

Borders, Inc. owns and operates retail book outlets throughout the United States. In 1997, Borders opened its first overseas location in Singapore. Three stores in the United Kingdom and one in Australia opened in 1998. Borders stores feature books, music, and videos, and host series of in-store appearances by authors, musicians, and artists. Most Borders stores also offer a casual espresso cafe.

Borders began in 1971, when Tom and Louis Borders opened a *serious* bookshop in the heart of Ann Arbor, an academic community in southeast Michigan. In the early 1990s, Borders began selling music in addition to books. Now, several companies are opening Borders-style book and music superstores at a furious pace, and the market is expanding rapidly. Since 1991, national bookstore sales have grown from $7.8 billion to over $10 billion in 1994. By late1999, Borders had nearly 300 stores.

In 1997, the Borders Group launched a new subsidiary, Borders Online, Inc. This company oversees the production of the Borders.com Web site.

FIGURE 5.3 The Borders Online, Inc. home page (reprinted with permission from MUZE Inc., © 2000).

CHECKFREE CORPORATION

> Corporate Headquarters
> 4411 East Jones Bridge Road
> Norcross, GA 30092
> E-mail: payinfo@checkfree.com
> Telephone: 1-678-375-3000
> www: http://www.checkfree.com/

CheckFree was founded by Peter J. Kight in 1981 in Columbus, Ohio. The company is now headquartered in Atlanta, and has offices in Dublin, OH; Austin, TX; Baltimore, MD; Ashburn, VA; Aurora, Downers Grove, and Chicago, IL; Jersey City, NJ; San Diego, CA; Raleigh, NC; and Phoenix, AZ. They provide electronic bill payment processing services to more than 350 financial institutions, including 9 of the top 10, 23 of the top 25, and 40 of the top 50.

The company has more than 1100 connections with merchants for the delivery of electronic payments. They recently consolidated four separate processing platforms into one capable of processing payments for 33 million U.S. households.

CheckFree E-Bill is used by dozens of major billing companies. Through the acquisition of BlueGill Technologies, CheckFree now offers a turnkey solution for billers who want to electronify their billing system.

They manage 700,000 portfolios totaling more than $400 billion in assets. Institutions that use these systems include Charles Schwab Inc. and Rittenhouse Financial Services, a division of John Nuveen Inc. More than

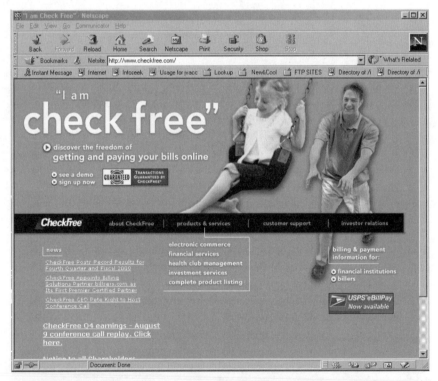

FIGURE 5.4 The CheckFree Corporation home page (reprinted with permission from CheckFree Corporation, © 2000).

two-thirds of the nation's 6 billion Automated Clearing House (ACH) payments are processed each year through CheckFree's ACH software and services. CheckFree also has a strong ACH presence in Australia, Chile, Panama, Guatemala, Colombia, and Malaysia. Nearly 400 banks and businesses use CheckFree's reconciliation products and services.

COMMERCENET, INC.

10050 N. Wolfe Road
Suite SW2-255
Cupertino, CA 95014
Telephone: 1-408-446-1260
Fax: 1-408-446-1268

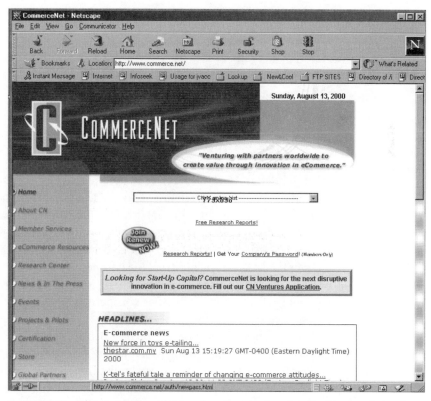

FIGURE 5.5 The CommerceNet, Inc. home page (reprinted with permission from CommerceNet, © 2000).

E-mail: bizdev@commerce.net
www: http://www.commerce.net/

Launched in Silicon Valley, California in April 1994, CommerceNet's membership has grown to over 600 companies and organizations worldwide. They include the leading banks, telecommunications companies, VANs, ISPs, online services, software and services companies, as well as major end users. See Chapter 9, "Strategies, Techniques, and Tools," for more details about this organization.

CYBERCASH, INC.

Corporate Headquarters
2100 Reston Parkway
Reston, VA 22091
Telephone: 1-703-620-4200
Fax: 1-703-620-4215
Alameda Office
1201 Marina Village Parkway, 3rd Floor
Alameda, CA 94501
Telephone: 1-510-263-4300
E-mail: investor@cybercash.com
www: http://www.cybercash.com

Founded in 1994, CyberCash is a pioneer in electronic commerce software and services for merchants. Today, the company supports over 22,500 e-commerce merchants through its CashRegister service, and processes over 10 million online transactions per month. The success of this service is shown by the 300-percent growth CyberCash has seen in payment activity over the last year. In addition, the company has sold over 145,000 copies of its payment software, making CyberCash one of the most widely used payment software for the PC. The company offers a wide range of software and service solutions for payment processing, for both Internet and physical store retailers. This allows CyberCash to provide solutions for payment processing that comprise services operated by an operations center and software that can be managed by the merchant customer.

The CyberCash payment system is described in greater detail in Chapter 6, "Electronic Payment Systems."

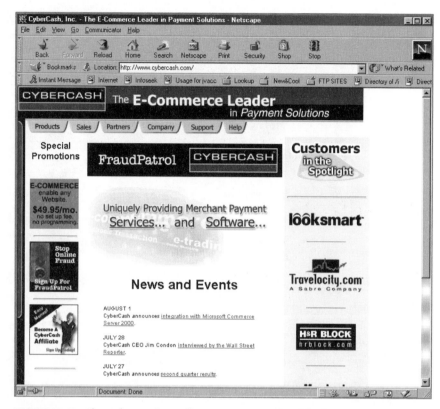

FIGURE 5.6 The CyberCash, Inc. home page (reprinted with permission from CyberCash, Inc., © 2000).

eBAY INC.

> Headquarters
> 2145 Hamilton Avenue
> San Jose, CA 95125
> Telephone: 1-408-558-6162
> Fax: 1-408-558-6162
> E-mail: safeharbor@ebay.com
> www: http://www.ebay.com/index.html

eBay was conceived initially as a result of a conversation between Pierre Omidyar and his wife, an avid Pez™ collector (she currently covets a

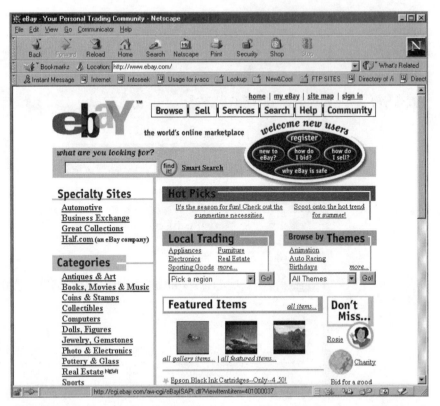

FIGURE 5.7 The eBay home page (reprinted with permission from eBay Inc., ©
2000).

collection of more than 400 dispensers). She commented to Pierre how
great it would be if she were able to collect Pez dispensers and interact with
other collectors over the Internet. As an early Internet enthusiast, Pierre
knew that people needed a central location to buy and sell unique items
and to meet other users with similar interests. He started eBay to fulfill this
need.

Pierre launched eBay on Labor Day in September 1995. eBay is the
world's largest personal online trading community. eBay created a new
market: one-to-one trading in an auction format on the Web.

Individuals—not big businesses—use eBay to buy and sell items in
more than 4320 categories, including automobiles, collectibles, antiques,
sports memorabilia, computers, toys, Beanie Babies, dolls, figures, coins,
stamps, books, magazines, music, pottery, glass, photography, electronics,
jewelry, gemstones, and much more. Users can find the unique and the

interesting on eBay—everything from china to chairs, teddy bears to trains, and furniture to figurines. They provide over 4 million new auctions and 450,000 new items every day from which users may choose.

eCASH TECHNOLOGIES, INC.

19015 North Creek Parkway
Suite 105
Bothell, WA 98011
Telephone: 1-425-415-5000
Fax: 1-425-415-1060
E-mail: info@ecashtech.com
www: http://www.digicash.com/

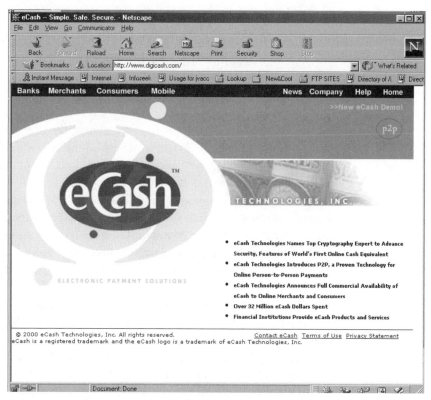

FIGURE 5.8 The eCash Technologies, Inc. home page (reprinted with permission from eCash Technologies, Inc., © 2000).

eCash Technologies, Inc. develops, markets, and supports the eCash software suite for secure, private, and nonrepudiable (that is, nonfraudulent) electronic cash transactions on the Internet. ECash Technologies owns and uses the patented blind signature™ encryption technology.

eCash products and services are provided to consumers and merchants through financial institutions. eCash is an open, nonexclusive system, available for implementation by any financial institution and usable by any customer or merchant. eCash is currently issued by financial institutions, and used by consumers and merchants around the world.

FINANCIAL SERVICES TECHNOLOGY CONSORTIUM

N. Michigan Avenue
24th Floor
Chicago, IL 60611
Telephone: 1-312-527-6724
Fax: 1-312-527-6724
E-mail: fstcadmin@fstc.org
www: http://www.fstc.org/

The Financial Services Technology Consortium (FSTC) is a not-for-profit organization whose goal is to enhance the competitiveness of the United States financial services industry. Members of the consortium include banks, financial services providers, research laboratories, universities, technology companies, and government agencies.

FSTC sponsors project-oriented collaborative research and development on interbank technical projects affecting the entire financial services industry. Particular emphasis is placed on payment systems and services, and leveraging new technologies that help banks cement customer relationships, boost operational efficiency, and expand their market reach.

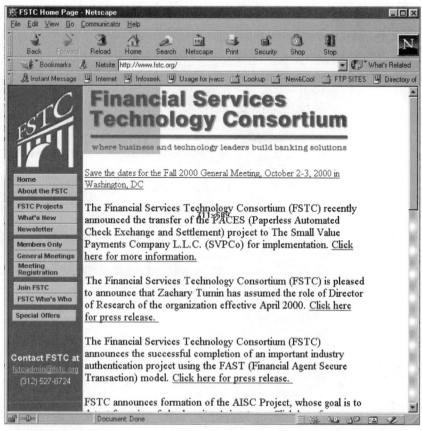

FIGURE 5.9 The Financial Services Technology Consortium home page (reprinted with permission from Financial Services Technology Consortium, © 2000).

IBM CORPORATION

Corporate Offices
New Orchard Road
Armonk, NY 10504
Toll-free number (U.S.): 1-800- IBM-4YOU
www: http://www-4.ibm.com/software/webservers/commerce/

IBM WebSphere™ Commerce Suite allows you to create e-marketplaces that integrate Web sites with business-critical systems like inventory, order processing, and shipping.

FIGURE 5.10 The IBM Corporation home page (reprinted with permission from IBM Corporation, © 2000).

INTERNET SHOPPING NETWORK

Corporate Office
500 Macara Avenue
Sunnyvale, CA 94086
Telephone: 1- 408-617-7400
E-mail: nfo@firstauction.com
www: http://www.isn.com/

Internet Shopping Network had the distinction of being the first online retailer in the world when it was launched in April 1994. In June 1997, Internet Shopping Network launched First Auction, at http://www.firstauction

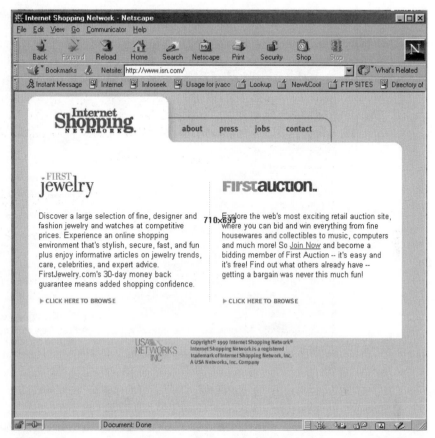

FIGURE 5.11   The Internet Shopping Network home page (reprinted with permission from Internet Shopping Network, © 2000).

.com. First Auction features new computers, consumer electronics, home furnishings, apparel, sporting goods, toys, jewelry, and health and beauty products in an online auction format.

MASTERCARD INTERNATIONAL

Global Headquarters
2000 Purchase Street
Purchase, NY 10577 U.S.A.
Telephone: 1-914-249-2000
www: http://www.mastercard.com

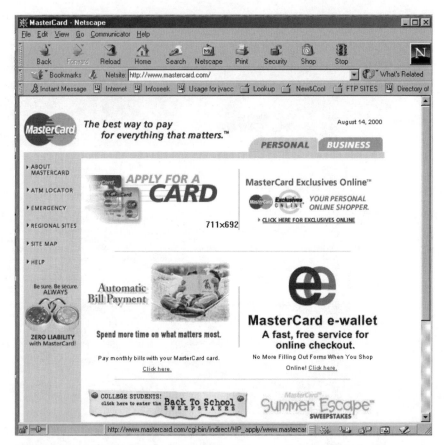

FIGURE 5.12 The MasterCard International home page (reprinted with permission from MasterCard International Incorporated, © 2000).

MasterCard has expanded globally to bring you the MasterCard/Cirrus ATM network. MasterCard International is also heavily involved in the development of smart card technology, discussed in Chapter 8, "Digital Currencies."

MICROSOFT CORP.

1 Microsoft Way
Redmond, WA 98052-6399
Telephone: 1-425-882-8080
www: http://www.microsoft.com

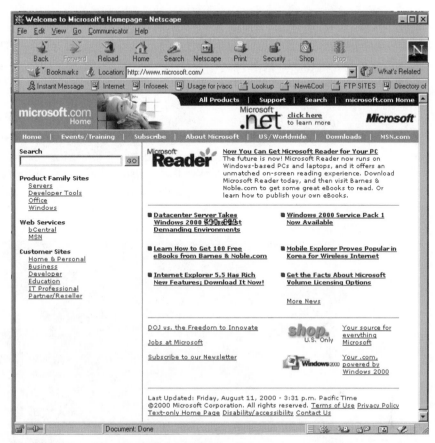

FIGURE 5.13 The Microsoft Corporation home page (reprinted with permission from Microsoft Corporation, © 2000).

Although it was not one of the first companies to develop products and services for the Internet, today Microsoft is a dominant player. Microsoft offers both an Internet browser for the end user and several commerce and information servers with which to build electronic commerce applications.

MONDEX INTERNATIONAL

London—Head Office
47–53 Cannon Street
London EC4M 5SH
England

Telephone: +44-0-20-7557-5577
Fax: +44-0-20-7557-5588
E-mail: customer.support@mondex.com
www: http://www.mondexinternational.com/

Mondex International Ltd. is a major subsidiary of MasterCard International. It develops smart card products and services. An idea invented in 1990, Mondex International Ltd. is one of the main providers in smart card technology. Incorporated in July 1996, Mondex International now has 180 employees in over five divisions (Market Management, Products and Marketing, Operational Infrastructure, Technology and Development,

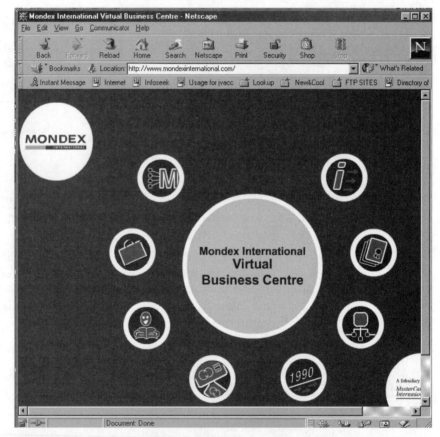

FIGURE 5.14 The Mondex International home page (reprinted with permission from Mondex International Ltd., © 2000).

and Business Infrastructure). They have offices in London, Japan, the United States, and Australia.

Mondex International is owned by MasterCard International and 17 major organizations worldwide, including leading banks in the United Kingdom, United States, Asia Pacific, Australasia, and Canada:

- MasterCard International Incorporated
- Mondex Australasia Pty Ltd.
- Mondex Canada
- The Chase Manhattan Corporation
- Bank One Corporation
- The Hong Kong and Shanghai Banking Corporation
- HSBC Bank Plc
- National Australia Bank Limited
- National Westminster Bank Plc
- Ulster Bank Limited
- Universal Holdcorp Inc.
- Wells Fargo & Company
- Banque Federative du Credit Mutuel
- The Sanwa Bank Limited
- Banco Nacional de Mexico S.A.
- Banomer S.A.
- Banco Internacional S.A.

Mondex offers an electronic cash system and security architecture as part of their electronic cash scheme. Mondex can be used for simple, everyday cash transactions. The Mondex electronic cash system operates on a smart card—a plastic card that looks like an ordinary debit or credit card and stores information on a microchip. The microchip contains a *purse* in which Mondex value is held electronically. The purse is divided into five separate pockets, allowing up to five different currencies to be held on the card at any one time. The microchip also contains the Mondex SECURITY program, which protects transactions between one Mondex card and another.

Being electronic, the Mondex card can be transferred over a telephone line or the Internet. The microchip maintains a record of the last 10 transactions, and the electronic cash can be locked into the Mondex card using a code chosen by the user.

Mondex electronic cash can be transferred directly to a retailer, merchant, or other outlet to pay for goods or services, and like cash, Mondex

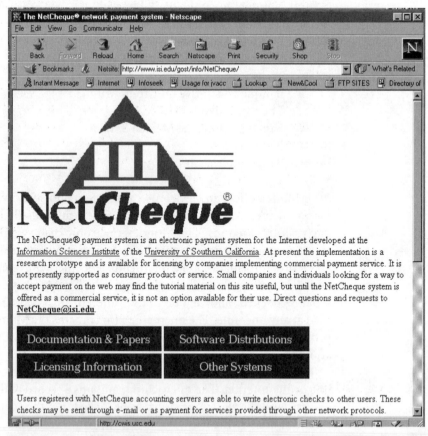

enables transactions between individuals, without the need for banks or other third parties.

NETCASH/NETCHEQUE

NetCheque Project
USC Information Sciences Institute
4676 Admiralty Way
Marina del Rey, CA 90292-6695
Telephone: 1-310-822-1511
Fax: 1-310-823-6714

FIGURE 5.15 The NetCheque® home page (reprinted with permission from the University of Southern California, © 2000).

E-mail: NetCheque@isi.edu
www: http://www.isi.edu/gost/info/NetCheque/

The NetCheque payment system is an electronic payment system developed at the Information Sciences Institute of the University of Southern California. The strengths of the NetCheque system are its security, reliability, scalability, and efficiency. Signatures on checks are authenticated using Kerberos. Reliability and scalability are provided by using multiple accounting servers. The NetCheque system clears micropayments; its use of conventional cryptography makes it more efficient than systems based on public key cryptography.

The NetCash research prototype is a framework for electronic currency developed at the Information Sciences Institute of the University of Southern California. NetCash will enable new types of services on the Internet by providing a real-time electronic payment system that satisfies the diverse requirements of service providers and their users. Among the properties of the NetCash framework are security, anonymity, scalability, acceptability, and interoperability.

When used in combination with NetCheque, service providers and their users are able to select payment mechanisms based on the level of anonymity desired, ranging from non-anonymous and weakly anonymous instruments that are scalable, to unconditionally anonymous instruments that require more resources of the currency server.

NetCash provides scalable electronic currency that is accepted across multiple administrative domains. Currency issued by a currency server is backed by account balances registered with NetCheque to the currency server itself. NetCash currency servers also use the NetCheque system to clear payments across servers, and to convert electronic currency into debits and credits against customer and merchant accounts. Though payments using NetCheque originate from named accounts, with NetCash the account balances are registered in the name of the currency server, and not the end user. The USC NetCash Research Prototype was developed by USC/ISI's GOST Group.

THE NETMARKET COMPANY

Corporate Headquarters
595 Summer Street
Stamford, CT 06901

FIGURE 5.16 The NetMarket Group Inc. home page (reprinted with permission from NetMarket Group Inc., © 2000).

Telephone: 1-888-696-2753
E-mail: info@netmarket.com
www: http://www.netmarket.com/

NetMarket is a one-stop shopping site where members and non-members can browse eight diverse superstores to find more than 800,000 name brand products.

NETSCAPE

America Online, Inc.
22000 AOL Way
Dulles, VA 20166
Telephone: 1-703-265-0094
E-mail: permissionteam@aol.com
www: http://home.netscape.com

Started in April, 1994, Netscape is now owned by America Online, Inc. Netscape's first products were Netscape Navigator, a widely distributed

FIGURE 5.17 The Netscape home page (reprinted with permission from America Online, Inc., © 2000).

World Wide Web browser, and the Netscape server line, including the first secure World Wide Web commerce server.

Netscape developed a secure protocol, Secure Sockets Layer (SSL), to encrypt and decrypt World Wide Web data as it is sent and received by underlying Internet software, rather than using the Secure HTTP (S-HTTP) protocol to provide security enhancements within the World Wide Web applications themselves. This protocol has been made available to the public and has been proposed as an Internet standard.

Netscape's secure servers are discussed at greater length in Chapter 7, "Online Commerce Environments," and their protocols are discussed at greater length in Chapter 4, "Protocols for the Public Transport of Private Information."

OPEN MARKET, INC.

One Wayside Road
Burlington, MA 01803
Telephone: 1- 781-359-3000
E-mail: webmaster@openmarket.com
www: http://www.openmarket.com/cgi-bin/gx.cgi/AppLogic+FT-ContentServer?pagename=FutureTense/Apps/Xcelerate/Render&c=Collection&cid=OMI9U1F9EZB&live=true

Founded in 1994, Open Market, Inc. (NASDAQ: OMKT) is focused on e-business solutions that enable universal customer relationship management (UCRM) through an integrated suite of applications for managing online content, commerce, and e-marketing worldwide.

Headquartered in Burlington, Massachusetts, Open Market is an $83 million company with an international presence in 30 nations, including offices in the United Kingdom, Australia, Canada, France, Germany, Italy, Japan, and The Netherlands. The company serves both the business-to-business and business-to-consumer markets, and has sold more than 35,000 licenses worldwide, with more than 10,000 Web merchants in production with more than 60 Commerce Service Providers (CSPs) and 120 Internet Service Providers (ISPs) in 26 countries. Open Market's global customers include many of the most popular domains on the Web, including Lycos.com, AOL.com, and the Wall Street Journal Inter-

FIGURE 5.18 The Open Market home page (reprinted with permission from Open Market Incorporated, © 2000).

active Edition; major industrials such as Acer, Ingram Micro, Milacron, and Siemens; as well as 10 of the world's top 13 national telephone companies.

In October of 1999, Open Market merged with FutureTense, a privately held provider of content management technology. This merger brought together technologies in content management and commerce management to provide the foundation of its e-business suite. Open Market's Integrated Commerce Environment is an infrastructure for Internet commerce and is described in greater detail in Chapter 7.

RSA SECURITY

Corporate Headquarters
20 Crosby Drive
Bedford, MA 01730
Telephone: 1-877-RSA-4900 or 1-781-301-5000
Fax: 1-781-301-5170
E-mail: pr@rsasecurity.com
www: http://www.rsasecurity.com/

RSA Security Inc. is helping organizations build secure, trusted foundations for e-business through its two-factor authentication, encryption,

FIGURE 5.19 The RSA Security home page (reprinted with permission from RSA Security, © 2000).

and public key management systems. With the global integration of Security Dynamics and RSA Data Security, RSA Security has more than 5000 customers. The company's RSA SecurID enterprise authentication products are protecting information in the majority of the Fortune 100 today, addressing the important need for easy, hacker-proof user authentication both inside and outside the corporate network.

These same products are similarly used by leading electronic commerce businesses, including securities trading and banking applications, to protect against external attack and fraudulent activity. The company's RSA BSAFE line of encryption-based security technologies are embedded in over 450 million copies of today's most successful Internet applications, including Web browsers, commerce servers, e-mail systems, and virtual private network (VPN) products.

RSA Security now offers its customers the RSA Keon family of PKI products for public key authentication and encryption security in today's leading e-mail, Web browser, Web server, and VPN applications. Headquartered in Bedford, Massachusetts and with offices around the world, RSA Security is a public company (NASDAQ: RSAS) with yearly revenues in excess of $200 million.

SECURE COMPUTING

Corporate Headquarters
Sales and Marketing
One Almaden Boulevard
Suite 400
San Jose, CA 95113
Telephone: 1- 800-692-5625
Fax: 1-408-918-6101
www: http://www.sctc.com

Secure Computing is a global provider of e-business security products to organizations of all sizes, including Fortune 500 enterprises, application and Internet service providers, and government agencies. Secure Computing's suite of network security product's—Sidewinder™, SafeWord™, and SmartFilter™—help enable safe, secure extranets for e-business.

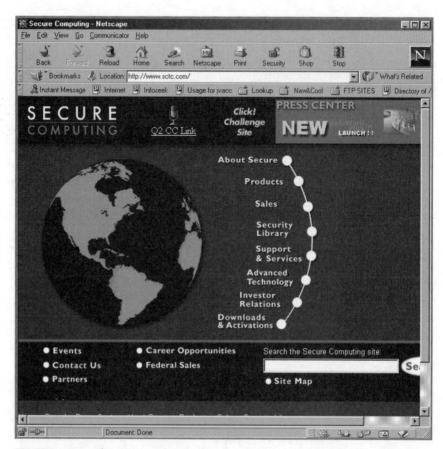

FIGURE 5.20 The Secure Computing home page (reprinted with permission from Secure Computing Corporation, © 2000).

SURETY.COM INC.

1890 Preston White Drive
Reston, VA 20191
Telephone: 1-703-264-8818
Fax: 1-703-264-2788
E-mail: info@surety.com
www: http://www.surety.com/index-nn.html

Surety.com is an Internet company providing notary service for digital data. The company's Digital Notary ™ Service allows customers to prove

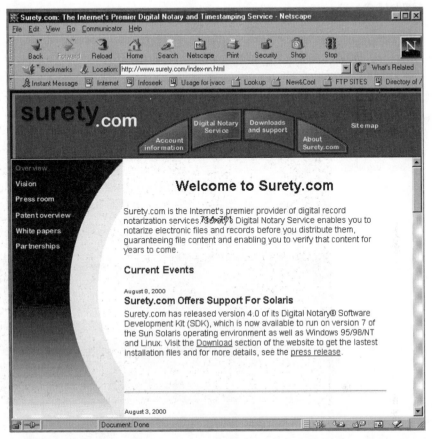

FIGURE 5.21 The Surety.com Inc. home page (reprinted with permission from Surety.com Inc., © 2000).

conclusively that digital information existed in an exact form at a specific moment in time. Digital Notary Service is used in a wide variety of business applications, including protection against repudiated e-commerce transactions, creating secure audit trails for regulatory compliance, and the protection of intellectual property. Digital Notary Service notarizes, time-stamps, and validates any electronic record, including e-commerce transactions, e-mail correspondence, database records, word processing documents, spreadsheets, images, audio samples, and video clips.

VERIFONE

Corporate Headquarters
Hewlett-Packard
3000 Hanover Street
Palo Alto, CA 94304-1185
Telephone: 1-650-857-1501
Fax: 1-650-857-5518
www: http://www.verifone.com

VeriFone is a division of Hewlett-Packard Co. and a global provider of secure electronic-payment solutions for financial institutions, merchants,

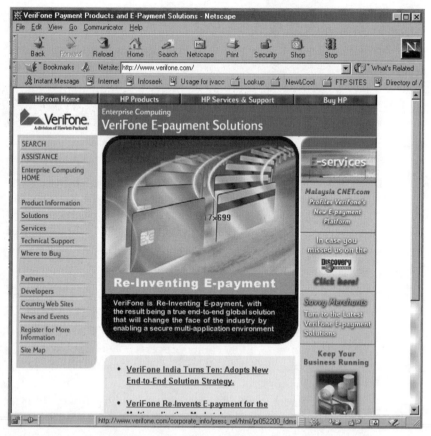

FIGURE 5.22 The VeriFone home page (reprinted with permission from VeriFone Inc., © 2000).

and consumers. They have shipped more than 7 million payment systems, which are used in more than 100 countries.

VERISIGN, INC.

Worldwide Headquarters
1350 Charleston Road
Mountain View, CA 94043
Telephone: 1-650-961-7500
Fax: 1-650-961-7300
E-mail: internetsales@verisign.com
www: http://www.verisign.com

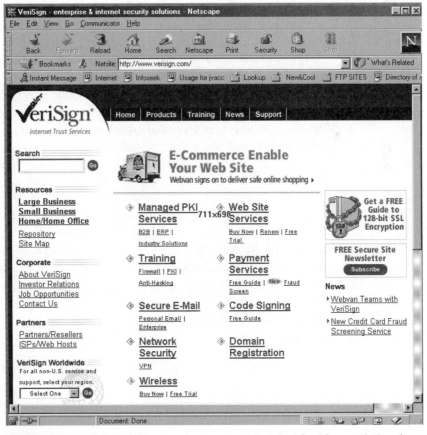

FIGURE 5.23 The VeriSign, Inc. home page (reprinted with permission from VeriSign, Inc., © 2000).

VeriSign, Inc. (NASDAQ: VRSN), headquartered in Mountain View, California is a provider of Internet trust services—including authentication, validation, and payment—needed by Web sites, enterprises, and e-commerce service providers to conduct trusted and secure electronic commerce and communications over IP networks. The company has established strategic relationships with industry leaders, such as AT&T, British Telecommunications, Checkpoint Technologies, Cisco, Microsoft, Netscape, Network Associates, Network Solutions, RSA Security, and VISA to enable widespread utilization of digital certificate services and to assure interoperability with a variety of applications and network equipment.

VeriSign's trust services for Web sites, developers, and individuals are available through http://www.verisign.com and through a growing number of ISPs and Web hosting companies. To date, VeriSign has issued over 215,000 Web site digital certificates and over 3.9 million digital certificates for individuals. The company's Web site digital certificate services are used by all of the Fortune 500 companies with a Web presence. VeriSign also offers a suite of technologies, services, and key industry alliances to accelerate the deployment of trust in next-generation applications for wireless Internet e-commerce.

VeriSign's managed digital certificate services allow enterprises and electronic commerce service providers to deploy digital certificates for employees, customers, and partners, and are available through regional account representatives, resellers, and global affiliates. Customers include Bank of America, Barclays, Hewlett-Packard, the Internal Revenue Service, Kodak, Southwest Securities, Sumitomo Bank, Texas Instruments, VISA, and US West.

The company's network of more than 20 affiliates, which provide trust services under licensed co-branding relationships using VeriSign technology and business practices, includes Arabtrust in the Middle East, British Telecommunications in the United Kingdom, CIBC of Canada, CertiSur of Argentina, Certplus of France, eSign of Australia, HiTrust of Taiwan, KPN Telecom of the Netherlands, Roccade of the Netherlands, the South African Certification Agency in South Africa, and VPN Tech of Canada.

VISA

900 Metro Center Boulevard
San Francisco, CA 94404
Telephone: 1-650-432-3923
www: http://www.visa.com
E-mail: AskVisa@visa.com

VISA, in conjunction with more than 170 banks around the globe, has over 23 million chip cards in the market today. Currently, more than 150 VISA members in over 38 countries have secure Internet shopping programs utilizing the Secure Electronic Transaction™ co-developed by VISA.

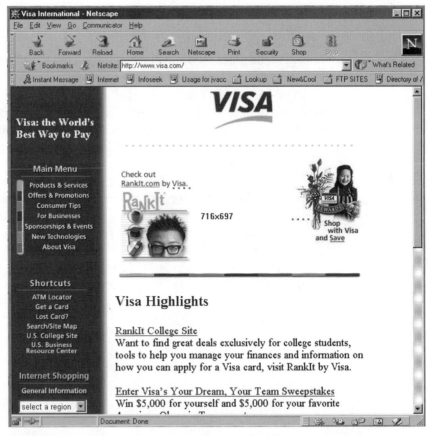

FIGURE 5.24 The VISA home page (reprinted with permission from VISA International, © 2000).

VISA is also heavily involved in the development of smart card technology, discussed in Chapter 8.

A HOST OF OTHERS...

These companies are among the more interesting, and in many cases, more likely to succeed in the long run. There are many, many more companies that are providing Internet commerce services in one form or another, as described in the section on services in Chapter 3, "Electronic Payment Methods." There are various associations, research groups, agencies, and consortia, all providing some type of service or support to the issues of electronic commerce. There are also less formal proposals; for example, individuals or groups offering to start their own electronic currencies, possibly based on barter of products or services. Others include payment systems instituted by online malls for use only at those malls, using telephone, fax, or other methods for collecting credit card information, and user IDs and passwords for making purchases.

To get more information about all of these companies (and all of the new ones that have surely sprung up since this book went to press), the best place to start is with an online search engine such as Yahoo!

http://www.yahoo.com

The pointers provided in the companion CD-ROM should also be useful to anyone wishing to get more complete information and, in particular, the latest news and developments from participating organizations.

6 Electronic Payment Systems

In God we trust—all others pay cash.

—THE SIGN OVER THE CASH REGISTER AT THE STORE AROUND THE CORNER.

Anything that makes it possible for a consumer to spend money online can be construed as an electronic payment system. As discussed in earlier chapters, these payment systems can be electronic checking systems, third-party systems, or electronic currency systems. All of these provide for the exchange of values between individuals. Some require prior arrangements by all participants, although this is changing. This chapter describes in detail how three representative payment systems work on the Internet.

DIGITAL PAYMENT SYSTEMS

Digital payment systems, unlike electronic commerce environments, focus on getting a payment from a customer to a merchant. The emphasis is on the customer: At least so far, the customer is required to make some type of commitment to the payment system in question in order to use it. For example, the customer may need to acquire and install some software, or make some type of contact with the digital payment system provider in order to register as a user of that service. Merchants also must make a specific commitment to one or more providers of digital payment services.

Neither customer nor merchant is bound by any single commitment, however. Just as the average consumer in a typical suburban mall may have a pocketful of credit cards (as well as a checkbook and cash), so the typical online consumer may very well use several different methods to pay for products purchased on the Internet. The same goes for merchants, who both online and offline are usually willing to accept a variety of different payment options.

Although digital payment systems require a higher level of activity and commitment from both consumers and merchants, the reward to providers of such systems is very attractive. Software publishers offering secure World Wide Web servers earn a profit on each sale of their server software, but companies offering a digital payment system are able to earn a profit on each sale made using the service itself.

This chapter examines three very different digital payment systems. CyberCash uses a straightforward interpretation of digital commerce, basing its service on the need for secure, private, and reliable transactions. CyberCash offers a digital payment mechanism that uses modern cryptographic technologies, including public and private key encryption and digital signatures, implemented through special client and server software.

Consumers store their payment information in an encrypted digital wallet, and they can make credit card payments as well as digital cash transfers through CyberCash. CyberCash can be accepted for virtually any type of transaction, from small to large purchases, although peer-to-peer digital cash transfers may be preferable for smaller purchases. Consumers need special free client software to set up a "digital wallet," while merchants must install free server software. Although the end-user application can be installed and configured in a few minutes, installing and configuring a merchant's World Wide Web server to accept CyberCash payments is more complicated.

Microsoft, on the other hand, approaches digital commerce by using a significant portion of the majority of corporate Web sites. As such, Microsoft has moved rapidly to digital commerce-enable its software offerings on the desktop and server. The result is a comprehensive desktop and server Internet digital commerce offering that enables business-to-consumer and business-to-business digital commerce applications.

Digital commerce functionality has been integrated into the Microsoft® BackOffice™ family to provide a digital commerce-enabled sever backend. Microsoft Site Server, Enterprise Edition, a BackOffice product, provides a comprehensive Web-site environment for enhancement, deployment, and the advanced management of digital commerce-enabled Web sites. Site Server, Enterprise Edition includes Commerce Server, an

Internet-selling software product adopted by thousands of customers worldwide since its availability in December 1996.

Support for digital commerce has also been integrated into Microsoft Internet Explorer and the Microsoft Windows® operating system, creating a digital commerce-enabled desktop offering. The Microsoft Wallet provides secure purchasing on the Internet, and is available for download from the Web.

Finally, you have MasterCard's digital e-Wallet payment strategy. MasterCard is continuing to develop and promote several different digital wallets so members can choose a program that best meets their market needs. In each case, members implementing a digital wallet program must address certain questions: Who controls the cardholder data, the issuer or the vendor? Does the digital wallet reside on the customer's computer or the issuer's server? Should members develop their own custom wallet or work with third-party vendors? Is there sufficient awareness and interest among merchants and consumers to merit a digital wallet launch?

MasterCard works with its members to answer the preceding questions and create a digital wallet program that best suits their business and customer needs. Their digital wallet strategy rests on three principles:

- They support both client-based and server-based vendors, but both must promote an issuer-centric wallet.
- They are committed to the continuing development of digital wallet standards and *best practices*.
- They will create and support branded digital wallet enhancements.

In partnership with IBM, MasterCard has introduced a single-click consumer e-wallet to member banks. PC based, the IBM program offers an implementation of the wallet while leaving the issuer in total control of its program. The single-click feature is based on the Electronic Commerce Modeling Language (ECML) standard and reduces the amount of information a consumer must input on a Web site in order to make a purchase. The wallet uses both SSL- and SET-enabled security functions. Available in 26 languages, it can be fully branded by the issuing bank.

Also, with its Trintech alliance, MasterCard is following an approach to online payment software that emphasizes the primacy of the member/customer relationship and the importance of branding. This is a server-based software package that puts the financial institution in control of wallet-oriented marketing programs, data mining, and distribution. The onscreen icon for this e-wallet can be a replica of the member's card, sitting on the computer desktop as an ever-present payment tool.

This chapter first examines Microsoft, then MasterCard, and finally CyberCash, describes them and their products, and explains how they work.

MICROSOFT'S INTERNET E-COMMERCE PAYMENT SYSTEM STRATEGY

Electronic commerce is not a new concept. Companies and consumers have been using electronic media to conduct commercial transactions for years. To date, high cost and complexity have inhibited electronic commerce. The complexity arises in establishing lines of communication and even more by the lack of standard applications for viewing and sharing information once connected. The Internet, specifically the World Wide Web, has changed this scenario radically. Connectivity over the Internet is cheap, increasingly secure, and built on standards that make communicating with anyone a straightforward task. Now, Internet commerce (the exchange of goods and services for value on the Internet) is evolving into a more cost-effective and powerful way to do business.

Internet commerce represents a market worth potentially hundreds of billions of dollars in just a few years. It presents tremendous opportunities for businesses (see Table 6.1).[1] First, a growing standard means for businesses to automate and streamline how they trade with other businesses: *business-to-business commerce*. Business-to-business commerce includes online wholesaling, where businesses sell goods and services to other businesses on the Web. In Internet-based corporate purchasing, wholesaling merges into a system where individual employees make purchases of office materials and supplies using the corporate intranet. With Internet-based supply chain trading, businesses work closely together via the Internet to automate and streamline the supply of goods for production and distribution.

Internet commerce also provides businesses a growing, dynamic channel for efficient delivery of goods and services to consumers: *business-to-consumer commerce*. In business-to-consumer commerce, digital commerce companies market physical goods to consumers online in a more personalized, dynamic environment. Business-to-consumer digital commerce will increasingly include the delivery of digital goods—software,

TABLE 6.1 Internet Commerce Opportunities

	Hard Goods	*Digital Goods, Services*
Business-to-Consumer	Retail	Information
	Direct	Media
		Software
		Ticketing
		Reservations
		Financial Services
Business-to-Business	Wholesale	Corporate Subscriptions:
	Corporate Purchasing	Professional Services
	Supply Chain Trading	

electronic media, and information. Consumers will also look more frequently to the Internet for the delivery of services, including ticketing, reservations, and financial services. In short, Internet commerce (business-to-business and business-to-consumer) will dramatically impact the way goods and services are managed, bought, and sold, all the way from manufacturer to consumer.

The Microsoft Internet Commerce Payment System Strategy (see Figure 6.1) is based on the following three components:[2]

- Server Foundation
- Payment
- Solutions with Commerce Partners

SERVER FOUNDATION

Server Foundation is a server and tools digital commerce foundation based on Site Server, Enterprise Edition. It is also based on BackOffice server components and tools for rapidly deploying and managing commerce applications (business-to-consumer and business-to-business) that extend Microsoft's Web platform, Active Server Pages, and Microsoft Transaction Server, and integrates Windows NT® Server security.

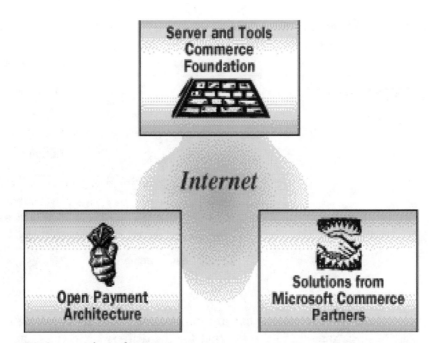

FIGURE 6.1 Microsoft Internet commerce payment system strategy.

Site Server, Enterprise Edition provides comprehensive functionality for commerce-enabling Web sites. The product supports electronic catalog management, online order processing, and the creation of dynamic product and price promotions. The Order Processing Pipeline provides an extensible data structure for managing orders. Its broad API allows any developer to create components to extend order-processing functionality or integrate with existing systems. Site Server, Enterprise Edition employs new tools, such as the StoreBuilder Wizard, that dramatically simplify the process of creating and managing online commerce sites. Site Server, Enterprise Edition also introduces a new capability called Buy Now. Buy Now allows the embedding of product information and order forms inline within most any context (such as an online ad banner), allowing businesses to promote and sell without the need for complete online stores.

Future versions of Site Server, Enterprise Edition will help business digital commerce solution developers dramatically lower the cost of development with a number of new built-in functions, including the Commerce Interchange Pipeline. The Commerce Interchange Pipeline is a workflow system that supports the exchange of EDI and other business document types over multiple transports, including the Internet.

PAYMENT

Payment is an open payment architecture based on Site Server Enterprise Edition and the Microsoft Wallet. The Wallet is simple-to-use client software that enables consumers to securely make purchases over the Internet. The Microsoft Wallet has an open design that allows Wallet Payment Modules created by independent payment technology companies to be plugged in dynamically. This open payment architecture gives consumers freedom of choice in how they choose to pay for goods and services online. It also establishes a framework for interoperability between banks, merchants, and consumers. Microsoft will support standards for next-generation payment protocols, such as Secure Electronic Transaction (SET), by distributing the Wallet with Internet Explorer 4.0 and higher; and, the next version of the Microsoft Windows operating system.

SOLUTIONS WITH THE COMMERCE PARTNERS

Solutions with the Commerce Partners is a creation of solutions with Microsoft Commerce Partners.

Microsoft's Internet commerce offering is a commerce platform. Hundreds of companies worldwide are extending Microsoft's offering to create complete solutions. Commerce partners include solution providers, hosting Internet Service Providers (ISPs), independent software companies, payment software companies, and banks and financial institutions. Industry leaders in these categories are working closely with Microsoft to create new kinds of business-to-business and business-to-consumer commerce solutions on the Internet.

INTERNET COMMERCE OPPORTUNITY IS PHENOMENAL

Internet commerce opportunity phenomenal growth has occurred and is expected to continue for the Internet World Wide Web. Estimates for the numbers of consumers and businesses online vary considerably for markets around the world. Still, experts believe that more than 47 million households will have access to the Web by the year 2001 in the United States alone. This number is lower in Europe, based on lower penetration of personal computers, but still approaches a dazzling figure of near 31 million households. In Japan, approximately 23 million households will have access to the Web in the year 2001.

The number of business Web sites is equally impressive, reaching more than approximately 3 million by the year 2001 in the United States, and as many as 2 million each in Europe and Japan. This significant adoption of the Internet World Wide Web by businesses and consumers presents two tremendous opportunities for businesses. First, a growing standard means for businesses to communicate transactional information with other businesses more cost-effectively: *business-to-business commerce*. Second, a growing channel for efficient delivery of goods and services to consumers: *business-to-consumer commerce*. Let's take a quick look at trends in these two areas of opportunity. Common requirements are then explored.

BUSINESS-TO-BUSINESS COMMERCE OPPORTUNITY
EDI FOR ALL BUSINESSES

Businesses today transact with trading partners in one of two generalized fashions. First, the majority of businesses use nonautomated means of communicating commerce-related information with trading partners: mail, telephone, and fax. Second, a small number of primarily the largest companies in the world (fewer than 50,000) conduct a significant portion of their transactions in an automated fashion such as Electronic Data Interchange (EDI). EDI (conducted either with leased lines or, more commonly, through Value Added Networks (VANs)) can be costly and complex. Large companies maintain full-time EDI staff for the ongoing management of translation systems and auditing of the operation. EDI VAN-based systems, because of their complexity and ensuing cost, exclude small and medium-sized businesses from participation in automated trading communities.

The Internet will bring radical change to automation in trading. By providing a ubiquitous public network and standards for communication, the Internet will help businesses lower costs in EDI-like transactions. More importantly, the Internet will make it easier for small and medium-sized businesses to participate in automated commerce transactions. Many businesses (small, medium, and large) will soon send and receive the majority of their purchase orders and invoices over the Internet.

FORMATION OF VIRTUAL ENTERPRISES

Increased ease of automating commerce will provide opportunities for businesses to work increasingly closely with other businesses for the supply of goods and information, either for the direct manufacturing process or indirect operation of the business. The impact on businesses of such improved commerce relationships is the formation of *virtual enterprises.*

Virtual enterprises are best described as business activities that span the business processes of more than one company. The formation of virtual enterprises represents the opportunity for businesses on the Internet. By establishing intimate business relationships with vendors and suppliers, companies can lower operational costs, improve customer service, and focus on their core value add in the marketplace. The Internet provides a means for companies of all sizes to participate in virtual enterprises.

Business-to-Consumer Commerce Opportunity Growth of a New Direct Channel

Every year, consumers spend more than $3.3 trillion on goods and services in the United States alone. About one fifth of this astronomical amount, or $660 billion, is spent as a result of direct marketing—mail order telephone order, catalogs, business reply card inserts, television, and online digital commerce. Within the online digital commerce category are included direct sale and marketing of physical goods, digital goods (such as software, media, and information), and services—ticketing, reservations, and financial services.

For many businesses, the Internet is a fast-growing channel of distribution. 1-800-FLOWERS, one of the world's largest florists, has seen their online business grow to 20 percent of their overall $400 million business. Their Web site has grown faster than any other online venue. Not all businesses have seen this kind of success in early ventures into online selling. Critical mass of consumers on the Web is still accumulating. The adoption of new technology and corresponding change in consumer behavior will take time.

PERSONALIZATION AND THE BEGINNINGS OF MASS CUSTOMIZATION

The Web offers a rare disconnect with traditional means of distribution, enabling forward-thinking businesses to create new value-added product and service offerings. Such value add will increasingly mean personalized, tailored service for the mass of buyers—mass customization. For example, visitors to @Tower, Tower Records' Web store, can click on the New Releases link and view the current week's releases for all genres—typically hundreds of CDs. Better yet, registered shoppers enjoy a personalized view of new releases when they click on the same link: They see a special call-out graphic that appears when their favorite artists have issued a new release in the last several weeks.

Web sites can also significantly improve a customer's experience. On the Web, buyers have direct access to sources of information and the opportunity for direct communication with the seller. Many sites have established communities, allowing buyers to interact with other customers. Such examples of value-added service to customers will help separate successful from less successful businesses.

CONTEXTUAL TRANSACTIONS

A significant opportunity for consumer marketers exists in the marrying of informational content with transactions. The most successful selling sites provide all kinds of information around the sale of a product—digital commerce and community merged. Many marketers will soon go even further. Rather than waiting for consumers to visit their selling sites, they will begin to embed product and service offers in other contexts and contextual transactions. Contextual transactions will be embedded in online banner ads, articles or stories, and even directly in a consumer's HTML desktop. They will be unobtrusive, leaving the content viewer in place once the transaction is complete. Contextual transactions will enable impulse buying, taking advantage of a consumer's peak moment of interest.

Mass customization and contextual transactions are just the beginning of what will be a radical new way of executing direct online marketing. In the future, the push model will supplement the pull model of the Web site. In the push model, consumers will be actively sought out based on special interests that they willingly publish. Internet digital commerce will become a part of each consumer's everyday life.

Requirements for digital commerce businesses need solutions to take advantage of the multitude of opportunities described previously. To date, there has been a lack of comprehensive software, expertise, infrastructure, and mature standards to support Internet digital commerce applications. The following are critical requirements for customers creating digital commerce solutions:

- Lower-cost deployment and management of custom Internet commerce
- Simpler integration with existing systems
- Flexible support for payment
- Secure access
- Simpler, lower-cost business document processing, EDI-compatible
- Dynamic, promotional, searchable content management
- Contextual transactions for online direct marketing
- Standards-based solutions

Lower-Cost Deployment and Management of Custom Internet Commerce Sites

Until fairly recently, the average company spent millions of dollars implementing digital commerce-enabled sites. Part of this cost derives from fees for software packages. More so, it derives from the cost of consulting services to develop code from scratch in order to meet custom needs, making up for the lack of effective tools. Businesses need lower-cost software that also reduces the amount of custom development required. They need tools to improve deployment and support ongoing change and management of site content and data. Businesses need a low-cost investment that can scale as their Internet business grows.

In many cases, shared hosting scenarios will keep costs low. In such a scenario, a hosting ISP will manage multiple sites on one configuration. To help lower costs, support for shared hosting is needed.

Simpler Integration with Existing Systems

Internet digital commerce sites will often need to mirror and use data from companies' existing business processes. Businesses need simpler ways to set up systems that reflect inventory, write out to accounting systems, or track fulfillment.

Flexible Support for Payment

Businesses and consumers need standards for secure, Internet-based payment. Solutions are needed to support payment between businesses, and between consumers and businesses.

Secure Access

A highly visible issue, security affects a number of aspects of Internet digital commerce solutions. Businesses need secure digital commerce sites to allow controlled access for consumers, business trading partners, and administrators.

Simpler, Lower-Cost Business Document Processing, EDI-Compatible

Businesses need to manage and improve structured communications with other businesses. However, the shift to the Internet cannot mean an end to EDI. Businesses need backward compatibility with traditional EDI to ensure continuation of business that affects the bottom line.

Dynamic, Promotional, Searchable Content Management

Businesses that sell need to manage electronic catalogs that display product and service offerings to customers in a clear, compelling, searchable fashion. In a consumer environment, such content needs to be highly promotional, supporting price and product promotions. Content must also support personalized service.

For businesses with complex offerings, customers need to make selections easily, sometimes configuring product options on the fly.

Contextual Transactions for Online Direct Marketing

Consumer marketers need simple tools for embedding product information. They also need order forms in any context.

Standards-Based Solutions

Businesses need to make investments in open, standard platforms and protocols. This lowers risk and ensures maximum interoperability between various components of a complete system.

For more information on Microsoft's Internet Commerce Strategy, see Chapter 7, "Online Commerce Environments." Now, let's look at MasterCard's digital payment system.

MASTERCARD'S DIGITAL PAYMENT SYSTEM STRATEGY

The Internet is changing customer expenditure patterns. Worldwide, in 1999 (the most recent year for which figures are available), expenditures on personal consumption approached $29 trillion, but only 17 percent of that was transacted using cards. In retail, only one household dollar in four is spent using payment cards, but on the Internet, consumers pay almost exclusively with cards. E-payment cards are the future of online retail.

The Internet is also changing the nature of the payment environment in that proportionately fewer transactions are face-to-face transactions in which a physical card is actually needed. More and more transactions are remote (mail order, telephone order, Internet order); in other words, they take place in a virtual environment.

VIRTUAL MASTERCARD PROGRAM ENVIRONMENT

Many trends, including the growth of *remote* or *card-not-present* transactions, have given rise to the Virtual MasterCard Program. This program enables a member to create a MasterCard-branded program intended for use in remote payment environments, where a physical card is not presented to a merchant. It may be used for any remote environment transaction, such as the Internet, mail, or telephone orders.

For consumers, the benefits of the Virtual MasterCard Program are clear: The program may be used to isolate online transactions from those made in the physical world, giving consumers a stronger feeling of security. Consumers get the peace of mind that comes from knowing that if their virtual MasterCard account is compromised, their other card accounts will not be affected.

Benefits for members are clear as well: As an acquisition channel, the Virtual MasterCard Program can help members sign up new accounts, increase transaction volumes, and expand their portfolio. As a customer retention initiative, the program can help strengthen existing customer loyalty by meeting the needs of consumers who are Internet-savvy and attuned to virtual purchasing channels. This can lead to increases in incremental transaction volume as well as increased profits per customer. Variations of the Virtual MasterCard Program include a virtual MasterCard account with an option for a physical MasterCard card, and a virtual MasterCard account with the option to link to another MasterCard card.

The Virtual MasterCard Program can coexist with all other MasterCard programs, including co-branded and affinity cards.

E-WALLETS

Digital wallets or e-Wallets, are software programs that reside either on a cardholder's PC or at the server computer of a member or online service provider. They contain all necessary payment, billing, and shipping information for an online purchase—information that is automatically transferred to an e-merchant's order form (see the sidebar, "Shop Online with an E-Wallet").

Shop Online with an E-Wallet

An electronic wallet is basically an online version of your physical wallet. Your payment and personal information is stored safely in one place for you to access when you need to pay for something online. Your electronic wallet will help you fill online order forms quickly and easily whenever you shop.

In addition to filling out online forms, electronic wallets can do even more. For example, some offer additional handy features such as:

- Password storage for multiple Web sites
- Wallet transaction history
- Storage of multiple shipping addresses
- Store directories
- Automatic notification of special offers and discounts

In short, electronic wallets are ready to serve as full-fledged shopping assistants.

Which Type Is Best for You?

You can choose from several electronic wallets, each with specific features and benefits. However, electronic wallets fall into two general categories: server-based and client-based. For the pros and cons of each type, see Table 6.2 for a comparison. You may want to download more than one wallet to see which one better suits your needs.

Are Electronic Wallets Secure?

Most wallets are protected by multiple layers of security. To use them, you need to provide both an ID and password. Wallets rely on sophisticated encryption methods such as SSL to safeguard the information being transferred.

For even greater security, some wallets, such as the *client-based* one offered by IBM and MasterCard, also employ a new, even more advanced security standard known as SET that offers you, merchants, and banks an even higher level of protection.[3]

TABLE 6.2 Comparison of Server-Based and Client-Based Wallets.

Wallet Type	*Server-based* (main software resides on computer servers run by a bank or service bureau)	*Client-based* (software resides entirely on your computer)
Features tion	Order form completion (usually with a *single click*).	Order form completion (mainly through *drag and drop*).
	May also store transaction history, remember passwords, and provide additional services such as store directories, comparison-shopping and automatic notification of special offers and discounts.	
Downloading time and installation requirements	Less time required for installation.	More time required for installation.
	Upgrades done quickly online.	Upgrades may not be automatic.
Information Storage	Information stored on home PC as well as on computer servers run by wallet provider.	Information stored solely on home PC.

The MasterCard Wallet (IBM Wallet v2.1) is one of the first Electronic Commerce Modeling Language (ECML) compatible wallets on the market. ECML is the standardization of online merchant order forms that allows wallets to automatically fill in customer information. It supports both SSL and SET (e-commerce encryption and security protocols). See the sidebar, "Downloading the MasterCard Wallet," for step-by-step instructions on how to actually download the Wallet.

Downloading the MasterCard Wallet

The following instructions will show you how to download the MasterCard Wallet:

- System Requirements
- Download Installation Instructions
- How to Use the Wallet
- Additional Wallet Information

System Requirements

- Windows 95/98 or Windows NT 4.0
- Personal computer using a 386 or better microprocessor (486 recommended)
- Minimum 16MB of RAM
- 7MB of free disk space
- 15MB of temporary disk space for the install process
- Netscape Navigator 2.0 or later, or Microsoft Internet Explorer 3.0 or later

Download Installation Instructions

1. Print these instructions (this page) before proceeding.
2. Click the icon to initiate download process.
3. Select Save *This Program to Disk*.
4. Select a directory or create a new directory to receive download. Write down the directory name.
5. Click the *Save* button.

6. File download will proceed.

7. When download completes, close your browser window.

8. In *My Computer*, open the directory that received the download.

9. Run *MasterCard_Wallet.exe*

10. Follow the directions on the screen.

11. You may choose a final directory or allow the MasterCard Wallet installation process to choose a directory for you.

12. When the Setup process is complete, choose the *Install Wallet* option. You may view the demo first, but the demo will automatically run after you complete the wallet installation process. During the installation process, the Wallet gives you several choices. It will suggest a default choice. It is suggested that you accept the defaults when provided. Fill in your shipping and credit card information as instructed. All of this information stays securely on your personal computer's hard drive in encrypted form—ready for you to use for online shopping. You are now ready to shop online.

How to Use the Wallet

1. Open your MasterCard Wallet when you have selected items to purchase online. The next step is to fill out the online order form.

2. Your MasterCard Wallet will place an icon on your desktop and in the tray at the bottom right corner of your screen. YOU MUST DOUBLE-CLICK ON EITHER ICON TO OPEN YOUR WALLET.

3. Sign in by selecting your User ID and typing in your password.

4. Two wallet screens will open—your Main Wallet on the left and your Shopping Assistant on the right. Before shopping, use your Main Wallet to add or edit your personal information if necessary.

5. If your current information is correct, you should select the *Hide the Window* option from the FILE menu in the upper left-hand corner of the Main Wallet screen. This will allow you to view the merchant order form. You may also minimize the Main Wallet window, but do not close it—doing so will close the Wallet totally.

6. Use the Shopping Assistant to fill out Merchant Forms. First, use the drop-down boxes (in both People and Cards) to ensure that you have selected the correct shipping address and payment card for this transaction.

7. Click the *Auto-Fill* button at the bottom of the Shopping Assistant screen. The Wallet will fill in as much of the form as it can. DRAG

AND DROP any unfilled information into the appropriate space on the Merchant Form.

Additional Wallet Information

- Use the Memo fields to store passwords and other information.
- Use the icons in the top left corner of the Main Wallet screen to move between your Payment Card Storage screen and your Shipping Addresses Information screen.
- You can open the Shopping Assistant by clicking its icon in the top left corner of the Main Wallet screen.
- There is no limit to the number of cards or addresses that you can store in the Wallet.
- Use the Options menu at the top of the Shopping Assistant to customize its functionality. For instance, you can have the Shopping Assistant always stay on top of the Merchant Form or choose to hide the labels for more room.[4]

SMART CARDS

Smart cards are nothing less than a revolutionary business opportunity for members. MasterCard's smart-card migration strategy is enabling members to deliver multifunctional financial services (including debit, credit, and prepaid payment solutions) via three of the most powerful devices for reaching customers: the telephone, the television, and the PC.

Already, many markets (including Argentina, Brazil, France, Germany, Japan, Korea, Mexico, South Africa, and the United Kingdom) are moving rapidly to migrate their card bases to a chip platform.

Smart cards give issuers and acquirers the single best tool for overcoming transaction fraud. This is an embedded digital certificate that securely authenticates the cardholder and each transaction. Embedded chips, moreover, will increasingly allow for the easiest, most flexible forms of payment. They will support applications (such as loyalty and reward programs, electronic vouchers, e-ticketing, and digital identification) that far exceed anything possible with magnetic stripes.

As consumers and corporate customers become ever more demanding, smart cards are the platform upon which to deliver more and better-personalized products and services.

A single card lets businesses manage travel and entertainment (T&E) reporting, purchasing, and fleet expenses. As new technologies open more channels for payment, smart cards will deliver additional revenue streams.

E-CASH

MasterCard's Mondex e-cash program provides an optimal cost-effective solution for low-value purchases. Mondex continues to outpace the competition, with 17 franchises having been sold in 90 countries to date. In nine of those countries, 24 program launches are now under way.

Mondex opens channels for new revenue, such as fast-food chains, coffee shops, news agencies, and even coin-operated self-service outlets (vending machines, parking meters, laundromats). Mondex can secure value for up to five different currencies simultaneously, and operation is icon based, so language is no barrier. Value can be transferred immediately, directly, and securely between one chip and another—and between individual users, card to card.

E-SECURITY

Security is essential for unlocking e-business. Smart cards and smart-card readers are the ultimate solution to making online transactions safer. In addition, software solutions provide an immediate, cost-effective, and practical alternative. MasterCard supports a multitude of security tools for e-business.

Chip And MULTOS™

MasterCard has been a pioneer in the development of smart cards, including the chip technology that enables the inclusion of different payment methods on a single MasterCard or Maestro® card. It also includes helping to establish MULTOS as the de facto standard operating system for smart cards. MULTOS is the heart of Mondex electronic cash, one of the only e-cash products currently available with multicurrency functionality. Moreover, MULTOS is one of the first commercial products to be awarded the highest possible security classification, ITSEC6.

MULTOS as the De Facto Standard

MasterCard helped establish MULTOS as one of the most widely recognized operating system for smart cards. A nonproprietary, open, industry-controlled standard, it provides one of the best high-security, multi-application operating systems available today. Multiple programs or services can run on one card at the same time, in a secure manner, and its functionality is not limited to the payments industry. It is being actively promoted and is well received across financial services, government, telecommunications, health care, retailing, and transportation. Other payments organizations backing MULTOS are Mondex International, Europay, American Express, Discover, and JCB. MULTOS will lead eventually to the emergence of the Lifestyle Card™ — a card that allows consumers to choose the products and services they need most at any given time, such as health records and membership renewals.

The Complete Chip Solution™

MasterCard has developed a turnkey strategy for helping members migrate their credit and debit cards to a chip platform. Called The Complete Chip Solution, it ensures that members are positioned to take advantage of the rapidly changing marketplace. The strategy is built upon the global inter-operability, multiple-application capability, and product flexibility of MULTOS that enable members to design the best programs for their markets. All of MasterCard's smart card offerings are forward migratable from the outset, so members need only make a single investment in the chip solution.

France Fights Fraud with Chips

Within six months of the implementation of chip-based cards at Cartes Bancaires in France (in November 1992), fraud was cut in half. Since then, it has fallen by a full 86 percent. The French experience is significant, too, in light of another key challenge: the high cost of online authorizations. Today, 9 out of 10 smart-card transactions at Cartes Bancaires are authorized offline—directly between the card's chip and the POS terminal.

The SET Secure Electronic Transaction (SET) Protocol

At worst, consumers may have limited liability, if any at all, should their card number be fraudulently used. Still, it is no secret that consumers are uneasy about putting their card numbers out into cyberspace.

Today, Internet shoppers view the potential abuse of card information as the leading barrier to shopping on the Internet. They are especially concerned about the legitimacy of merchants; for example, are they a *fake storefront* (simply collecting card numbers and personal information)?

Consequently, to successfully market online, Internet merchants must provide their customers with a fast, easy payment process that is convenient, spontaneous, and universal, while guaranteeing security and privacy. As previously discussed in earlier chapters and reiterated here, SET is that secure payment process.

What Is SET?

The SET protocol is an open industry standard developed for the secure transmission of payment information over private and public networks, including the Internet. SET uses digital certificates that authenticate and protect all parties in an electronic transaction. Industrial-strength encryption is provided in SET through a combination of public key encryption and digital certificates. This technology ensures confidentiality of the payment information exchanged between the parties during a transaction.

Since its inception in 1996, SET has been establishing its viability in implementations worldwide. It secures the Internet for the advancement of e-commerce, it protects MasterCard's members from the threat of disintermediation, and it leverages the existing payment card infrastructure to yield new value. It also positions bankcards as the preferred method of payment, and it positions MasterCard's members as the guardians of the financial trust between themselves and their cardholders.

SET development is governed by SETCo LLC, a nonprofit entity run by and composed of resources from MasterCard and VISA. SETCo oversees compliance testing of third-party vendor software, and it coordinates work to encourage SET adoption as the global e-commerce payment standard. MasterCard is now working with SETCo to improve support for multiple cardholder authentication schemes, such as digital signatures, PIN, chip, cryptograms, and non-SET certificates.

A new model for SET (the Three Domain Model, or 3D-SET) accommodates the preferences of issuers who want to create their own cardholder authentication and security schemes. It will support all meaningful methods of credit and debit payments, including digital signatures, PIN, chip, and cryptograms. This will provide members with a flexible Internet payment platform from which they can implement any or all of the components.

Advanced Cryptography Is What Makes SET So Secure

Cryptography has been used for centuries to protect sensitive information as it is transmitted from one location to another. In a cryptographic system, a message is encrypted (or scrambled) using a key. The resulting ciphertext (scrambled message) is then transmitted to the recipient where it is decrypted (unscrambled) using another key to reproduce the original message. As previously mentioned, SET uses the two primary encryption methods in use today: private (or secret) key cryptography and public-key cryptography.

Here's How SET Works

The SET Internet payment system relates to today's physical world payments. In fact, SET's goal is to make MasterCard accounts as easy to use in cyberspace as they are to use at the local store. For Internet payments, consumers will need two things: SET-compliant Electronic Wallet software to store MasterCard account information, and a digital account ID used for electronic payment slips.

As previously explained, Electronic Wallets have been bundled into new Web browsers. Cardholders who do not upgrade to a new browser will be able to download an Electronic Wallet off the Internet.

Consumers will be encouraged by card-issuing banks to obtain their digital account IDs. To be certified for a digital account ID, cardholders will be directed to a World Wide Web site connected to the banks' Certificate Authority (CA), which will ask a series of questions that only the true cardholder can answer.

After the card-issuing bank verifies the information, their CA will issue a digital account ID certifying the cardholder account. The account ID will be stored along with the credit card account number in the cardholder's Electronic Wallet. See the sidebar, "Walking through a Typical Online Transaction," to see how SET works.

Walking through a Typical Online Transaction

1. The cardholder browses for items to purchase. This may be accomplished in a variety of ways, such as:

   • Using a browser to view an online catalog on a World Wide Web page

   • Viewing a CD-ROM catalog.

   • Looking at a paper catalog

2. The cardholder selects items to be purchased.

3. The cardholder is presented with an order form containing the list of items, their prices, and a total price including shipping, handling, and taxes.

4. The cardholder opens an onscreen Electronic Wallet and selects a MasterCard account for payment.

5. The Electronic Wallet will then initiate a message to the merchant indicating that the consumer wants to use a MasterCard account for payment.

6. The merchant responds with a message to the consumer's Electronic Wallet with the merchant's MasterCard certificate, which has the merchant's public key and the acquirer's certificate with the acquirer's public key.

7. The Electronic Wallet verifies the merchant certificate and acquirer certificate, and then uses the public key to encrypt a message to the merchant.

8. The merchant can determine if the message is authentic and has all of the purchase order information.

9. At this time, the merchant will not be able to decrypt the electronic slip or the card number.

10. The merchant sends the encrypted electronic slip to their acquiring bank.

11. The acquiring bank receives the encrypted information, decrypts the electronic slip, authenticates the cardholder certificate, and sends the card number out for authorization using existing authorization systems (MasterCard's Banknet), just as they do today in a physical point-of-sale.

12. The merchant receives the authorization response from the acquirer that, at the acquirer's option, may or may not contain the card number.

13. The merchant sends authorization status to the cardholder.

14. If authorized, the merchant ships the goods or performs the requested services.

15. The merchant receives payment from the merchant's financial institution.[5]

Merchants Will Also Be Certified

Just as consumers need to have digital account IDs and special software, so too will merchants. Merchants need to obtain SET server software to store their digital account IDs along with their acquirer's key.

SET reinforces the relationship between a merchant and an acquirer to enable the merchant to deal directly with their acquirer for secure electronic commerce. The merchant will contact their acquiring bank to obtain their digital account ID and a copy of their acquirer's key.

After merchants obtain their SET certificate, they will need to upgrade their systems to process SET transactions. This software most likely will be purchased from a SET certified provider.

A Word about RSA Technology

As previously mentioned, SET is built upon RSA encryption. To take advantage of this technology, there is a mathematically interrelated private and public key pair.

Private keys are used and held ONLY by their owner. If a private key is compromised, it must be replaced immediately.

Public keys are used to encrypt or decrypt information, and are provided by the private key holder to everyone who needs them. Unlike a private key, a public key is open for anyone to see and there are no adverse effects.

Other Security Measures

In addition to SET, MasterCard has implemented CVC2 (Card Validation Code) verification. The CVC2 code consists of a three-digit value that is uniquely derived for each account, and it is printed rather than embossed on the signature panel of all MasterCard cards. In a card-not-present environment, such as a telephone order, CVC2 lets a merchant verify that the cardholder does have the card in his or her possession. MasterCard has also contributed to a fund for the National Consumers League for the launch of the Internet Fraud Watch. This is a program for monitoring, reporting, and preventing online fraud. It is designed to assist law-enforcement agencies in gathering complaints about online fraud. Consumers can access the Internet Fraud Watch Web site at http://www.mastercard.com/shoponline/set/fraudwatch.html.

Finally, let's look at CyberCash's digital payment system strategy.

CYBERCASH

Starting out in August 1994, its founders set for CyberCash the goal of working with financial institutions and merchants to provide an accessible and acceptable payment system for the Internet. CyberCash offers a secure conduit to deliver payments between customers, merchants, and banks. CyberCash has been described as the Federal Express of the Internet payment business, since it offers safe, efficient, and inexpensive delivery of payments across the Internet—practically instantaneously.

CyberCash makes available the software and services needed to exchange payments securely across the Internet with its Secure Internet Payment Service. Using a procedure that incorporates encryption and digital signatures, CyberCash gives consumers a "digital wallet," (the CyberCash Wallet) and merchants a conduit to Internet payment processing through their own banks. Customers are able to authorize payments out of their digital wallets. The payments are signed, encrypted, and then sent through the merchant back to CyberCash, which in turn passes the transaction to the merchant's bank for processing. The digital wallet initially supported only credit cards, but now supports digital cash transfers for small dollar amounts for products and services that are too inexpensive to justify using a credit card.

CyberCash makes its software available at no charge, both for the client and the server applications. Neither the customer nor the merchant is charged directly for transactions: CyberCash charges participating banks and credit card processors fees similar to those charged by traditional methods. These fees are covered by the banks' or processors' standard service charges to merchants.

THE CYBERCASH MODEL

Very simply, CyberCash acts as a conduit for transactions among the Internet, merchants, consumers, and banking networks. Merchants wishing to use CyberCash to securely process credit card transactions must establish a merchant account with a bank offering CyberCash to its merchants, and modify their servers to include the CyberCash PAY button. Customers wishing to use CyberCash have several options for obtaining the client software. Customers can initialize their CyberCash identity by linking at least one credit card or checking account to the service—there is no charge to consumers for this service.

CyberCash client software is available from several sources, including CyberCash's World Wide Web site; some Internet browser software programs will include the CyberCash wallet, and select banks have begun offering CyberCash client software to their customers.

When the customer completes a purchase and begins a CyberCash transaction by clicking the CyberCash PAY button of a merchant's World Wide Web site, the merchant receives information about the customer's order, as well as an encrypted message from the customer's CyberCash client. The encrypted data includes the customer's payment information. The merchant's CyberCash software verifies that neither the order nor the encrypted payment information has been modified during transmission, and then forwards the encrypted message to CyberCash.

Once CyberCash receives the encrypted payment message and verifies that no modifications have been made to it in transit, CyberCash determines if the transaction is a CyberCash credit-card-based transaction or CyberCoin transaction. With CyberCash (credit card) transactions, CyberCash decrypts that message, reformats it, and forwards it to the merchant's designated bank or credit card processor. The bank or processor responds almost immediately to CyberCash, which in turn forwards the approval (or refusal) to the merchant's server. Once the merchant's server receives approval, it notifies the customer. The whole process, from the customer initiating the payment to getting approval, takes less than 17 seconds.

With CyberCash, the wallet is used to manage your credit cards. In a sense, the CyberCash process electronically presents your credit card payment to the merchant in the process described previously, just like the last time you physically pulled the card out of your wallet and presented it to a merchant.

With CyberCoin, your electronic wallet essentially holds digital money, which can be added to your wallet using the credit card used for other transactions or your checking account, which can be linked to your wallet. Once one of these accounts is linked to your wallet, you can request dollars to be transferred to your CyberCoin wallet in US$20 increments.

Your CyberCoin money is placed into an account at CyberCash, and as you make CyberCoin transactions, money is pulled from your wallet and sent to the CyberCoin merchant's wallet.

The CyberCash client software manages all of this for the consumer, including setting up an identity, or CyberCash Persona, linking credit cards to that persona, and keeping track of CyberCash transactions through a transaction log. In addition, the software includes other administrative and configuration options for customizing and managing the CyberCash service, for backing up the CyberCash persona information, and for downloading the latest version of the client.

The CyberCash merchant server must be properly set up before the merchant can accept CyberCash transactions. This process includes installing the CyberCash software and embedding the CyberCash PAY button into the ordering pages on the World Wide Web server. Once tests have been successfully completed, the merchant can begin accepting CyberCash. If the merchant's bank is already a participant, the entire process can be completed in a few days; if the merchant's bank is new to CyberCash, the process may take a couple of weeks to a month.

CYBERCASH SECURITY CONSIDERATIONS

CyberCash uses a combination of RSA public key and DES secret key technologies to protect and guarantee data through encryption and digital signatures. The CyberCash software has been approved for export from the United States, even though it employs a very strong version, using 768-bit RSADSI keys. This high level of encryption is intended to protect the sensitive portions of commercial transactions.

The CyberCash software uses the strongest encryption approved so far by the U.S. Government for worldwide use. It uses full 768-bit RSA as well as 56-bit DES encryption of messages. All transactions are authenticated with MD5 (a message digest procedure) and RSA digital signatures.

Customer Protection

With the use of digital signatures and encryption, CyberCash is able to keep transmissions secure for all practical purposes, as discussed in Chapter 2, "Security Technologies." It can be asserted that CyberCash is free from any danger of hackers intercepting or modifying transmissions between the merchant and the customer, or between the merchant and CyberCash. However, since the customer must provide his or her own password, attacks on individual accounts are possible, just as they are in any system that uses passwords for access. This exposure is limited to the systems on which the customer has installed the CyberCash client software—sensitive customer information is not stored on servers from which the customer has made purchases.

USING CYBERCASH

CyberCash offers significant advantages to both the customer and the merchant. For the customer, there is no need to register each time he or she first shops with a merchant, mall, or payment system. Unlike secure Web browser/Web server combinations, CyberCash does not require the customer to reenter credit card information for transmission to the merchant. In addition, the customer does not have to worry about possible security issues with the merchant's own server, since the payment information is not decrypted until it arrives at the CyberCash payment server.

The CyberCash-enabled merchant gets the benefit of offering a convenient payment method to customers, without limiting the customers' choice of Internet browser. The merchant can install CyberCash on any existing World Wide Web server system without having to purchase a new server program. In addition, CyberCash transaction approvals are virtually instantaneous.

CyberCash Availability

Starting with a single participating bank, Wells Fargo & Co. in 1995, CyberCash has lengthened its list of banks to several dozen. CyberCash is also working directly with third-party services and expects to serve several hundred banks.

The number of merchants offering CyberCash is also growing. During its first few months of operation, only a handful of places would accept CyberCash, but that is changing rapidly. With the addition of the CyberCoin feature, merchants of digital information such as software, images, and computer-based information that are traditionally smaller items are able to offer their products online. CyberCoin is offered primarily for items that sell for less than $10 where using a credit card would not make sense for the merchant or shopper. The term *micropayment* is often used to describe CyberCoin transactions.

CYBERCASH CLIENT APPLICATION

Before you can use CyberCash, you must install and configure the CyberCash Client application. This program is actually an Internet application, capable of communicating with merchants and with CyberCash over your TCP/IP connection to the Internet. This is the piece of software that manages your "electronic wallet," keeping track of your credit cards, electronic cash, and tracking transactions. It also applies all the cryptographic tools necessary to encrypt transaction information and transmit it securely.

Getting the Software

CyberCash distributes its client software in several ways. It has been bundled with Internet startup kits and browser software. Some large banks now provide back-end support for CyberCash merchants, and distribute the CyberCash client for consumers. You can find the CyberCash client on the accompanying CD-ROM, or you can download the software from the CyberCash World Wide Web site at:

> http://www.cybercash.com

Once the software is installed, consumers can use the CyberCash PAY buttons that participating merchants include in their World Wide Web documents to pay for selected items.

Installing the Software

The Windows version of the Client Application is a single, compressed, and self-extracting program: executing the program causes it to uncompress the component files. One of these files is a setup program that takes the customer through the process of installing and initializing the software.

Running the setup program should be routine to anyone who has installed software before. Under Windows, the program first asks the user where to install the CyberCash client: The default is the directory C:\CYBER. The files are then copied to the indicated directory.

Next, the CyberCash application offers to search the system for Internet browsers so it can add CyberCash functionality to them. At the start of the process, the user is cautioned to exit any Internet browser that may be running on the desktop, since the following lines are added to the browser INI file:

```
[Viewers]
Type0=application/x-cybercash
application/x-cybercash=C:\Cyber\cyber.exe
Type1=application/cybercash
application/cybercash=C:\Cyber\cyber.exe
[Suffixes]
application/x-cybercash=cym
application/cybercash=cym
```

Code snippets are subject to change without notice by the vendor or organization providing them. The preceding code snippets are included here for demonstration purposes only.

These lines ensure that when the customer is browsing a CyberCash-enabled Web page, the browser will do the right thing whenever a Cyber-Cash PAY button is clicked. When the customer clicks the CyberCash PAY button, the browser needs to be able to interpret the data that will be sent from the server. It also needs to be aware that the data must be handled by calling up the CyberCash application. The original INI file is saved with the file extension CYB.

Running the Software for the First Time

Keeping with the popular trend among software vendors of using wizards—organized programs within a program—CyberCash includes several wizards to walk users through the installation process.

The first wizard presented is the Welcome wizard, which helps you indicate whether the network you are using to connect to the Internet has a proxy-based server. A proxy-based server can be several things, but is traditionally a firewall. Most Internet service providers do not use proxy-based servers, and most large corporate networks should. If you have questions, contact your ISP or system administrator. The second question is whether you are creating your first wallet, or wish to reinstall a previously established wallet.

At this point, the software will connect to the CyberCash administration server via the Internet and will start the New Wallet wizard, which will let you create your persona and attach at least one credit card to your wallet.

Figure 6.2 shows the screen where you can request a wallet ID (i.e., name) and tell CyberCash what your e-mail address is.[6]

The next two screens prompt you to enter and confirm both a password for use when using the wallet and a verification ID you can supply now so that CyberCash customer service employees can confirm who you are should you need to call for assistance. With other products and services, your mother's maiden name is commonly used as a verification ID. The next screen prompts you for the currency you would like with your wallet. At the time this edition of the book was written, despite plans to add others, only the U.S. dollar is supported with the CyberCash wallet. Figure 6.3 shows you a summary screen of your selections at this point in the process and offers you a chance to make any changes.

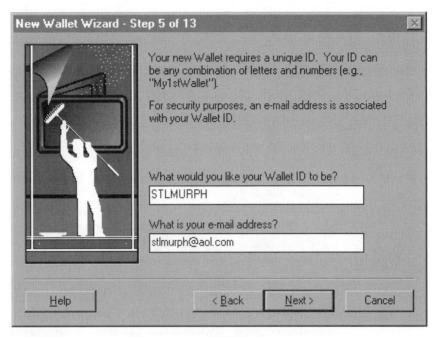

FIGURE 6.2   New Wallet setup screen 5.

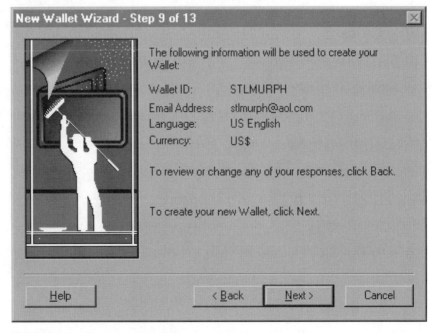

FIGURE 6.3   Summary screen.

FIGURE 6.4 Key generation screen.

The next thing you will see is a CyberCash screen informing you that the Security keys are being generated (Figure 6.4). Once the keys are established, they will be used to encrypt your data and send it off to CyberCash.

CyberCash will respond with a screen similar to Figure 6.5, confirming that your information has been received and what your new wallet ID is.

There are two more tasks before completing the new wallet process. First, CyberCash allows for a confirmation message with all transactions. If you are going to make a lot of small transactions and do not want to be bothered with confirmations below a certain transaction total, you

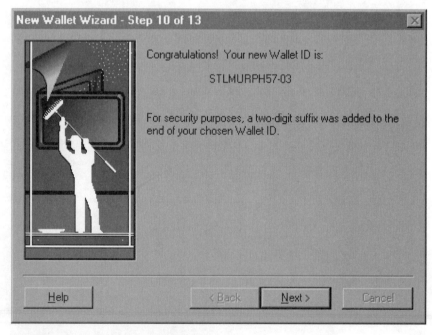

FIGURE 6.5 New Wallet confirmation.

can set that threshold as well. Of course, all transactions appear in the transaction log.

The final task with this first wizard is to make a backup of your Cyber-Cash persona information (Figure 6.6). This is very important in case you have a computer failure and cannot retrieve the keys and information in your digital wallet.

Linking Payment Information

Now that you have established your account or persona with CyberCash and your wallet is in place, the next thing to do is attach a credit card and/or a checking account to pay for the goods you purchase online.

With the credit card you can pay for goods paid for with CyberCash and add money to your CyberCoin wallet. You can also add money to your CyberCoin wallet by linking a checking account to your CyberCash persona.

Attaching a credit card or checking account to your CyberCash persona is very easy. The process of adding the credit card begins with the Add Credit Card wizard (Figure 6.7).

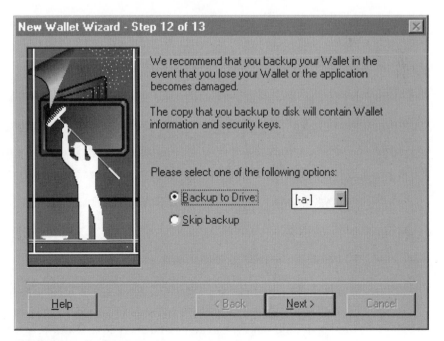

FIGURE 6.6 Backup screen.

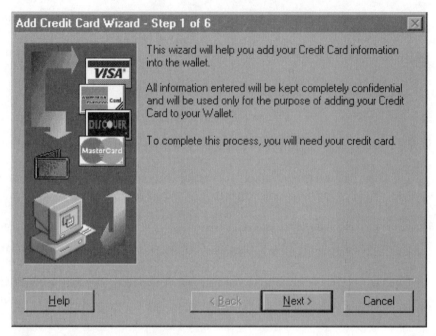

FIGURE 6.7 Add Credit Card screen 1 of 6.

The next step is to name the credit card to be used (Figure 6.8) and enter your credit card billing information as it appears on your monthly credit card statement (Figure 6.9).

In Figures 6.10 and 6.11, we enter the actual credit card number and expiration date.

When the process of adding the credit card to your wallet is complete, CyberCash will reply with a confirmation, and you will be ready to use the service at any merchant offering CyberCash as a payment mechanism.

CyberCoin

With your wallet established, and at least one credit card attached to it, you can also set up the CyberCoin portion of your wallet by simply adding money. The process begins with Figure 6.12.

The next step is to choose the amount of money you want to place in your CyberCoin wallet. Transfers can occur in US$20 increments (Figure 6.13).

In Figure 6.14, you can choose either credit card or checking account as the source for the money.

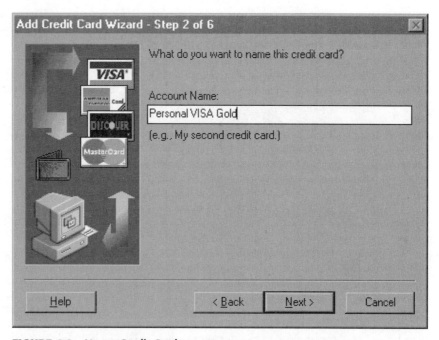

FIGURE 6.8 Name Credit Card screen.

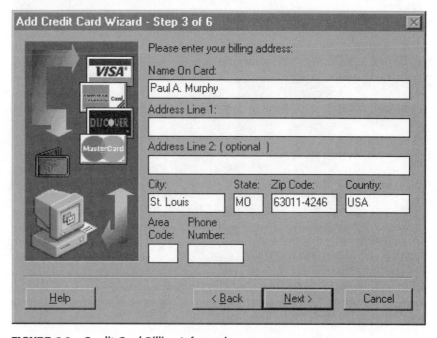

FIGURE 6.9 Credit Card Billing Information screen.

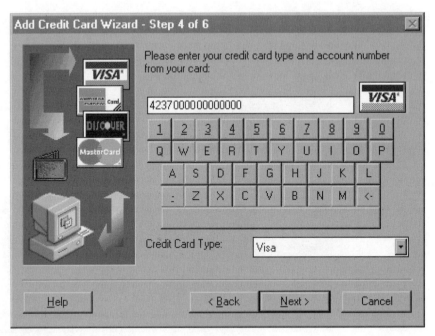

FIGURE 6.10 Credit Card Number Entry screen.

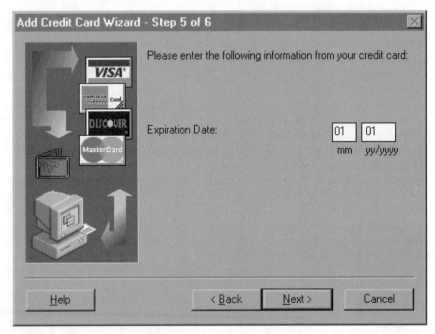

FIGURE 6.11 Credit Card Expiration Date Entry screen.

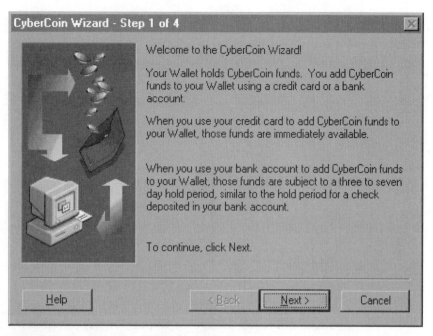

FIGURE 6.12   CyberCoin Wizard screen 1.

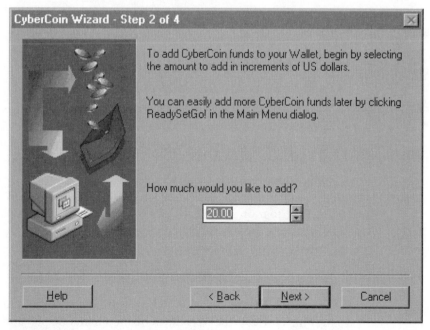

FIGURE 6.13   CyberCoin Wizard screen 2.

FIGURE 6.14   CyberCoin Wizard screen 3.

You finally see a confirmation screen (Figure 6.15) where you double-check your request and then press FINISH.

Configuration and Administration

The CyberCash client application allows the user to manage credit card information and links to add new cards or remove old ones. Administration functions include everything from modifying persona information, to backing up or restoring CyberCash data, to getting the latest version of the application. Figure 6.16 shows the choices available.

More important, the client keeps track of transactions in a transaction log. Information about each transaction is maintained in a log and can be printed or canceled if desired. The transaction log in Figure 6.17 simply shows a record of linking credit cards to a persona.

Making a Purchase

CyberCash customers can purchase products over the Internet by browsing the World Wide Web sites of merchants displaying the CyberCash logo. CyberCash merchants range from Virtual Vineyards (the first Cyber-

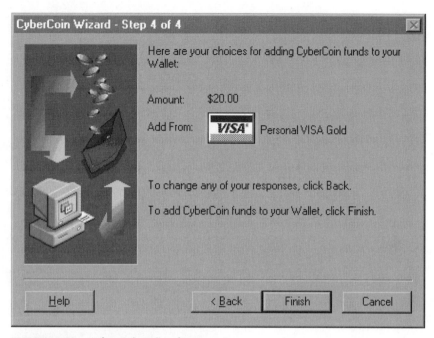

FIGURE 6.15 CyberCoin Wizard screen 4.

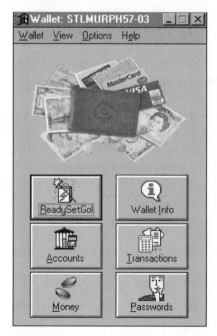

FIGURE 6.16 The CyberCash Client application administration panel.

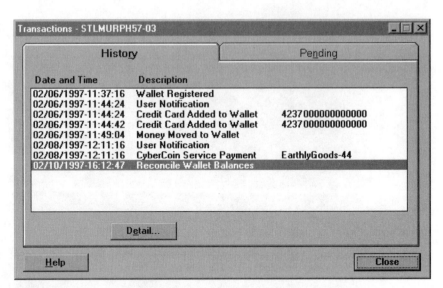

FIGURE 6.17 A CyberCash Client application transaction log.

Cash merchant), offering premium wines and food, to alternative music vendors, and scores of companies in between.

The customer selects items for purchase, proceeds to the merchant's payment page, which is frequently referred to as the "shopping cart," and clicks the CyberCash PAY button. This initiates a transmission of information about the transaction from the merchant's server to the customer's system. The CyberCash Client application is started. It responds by displaying a payment request summary, including an order number, the merchant's CyberCash ID, and the purchase amount, as shown in Figure 6.18. The customer can also choose the payment method, which in Figure 6.18 is a VISA card.

The customer at this point can still decline the sale by clicking CANCEL or proceed with the transaction by pressing PAY. At this moment, the transaction occurs and can take up to 17 seconds for an authorization. As is clear from the example, this panel displays an order number, as well as the credit cards that may be accepted for the order. Note that only accepted cards are displayed.

When the customer chooses to continue, the CyberCash application software puts together all the information received from the merchant (price, credit cards accepted) with the customer's payment information, and the transaction occurs.

FIGURE 6.18 CyberCash payment request summary.

Once a credit card is chosen, the software encrypts and signs that information and sends it on to the merchant.

The merchant receives a signed message indicating what products are to be purchased, as well as an encrypted and signed copy of the payment information. Both are verified, and the (still-encrypted) payment information is forwarded to the CyberCash payment server. At that point, the process of credit card authorization is almost the same as if the customer were presenting the credit card at a shop: The same information is sent on to the bank by CyberCash, and the merchant receives an authorization within seconds. As shown in Figure 6.19, successful completion of the transaction is reported back to the client, with a transaction summary. Besides the obvious difference that the transaction between customer and merchant takes place entirely online, another important difference to note is that the merchant does not have access to the customer's actual credit card account information.

FIGURE 6.19 Transaction authorization notification from the CyberCash Secure Internet Payment Service includes purchase and payment summary information.

SELLING THROUGH CYBERCASH

Although the CyberCash client application is quite simple to install and use, even for early implementers, the first CyberCash merchants did not have it quite as easy. The first version of the CyberCash merchant server software was for UNIX systems only. Current releases include support for Solaris, BSDI, SGI Irix, NT, SunOS, Digital UNIX, SCO, and Linux. The CyberCash World Wide Web site is very complete with merchant software and installation information.

CyberCash is supporting the VIP (Value-added Integration Provider) program, which brings together prospective merchants with companies that have already developed sites with CyberCash functionality and are offering related services to other merchants. Another option for merchants is to purchase an integrated package from one of the systems integrators working with CyberCash to include CyberCash functionality in a ready-to-use, integrated server.

Merchants setting up to accept CyberCash payments have three general tasks:

- Open an account with a bank offering CyberCash services
- Modify server home pages to include the CyberCash PAY button
- Install the related CyberCash software on the server

CyberCash Merchant Code

The merchant code functions in support of both shopping and administration. This code is invoked only when a customer makes a purchase decision. When the customer initiates the purchase payment process, the merchant code responds by sending an encrypted message to the customer's system to begin. The process, as described earlier, moves information between the customer, the merchant, and the CyberCash payment server.

The merchant software includes administrative functions, allowing merchants do the following:

- Check on an order database to review orders
- Process supporting transactions such as voids, credits, and authorizations
- Perform merchant-originated transactions, as when the merchant has received a telephone order

Other parts of the software perform the cryptographic functions necessary for encryption, decryption, digital signatures, and verification. Also included are information files, test software, a database program that can log orders, and sample merchant shopping pages.

The process of getting a merchant site online with CyberCash can take as little as a few days if the merchant's bank is already set up to provide CyberCash services. As the merchant software becomes available for more platforms, the process could become even simpler.

OTHER CYBERCASH PRODUCTS

CyberCash is uniquely positioned as a vendor that offers a complete range of products for both the physical world and the virtual world. To meet the broad needs of their customers, their solutions are offered as both software and services.

Payment Services and Processes for Online Business

The following are payment services for online business:

- CashRegister
- FraudPatrol
- Affiliate Marketing
- PayNow

CashRegister

CashRegister is a platform that allows merchants to accept payments over the Internet with a minimum of software. Through remote secure interactions with the CashRegister server, a merchant can process credit cards through the merchant's bank of choice.

FraudPatrol

FraudPatrol provides complete credit card fraud detection to minimize costs associated with chargebacks and lost goods. Once a subscriber to the service defines a level of fraud detection, the FraudPatrol system evaluates all e-commerce transactions for that subscriber and authorizes only those that meet an acceptable level of risk—automatically, and in real time. The service uses a combination of consumer data, merchant data, and fraud trend information that is constantly updated. These factors are entered into a neural network that identifies and adapts to new fraud trends.

Affiliate Marketing

Affiliate Marketing is a program where merchants gain access to more than 130,000 Web sites that promote their products and services for commissions. Offered in partnership with Commission Junction, this service allows merchants to increase revenues, but they pay commissions only when a sale is made.

PayNow

With the Cybercash model, we have seen how to establish a digital wallet or secure channel for sending instructions to a third party and securely send funds to a merchant at the time of a sale. We have also seen a way to securely designate a checking account and/or a credit card as the source of the money sent on our behalf.

So, what else can we do with this technology? That is exactly what the folks at CyberCash were thinking when they created PayNow, an electronic bill-payment process.

On the consumer side of the electronic commerce equation, online banking and bill payment for consumers is a growing trend in North America. The online bill payment process begins with the creation of a relationship between a consumer, or a business for that matter, and a financial institution (e.g., bank, S&L, credit union) for the purpose of paying bills.

With online banking, you can use either your computer or telephone to instruct the bank to send money to just about anyone you would normally pay with a check, after a relatively painless enrollment and setup process. The benefit for the consumer is convenience, as there are no checks to buy or write, no postage to pay, and greater control over when your payments are processed.

The PayNow concept is that once you have established your relationship with CyberCash and have attached a checking account to your CyberCash wallet, there is no reason why CyberCash can't be used to execute an electronic payment to a participating PayNow merchant. For example, suppose your electric company signs up for this program and installs the CyberCash merchant server on the company Web site. Either through the traditional bill you would receive in the mail or through online bill presentment (a financial e-mail, if you will), you make your payment with your CyberCash wallet instead of a traditional check.

Your payment would be protected with all of the software-based encryption, which is at the heart of the CyberCash wallet, to complete the transaction.

The PayNow Secure Electronic Check Service reduces costs for companies like the electric company by eliminating paper check processing costs. You will enjoy lower mailing fees, and PayNow increases the accuracy of bill remittance.

For the current or future online merchant, CyberCash now offers a complete online payment suite of digital cash (CyberCoin), use of existing credit cards (CyberCash), and now secure checks (PayNow).

As the third edition of this book goes to press, the process continues to hold great potential and is a great example of several technologies coming together to create new applications.

Payment Software for Online Business: WebAuthorize

WebAuthorize is a software product designed for Enterprise and Hosting environments. It is useful for CSPs and ISPs who want to offer payment processing to their customers.

Payment Software for Physical Stores

Finally, the following are payment software for physical stores:

- ICVERIFY
- PCAuthorize
- MacAuthorize

ICVERIFY

ICVERIFY is a credit authorization product for use in point-of-sale environments, such as retail stores, mail order companies, and call centers. Using a personal computer (PC) or PC-based electronic cash register (ECR), ICVERIFY authorizes and automatically captures deposits for all major credit cards, including ATM/debit cards, corporate purchase cards, and private label cards. Check processing is also supported.

PCAuthorize

PCAuthorize is a stand-alone application that integrates credit authorization and electronic deposit into your sales system. It is ideal for retailers, mail-order houses, or merchants who don't want the additional expense of stand-alone terminals.

MacAuthorize

MacAuthorize is the software product equivalent of PCAuthorize for Macintosh systems. Transactions are stored in batches on the Macintosh and may be reviewed, printed, imported, exported, and saved back as far as your disk will hold. Import, export, allow batch processing and AppleEvents/AppleScript provides real-time authorization from your favorite database application.

SUMMING UP THE CYBERCASH SYSTEM

CyberCash offers some real values to the consumer:

- It keeps payment information private, even from the merchant.
- It offers a convenient electronic wallet to store payment information, so the information need not be reentered every time a purchase is made.
- It maintains a transaction log to handle, track, and document every transaction.

Likewise, CyberCash is attractive to merchants:

- There is no extra charge for using CyberCash.
- It is a convenience for customers who may prefer not to have to reenter credit card numbers on the Internet.
- It offers merchants useful tools for tracking and transacting business on the Internet.
- It has been widely supported by banks and credit card companies.

Most important, CyberCash is committed to complying with the VISA/MasterCard standards for credit card transactions across the Internet. CyberCash is committed to providing a secure, simple, and accepted solution for Internet commerce.

END NOTES

[1] NetConcept, 3600 S. Harbor Blvd., #513, Oxnard, CA 93035, 2000.
[2] Ibid.
[3] MasterCard International, Inc., Global Headquarters, 2000 Purchase Street, Purchase, NY 10577, 2000.
[4] Ibid.
[5] Ibid.
[6] Reprinted with permission from CyberCash, Inc., © 2000, Corporate Headquarters, 2100 Reston Parkway, Reston, VA 20191.

7 Online Commerce Environments

He who pays the piper calls the tune.

—Traditional Proverb

Since the online merchant pays the Internet marketing piper, the merchant gets to call the electronic commerce tune. The merchant decides what products to offer online, how those products will be described and depicted, and what options for payment are available to customers.

An online commerce environment is differentiated from an electronic payment system most notably by the use of a secure server. The secure server provides a secure channel between customer and merchant over which business can be securely and reliably transacted. The merchant may also choose to accept other types of electronic payment, as well as offer support for mail orders and telephone orders. However, by setting up a secure World Wide Web server, the merchant makes it possible for anyone with a credit card to place an order immediately and directly over an Internet link.

In a sense, the online commerce environment is an invention of the industry, offering a method of packaging all the products necessary to sell online. Rather than starting and stopping at the point of taking an order in exchange for payment information, the online commerce environment can include much more. Online commerce integrators may be able to supply the hardware, software, and network connection for the merchant's World Wide Web server, the labor and programming involved in creating the digital storefront, the payment and settlement mechanisms, and programming to link online transactions with existing organizational systems.

This chapter examines some secure World Wide Web browser and server offerings.

One word describes the electronic commerce server market circa 2000: *competition.*

To begin with, there is tremendous competition for Internet servers in general. Regardless of the need for secure transactions, companies such as Microsoft and Netscape (now part of AOL) are developing and supporting entire categories of new software products and development tools. All share the same goal of helping companies and individuals place their information on a computer accessible by the Internet.

In addition to offering Internet browser software, they offer Internet server software, including secure servers, and a host of development tools that enable software developers to create end-user applications.

Although they do not offer an Internet browser software program, Open Market is an example of the many companies offering a line of Internet commerce products, including a secure World Wide Web server and other supplemental tools and services.

This chapter examines the secure server and browser offerings from Netscape Communications and Microsoft and looks at the Open Market softgoods transaction model to demonstrate how a commercial environment can handle online transactions.

SERVERS AND COMMERCIAL ENVIRONMENTS

Although it is the centerpiece of an online commercial environment, the secure World Wide Web server cannot stand alone. It must be implemented on a secure and reliable hardware platform and connected to the Internet securely and reliably, and orders must be processed securely and reliably once the merchant receives them. However, without a secure server, secure transactions would require some other secured mechanism, either electronic payment systems like CyberCash (Chapter 6, "Electronic Payment Systems") or digital money (Chapter 8, "Digital Currencies").

Choosing Payment Methods

Merchants have traditionally allowed their customers to use a variety of payment methods: cash, credit card, personal check, travelers' check, or store credit are all common. Limiting customers to one or two payment methods would likely cost a merchant some business. The same goes for the online shop: Limiting shoppers to a single method will also limit the number of sales possible online.

Many online merchants offer at least a telephone number to call in an order, and a fax number or postal address where customers can send a copy of an order form. Those willing to accept orders online may be using one or more payment systems as well as a secure server. This gives the customer a range of options: offline ordering by telephone, fax, or mail; online ordering with a payment system; or online ordering through the secure channel provided by a secure server.

The advantage of a secure server is that it serves the casual Internet consumer who has a new World Wide Web browser and a credit card but has never set up to use any electronic payment or digital money system. Since software publishers are continuing to incorporate SSL, S-HTTP, and other secure protocols (Chapter 4, "Protocols for the Public Transport of Private Information") into their World Wide Web browser products, the number of secure servers supporting those protocols is also growing.

At the same time, merchants are free to offer other payment methods: Electronic payment systems or digital money systems generally operate in any transmission medium. The result is that a merchant can offer the simplest payment method, entering credit card information directly into a form maintained on a secure server, and still allow the more serious Internet consumer to do business wielding an electronic wallet.

Server Market Orientation

World Wide Web server software comes in all shapes and sizes, particularly since any server product must conform to a well-known set of rules—HTTP.

Web browsers that support S-HTTP can be used with servers that support S-HTTP to produce a secure channel; browsers and servers that support SSL can also produce a secure channel. Microsoft and Netscape have incorporated roughly equivalent support for S-HTTP and SSL into their browsers. If you want to conduct secure business with the vast majority of Web-browser users on the Internet, your server must implement SSL.

Since these two browsers are the current de facto standard for the Web browser market, and are so widely available, they outnumber other browsers in general use.

Other World Wide Web servers support S-HTTP, or secure commercial transactions by implementing PGP (Pretty Good Privacy, an implementation of public key encryption and digital signature technology) between consumer and merchant, but they are not as compelling to merchants because they are not perceived as being as widely and broadly implemented either in servers or in browsers.

NETSCAPE

With an incredibly successful initial public offering in the summer of 1995, Netscape's shares rocketed from an original estimated offering price of $13 for 3.5 million shares to an actual offering price of $28 for 5 million shares. On the first day of trading, the shares opened at over $70, and finally settled down to the mid-50s.

Netscape's attractions include its highly acclaimed Netscape 6 or higher World Wide Web browser, and its history in the commerce server area.

Netscape has organized its commerce server strategy around three basic components: Netscape Client Products, the Netscape Commerce Platform, and Netscape Commercial Applications. These three elements piece together a commerce model, including everything needed to begin an Internet commerce site. This model leaves the door open for new technologies in Internet commerce from Netscape and other Internet vendors.

The Netscape Client Products include the Netscape 6 or higher Client Products, also referred to as the *browsers*. To develop commercial Web sites, Netscape offers the Netscape Commerce Platform, a set of servers. This includes a family of integrated software applications that enable you to bring up a full-scale commerce site quickly. These applications can be used individually or together to create different online businesses. The two basic applications systems include the Netscape Publishing System and the Netscape Merchant System.

By distributing its browser over the Internet at no charge for evaluation or educational purposes, Netscape helped ensure its wide distribution. Server products are also available for a limited evaluation period, which also helps to secure market share. Netscape delivers to merchants shopping for a World Wide Web server a broad installed base of potential customers using browsers that support the SSL security protocol.

Netscape produced SSL, a method of obtaining a secure channel between client and server, at a time when others were working on a different solution: S-HTTP. Rather than wait for customers and merchants to start installing S-HTTP servers and clients, Netscape implemented SSL in its products and made them widely and easily available.

Netscape's Approach to Building Business

Netscape's approach to developing its business as an Internet commerce environment provider has so far proven successful: Actively put client and server applications into the hands of online consumers and merchants, and actively develop standards and contribute them to the industry. The Netscape browser is easily accessible from Netscape's Web site, as is a fully functional evaluation version of their secure server. This ensures that Netscape's products are widely distributed and installed—which makes the final sale that much more likely.

As mentioned before, by making public its security protocol specifications, Netscape guarantees that anyone can create a browser that will be compatible with the Netscape secure servers. It also guarantees that anyone can create a server that will be compatible with Netscape secure browsers—and many have. Netscape retains a head start in developing software, while allowing potential buyers the freedom to choose other products. Making the protocols public and allowing other software developers to produce Netscape-compatible browsers and servers has been good for Netscape and the industry in general.

Netscape has generated sufficient interest in its products for individual users to make its name synonymous with World Wide Web browsers. At the same time, Netscape has defined the protocols needed to do business with all the people who use the Netscape browser, so merchants looking for a way to sell to them will naturally consider Netscape, too.

The next section examines the Netscape product line, looking first at the features, particularly security and commerce options, of the Netscape 6 or higher World Wide Web browser. The features and use of the Netscape Commerce Server are discussed next, followed by an overview of some of Netscape's other Internet products.

NETSCAPE PRODUCT LINE

This section looks at the Netscape 6 or higher browser, particularly at the way it implements secure commercial transactions, and briefly describes the Netscape Commerce Server, again focusing on secure commercial transactions.

A great source for ongoing information on Netscape is to frequently visit its World Wide Web site:

http://home.netscape.com/

Netscape Browser Update

The Netscape 6 browser combines Netscape Communicator and Netscape Navigator with a suite of Internet tools for high-performance Internet mail, Web page creation, and instant messaging. If you are using an older version of Netscape Navigator or Netscape Communicator (version 4.05 or earlier), you may wish to update your Netscape browser to ensure a continued smooth experience when conducting secure online transactions. The current version of Netscape Communicator (4.7 or higher) is free via download, or you can order it on CD-ROM. Again, if you use Netscape versions 4.06, 4.07, 4.08, 4.51, 4.6, 4.61, or the current version (4.7 or higher), you do not need to upgrade.

Netscape Browsers

To recap the discussion from Chapter 3, "Electronic Payment Methods," a World Wide Web browser must be able to send requests for documents and services residing on World Wide Web servers, and interpret and display those documents appropriately. As discussed earlier, the most basic Web browser must be able to handle three protocols:

- **Uniform Resource Locator (URL)**–This is the format defining a syntax for pointing at Internet and World Wide Web resources. Most URLs point at resources with three parts: the scheme or protocol (for example, HTTP or FTP), the server offering the resource (an Internet host name, or less often an Internet Protocol numerical address), and the resource itself (often a specific file, or simply the root of the specified Web server).
- **Hypertext Transfer Protocol (HTTP)**–This protocol defines the interaction between Web browser and server. Based on the protocols that define electronic mail, it basically defines a set of queries and responses between the browser (client) and the server. The client makes a connection and requests a document or resource; the server responds either by sending the requested resource or by sending an error message indicating why the resource is not available.
- **Hypertext Markup Language (HTML)**–This protocol defines the way in which Web documents are expected to display; HTML consists of tags that are used to define different functional parts of the resource. The browser must be able to interpret the different tags in an appropriate way and then display the resource to reflect the

different tags' values: A block of text defined as a paragraph is displayed as a paragraph using the default text display font, and a block of text defined as a heading is displayed using the font defined for use as a heading.

The Netscape 6 (or higher) browser (which consists of Netscape Communicator and Navigator) fulfills all of the preceding functions, just as any other World Wide Web browser does.

In addition to the previously explained features, Netscape 6 also supports numerous software add-ons for everything from spell-checking your e-mail, to running small applications called *applets*, to playing music files from the Internet. New add-ons are being introduced all the time, and those already in distribution are undergoing constant development and updates. Properly describing some add-ons can fill an entire book and is outside the scope of this one. The use of online information resources such as newsgroups and mailing lists is one of the best ways to learn more and stay current in this changing business.

Netscape 6's (or higher) most important value-added feature, however, is the ability to support secure transactions with SSL encryption of sensitive information. More important to users, securing the transmission of sensitive information is done automatically, with the browser being alerted to the need for SSL by a URL with the scheme type HTTPS instead of HTTP. The browser and the server negotiate keys for secure transmissions, without involving the user.

Getting Netscape 6 Browser

The Netscape 6 or higher browser software is available through Netscape's own World Wide Web server and at various other FTP sites on the Internet. Although the product is increasingly available as a shrink-wrapped software package from retailers and as software preloaded when you purchase a new computer, the entire group of browser software is available for sale online (see the sidebar, "Netscape 6 and Beyond").[1]

Getting Netscape Communicator

Netscape also supports a program to distribute the software through Web sites run by Netscape server products, called "Netscape Now." Netscape servers can support special features such as tables, backgrounds, and dynamic documents (for graphics that may change over time, like weather maps), but these may only be viewed with the Netscape browser (or with some other browser that supports Netscape's extensions).

Netscape 6 and Beyond

The Internet has evolved at an extraordinary pace, and browsing software has brought easy information access to millions of people. While early browsers revolutionized the Internet, browsers have grown in size and complexity with every release and have failed to implement Web standards consistently, thereby holding back the development of richer Web applications and content.

Netscape is fulfilling its promise to deliver a new browser that is small in size, leads the industry in standards compliance, and can run across a wide variety of platforms from traditional PC desktops to new computing devices. This new groundbreaking browser is Netscape 6.

Netscape 6 offers users unmatched convenience features and the ability to stay connected to important information, while offering users the flexibility to deeply customize the browser to fit their individual needs and personality. To deliver these benefits, Netscape 6 offers innovative functionality in these key areas:

- Small download size and speed
- Standards support
- My Sidebar
- Search
- Same-time messaging integrated with browsing and mail
- Themes

Small Download Size and Speed—Quickly Install the Internet Software You Want

Netscape 6 is a full-featured yet lean browser that bucks the trend in software bloat. Netscape 6 was developed from the ground up to be as small as possible but still provide a rich feature set. The result is a very powerful product that you can download quickly, even over a modem. For example, a small size for faster download allows:

- The Installer is less than a 300k download and allows you to customize your installation with just the components you want.
- The browser is only 7.5MB download, smaller than a comparable install of Internet Explorer.
- Typical installation is only 9.6MB, smaller than a comparable installation of Internet Explorer 5.

Best Standards Support from Desktop PCs to Home Appliances

As content developers take advantage of accepted Web standards, the result is a richer Internet for developers and consumers. The revolutionary Netscape Gecko Technologies, developed as an open source project, provide the basis for Netscape 6. With full support for XML, CSS level 1, and DOM (among others), a new class of rich Web applications is possible. Netscape also delivers support for rich Web content and applications across a variety of desktop platforms (such as Windows and MacOS), and across a new class of Web appliances that run on the Linux platform.

My Sidebar Keeps You Connected to What's Important

Located on the left side of the Netscape 6 interface, My Sidebar gives you a convenient place to keep track of the things that are important to you. Read the latest news, set up a custom stock portfolio, check your Buddy List for instant messaging, track auctions, or listen to music. With over 400 tabs available from Netscape and third parties, My Sidebar is your customized connection to the sites and people you care about. Hundreds of My Sidebar tabs give you the power to customize the Internet with:

- Over 400 Netscape tabs, including Stocks, News, Calendar, music and more!
- Instant Messaging Buddy List tab lets you keep track of your buddies and allows you to communicate with them in real time.
- Third-party tabs from CNN and other Web sites from around the world.
- Open architecture enables Web developers to easily create My Sidebar tabs and link them from their sites.

Same-Time Messaging Integrated throughout the Browser and Mail

Instant messaging is the third "killer app" on the Internet, after browsing and e-mail. Netscape 6 is the first Internet software suite to seamlessly combine browsing, e-mail, and instant messaging. You can now manage multiple e-mail accounts and communicate with friends who use the popular AOL Instant Messenger service (over 40 million users and growing)—all in an environment integrated with the Navigator browser. Integrated communication keeps you connected with:

- Multiple e-mail accounts, including Netscape Webmail and AOL e-mail accounts

- Integrated instant messaging with Buddy presence in My Sidebar and Mail messages
- Automatic collection of contact information from the people you communicate with in the Netscape 6 address book

Fully Customizable, Integrated Search

Netscape Navigator now includes a search field in the main toolbar. That means that at any time, from anywhere on the Web, you can type what you want and click "Search"—you no longer have to take the time to load a special search page or open a frame.

This search field doubles as the Web address field, so whether you have a Web address, an Internet keyword, or a word or phrase to search for, enter it in the search field and get what you want quickly. Search highlights include:

- The Netscape Search service (powered by the Google search engine) and Netscape Open Directory Project (search directory).
- Customizing with your choice of Search services.
- Search results are opened in My Sidebar, allowing you the flexibility to check multiple results without time-consuming return trips to a search engine.

Themes Add Personality to Your Browser

With Themes, you can personalize the look of your browser. Consumers can choose a custom appearance for their Netscape 6 software that best suits their personality. Web sites and businesses can create custom browsers to best suit their customers and allow them to:

- Customize the browser interface.
- Quickly and easily change the appearance of your browser.
- Any organization can create and distribute a custom browser.

The Netscape Now program allows merchants (or other Web site sponsors) to add a button to their Web documents that, when clicked, will allow the person browsing the document to retrieve a copy of Netscape Communicator. A special graphic button is made available to these sites that allows visitors to the site to download the latest version of the Netscape browser directly.

Clicking on the Netscape Now! button results in a sequence of screens that walk you through the process of selecting and downloading the software, first by indicating which Netscape product you want to download. Next, you are prompted to indicate which operating system you are using, your desired language, and what continent you are connecting from. This helps point you to the nearest FTP sites that store copies of the distribution file, which is a self-extracting executable file. Execute the file, and it uncompresses the Netscape Communicator program and related files. Finally, you are pointed to a text file that contains some installation instructions and program notes.

Using Netscape Communicator

The Netscape Communicator program works roughly like any other World Wide Web browser. Under Windows, it requires that Internet connectivity be established by some means, whether a LAN connection or a telephone (SLIP or PPP); see the glossary in Appendixes, connection through an ISP. Once connectivity has been established, starting Navigator initially will connect the user directly to the Netscape URL noted earlier.

Figure 7.1 shows Netscape Communicator version 4.75 (or higher) using the default configuration.[2] Starting from the top of the display, the user can manage the session using the pull-down menu bar options (File, Edit, View, Go, and so on). Directly below the menu bar is the toolbar, which includes icons that represent some of the most commonly used functions (Back and Forward to move between Web pages, return to the home page, and so on). The menu-bar and toolbar functions are described in greater detail later.

Beneath the toolbar is the Location field or window, containing the URL of the currently displayed resource. Just above the actual browser display is a series of directory buttons that connect to areas of the Netscape Web site that correspond to the directory button title ("What's Related" refers to items related to this Web site). Displaying the toolbar, location, and directory buttons are options, although the default is to display all of them.

Communicator users can browse the Internet immediately, simply by clicking links highlighted in the display on the home page. The user can also double-click the Location box, enter a new URL, and press the Enter key to connect. Clicking one of the directory buttons connects the user to the appropriate page on Netscape's Web site.

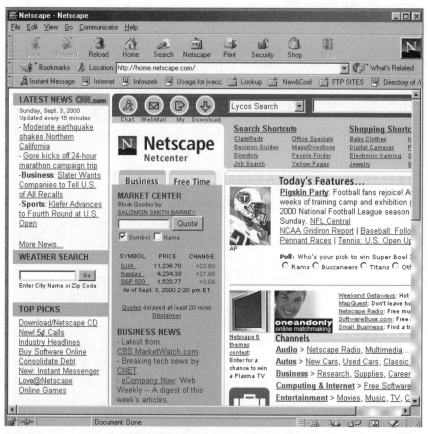

FIGURE 7.1 The Netscape Communicator browser display is, on the surface, much like other browsers, displaying World Wide Web resources with supporting functions.

Toolbar tools include the following:

- **Back**–For moving back to the previous Web document retrieve.
- **Forward**–For moving forward along a path already taken (this button is active only when a forward path is possible).
- **Reload**–To load a fresh copy of the current document (to reflect changes made between the time the document was originally loaded and the current time).
- **Home**–For returning to the default home page.
- **Search**–On the Internet.

- **Netscape**–Go to your personal start page.
- **Print**–For printing the current document.
- **Security**–Shows security information.
- **Shop**–Go to Shop@Netscape.
- **Stop**–For terminating a query in progress.

It is not unusual for users to be able to use any type of browser with little or no instruction or documentation. This is a tribute to browser designers, who have managed to make most World Wide Web functions sufficiently graphical and intuitive, and to the designers of World Wide Web pages who have made the documents themselves sufficiently intuitive and graphical by using HTML to create them.

There are quite a few more functions, accessible through the menu bar. Very briefly, they include functions listed under the File menu:

- **New**–Opens a new instance of the browser, so more than one Web document can be displayed at once.
- **Open Page**–Has the same function as the Open button (or as typing a URL into the Location box)—it retrieves the designated resource.
- **Save–As** Saves the current Web document as a file on the local computer.
- **Send Page**–Allows you to mail a Web page.
- **Edit Page**–Allows you to edit a Web page.
- **Offline**–Allows you to work offline and/or synchronize work between off and online.
- **Page Setup**–Lets you define how a Web resource is to appear if printed on the local computer.
- **Print Preview**–Lets you see how the Web resource would look if printed.
- **Print**–Sends the displayed Web resource to a printer.
- **Close**–Closes the current window; if only one browser window is open, it exits Navigator.
- **Exit**–Ends the program and closes all windows.

The Edit pull-down menu includes the same editing functions you would normally find in a Windows application, including Undo, Cut, Copy, Paste, and Find.

The View pull-down menu includes Reload, which does the same thing as the Reload toolbar button—gets a fresh copy of the resource. Refresh causes the browser to redraw the current resource, and the Page Source function causes the browser to display the actual HTML-tagged Web document in a window.

The Go pull-down menu includes many of the navigating functions of the toolbar tools; for example, Back, Forward, and Home. Also displayed under the Go pull-down menu is a list of the most recently viewed documents, listed by number (the current one is "0" and the one before that is "1") and document title.

The Bookmarks pull-down menu is used either to view the current list of bookmarks or to add to it. Help provides access to help documents using the browser interface.

This is hardly an exhaustive set of instructions for using Communicator, but it briefly covers most of its functions—except for those relating to security and secure commerce.

Securing Your Netscape Browser and Site for E-Commerce

The Web presents a unique set of security issues for online merchants (issues that were initially discussed in Chapter 4). Customers will provide personal information, such as credit card numbers, only if they are confident that the information will remain secure. Web transactions lack the reassuring physical merchandise and face-to-face interaction with salespeople familiar from traditional stores.

The Risks

In the anonymous world of the Web, customers and Web merchants must deal with a new array of faceless threats:

- **Unauthorized access**–Someone accesses or misuses a computer system to intercept transmissions and steal sensitive information.
- **Data alteration**–The content of an e-commerce transaction (usernames, credit card numbers, and dollar amounts) is altered en route.
- **Monitoring**–A hacker eavesdrops on confidential information.
- **Spoofing**–A virtual vandal creates a fake site masquerading as yours to steal data from unsuspecting customers or to disrupt your business.
- **Service denial**–An attacker shuts down your site or denies access to visitors.

- **Repudiation**–A party to an online purchase denies that the transaction occurred or was authorized.

The preceding dangers pose the threat of fraud, service disruption, lost sales, theft of confidential information, and most damaging of all, loss of your customers' trust.

The Solution: Digital Certificates

Fortunately, the most important thing you can do to secure your e-commerce site is also the simplest: Just install an electronic file called a *digital certificate* on your Web server. As discussed in Chapter 4, digital certificates are a kind of online passport issued by a trusted third party, a *certificate authority* (CA) who verifies the identity of the certificate's holder. See the sidebar, "Netscape's Certificate Authority Program," for additional information on CAs.

Digital certificates, SSL, and S/MIME are several of the technologies that form the foundation for Internet Security.

Netscape's Certificate Authority Program

Certificate authorities (CAs) are the digital world's equivalent of passport offices. They issue digital certificates and validate the holder's identity and authority. CAs embed an individual's or an organization's public key along with other identifying information into each digital certificate and then cryptographically *sign* it as a tamper-proof seal, verifying the integrity of the data within it and validating its use.

The Certificate Authority Program is designed to make it easier for Netscape customers to get and use digital certificates. The program offers both client and server certificate services:

- Client certificate authorities
- Server certificate authorities

This program is open to certificate authorities who bundle their root public keys with Netscape Communicator.3

Digital certificates are tamper-proof and cannot be forged. They do two things:

- Authenticate that their holders (people, Web sites, and even network resources such as routers) are truly who or what they claim to be
- Protect data exchanged online from theft or tampering

Learn more about how digital certificates work by taking a brief look at the sidebar, "How Digital Certificates Work."

There are two types of digital certificates that are important when building secure Web sites: *server certificates* and *personal certificates*. Let's look briefly at these two certificates.

How Digital Certificates Work

Digital certificates are based on public/private key technology, the same technology used to protect nuclear missile sites. Each key is like a unique encryption device. No two keys are ever identical, which is why a key can be used to identify its owner.

Keys always work in pairs, one called the *private* key, and the other called the *public* key. What a public key encrypts, only the corresponding private key can decrypt, and vice versa. Public keys are distributed freely to anyone who wants to exchange secure information with you. Your private key is never copied or distributed and remains secure on your computer or server.

Digital certificates automate the process of distributing public keys and exchanging secure information. When you install a digital certificate on your computer or server, your computer or Web site now has its own private key. Its matching public key is freely available as part of your digital certificate posted on your computer or Web site.

When another computer wants to exchange information with your computer, it accesses your digital certificate, which contains your public key. The other computer uses your public key to validate your identity and to encrypt the information it wants to share with you using SSL (Secure Sockets Layer) technology. Only your private key can decrypt this information, so it remains secure from interception or tampering while traveling across the Internet.[4]

Server Certificates

Server certificates let visitors to your Web site send you personal information, such as credit card numbers, free from the threat of interception or tampering by encrypting the information exchanged between their Web browser and your service. Server certificates also let visitors to your site authenticate your identity so they can feel secure that they are communicating with you and not with a rogue site impersonating you. Server certificates are necessary for anyone building an e-commerce site or a site designed to exchange confidential information with clients, customers, or vendors.

You should encourage visitors to your site to upgrade their browsers to the current version. Doing so lets them take advantage of powerful 128-bit SSL encryption, as well as a variety of new features. Upgrading also will allow a small percentage of people using older versions of Netscape browsers to avoid a dialog box regarding root CA certificate expiration.

Personal Certificates

Personal certificates let you authenticate a visitor's identity and restrict access to specified content to particular visitors. You can also use personal certificates to send secure e-mail for private account information.

Personal certificates are perfect for business-to-business communications such as offering your suppliers and partners controlled access to special Web sites for updating product availability, shipping dates, and inventory management. Also, several security standard protocols are being widely adopted for electronic communication that rely on digital certificates:

- **SSL (Secure Sockets Layer)**–Developed by Netscape Communications Corporation, SSL is the standard for Web browser and server authentication and secure data exchange on the Web. All the leading servers and browsers, including Netscape Communicator, are optimized to enable SSL encryption.
- **Secure Multipurpose Internet Mail Extensions protocol (S/MIME)**–S/MIME is the standard for secure e-mail and Electronic Data Interchange (EDI).
- **Secure Electronic Transactions protocol (SET)**–SET secures electronic payments.

■ **Internet Protocol Secure Standard (IPSec)**–IPSec authenticates networking devices.

MICROSOFT

This section looks at the Microsoft Internet Explorer browser, particularly at the way it implements secure commercial transactions, and briefly describes the Microsoft Back Office series of servers and products focusing on secure commercial transactions.

Visit Microsoft's Web site for information on updated products at:

http://www.msn.com

Microsoft Internet Explorer

There is still a great deal of competition between Netscape (AOL) and Microsoft in the battle for Internet market share. Microsoft, in its truly competitive form, has taken the precedence set by Netscape and has tried to build a better mousetrap. Like Netscape, Microsoft has developed both Internet browsers and servers.

The Microsoft Internet Explorer is an Internet browser that meets the same requirements for supporting the URL, HTTP, and HTML protocols described earlier in this chapter and in Chapter 3.

Microsoft Internet Explorer supports most if not all of the plug-ins, add-ons, and related functions offered in the Netscape browser software. Explorer also offers support for the SSL security protocol. For the average user, it can be hard to tell a functional difference between Navigator and Explorer.

Getting Microsoft Internet Explorer

Bill Gates once described Explorer as "priced to sell." This was a comical reference to underscore the fact that Internet Explorer comes with every copy of Windows 2000 and is available as a free download from Microsoft at

http://www.microsoft.com/downloads/

Microsoft has a program for Web designers to add a button to lead visitors to a Web page where they can download the software.

The process is very similar and begins at the "Microsoft.com Downloads Center" page. Select the Internet product, which in this case is Internet Explorer. You can select one of the following versions: 4.0 for Windows

95 and NT, 5.0 for Mac, or 5.5 for Windows 2000. You will then be given a choice of which products and add-ons you would like to receive. Your next choice is which language version (for example, U.S. English) you would like to receive. Finally, you are given a choice of servers around the world from which to download your file.

The file you receive is a compressed program that will uncompress and install when you run the program.

Using Microsoft Internet Explorer

Explorer works like any other Web browser requiring a modem or local area network connection. Upon running Explorer for the first time, you will see the default configuration shown in Figure 7.2.[5]

Like other browsers, the user can immediately connect with other sites on the Internet by clicking on any available link. The user can also

FIGURE 7.2 The Microsoft Internet Explorer browser.

double-click on the Address box, enter a new URL, and press the Enter key to connect.

The Toolbar tools include the following:

- **Back**–To move back to the previous Web document retrieved.
- **Forward**–To move forward along a path already taken (this button is active only when a forward path is possible).
- **Stop**–To terminate a query in progress.
- **Refresh**–To load a fresh copy of the current document (to reflect changes made between the time the document was originally loaded and the current time).
- **Home**–To return to the default home page.
- **Search**–A quick link to a Microsoft-prepared Web page providing a quick way to find material on the Internet through the use of one or many of the Internet search engines currently available.
- **Favorites**–To access to a tool for creating and managing a list of your favorite Web sites; this is also referred to as *bookmarks*.
- **History**–A list of the latest URLs you accessed.
- **Channels**–A channel guide that highlights the top content partners in the industry and lets you search for channels from around the world.
- **Fullscreen**–Brings up a full-screen display of the Web page you are looking at.
- **Mail**–To access the Internet mail and newsreaders.
- **Print**–To print the current document.

There are quite a few more functions accessible through the menu bar. Very briefly, they include functions listed under the File menu:

- **New**–Opens a new instance of the browser, so more than one Web document can be displayed at once.
- **Open**–Has the same function as the Open button (or as typing a URL into the Location box)—it retrieves the designated resource.
- **Save** and **Save As**–Saves the current Web document as a file on the local computer.
- **Page Setup**–Lets you define how the page is presented (for example, portrait versus landscape, height, width).
- **Print**–Sends the displayed Web resource to a printer.
- **Send**–Allows the user to send a shortcut to someone else through several different means.

- **Properties**–Displays the properties for the document, including the security information.
- **Work Offline**–Allows you to work offline within the browser.
- **Close**–Simply closes the current window; if only one browser window is open, it exits Explorer.

The Edit pull-down menu includes the same editing functions you would normally find in a Windows application, including Cut, Copy, Paste, and Find.

The View pull-down menu includes the ability to toggle on or off the toolbar or status bar. Fonts acts just like the icon on the toolbar, allowing the screen font to be changed. Stop, like the icon, will stop the query in process, and Refresh causes the browser to redraw the current resource. The Source function causes the browser to display the actual HTML-tagged Web document in a window. Internet Options brings up a page of different settings and switches that will tailor the way the browser displays Web pages.

The Go pull-down menu includes the Back, Forward, and Home functions. Search the Web takes you to Web pages developed by Microsoft to help you find information on the Web. Access to Internet mail and newsreaders is listed next, followed by a listing of the last few URLs you visited.

The Favorites pull-down menu is used either to view the current list of bookmarks or to add to it. Finally, Help provides access to help documents using the browser interface.

This is just an overview of Internet Explorer, briefly covering the major functions with the exception of those relating to security and secure commerce.

Sanity Check

If you are finding the overview of the Microsoft Internet Explorer to be very similar to the overview of Netscape's Communicator, you are on the right track. What was once a horse race that Netscape led by several lengths, the fight for market share in the browser business, is a very close race to call in 2001. This is one of the strongest examples of the competition between Netscape and Microsoft.

Microsoft Internet Servers

Microsoft outlines its Internet Commerce Strategy on the Web at http://www.microsoft.com/commerce. See the sidebar, "Microsoft's Internet

Digital Commerce Payment System Strategy," for a detailed discussion of Microsoft's e-commerce startegy.[6] A white paper detailing their strategy is also available from that site.

Microsoft's Internet Digital Commerce Payment System Strategy

Microsoft is providing a comprehensive Internet digital commerce offering to meet the demanding needs of businesses creating digital commerce solutions. This includes the delivery of best-of-breed digital commerce products (components, tools, APIs to enable extension), an open secure payment architecture, and complete solutions through partnerships with industry leaders (see Figure 7.3).[7]

Microsoft is currently delivering a server and tools digital commerce foundation based on Site Server, Enterprise Edition. Site Server, Enterprise Edition runs on the Windows NT Server operating system, and extends Microsoft's Active Server platform—Internet Information Server, Microsoft Transaction Server, and the Component Object Model architecture. Site Server, Enterprise Edition integrates with the Microsoft Internet Security Framework and Windows NT security to support secured access, authentication, and nonrepudiation.

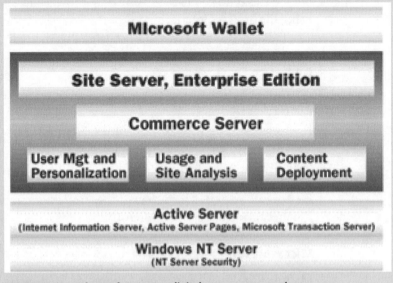

FIGURE 7.3 Microsoft Internet digital commerce products.

To support secure Internet-based payment for consumers, Microsoft is currently delivering an open payment architecture based on Site Server, Enterprise Edition and the Microsoft Wallet. The Wallet is available free on the Web and will be part of future releases of Microsoft Internet Explorer and Microsoft Windows. Microsoft's payment architecture enables the exchange of products, information, and services for different forms of payment on the Internet. Microsoft supports standards such as Secure Electronic Transaction (SET) and SSL to ensure interoperability of secure payment systems between banks and financial institutions, businesses, and consumers.

The creation and ongoing management of Internet digital commerce sites involves the efforts of multiple participants and the combination of several software offerings for a complete solution. Microsoft is working with leading software companies, banks and financial institutions, systems integrators, site developers, and hosting service providers to make it easier for customers to build and manage complete Internet digital commerce solutions.

Server and Tools Foundation for Digital Commerce
Site Server, Enterprise Edition

Microsoft Site Server, Enterprise Edition is a comprehensive Web site environment for the enhancement, deployment, and advanced management of commerce-enabled Web sites on Windows NT Server and Internet Information Server. Site Server, Enterprise Edition consists of tools and components to digital commerce-enable your site, deploy content reliably between staging and production environments, and manage and conduct data analysis of your site. Digital Commerce Server, the follow-on release to Merchant Server 1.0 and higher, is a Site Server, Enterprise Edition feature that provides horizontal digital commerce functionality.

Digital Commerce Server provides the following key features:

- Server components for managing electronic catalogs, users, and orders.
- Order Processing Pipeline to manage the order process workflow—more than 30 default components to allow price look-ups, product and price promotions, inventory look-up, and shipping and handling, among other functions.
- Order Processing Pipeline API enabling integration of software from independent companies, such as commercial tax calculation, Enterprise Requirements Planning, accounting, payment, shipping

modules, and applications. More than 30 independent companies have delivered or are planning to deliver compatible components.

- Site creation and management tools, including the StoreBuilder wizard, that enable easy, custom creation of commerce sites. These tools support remote creation and management for hosting service providers.
- Buy Now, a new online selling technology that allows companies to embed product information and order forms in almost any online context, such as online banner ads.

Figure 7.4 illustrates the functional elements of Digital Commerce Server.[8] In other words, it illustrates the Internet digital commerce functional components.

Digital Commerce Server Components

In conjunction with Active Server Pages, Digital Commerce Server components provide the run-time environment for the presentation and operation of digital commerce Web sites. Digital Commerce Server components are ActiveX Server components that supply the basic set of services for access to product information, access to user information, and creation of an order form for presentation to and processing by the order processing pipeline. In addition, there are Digital Commerce Server components for traffic collection, message management, and site debugging.

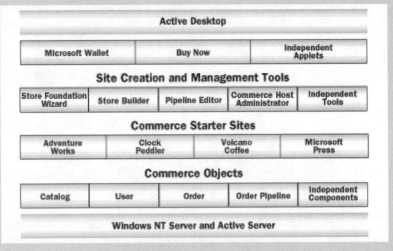

FIGURE 7.4 Microsoft Internet digital commerce functional components.

The Digital Commerce Server components allow developers to significantly shorten development time of sophisticated digital commerce sites.

Order Processing Pipeline

The Order Processing Pipeline (OPP) components are key to any digital commerce site as shown in Figure 7.5.[9] They allow businesses to enforce rules that direct the processing of orders through a specified sequence of stages and procedures. The OPP is a comprehensive data structure consisting of Component Object Model (COM) components that manage 14 stages in order processing.

Pipeline components included with Site Server, Enterprise Edition are optional and can be integrated with existing systems or replaced with components supplied by independent software companies, created to work with OPP interfaces. The interfaces of the Order Processing Pipeline are described in the Digital Commerce Server Software Development Kit (SDK). The Order Processing Pipeline, by enforcing rules for a specified processing sequence, ensures component interoperability, which lets customers create a multitude of custom solutions with off-the-shelf add-ons.

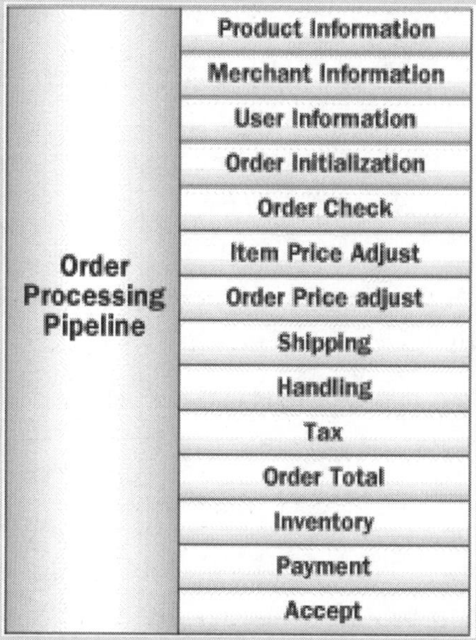

Order Processing Pipeline	Product Information
	Merchant Information
	User Information
	Order Initialization
	Order Check
	Item Price Adjust
	Order Price adjust
	Shipping
	Handling
	Tax
	Order Total
	Inventory
	Payment
	Accept

FIGURE 7.5   Order Processing Pipeline.

Tools and Starter Sites

Digital Commerce Server tools in Site Server, Enterprise Edition make it easier to build and maintain online sites that use Digital Commerce Server components and the Order Processing Pipeline. These tools integrate with other Site creation and management tools such as the Front-Page™ Web authoring and management tool, Visual InterDev™ Web development system, Internet Information Server Service Manager, and SQL Server™ Enterprise Manager. Together, these tools (Store Foundation wizard, StoreBuilder wizard, Commerce Host Administrator, and the Pipeline Editor) make it simpler for site developers to create and manage site virtual directories, site structure, database schema, and the Order Processing Pipeline configuration.

Starter Sites, Active Server Pages templates delivered with Site Server, Enterprise Edition, demonstrate the capabilities of the product to serve the needs of different businesses. Starter Sites are used as a tool for learning how to implement certain types of functionality in a digital commerce site. Future releases of Site Server, Enterprise Edition will support new starter sites to enable quick development of additional applications such as corporate purchasing, supply chain trading, and distribution of digital goods and services.

Client Components

Buy Now enables consumers to make quick purchases from any site on the Internet. When the shopper clicks an online banner ad, product name, or any other link, Buy Now opens a window within any browser window to facilitate purchasing. The user is left in the context of the current site or page to complete the purchasing process. Buy Now is integrated with the Microsoft Wallet on the client side, and with the Site Server, Enterprise Edition Digital Commerce Server database and Order Processing Pipeline on the server side.

NOTE: *Businesses can include links that initiate Buy Now from within their Digital Commerce Server-based store or catalog (for featured products, for example), or from sites or Web pages other than their own.*

Integration with Microsoft Wallet

Site Server, Enterprise Edition integrates with and uses the Microsoft Wallet. By providing this support out of the box, users of Site Server, Enterprise Edition can process transactions that are submitted by users of the Microsoft Wallet.

Site Server, Enterprise Edition for Business-to-Business Commerce

In order to meet the needs of businesses looking to lower the cost of creating business-to-business commerce sites, Microsoft continues to invest heavily in developing enhanced business-to-business functionality. Future enhancements include:

- Corporate Purchasing and Supply Chain Trading Starter Sites, to support rapid creation of solutions.
- Commerce Interchange Pipeline for managing communication of structured business documents, such as ANSI x.12 transaction sets, between companies.
- Integration of business-to-business payment modules such as Electronic Funds Transfer (EFT) solutions, together with independent software companies, allowing businesses to execute payments through the Internet.
- Enhanced ERP integration for tying in online commerce with existing Enterprise Resource Planning systems.
- Configuration and advanced search support for management of complex electronic catalogs, as well as support for dedicated configuration management solutions from independent companies.

Commerce Interchange Pipeline

The Commerce Interchange Pipeline (CIP) is a workflow system similar in concept to the Order Processing Pipeline, but designed to simplify the integration of structured business document communication into Internet commerce sites. The Commerce Interchange Pipeline is schema and transport independent. This gives developers of commerce sites a choice in the use of message formats—EDI or other—and transports—S/MIME, DCOM, EDI, or other. CIP will support document translation, including a plug-in interface for independent company EDI translation software; data encryption for transmission over the Internet; document authentication via digital signatures; and transport independence to allow sending and receiving of documents over the Internet, VANs, or other networks.

The Commerce Interchange Pipeline, business-to-business starter sites, improved facilities for managing complex electronic catalogs, and simpler

ERP integration will combine to form a powerful business-to-business commerce platform. Most important of all, businesses will develop sites more quickly and at less expense.

Microsoft Windows NT Server and Active Server
Internet Information Server and Active Server Pages

Microsoft Internet Information Server (IIS) is the only Web server integrated with the Microsoft Windows NT server operating system, providing a powerful platform for Web-based line of business applications. By optimizing around the Windows NT Server platform, Internet Information Server delivers high performance, excellent security, ease of management, and is up and running in minutes.

With IIS 4.0, Microsoft's Active Server Pages, an open, compile-free scripting environment, allows you to combine HTML, scripts, and server components to create dynamic HTML and to enable powerful Web-based business solutions. Active Server Pages support virtually any scripting or component language, and provide the easiest way for Web developers to create powerful, dynamic Web sites on Windows NT Server.

Site Server, Enterprise Edition runs on top of Internet Information Server and extends Active Server Pages. The starter sites that ship with Digital Commerce Server are a collection of Active Server Pages that call into commerce specific ActiveX server components.

Microsoft Internet Security Framework and Windows NT Security

The Microsoft Internet Security Framework (MISF) is a comprehensive set of cross-platform, interoperable security technologies that support Internet security standards. Developers and Webmasters can use this set of technologies for a variety of applications, including secure communications, Internet commerce, and controlled access to information or resources. MISF technologies support existing Internet security standards. Applications using MISF technologies will be able to interoperate with other standards-based software. Microsoft is also actively participating in standards bodies to ensure continued interoperability.

MISF technologies implemented to date include Authenticode technology, CryptoAPI 1.0 (or higher) and CryptoAPI 2.0 (or higher), support for client authentication, support for SSL 3.0 (or higher), and PCT-secure channel protocols. MISF technologies also include a certificate server and

Personal Information Exchange (PFX) 1.0 (or higher) protocol. Support is also incorporated for Transport Layer Security (TLS), the follow-on specification of SSL.

Microsoft Windows NT Server offers excellent security services for account management and enterprise-wide network authentication. Large organizations need flexibility to delegate account administration and manage complex domains. Internet security concerns are driving the development of public key security technology that must be integrated with Windows NT security. To meet these expanding needs, Microsoft is developing the Distributed Security Services Technology preview, a related white paper. This white paper examines the components of the Windows NT Server Distributed Services Technology preview and provides details on its implementation.

For user authentication, Digital Commerce Server integrates security mechanisms provided within Windows NT security and MISF:

- Windows NT Challenge/Response
- Hypertext Transfer Protocol (HTTP) basic authentication
- Personal certificates

Digital Commerce Server limits browser-based access to store management pages to users with Windows NT accounts that have been defined as administrators or store managers. In addition, Commerce Server has the capability of requiring account authentication for access to the store's file system, for users of the Windows NT file system (NTFS). It is recommended that customers use the Secure Sockets Layer support in IIS for the security of transactions between the client and the server.

Microsoft Transaction Server

Microsoft Transaction Server is designed to simplify the development of infrastructure needed to execute business logic. It provides services that make it easy for developers to handle security, directory, process and thread management, and database connection management. In addition, Microsoft Transaction Server provides a transaction monitor that enables transactional integrity across business components. Future versions of Site Server, Enterprise Edition will take advantage of Microsoft Transaction Server to enable transactional integrity as part of the Order Processing Pipeline.

Marble

"Marble" is the code name for commerce extensions for banks and financial institutions that need to create Web sites for the purpose of supporting financial transactions. Marble enables financial institutions to execute and complete banking and brokerage transactions in a more secure manner through the support of Open Financial Exchange (OFX)—a financial transaction protocol backed by Microsoft, Intuit, and CheckFree. Although Marble is available separately, it is fully compatible with—and relies on—BackOffice and Site Server, Enterprise Edition components.

Open Payment Architecture

Microsoft provides an open and extensible payment architecture on the client and server. For the server, the Site Server, Enterprise Edition APIs, or Order Processing Pipeline APIs enable commerce site payment integration. For the client, the Microsoft Wallet and Wallet Payment Modules architecture serves as the point of integration. Leading payment software companies around the world are supporting this architecture with a diverse set of payment methods.

Support for SET and SSL

Microsoft's payment architecture supports multiple payment methods and multiple secure payment protocols, including SSL and Secure Electronic Transaction (SET). SET, a standard driven by a number of leading industry companies including VISA and MasterCard, is a powerful secure payment alternative. SET is a three-way protocol and manages the interfacing of consumer, merchant, and financial institution in one single message. A number of independent payment software companies are delivering SET payment solutions based on the Microsoft Wallet and Site Server, Enterprise Edition API.

Microsoft Wallet Description

The Microsoft Wallet is a cross-server payment front-end solution. It can be integrated into any commerce site, even sites that are not based on Site Server, Enterprise Edition. The Microsoft Wallet is available as an ActiveX control for Internet Explorer users and as a Netscape plug-in.

The Microsoft Wallet consists of the Payment Selector control and the Address Selector control. The Payment Selector control provides for the entry, secure storage, and use of various types of payment methods for paying for online purchases. The Address Selector control provides for the entry, storage, and use of addresses that can be referenced for shipping and billing during online order entry. The Payment Selector control also provides a programmatic interface for Wallet Payment Modules—plug-in modules created by independent payment software companies. In addition to open credit card solutions, Payment Modules are created to support digital cash, private-label credit cards, check payment, and other methods.

For more information regarding Microsoft's Open Payment Architecture and to download the Wallet, visit http://memberservices.passport.com/.

Creation of Complete Solutions with Microsoft Commerce Partners

The creation and ongoing management of Internet commerce sites involves the efforts of multiple participants and the combination of several software offerings for a complete solution. Depending on the depth of any given solution, businesses may need to add order-processing extensions, integrate with existing systems, and interface with payment systems and financial institutions. Microsoft's commerce partners enable customers to create custom solutions. They provide payment solutions, software extensions, hosting services, and integration and consulting expertise.

Payment Solutions from Independent Software Companies, Banks, and Financial Institutions

Leading suppliers of payment software, credit card processors, banks, and financial institutions from around the world are working with Microsoft to make it easy for customers to incorporate their payment solutions into the Microsoft Wallet and Site Server, Enterprise Edition.

Microsoft Internet Commerce Strategy Solutions

Microsoft's Internet Commerce Strategy meets the demanding needs of businesses creating commerce solutions. Table 7.1 provides a summary of solutions to critical requirements identified previously.[10]

TABLE 7.1 Summary of Microsoft's Internet Commerce Strategy Solutions

Requirement	*Microsoft Internet Commerce Strategy Solution*
1.–Lower-cost deployment and management of custom Internet commerce sites.	•–Site Server, Enterprise Edition Commerce Server Components
	•–Tools: StoreBuilder wizard, Pipeline Editor
	•–Starter Sites
	•–Support for remote hosting by Internet Service Providers, allowing low-cost creation of commerce sites
2.–Simpler integration with existing systems.	•–Components offered by Microsoft Commerce Partner solutions that integrate with and extend Site Server, Enterprise Edition, including those from Enterprise Requirements Planning and accounting vendors: SAP, Baan, Great Plains et al
	•–Site Server, Enterprise Edition Order Processing Pipeline API, enabling custom integration
3.–Flexible support for payment.	•–Open payment architecture and multiple Microsoft Commerce Partners offering payment solutions (listed above)
4.–Secure access.	•–Integration with Microsoft Internet Security Framework and Windows NT security; Site Server, Enterprise Edition Commerce Server supports Windows NT Challenge/Response, HTTP authentication, and personal certificates.
5.–Simpler, lower-cost business document processing, EDI-compatible.	•–Planned enhancements including the Commerce Interchange Pipeline
	•–Leading independent EDI and electronic commerce software vendors providing solutions that will integrate with the Commerce Interchange Pipeline
6.–Dynamic, promotional, searchable content management.	•–Site Server, Enterprise Edition electronic catalog support
	•–Independent configuration management software companies that offer solutions that integrate with Site Server, Enterprise Edition
7.–Contextual transactions for online direct marketing.	•–Site Server, Enterprise Edition Buy Now feature.
8.–Standards-based solutions.	•–Support for TCP/IP, HTML, HTTP, COM / DCOM, Java, and ANSI X.12, SET, SSL, S/MIME.

For the Beginning of This Century

E-commerce is no passing fad. Many companies already engage in e-commerce: corporate purchasing; secure distribution of information; direct marketing, selling, and customer service; banking and billing; and marketplace trading. Pioneering entrepreneurs have mixed Internet technologies with imagination and invented new business models and service offerings that did not exist in the pre-Internet economy.

Conducting commerce via the Internet opens new markets, new opportunities for large and small companies worldwide. According to Nua, an Internet-strategy firm, the worldwide population of Internet users will expand from 282 million in 2000 to 600 million by 2004. The International Data Corporation (IDC) estimates that by 2004 the Internet will account for 8 percent of the gross domestic product of just the United States. Savvy enterprises that Web-enable their businesses and dot-coms are positioning themselves to take advantage of the potential—not only of larger markets but also of creatively expanded business uses of the Internet.

Trends

Several marketplace trends affect the opportunities and challenges for e-commerce:

- **Customer-focused outlook**–Companies are facing outward, focusing on the needs and demands of customers, and adapting products and services quickly to fulfill demand.
- **Business integration potential**–Development of new standards, such as the Extensible Markup Language (XML) and wireless protocols, expand the potential for businesses to share data easily and to offer new services to consumers.
- **Conflicting customer demands**–Customers want personalized services over the Web, but also want their privacy protected and their data secure. Companies that know their customers will be well positioned to navigate these shoals.
- **Expansion of broadband services**–New technologies, expanded telecommunication infrastructures, standardized protocols, and richer device capabilities are fueling the market for broadband services.

With the advent of e-commerce, competition has intensified. Companies are under increasing pressure to be more nimble so they can get to market quickly, respond to customer needs, and manage operational costs effectively.

The Microsoft Vision

The Microsoft vision for e-commerce is to enable every business to use the Internet to build richer customer experiences. Microsoft sees Internet commerce as more than just transactions over the Web; it is a means for establishing a closer relationship with customers and direct process links with trading partners. In particular, e-commerce lets a company understand, tailor, and deliver the services and information each customer and partner wants—anytime, anywhere, on any device.

Microsoft's goal is straightforward: to make the Internet a part of everyday operations. Its focus is an enabling platform for e-commerce (client devices, servers, and services) so that its partners can provide solutions that empower every business, large and small, to reap the benefits of e-commerce.

OPEN MARKET

Open Market's new e-Business Suite includes support for Java 2 Enterprise Edition (J2EE) and new modules to create and add features to an e-commerce site without extensive coding. Open Market offers an integrated suite of e-business applications for content management and commerce management, addressing the need for universal customer experience management (UCXM). Built upon an open and extensible platform, the suite enables enterprises to leverage existing and new assets to deliver a personalized, dynamic end-user experience while cost effectively managing overall e-business performance.

Open Market's packaged applications enable enterprises to quickly deploy full-featured e-business solutions while minimizing cost of ownership. With integrated content and commerce management, enterprises can increase revenue potential and maximize the value of online customer relationships. Additionally, customers can extend and expand systems more easily because of Open Market's open architecture. Key advantages of the overall suite include:

- Rapid deployment of full-featured solutions
- Control of site content and behavior by nontechnical users for fresher content and more interesting, compelling sites—eliminates the IT bottleneck

- Flexibility to accommodate diverse business models, including support for multiple business units and sales channels as well as support for catalogs, auctions, subscriptions, physical goods, digital goods, and microtransactions
- An open platform that easily extends and integrates with other applications such as ERP, customer service, and data warehouse systems
- Proven mission-critical stability including security, reliability, scalability, availability, and performance
- Enhanced features for global e-business

The suite includes products for:

- Content management and delivery
- Commerce management
- Online marketing and personalization

Now, let's look at the sidebar, "Demonstrating the Power of the Open Market eBusiness Suite," for a quick look at the power of the Open Market e-Business Suite!

Demonstrating the Power of the Open Market eBusiness Suite

1. Attract and Retain Customers/Visitors with Rich, Interactive Content.

The customer or visitor is presented with a rich Web site that serves up personalized content as shown in Figure 7.6.[11] Content Server manages and delivers the content and is based on an open application server. Because of its robust architecture, Content Server is able to handle the volume requirements of high-traffic sites such as the *Washington Post* and Chase Manhattan.

2. Enhance Visitor Experience and Increase Revenue through Total Coverage.

The site as shown in Figure 7.7 offers an intuitive navigational experience that combines compelling content with cross-references to related content and product information.[12]

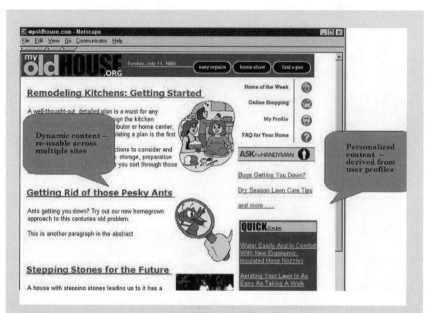

FIGURE 7.6 Personalized dynamic content.

FIGURE 7.7 Combined content and product information.

3. Transact Enabled.

The integration of Content Server and Transact allows the Web site to create a selling environment that is seamlessly integrated into the traditional content (see Figure 7.8).[13] By offering this compelling combination, businesses can increase their conversion rate—turning browsers into buyers.

4. Catalog Flexibility—Multiple Merchandising Paths.

The personalized content presented by Content Server includes specific promotional offers based on the business rules of the seller (see Figure 7.9).[14]

5. Enhance the Buying Experience with the Premier Commerce Application.

Open Market's Transact securely captures the order, making sure that the credit card owner is correct and that credit is available before accepting the order as shown in Figure 7.10.[15]

6. Streamline Production—Faster Time-to-Market.

Content Centre provides an interface for nontechnical content developers to create or modify content without the need for technical assistance (see

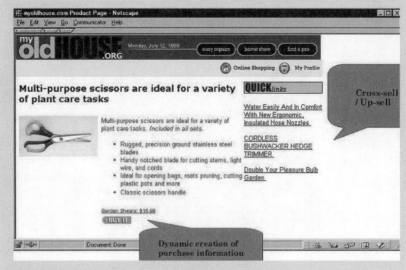

FIGURE 7.8 Cross-sell and up-sell.

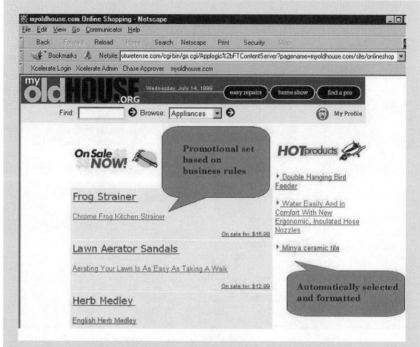

FIGURE 7.9 Targeted Web promotions.

Figure7.11).[16] The interface is designed for authors, editors, product managers, and anyone who has a stake in what is presented on the Web site.

7. Re-purpose Content Across Multiple Sites.

Before the updated content goes into production, the user can preview the resulting changes and even export the content for use in other sites (syndication) as shown in Figure 7.12.[17]

8. Just-in-Time Merchandising.

Marketing programs can be executed through the same intuitive interface. As shown in Figure 7.13, promotional coupons are ranked and grouped to provide a targeted program.[18]

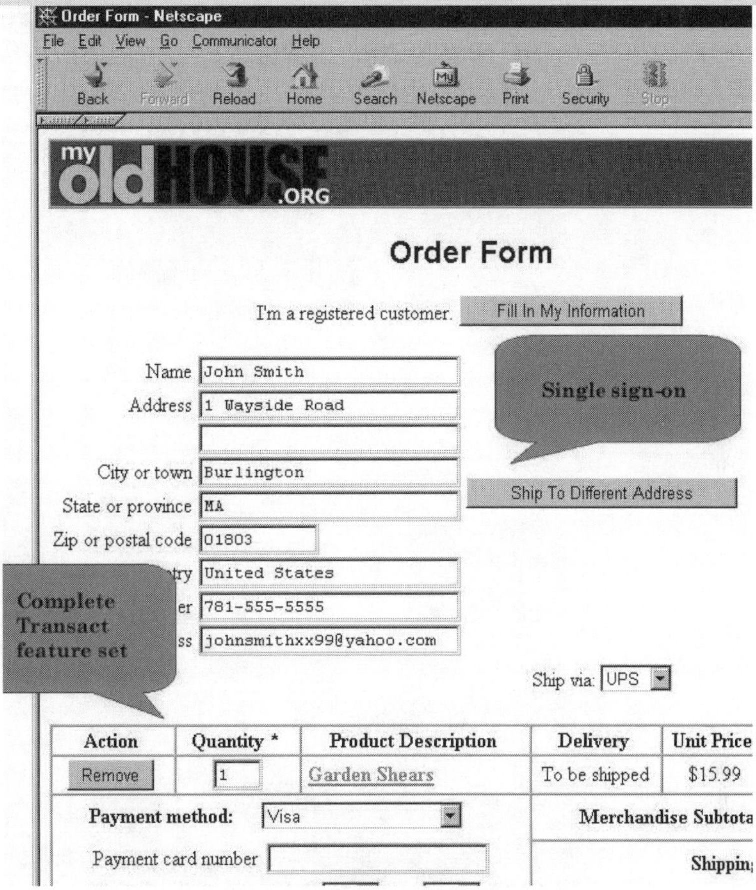

FIGURE 7.10 Robust commerce capabilities.

9. Personalized Outbound Marketing.

Coupons and other promotions can even be e-mailed to targeted prospects to help drive traffic and repeat purchases as shown in Figure 7.14.[19]

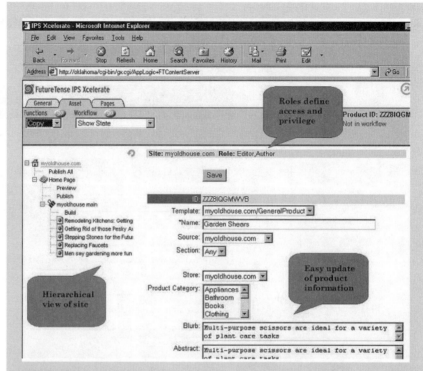

FIGURE 7.11 Easily update content.

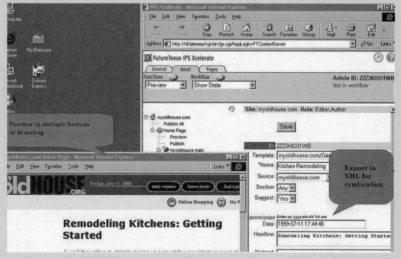

FIGURE 7.12 Re-purpose content (syndication).

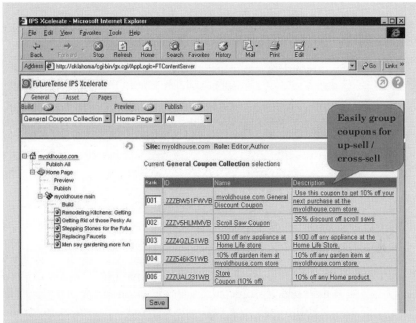

FIGURE 7.13 Powerful merchandizing.

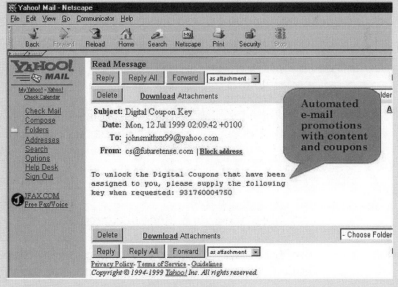

FIGURE 7.14 Targeted e-mail promotions.

Formal E-Business Model

Open Market Inc. uses a formal model for transacting business across the Internet or any other open network, with specific attention to purchase and sale of products that can be delivered over the network. Although Open Market sells a full line of commerce products for the Internet and the World Wide Web, including a secure server (supporting S-HTTP and SSL), its most interesting contribution is its comprehensive approach to producing an overall "commercial environment." This environment includes transaction services as well as tools for creating online stores, and it produces smart links to online products for sale.

One feature that differentiates Open Market's approach from other vendors' stand-alone secure servers is that Open Market separates the content server from the transaction server. The content server acts as a catalog and ordering station, offering users descriptions and prices on available products, as well as ultimately delivering those products once transactions have been completed. The transaction server processes the transaction, and if authorization is permitted, passes on notification to the content server.

The process begins with a customer browsing a content server. The customer initiates a transaction by requesting product information—an offer—from the content server. The model requires that this offer include the following information:

- A pointer to the transaction server handling the transaction
- An identifier indicating who gets paid when a sale is made (the merchant making the sale)
- Product price
- Product description, which points at the digital product's URL (this can also be a description of a physical product)
- A time limit on the validity of the offer being made
- The merchant's digital signature on the offer

When the customer decides to make a purchase, he or she clicks the appropriate purchase button and connects to the transaction server. At this point, the transaction server can request a user ID and password to identify the user or prompt the user to set up an account. Further authentication at this point is optional, but in any case, the transaction server has the option of denying service to "problem" customers at this point.

Assuming the customer has passed this point, the authorization process begins. This will vary depending on how payments are being made.

For example, if a credit card is being used, the transaction server can connect to an external financial processing network, pass along the transaction information to the network, and receive an authorization number (if the payment is authorized).

Other options are available, and payment methods could include digital currencies, payment systems, or even alternative "currencies." Open Market has a working relationship with CyberCash and supports Cyber-Cash and CyberCoin payment processing. For instance, a system could be set up to exchange frequent-flier miles online.

Once the transaction has been authorized, the transaction server sends back a "confirmation ticket" to the customer. This provides access to the digital product being purchased, and can include the following information:

- The product being purchased and the name of the content server it resides on.
- Some identifier to limit delivery to the purchaser. This could be the buyer's Internet (IP) address, or a public key, or a shipping address.
- A time limit on the fulfillment of the purchase. This can be used to provide online subscriptions.
- A digital signature on the confirmation ticket, so the content server can authenticate the ticket.

This is the model on which Open Market builds its commercial services. Additional services include special gateways that may be available for linking the transaction server to financial networks or other payment authorizers. In addition, both the merchant and the customer receive digital statements of their activities.

This model, illustrated in Figure 7.15, is useful because it demonstrates that simply having a secure World Wide Web server may not be sufficient to perform online commerce. There must be some means of keeping track of transactions and authorizing payments. Although it is possible to do these functions by hand, in the same way that telephone orders are handled, this becomes unwieldy when the number of orders is large—and it fails to capitalize on the benefits of automation that Internet commerce promises.

Open Market has enjoyed tremendous growth, much of which is due to the fostering of strategic relationships with business partners and several major companies selecting Open Market products to deploy Internet and intranet projects. A partial listing includes the following:

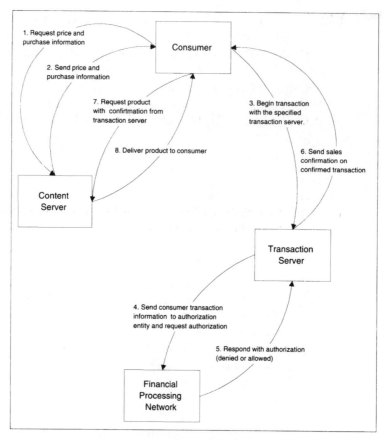

FIGURE 7.15   Open Market's softgoods transaction model allows customers and merchants to buy and sell online.

- Joined with RSA to conduct SET Transaction testing.
- Disney Online is using Open Market software for The Disney Store Online.
- AT&T's SecureBuy service has teamed with Open Market.
- Houghton-Mifflin Interactive selected Open Market for its Internet commerce solution.
- Novell licensed Open Market technology to support electronic commerce on intranets and the Internet.
- Barron's Online selected Open Market's innovative Internet commerce software.

END NOTES

[1] Reprinted with permission from Netscape © 2000.

[2] Ibid.

[3] Ibid.

[4] Ibid.

[5] Reprinted with permission from Microsoft Corporation © 2000.

[6] Ibid.

[7] Ibid.

[8] Ibid.

[9] Ibid.

[10] Ibid.

[11] Reprinted with permission from Open Market Incorporated © 2000, One Wayside Road, Burlington, MA, 01803.

[12] Ibid.

[13] Ibid.

[14] Ibid.

[15] Ibid.

[16] Ibid.

[17] Ibid.

[18] Ibid.

[19] Ibid.

8 ∷ Digital Currencies

Sing a song of sixpence, a pocket full of rye . . .

—NURSERY RHYME

The very idea of individuals being able to exchange values electronically using a digital currency seems impossible—how could the physical component be removed from the exchange of currency? And yet this is already happening, in small ways, and has been for some years. For example, certain public facilities accept coin-like tokens—mass transit systems in particular, but also many toll-collecting authorities. Some mass transit systems require the use of "farecards" that store value in a magnetic strip, instead of coins or tokens. Some toll road authorities place "tags" on your car that can be scanned at low speed so a complete stop at the booth is not required. Prepaid telephone cards represent another digitized currency.

Digital currencies are differentiated from electronic payment systems in two very important ways:

- Digital currencies can be used to maintain the anonymity of the customer in an online transaction, whereas users of online payment systems are usually identifiable, at least to the service to which they subscribe.
- Digital currencies themselves can support an actual transfer of value by themselves, without linking to some third-party credit provider or financial institution for authorization to complete the transaction.

The use of standard encryption and digital signature technologies makes it possible to safely and reliably transmit payment information between customer and merchant, or between customer and online payment service provider. Encryption, particularly public key encryption, makes the contents secure from prying eyes, while digital signature techniques ensure that forgery is not possible. However, both encryption and digital signature need to be two-way processes: If Alice and Bob are to exchange encrypted messages, they must identify each other with an encryption key. More critically, digital signatures work only if you can trace the public key of the person signing.

Actual cash transactions can be completely anonymous. When you purchase a sandwich from a restaurant, you exchange currency for the sandwich. The cashier does not ask you for any kind of identification, and as long as the currency you use does not appear to be counterfeit, your payment is accepted without question. Pay with a check or a credit card, and the process is considerably different: You may be asked for identification, for addresses or telephone numbers, and your signature may be compared to the one on your driver's license.

More to the point, that transaction becomes a matter of record. The restaurant can keep track of what kind of sandwiches you've been buying, and so can the credit card company. More frightening, the credit card company can build a fairly comprehensive consumer profile based on all your purchases over time: what kind of food you eat, how often you travel, how much gasoline you buy, whether your automobile is serviced regularly or adequately, and much more.

There is no reason why anyone but you should know how often you change the oil in your car, and you may wish to keep an anniversary gift secret from your spouse. While consumers who use several different credit cards to avoid having any significant profiles built up by the financial institutions might be viewed as paranoid, there are some who feel strongly about this issue. Cash is an excellent solution. Electronic currencies, fully negotiable and fully anonymous, are another.

DigiCash has been a ground-breaking organization in developing electronic currencies, and their electronic cash program, called eCash, is discussed in this chapter. eCash does not have any intrinsic value, nor is it exchangeable for any real currency, but since October 1994, 8 million CyberBucks have been placed into circulation for the purposes of testing and using DigiCash's electronic currency application. This chapter discusses the principles underlying this electronic currency and explains how it works.

HOW DIGITAL CURRENCY CAN WORK

Let's say you wanted to start your own Internet currency. You could run an electronic bank, or e-bank, taking cash deposits from customers and giving them some kind of electronic manifestation of cash on demand. They could spend that manifestation by giving it to others, who could in turn spend it themselves, or they could turn it back to the e-bank for actual money. This manifestation of value is what we look at in this section.

Using just the methods discussed in Chapter 2, "Security Technologies," this service should be fairly simple to provide. Whenever a customer wants to withdraw money from his or her account, he or she comes up with a randomly generated serial number and signs it digitally. The customer sends this to the e-bank, which uses the customer's public key to certify the serial number as coming from that customer.

The e-bank then digitally signs this serial number using a different public key varying by denomination: A $1 signature would be different from a $20 signature. The resulting signed serial number is sent back to the customer. And, of course, the e-bank debits the amount being withdrawn from the customer's account.

These manifestations of value are called *digital coins*, because each represents a discrete amount of value. When shopping, the e-bank customer can present a digital coin to a merchant in payment for goods or services. The merchant can certify that the digital coin is, in fact, currency and that it has a certain value by checking the e-bank's digital signature: The signature itself identifies the denomination, and if the signature is valid, the currency can be accepted for payment. The next step is for the merchant to submit the currency to the e-bank for payment into his or her own account. The e-bank credits the merchant's account for the amount and sends back a receipt to the merchant.

Each of these procedures can generate its own signed receipt or notification, so the e-bank customer gets unforgeable notification from the e-bank whenever a withdrawal is made, the e-bank gets an unforgeable withdrawal notification from the customer, and the merchant gets unforgeable notification that a deposit has been made.

Double-Spending, Part One

Unlike a piece of paper currency, serial numbers on digital coins change every time they change hands. Paper currency gets its legitimacy from the fact that each bill represents a certain amount of money. The physical presence of the bill determines whether it can be spent: If you forget your billfold at home, you cannot use any of the bills inside it. You cannot have your partner fax you a copy of a $20 bill to pay for lunch.

Digital currency, on the other hand, eliminates this limitation. In fact, it is in large part the reason why digital currencies were invented: the ability to transfer values with no physical interaction. Digital coins can be transmitted by e-mail, fax, telephone, or by any other method of communication. The downside to this is that while a merchant can independently certify that a digital coin represents some value simply by checking its digital signature, the issuing e-bank must be contacted to make sure that the coin has not already been spent.

Double-spending is a real concern of digital currency designers. There are many different ways it could be done, from submitting the same digital coin for payment simultaneously to different merchants, to intercepting someone else's digital coins while they are en route to online merchants. Unlike traditional currency, digital coins can be, and are intended to be, copied effortlessly; thus, requiring online and immediate authentication through the e-bank goes a long way toward reducing the risk of double-spending.

When the merchant, or anyone else taking a payment with digital coins, notifies the e-bank of the receipt of a digital coin, the e-bank can check its records to ensure that the coin has not already been spent.

More will be said about double-spending later, after we look at digital currencies in greater detail.

What's Wrong with This Picture?

The system described here would work, but is not significantly more attractive as a system than other online payment systems. Specifically, there is no anonymity. As the e-bank keeps track of transactions, it collects information about the specific transactions made by each of its customers. When the merchant's deposit is credited, that transaction inevitably points back to the original customer who made a purchase from that merchant. The result is that the e-bank can accumulate a lot of information about its customers' spending patterns, habits, and inclinations.

Many would claim that privacy and anonymity of transactions are necessary only for those who wish to circumvent the law. They argue that only those with something to hide would want their transactions kept private. The issue of criminal payments is addressed in the next section, but whether or not the desire for privacy is a culpable matter, there are many individuals who prefer to keep their business matters private between themselves and the people with whom they do business.

The fact is that anonymous transactions are possible using digital currencies, and customers can retain their anonymity even if both their merchant and their e-bank attempt to break it. This of course assumes that the customer uses an online identity (nom d'Internet) and does not provide merchants with true identity information.

Adding Privacy

To create truly anonymous digital currencies, it is necessary to add some method that allows the bank to certify serial numbers without knowing what those serial numbers are. This is relatively easy to do by having the customer add what is called a *blinding factor* to the serial numbers chosen for the digital coins.

Remember that the customer chooses the serial numbers at random. In the previous discussion, this number could be clearly linked with the customer generating the serial number, since the number accompanies account transactions: The request for digital coins must be linked to the account to be debited.

However, the customer can generate a set of serial numbers and then apply some other random factor to those numbers. In effect, the serial numbers are multiplied by some other number. The resulting (large) number is a product that cannot be easily factored (remember that factoring large numbers is difficult). This number can be signed digitally by the bank and sent back to the customer. The customer can divide the resulting signed number by the blinding factor, and the result is still digitally signed, but unrecognizable to the e-bank.

The result is a digitally signed digital coin with a serial number unknown to the bank. The coin can be certified by checking the e-bank's digital signature. When the coin is spent, the e-bank verifies that the signature is valid, and pays the coin amount to the person or merchant presenting it. When the coin is spent, the serial number is checked against a list of serial numbers of coins that have already been cashed. If the number is already on the list, that coin has already been spent; if the number is not on the list, it is paid out and the serial number is added to the list.

Anonymity is added to the system because the e-bank never knows actual serial numbers on digital coins until those coins are spent, and the e-bank is never able to connect any serial number to the person who spent it.

Breaking the Law

A merchant who accepts digital currency may ask for your name and address, but you can retain your anonymity by withholding any personal information from the merchant. The merchant cannot trace you based on the serial numbers you use in your digital coins, for the same reasons the e-bank cannot link you to your coins. Only you can prove that you spent a particular digital coin, but only if you choose to disclose the relevant information, such as whom you paid it to and when.

Opponents of digital currency object that anonymity can protect anyone who wants to transfer cash from one place to another for objectionable purposes: tax evasion, drug dealing, bribery, extortion, or any other criminal activity. However, only the person spending digital currency remains anonymous; the person receiving a payment is not anonymous. That person must still go through the e-bank to receive payment, and the person making the payment can incontrovertibly prove that the payment was made.

These features make digital currency inappropriate for receiving payment for criminal enterprises. For example, a drug dealer's customer could give proof that payments had been made to that person; similarly, with extortion or bribery payments, the person making the payments could easily implicate the person receiving the payments.

The result is that digital currencies might be attractive to people wishing to purchase illegal goods or services, but not to those who are selling them. On the other side, law enforcement agencies involved in "sting" operations would be unlikely to accept digital currency payments, since they guarantee anonymity to the person making the payments and would therefore not yield acceptable evidence.

Double-Spending, Part Two

As should now be clear, the risk of double-spending a digital coin is significantly reduced by requiring the recipient of a coin to authenticate it online directly with the e-bank. In this way, the e-bank can make a note of the serial number after certifying its digital signature. If the same serial number is submitted for payment again, the transaction is not permitted.

Additional refinements are possible that further reduce the risk of double-spending. It is possible to embed information that can point to the owner of an account in digital coins issued from that account, without having this information accessible in the normal course of events. This identifier is used in creating the digital coin, but cannot be determined unless the owner of the coin attempts to spend that same coin with more than one merchant.

The way this works is that the account holder's account number, along with the digital coin serial number, can be combined mathematically with some random number. If you know the random number being used in combination with the account number, and you know the resulting combination, you can easily figure out the identification.

Now, when a digital coin is generated, some random numbers can also be generated and combined with the account holder's identification. If you add a simple challenge/response to the purchase process, you can maintain anonymity of the account holder, but identify any account holder who attempts to double-spend. The merchant can ask the customer to give one of two pieces of information for each of the compound numbers described earlier (the mathematical combination of the account ID and some random number). For example, if there are 10 of these numbers, the merchant will request 10 pieces of information, either:

- The random number
- The combination of random number and account ID information

The result will be a list of 10 numbers, some of them random numbers, some of them account information essentially encrypted by some set of random numbers. Whether the merchant requests one or the other may itself be randomly determined, or it may be determined by giving every entity capable of accepting payments its own unique query pattern.

If the coin is spent once, the information acquired remains useless. However, if an attempt is made to spend the coin twice, the identity of the double-spender will be divulged. This is how: Because everyone accepting digital coin payments will select a different combination of the two values indicated earlier, there will be at least one instance where both the random number (essentially an encryption key) and the mathematical combination of account ID and that random number (essentially that information encrypted using the random number as a key) will be available.

The result is that trying to double-spend means fingering yourself as a criminal. This also means that the digital currency does not necessarily have to be authenticated online and immediately, since any attempt by the owner of the account to spend a coin twice will immediately point to that person.

Academic discussions of digital currency have been going on for some time, and there are many more subtleties involved in implementing it, but they are beyond the scope of this book.

DIGICASH eCASH TRIAL

The topics discussed so far in this chapter derive from work done by David Chaum, founder of DigiCash. In fact, these digital coins are more often referred to as *Chaumian coins*. While there have been other proposals for digital currencies that use other types of mechanisms, no other method has received as much attention—and no other mechanism has been tested as extensively and publicly on the Internet.

Starting in October 1994, DigiCash made available for testing purposes a digital currency client called eCash, a trademark (as is DigiCash). Users who requested a client from DigiCash were given a password and user ID that allowed them to download a copy of the software. Another password/ID pair entitled the user to 100 free CyberBucks (another trademark). No more than 1 million CyberBucks were to be issued, and these would be exchanged by participants in the experiment.

While there is no value behind a CyberBuck, other than its scarcity, participants have offered various products, including software, documents, pictures, and other items. Some participants asked for donations of Cyber-Bucks, while others set up electronic casinos accepting CyberBucks for wagers. Some participants have offered physical products of one kind or another in exchange for CyberBucks.

Like ordinary currency, digital currency can be exchanged between individuals, or used to make purchases from merchants. Since eCash is a peer-to-peer system, client software can handle the receipt or payment of funds. As a result, the ability to accept payments is not significantly more difficult or expensive to add than setting up to make payments. Although the exact form a digital currency implementation takes will surely be at least slightly different from the eCash software, there is no question that eCash offers a very interesting view of how digital currency can work.

USING eCASH

To get a copy of the eCash software, participants filled out a request form with their name, e-mail address, and information about their systems and their intended use for the eCash client, and waited for DigiCash to reply with username and password information. Equipped with these, the participant could connect to the DigiCash server and download software and instructions. Installing this software proved to be no more difficult than any other Internet application; the software was intuitive and easy to use.

eCash Client Software

Using eCash required an Internet connection; otherwise, supported platforms included Microsoft Windows, Macintosh, UNIX line mode, and UNIX X Window System. Installation under Windows was typical of other similar products. The eCash setup program installed the program files, offered the option of installing with or without sound support, allowed the user to specify a directory to install the program, and finished with a reminder that the eCash required a Winsock 1.1 (or higher)-compliant network link. When the installation was complete, an eCash folder was set up with an icon for the eCash program and a file containing release notes. Double-clicking the eCash icon started the program.

The first step when first running eCash is to accept the DigiCash license agreement, followed by entering personal information: your full name and your e-mail address. The next panel prompts the user for an account ID and a password for opening a new account. Once this information is entered, the software begins generating a digital signature key. Once this key generation has begun, a small "digital wallet" appears and a very small animation in the corner of the display indicates that activity is taking place. Once the key is generated, the user is prompted for a password to protect this key.

Because there is communication between the e-bank and the eCash client at this point, the initial registration of keys and setting up of accounts must be done with a live connection to the Internet. If the connection is down, an account cannot be set up. During the trial, each user received 100 CyberBucks, but in actual use, some other currency or currencies will be used and some acceptable mechanism for activating accounts will be necessary.

eCash Client Features

Using eCash once the software is set up is simple. When the eCash client is running, it appears as a small rectangle, with five icons on the bottom third and the upper two-thirds displaying the amount of currency being held in the local client next to a DigiCash symbol.

Click on any of the icons to interact with eCash. The first icon on the left looks like a bank building and is used to withdraw or deposit money to the eCash bank account. There are three options:

- Withdraw from eCash bank account
- Deposit to eCash bank account
- Withdraw from credit card

Only the first two options are available in the eCash trial client; the third is grayed out and cannot be selected. It does suggest that one way of "filling up" an eCash account might be through a credit card advance.

The next icon appears to be a flying banknote: Click here to handle an eCash payment. The same panel is used for paying money out and for receiving an inbound payment. When a user interacts with an eCash shop, the information in this panel is automatically transferred between the eCash clients, but this manual payment method is available, too.

The third, and middle, icon appears to be a notebook with a dollar sign on the cover. This is the eCash payment log. It lists the payments made to or from the account. A red arrow signifies deposits to the eCash account; other payments get a green check mark. Each entry in the log includes the following information:

- Payment number (starting from 1 and continuing sequentially)
- Amount of the transaction
- Date and time of the transaction
- The result of the transaction (for instance, whether the payment was verified, or paid into an account, or accepted)
- A description of the transaction (deposit or withdrawal, or a brief description of the shop or individual on the other end of the transaction)

Payments made (money paid out) are kept separate from payments received (money paid in) and are viewed separately.

The fourth icon appears to be a wallet or purse, with a dollar sign on the side and a banknote and coin sticking out at the top. This icon produces the eCash account status, displaying the account ID, the bank address, the amount of eCash in the bank account, and the amount of eCash in coins in the digital wallet.

The last icon, or the first on the right, is small pliers crossing a screwdriver: configuration tools. Click on this icon to set eCash preferences, including the default amount to withdraw from the e-bank, method of connection, passwords, and type of currency in use.

eCash Transactions

eCash exchanges through eCash-accepting shops on the World Wide Web become fairly automated and standardized. Whether the exchange is a payment to an eCash merchant (for example, to make a purchase) or a payment from an eCash merchant (for example, a refund or a payment on a wager), an eCash request panel appears.

A shop making a request for a payment sends an incoming payment request to the customer. This request includes the account ID of the shop in question, the amount being requested, and a very brief description of what the payment is for. The panel includes the question, "Make this payment?" along with No and Yes buttons. Another button, labeled "Policy," can be clicked to see and set a standard policy for making and receiving payments: For example, all incoming payments could be accepted without prompting, or all requests for payment could be automatically denied.

Once an outgoing payment is authorized, the digital coins are exchanged. If exact change is not available, the eCash client offers to exchange money at the e-bank. If the client doesn't have enough eCash to make a payment, it offers to make a withdrawal from the e-bank.

Setting Up a Shop Accepting eCash

In the eCash trial, setting up a store that can accept eCash payments was relatively simple. An eCash shop is essentially the combination of a standard Web page, through which your product can be distributed, with eCash payment software, through which payments are managed.

The payment software can run directly on the same system that handles the Web page, or the shop can use a remote server to handle payments. Installing the payment software locally requires running script files on the Web server, something that not everyone is permitted to do on supported systems that can run scripts, and something that no one can do on unsupported systems or systems that cannot run the scripts.

The way it works is that when a BUY Web link is selected, the server starts the eCash software and passes it the product price and description, and the address of the requesting eCash client. With this information, the eCash software negotiates payment on both systems: If the client has enough eCash available, and if the user agrees to make the payment, the transaction is completed. The eCash payment software on the server then can allow the Web server to pass along the requested product.

For those who cannot run the eCash payment software on their Web servers, or prefer not to, DigiCash maintains a remote shop server. This requires that the files for sale on the shop's Web server be restricted to access only from the DigiCash Internet domain; customers wishing to make a purchase then are referred to the DigiCash server, which collects the payment on behalf of the shop, passes the payment along to the shop's eCash account, and passes the desired files along to the customer after debiting the customer's account.

eCash Implementation

According to DigiCash's World Wide Web documents, the company wishes to license the banking software to organizations interested in running electronic banks. They have negotiated many such agreements lately. There are many eCash-like systems available today. However, there are still some issues that probably need to be resolved, including the following:

- It is still not clear how the sponsoring bank or financial organization will charge for the service, but payment standards are being worked out.
- It is still not clear how much the service would cost the customer, but fees are being negotiated between the financial institutions.
- Governments almost certainly will involve themselves in the way this type of service is implemented, for the same reasons that they are involved in other banking and financial services.

Once the preceding issues, and many others have been finally resolved, many financial analysts expect to see DigiCash software increase exponentially in general use under license to financial institutions.

SMART CARDS

The majority of our discussions in this text have focused on computer-based solutions to exchanging value. On the surface, the use of smart cards may seem out of context in this text, but is not.

Smart cards look very much like a traditional credit card with one major exception: There is a tiny microprocessor or computer chip on the face of the card. Smart cards are being offered to consumers for small purchases, normally less than US$20.

Outside of North America, smart cards have enjoyed great exposure for several different applications. Most notable is the use of smart cards as prepaid telephone cards. Simply slide the card into the telephone, read the value, and talk as long as the value on the card will allow. This is a very portable, quick, and easy way for you to use your money without fumbling with exact change. The point, which must not be overlooked, is that your money is on the card. It is not a credit card, it is not a check card, and it is not some sort of device representing money sitting in a bank. The most notable difference is that if you load the card with cash and you lose the card, you've lost your cash. Furthermore, to the merchants, once the transaction is complete, they have their money. There is no waiting to settle with the bank.

All over the world, consumer and merchant trials are beginning to see how consumers will change from using physical cash in paper and coin form to using a smart card. Some projects are already testing the addition of smart-card technology and function to drivers' licenses and college identification cards.

The Chip

The focal point of the smart card debate is the function of the chip on the face of the card. Potential applications for the card range from use as a simple prepaid telephone card, to the loading of digital currency, to the complex loading and executing of computer programs for use by the holder, to the collection of data every time you visit a certain merchant, earning you points that you can redeem later.

The financial world is beginning to form alliances around which methods will be employed to manage cash on the cards. For example, MasterCard purchased 51 percent of Mondex and is continuing to build products around the basic premise of smart-card transactions not requiring any central settlement like the traditional credit-card settlement process. VISA is working with smart cards as well. However, the VISA Cash program is focused on settlement of the transaction data by a central server, much like current credit card transactions.

Mondex

In 1990, Tim Jones and Graham Higgins of NatWest, a major bank in London, were looking for a way to exchange digital cash. Their idea was the first step in creating Mondex International. Mondex International is responsible for the assignment of Mondex licenses around the world and the development of new products based on Mondex. Mondex International is also responsible for ensuring interoperability among Mondex licensees around the world, security and risk-management issues, and the certification of all Mondex equipment for use around the world.

Mondex USA was formed in April 1997 to speed the commercial development and implementation of Mondex in the United States. The company is owned by seven equity partners: Bank One Corporation, Chase Manhattan Bank, Citibank Universal Card Services, Discover Financial Services (a unit of Morgan Stanley Dean Witter & Co.), MasterCard, Michigan National Bank, and Wells Fargo. The company consists of two separate organizations: Mondex USA Services and Mondex USA Originator.

A separate company, Mondex International, continues as the umbrella organization responsible for the global Mondex functions of branding, interoperability, security, risk management, and future technology development. In addition to Mondex USA, other regional franchises such as Mondex UK and Mondex Canada have formed around the globe to propel Mondex.

Smart Card Security

Security is focused on the chip embedded in the card and the software that controls the movement of value between smart cards. For example, the Mondex chip is a highly customized security application using the Hitachi H8/310 smart-card microprocessor, which was designed specifically to thwart unauthorized disclosure and modification of data. The cards are *personalized* with cryptographic keys, which sets limits on the card's use.

Mondex has programmed the chip with the Mondex Value Transfer Protocol (VTP) software. This software uses sophisticated encryption to protect value as it passes from one Mondex card to another. Mondex cash can only be stored on or transferred between Mondex cards. The VTP operates in two steps, both transparent to the user. First, two cards "validate" each other. This ensures that only registered cards receive value. Second, using digital signatures to authenticate both payment and receipt, value is transferred and the transaction completed. Each transaction has a unique sequence number.

Transactions

As mentioned earlier, the smart card transaction is normally less than $20. A cup of coffee, a newspaper, lunches, or bus fare are typical smart-card transactions. Simply go to the register, or ticket booth, select your purchases, and use your card. At that moment, the money is transferred from your card to the merchant. There is no delay waiting for an authorization or signing a receipt.

The merchant will require a device to transfer the money from your smart card. Most merchants will use a device very similar to the card reader used for your traditional credit card, and many have one device capable of processing smart card and credit card transactions.

We used the term *wallet* in Chapter 6, "Electronic Payment Systems," to describe the way CyberCash manages your money with software on your computer. With smart cards, wallets regain a physical meaning. However, a smart-card wallet is more like a small calculator used for peer-to-peer transactions. Assuming we were to exchange money, the party who owes would insert his or her smart card into a wallet, enter the PIN, and then enter the amount to be exchanged. The first card would be removed from the wallet and the second card would be inserted, a PIN would be entered, and the transactions would be complete.

Putting It All Together

Some smart cards will be programmed for use until the original face amount has been spent, and others will be programmed for reloading. Devices used to reload smart card will include ATM-style machines. Additionally, some smart card trials are exploring the use of telephones and personal computers—equipped with devices capable of reading and writing to smart cards for reloading value to the card.

It is quite probable that when you send your young child off to school in a few years, the school cafeteria will accept smart cards. When your child needs more money for lunch or snacks after school, you will access your bank account via the telephone or personal computer, insert the smart card, and download money right to your child's card from your home.

Much sooner than that, you will probably complete your first online purchase by placing your smart card in a device hooked to your telephone or personal computer and pay for goods and services on the Internet by transferring money from your smart card.

Since we now have the ability to complete a secure Internet transaction with SSL technology and the smart card has encryption built in for managing the specific task of exchanging money, the risks for you, your bank, and the merchant are very limited.

Electronic Data Interchange

The majority of this book has focused on developing or recently deployed standards and methods for conducting electronic commerce over the Internet. Electronic Data Interchange, or EDI, on the other hand, has been available for years as a method for exchanging business documents between companies. EDI could be considered one of the first truly electronic commerce applications, as it uses computers and software standards to manage the flow of business transactions.

Electronic data interchange is generally described as the transfer of business documents between computers. Many businesses choose EDI as a fast, inexpensive, and safe method of sending purchase orders, invoices, shipping notices, and other frequently used business documents.

EDI Basics

From a high level, the first requirement for using EDI is for a company to sign a trading agreement with the companies with which they wish to exchange EDI documents. The second step is to subscribe to a value-added network (VAN) that, acting as an electronic mailbox, manages the flow of your EDI documents. You will also need a translator or software to interpret the message and integrate into your existing software. The final step is for you to create the EDI documents and send them to your trading partner via the VAN.

After you, or the software hooked to your company's computer system, create a document, it is placed in an electronic or EDI envelope. The VAN is contacted with a modem and the envelope and message is "uploaded" to the VAN for distribution to your trading partner. You will also receive EDI messages addressed to you from your VAN. Depending on the size of your company and the complexity of the computer system used to manage this process, the EDI message will either be created with a stand-alone piece of software entered one at a time, or will be automatically generated from the computer system of a large company.

Documents that can be sent via EDI cover the entire spectrum of today's business world, ranging from a simple purchase order and acknowledgment to health care laboratory results, and from college transcripts to government documents such as customs forms.

EDI versus the Internet

EDI has a lot in common with the Internet. EDI relies on standards to make sure that information can be passed between trading partners regardless of the computer and software that are used by each trading partner. Like the Internet, the EDI industry also has a non-profit organization, the ANSI Accredited Standards Committee, that manages the development and publishing of EDI standards.

The biggest difference between the Internet and EDI is that EDI is more an application than it is a network. The VANs are the "network," although they are traditionally closed systems and are not directly connected to the Internet.

EDI costs can range from free to several thousands of dollars per month depending on your needs, volume of transactions, and your position in the trading relationship. Most EDI vendors charge annual maintenance, mailbox, and transmission/transaction fees.

EDI over the Internet

Since an absolute requirement of any EDI transaction is absolute security and guaranteed delivery of the EDI message, the Internet was not initially used as a part of the EDI process. However, with the continued development of Internet security protocols and systems capable of confirming e-mail messages, the Internet and EDI will continue to overlap. This overlap is being fueled by a constant flow of new Internet-based EDI solutions.

For example, Peregrine Systems, Inc. (http://www.premenos.com/) has introduced several products that use the Internet to exchange EDI messages.

It is hard to predict what portion of EDI business will migrate over to the Internet, but it will continue to grow.

9 Strategies, Techniques, and Tools

"Give us the tools and we will finish the job."

—Winston Churchill, radio broadcast (February 9, 1941)

The raw building blocks of a new Internet commerce are falling into place: protocols and standards for exchanging values electronically, secure Internet information servers, cryptographic tools necessary to keep transactions secure and safe, and business services necessary to support online commerce.

There is a continuous flow of information discussing the strategic issues of marketing on the Internet. Given that marketing on the Internet was once considered unthinkable, at least among the Internet community, it should be obvious that there are no time- and market-proven methods of selling products on it. While estimates of the size of the Internet range as high as 140 million users in 120 countries, the actual number of users who can profitably be considered to be "on the World Wide Web" may be considerably lower, at least for now. The higher estimates include anyone with any type of Internet connectivity, which can include those with e-mail–only connections, as well as those whose links are mediated through mainframes or other multiple-user systems that don't offer any kind of graphics capability—and that may not even have Web browsers implemented or installed.

The room for growth in use of the Internet is still huge, and the commercial uses of the Internet are still being developed. That said, there is still much to be said about strategies, techniques, and tools that have been proven over time and are available to merchants as well as customers.

INTERNET STRATEGIES

The Internet is a network of networks, and by its nature is the result of a co-operative effort of all participants. This statement can be applied to at least two different levels of meaning:

- At a very basic technical level, any internetwork depends on every connected network cooperating with every other network.
- At a content level, from the start there has been a feeling that people who use the Internet, particularly for gathering information, should also "give back" something by sharing information when they have something of interest to others.

Cooperation was considerably more important at all levels before the commercialization process began in earnest. For example, some organizations provided Internet connectivity to other organizations simply by allowing them to connect their networks together, and routing traffic properly.

When the focus of Internet participation was the use of newsgroups and e-mail distribution lists, where interaction between and among groups is the primary objective, cooperation was critically important: Participants might request information, which other participants would provide if they had it. The rule was that as long as you were willing to share the results of your queries, others were happy to share information.

Why Share?

Acceptable-use policies once restricted the use of the Internet for any commercial activities, and newsgroups on virtually every topic included at least some discussion of what was acceptable and what was not. These were usually prompted by an inappropriate posting, which may have been as innocuous as a new product announcement from a networking company in a newsgroup devoted to networking. Now, however, individuals and companies are generally free to pursue their activities without apologizing for any attempts to make a living using the Internet.

However, attempting to make every bit you send across the Internet pay off is a self-defeating strategy. Similarly, attempting to cost-justify Internet expenses, particularly in the short term, will very likely fail to capture the value gained from Internet activities. Consider that no executive would ever require a cost-justification study to determine whether a new plant should be equipped with telephones, although what kind and how many telephones is definitely open to discussion. Similarly, customer service is a requirement for virtually any organization selling a product to customers, but the form that support will take can vary.

The bottom line is that potential customers are already paying some kind of access fee to an Internet Service Provider (ISP) before they even know about online merchants' World Wide Web sites: attempting to make them pay up front for nonessential services can be counterproductive.

Success Stories

Consider the Yahoo! Web site. Originally started by two students at Stanford University as a free service to the Internet community, Yahoo! became one of the most popular sites on the World Wide Web. At first it was maintained on systems to which the students had access, but the very high traffic it generated made it a drain of resources even though it offered an important service. One obvious solution, making Yahoo! a for-pay service, turned out to be completely inappropriate. Setting aside the technical difficulty of limiting access to subscribers, billing those subscribers, and doing it all at a reasonable cost both to the customer and the service operators, there was a feeling that paying subscribers would be much more demanding, and many users would avoid the service altogether.

Another option was to charge a listing fee to the sites listed in the catalog and continue to offer free access to the links. This, too, raises problems, particularly in terms of sites that offer very important information, but that are operated by individuals or by nonprofit organizations. Charging fees for listings would tend to drive out hobbyists and charitable organizations while making "better" listings (bigger sections or listings under more categories) available to those with deeper pockets.

Free access to both users and maintainers of Web sites was retained by offering corporate sponsorship of the site, along with paid advertisement links. The advertisements do not interfere with the operation of the catalog, but do give the advertisers exposure on one of the most accessed sites on the World Wide Web. The costs of maintaining Internet links sufficient to provide fast and consistent access are taken on by the sponsors, and what was a resource drain becomes a potential profit center. Yahoo! is, so far, a success story. However, Yahoo! earnings have been down recently.

Making It Work for You

The Internet has been, in many ways, a demonstration that certain types of altruism can be in the individual's self-interest as well as the interest of the community. However, setting up a digital storefront does not absolve the merchant from providing responsive, personal service whenever necessary, nor does it absolve the merchant from the responsibility of keeping that storefront current and up to date. Getting customers in the door is of no use if, once in, they find nothing of value. Some important points that merchants and vendors do not always consider as they set up an Internet presence include, but are certainly not limited to:

- Putting an electronic version of a corporate brochure online is useful, as long as there is more information available online as well.
- Using automatic mailers referenced on a Web site to e-mail copies of the documents published on the Web site is generally a waste of time.
- Your business cannot run by itself, and there will be potential customers who need to speak with you. The more they need to speak with you, the more likely you are to want to speak with them—for example, the customer who needs 40,000 licenses of your software, or the one who needs your product today and will pay a premium for it.
- Giving your World Wide Web site appeal for anyone who might want to buy your product will bring them back, and will give you increased market awareness.
- The Internet is an ideal way to get up-to-the-second information to your customers; if your online catalogs are a year old, it is worse than having no presence at all, since it makes you look bad and costs you sales of your newer products.

There are many forums for discussing marketing techniques and strategies, including Internet mailing lists and Web sites, magazines, books, and organizations. Some of these are referenced in Appendix B, but the reader is urged to check Internet search engines and mailing lists, since the available resources change constantly and new ones appear daily.

IMPLEMENTING MERCHANDISING STRATEGIES

The art of merchandising has enjoyed decades of refinement in offline retail. Today, e-commerce retailers have just begun to figure out how to merchandise effectively online. This is an important area of study: A recent Forrester survey reported that 84 percent of e-tailers consider merchandising one of their most important objectives.

One way to think about online merchandising is to compare it to what works best offline: the salesperson. A good salesperson can identify the customer's needs, recommend relevant products, and give advice on how to use the products.

A literal translation of the live salesperson to the Internet, however, usually creates a bad customer experience. By not recognizing the technological constraints of the medium, sites that have tried to emulate the salesperson with *virtual sales assistants* have mostly failed in their merchandising attempts.

An effective merchandising strategy would use the best aspect of the salesperson (understanding the customer's needs) without making a mess of the technology in the process. The site should understand, either intuitively or through direct questioning, what products to suggest (and when) to the customer.

Another Forrester report found that targeting is the most important factor of success for online promotions. For perfect targeting, the retailer would have complete information on the specific shopper, including past purchases at other stores, known needs, and even unarticulated desires. Obviously, it's unreasonable for e-tailers to expect to capture that much information about their customers. Without a huge database of information, though, there is still a way that e-tailers can merchandise effectively.

A Formula for Product Recommendations

Now, let's look at an algorithm that calculates, with relatively limited data, the best products to recommend to each customer. By selecting the most appropriate products, the promotions are then targeted to the right customers, at the right time. It's also much easier to develop occasion-based sales scenarios around the products, once a company has done the work to create the merchandising algorithm. Steps to create the algorithm are outlined in the following sections.[1]

Step 1

The most important step is to identify those success criteria that will help you make a decision about whether to include a certain product or, in the case of occasion-based promotions, a certain occasion. These decision criteria must be aligned with the overall goals of the merchandising strategy. For example, do the products promoted:

- Appeal to target customers?
- Aid with overstock clearance?
- Optimize margins?
- Introduce new products or new product categories?

- Increase average order size (such as through multiple product bundles)?
- Aid with load balancing (promote orders at a certain time of day or week)?
- Conform with typical customer purchases (based on transaction data)?[2]

Step 2

Check to ensure that you have data to support each decision criterion. For example, to test whether there is appeal to target customers, you might refer to demographic or psychographic information, or you might use survey data if it is available.

If there's not enough quantitative data available, you can rely on qualitative data. For example, you can use your industry knowledge and common sense to decide whether a certain product would promote orders during the week rather than the weekend.

Step 3

You should assign each criterion chosen a relative weight in percentage terms. For example, if a primary company strategy is to attract a different customer segment, the *target customer appeal* criterion may be weighted more heavily than whether the products *conform to typical customer purchases*.

Step 4

You should construct an analytical model that can evaluate each product (or occasion) using the criteria identified. You should also rank how well each will meet the company's merchandising goals.

Step 5

Launch the algorithm. Run various promotions on the site, using the merchandising algorithm to choose which products (or occasions) to use within each promotion.

Step 6

Once the algorithm is running, test its effectiveness by tracking customer usage. Because of the Internet's unique ability to allow real-time product adjustments (pricing, placement, etc.), it has an advantage over the offline retail environment. You should track changes in conversion rate, average order size, and sales by category.

The Algorithm in Action: A Hypothetical Example

As an example, let's imagine how a fictional apparel retailer, EZClothes-RUS.com, might implement this merchandising algorithm. EZClothesRUS wants to decide what products it should promote on its home page. Its strategy has three main components:

- Attract men who dress *business casual* at the office
- Introduce its new line of professional luggage
- Increase its average order size and optimize gross margins[3]

Step 1

The company chooses decision criteria that are aligned with its strategic goals:

- Appeal to target customers
- Introduce new product category
- Increase margins
- Increase average order size[4]

Step 2

Fortunately, EZClothesRUS has focus-group data that suggests what apparel is most appealing to the male business-casual segment. The company also knows its revenue and margin on each product, so it has all the data it needs for a simple algorithm.

Step 3

Since its most important objective is capturing the profitable customer segment of professional men, EZClothesRUS weights this criterion at 40 percent, while the other criteria are weighted at 20 percent each.

Step 4

Using office-suite software, EZClothesRUS builds a model that lists all of its product Stock-Keeping Units (SKUs (though product categories would be sufficient if the data are similar across the category)). Along the four decision criteria, each product is given a score on scale of 1 to 5—5 if it best fulfills the criterion.

For yes/no decisions, 5 stands for yes, and 1 for no. For example, a pair of cargo pants might get a score of 4 on appeal to target customers and a score of 1 for the yes/no introduce new product category criterion. The scores are then weighted and the result is a final ranking score for each product SKU.

Stock-Keeping Unit (SKU) refers to retail merchandising jargon for what the aerospace industry would call a part number. A code number assigned to a particular style, sometimes in a particular size.

Step 5

Based on the results of the algorithm, EZClothesRUS decides to promote on the home page a picture of a man wearing flat-front khaki pants and a casual blue oxford and carrying a canvas briefcase.

Step 6

EZClothesRUS tracks customers' click-paths and conversion rate and determines that the oxford should be replaced with a spring polo shirt. Sales continually increase as EZClothesRUS monitors the data and continually improves its merchandising.

Now that we've created, tested, and implemented the merchandising algorithm, let's look at some hands-on examples of how to implement real e-business merchandising strategies.

IMPLEMENTING NEXT-GENERATION E-BUSINESS MERCHANDISING STRATEGIES

Web sites are accommodating a new business model based on e-commerce that encompasses much more than Internet sales. According to Zona Research, 85 percent of organizations surveyed had implemented or planned to implement this e-business model.[5]

Also, according to International Data Corp. (IDC), the worldwide market for Internet-related services is expected to explode from $5.6 billion in 1998 to $54.7 billion by 2003. The main impetus for this trend is the rush to implement e-commerce Web site merchandising strategies.

E-business is more integrated with back-office systems than typical e-commerce efforts, increasing customer satisfaction with faster service and lower operating costs. In addition, adopting e-business can generate new marketing opportunities, reduce time-to-market, and increase return on investment (ROI).

In other words, the important thing to remember when implementing next-generation e-business merchandising strategies is to distinguish e-commerce from e-business, and discuss the differences between business-to-business (B2B) e-commerce and business-to-consumer (B2C) e-commerce. The role of e-business must be emphasized when implementing merchandising strategies for the entire enterprise, by presenting a seamless integration among company systems and with partners' and third-parties' systems. The following are issues that implementers must consider in their merchandising strategies:

- The market for B2B and B2C commerce
- Widely adopted e-business applications
- Centrality of the customer
- Preventing initial implementation disruptions
- Common characteristics of e-business Web sites
- Creating a strategy for supporting an e-business site

Implementing E-Business Merchandising Strategies

E-business offers numerous benefits, but is often accompanied by complex concerns such as security, researching supportive products and vendors, and selecting the most appropriate technologies such as programming languages. In addition to e-business' philosophical basics and related in-depth case studies, enterprises must also be concerned with detailed information regarding e-business principles, tools, and merchandising implementation techniques:

- Electronic bill presentment and payment (EBPP)
- Electronic data interchange (EDI)
- The role of Secure Sockets Layer (SSL)
- *E-merchandising* the supply chain locally and globally
- Using extranets to relate to partners
- Extensible markup language (XML)
- E-business application server, tool, and software vendors
- How to measure e-business and advertising ROI

Fulfillment Merchandising Strategies for E-Commerce

The Internet has dissolved traditional market boundaries and given firms the ability to market their products and services to an enormous collection of potential buyers. Realizing this as an opportunity to make additional sales, firms have raced to develop an e-commerce offering without really understanding the strain this new business model places on fulfillment capacity and fulfillment execution. Many start-up enterprises have generated healthy sales numbers via the e-commerce channel. However, several of these firms have begun to flounder due to a poorly planned fulfillment model. According to a recent study conducted by Forrester Research, a significant number of firms engaged in e-commerce are losing money on every package they ship. Other firms cannot gauge the profitability of their online presence because they fail to accurately capture the costs associated with order fulfillment. As competition in the e-commerce channel continues to intensify, firms will be forced to develop an end-to-end fulfillment merchandising strategy if they wish to remain viable. This merchandising strategy should take into consideration the following questions:

- Where will our products be inventoried—in our warehouses, or will we drop ship from another source?
- How much fulfillment capacity will we need to handle variant demand?
- Should our capacity be centralized, or should we operate multiple distribution points?
- What are the components of our supply chain, and how does each component interact?
- How much control do we have over each component of our supply chain?
- Does e-commerce require a fundamental change in our supply chain strategy?
- What method of distribution will we use to reach our customers?
- Does it make sense to offer all our products to online customers?
- Can we measure the profitability of each shipment?
- How will our e-commerce fulfillment merchandising strategy be supported by technology?[6]

Strategic Positioning

A merchandising strategy usually begins with a hard look at the marketplace and a closer look at what the customer wants. Strategy also demands a blunt examination of the economics and logistics of the entire supply chain to understand the true costs and the real opportunities for growth. The challenge is to create a real-world competitive advantage that can be executed in the routine practice of daily operations. The following strategic positioning services (see the sidebar, "Strategic Positioning Mini Case Studies") should be offered:

- Channel Planning
- Competitive Analysis
- Supply Chain Management
- Modeling of Strategic Alternatives
- Product Portfolio Strategy
- Acquisition Strategy and Business Valuation.[7]

Strategic Positioning Mini Case Studies

Competitive Positioning

Situation:

Eroding margins: A major Canadian dairy-foods producer faces heavy competition. Problem: How to position the company to be competitive in the future and preserve profitability in spite of severe margin pressure.

Action:

Redesign distribution systems, company logistics, and product pricing strategies. Redefine service levels and delivery methods. Identify and develop alternative distribution channels. Revamp the pricing structure for food service accounts, and change compensation to distributors based on the actual cost of service.

Results:

Total costs were reduced by more than $8 million. Payouts to distributors have increased and margins improved.

Partnering within the Supply Chain

Situation:

A premier international consumer goods company is asked to participate in an Efficient Consumer Response (ECR) test with one of its major customers. An alternative distribution and warehousing approach is to be tested, and a cost-benefit analysis is required.

Action:

Conduct an analysis of the functions, activities, and time associated with the current and anticipated system. Develop a cost implications model and use mapping technology to validate the anticipated cost impact.

Results:

The anticipated approach failed to yield system cost savings and identified additional unanticipated costs for the customer. The implications identified in the study altered the initial strategy and redirected the implementation plan.

Evaluating Distribution Channels

Situation:

A Fortune 500 food products company wants to assess the potential for distributing an established product line through alternative channels.

Action:

Conduct a study of alternative distribution channels and evaluate the practices and economics of supplier/distributor relationships.

Results:

Analysis revealed that use of alternative channels was unlikely to succeed in the current business environment. The information enabled the company to make a clear choice: to divest the product line and refocus resources elsewhere.

Product Portfolio Strategy

Situation:

Product portfolio expansion: A large multinational snack-food company wants to identify the incremental costs and profitability of new products and SKUs. Management must identify how adding new SKUs affects incremental time in the trade.

Action:

Define the sales and *e-merchandising* activities in the trade. Conduct audits of retail space and time studies of activities. Develop a modeling tool that predicts time requirements based on package size and space available.

Results:

Alternative merchandising methods and shelf management systems were developed and implemented. The decision model helps the company evaluate the potential success of new products.[8]

Service Strategy and Customer Relationship Management

The basis of customer service strategy is understanding which services the customer values, and knowing the cost of those services. A sound customer service strategy provides a clear map: the right approach for the right customer. The following are service strategy and customer relationship management services (see the sidebar, "Service Strategy and Customer Relationship Management Mini Case Studies") that should be offered:

- Customer Surveys
- Customer Value Analysis
- Cost-to-Serve Analysis: Direct Activity Costing, Formal Service Policy
- Inside Sales and Call Center Effectiveness
- Customer-Focused Sales Strategy
- Account-Based Sales/Service Teams.[9]

Service Strategy and Customer Relationship Management Mini Case Studies

Focusing Sales Strategy

Situation:

A Fortune 100 food products company had their distribution costs evaluated and assessed the need for route engineering technology. Analysis showed that high distribution costs were driven by a sales problem that could not be solved with route engineering. Problem: improper targeting of retail customers.

Action:

Reengineer sales, distribution, and customer service functions.

Results:

Distribution costs were reduced by 26 percent, while volume per stop increased 29 percent. Significant improvements were made in the quality of customer service. In addition, the sales organization got the information needed to pursue profitable business.

Increasing Customer Demands

Situation:

A product-focused industrial supply company encounters customers who are demanding more service. Competitors are capitalizing on this opportunity by selling products and services bundled together, while the company concentrates on individual product line sales.

Action:

Survey the customer base and identify what the customer values. Break down product line barriers and create cross-product-line account teams that are dedicated to serving the needs of specific clients. Establish account team managers who ensure the teams are providing integrated products and services that add value to their customers.

Results:

A greater understanding and awareness of the customer was translated into increased sales and profitability.

Customer-Focused Sales Strategy

Situation:

A major international brewery with over 400 distributors wants to implement consumer-marketing techniques and improve sales and distribution systems through distributors.

Action:

Develop a salesperson tool kit that directs sales activities and expectations. Revise the company's distributor performance standards to reflect objective rather than subjective expectations. Refine channel strategies, based on the account's opportunities, size, and consumer profile. Link the company's corporate marketing strategy to its distributors' street-level tactical execution.

Results:

In a highly competitive market, the company strengthened its distribution network and gained market share.[10]

Logistics, Distribution, and Warehousing

Distribution planning and design is much more than shipping or transportation, it is an integral part of the service offering provided to your customers. Managing logistics costs is not just about finding the lowest-cost solution; it's about developing an overall strategy for going to market and executing that strategy without wasting limited resources. The following logistics, distribution, and warehousing services (see the sidebar, "Logistics, Distribution, and Warehousing Mini Case Studies") should be offered:

- Operations Research
- Network Logistics
- Route and Territory Engineering
- Inventory Management
- Warehouse Flow and Layout
- Warehouse Management Systems.[11]

Logistics, Distribution, and Warehousing Mini Case Studies

Improving Performance

Situation:

Profit squeeze: A major linen and uniform supply company has a block of customers that consumes over 25 percent of delivery costs, while contributing a scant 3 percent of total gross profit dollars. Fleet utilization is low and customer service is weak.

Action:

Redesign delivery service to boost service quality and reduce unproductive time. Trim distribution activities that add no value. Increase weekly face time on each account.

Results:

Revenue per route increased 22 percent. Overall delivery cost was trimmed by 19 percent, and retention of profitable customers showed dramatic improvement.

Streamlining Distribution

Situation:

A retail grocer has two dairy production plants approximately 100 miles apart. Each plant produces distinctly different products. Direct-store deliveries and empty case pick-ups are made from both locations. Consequently, there are duplications of delivery expenses.

Action:

Using computerized modeling tools, the customer structure is analyzed to determine which customers should be shipped direct from each location, which customers should have combined cross-docked deliveries, and which customers should go through third-party affiliated distribution.

Results:

By assigning the right services to each customer, distribution costs were reduced by 22 percent while the frequency of delivery was increased to many stores.

Network Modeling

Situation:

A New England soft-drink bottler with multiple distribution centers (DCs) in close proximity has excess distribution capacity and expense. The company wants to determine the optimal number and locations of the DCs to achieve the lowest-cost network.

Action:

Compile direct activity cost information for each part of the supply chain. Develop a model of the current supply chain network and test the impact of alternatives.

Results:

Twenty-five percent of the DC locations were eliminated, creating a more efficient supply chain network with a stronger customer service orientation.

Inventory Management

Situation:

A wholesale distributor gets inadequate returns on its investment in inventory, and the sales force is diluted by an unmanageable book of products to sell.

Action:

Direct a strategic initiative to evaluate and streamline the company's product portfolio and fine-tune its product addition/deletion policy.

Results:

The company achieved a 40-percent reduction in SKUs, reducing inventory by 31 percent with a 3.2-percent increase in sales volume over the prior year.[12]

Organizational Infrastructure

The customer landscape and a company's strategy for going to market should be the driving forces in defining positions and justifying every role in the organization. We've seen what can happen when time is invested prudently and people are positioned, equipped, and compensated to support company strategy. The following organizational infrastructure services (see the sidebar, "Organizational Infrastructure Mini Case Studies") should be offered:

- Work Measurement
- Organizational Analysis and Design
- Market-Focused Job Design
- Manpower Planning
- Productivity Improvement.[13]

Organizational Infrastructure Mini Case Studies

Raising the Bar for the Sales Force

Situation:

An emerging national consumer packaged goods producer has a small but skilled sales force and an expanding distributor network. The problem: How to help the two interface effectively, to leverage efforts of the distribution network.

Action:

Make structural changes in the sales organization to redefine roles. Establish criteria for more productive interaction with the independent distributor network. Develop specific training tools to help the sales force understand the distributor perspective.

Results:

Volume has increased across the distributor network. The sales force is viewed as more knowledgeable and providing greater value. The product lines have become the leaders in the producer's niche market.

Market-Driven Job Design

Situation:

Sales burnout, high turnover: A large regional distributor is caught between budget constraints and increasing retail merchandising demands. Solving the workload problem by expecting salespeople to work more hours results in employee turnover, which damages trade execution and customer service.

Action:

Realign account service based on account profitability. Clearly define workloads and build jobs around actual work requirements rather than commissions. Revise compensation plans and commission structures to ensure that job skills and pay levels are properly aligned.

Results:

The sales day was trimmed from 13-plus to an average of 10 hours. Sales compensation is up 5–10 percent. Branch operating expenses are virtually unchanged. Turnover has been cut dramatically, and salespeople who quit have reapplied.

Work Force Planning

Situation:

Insufficient work force: An international industrial manufacturing company faces increased demand and a shortage of highly skilled company representatives. The customer is receiving inadequate service, and the company representatives lack focus, accountability, and the ability to form partnerships in key accounts.

Action:

Develop a streamlined sales system with clarified accountability and responsibilities. Activities in the sales organization are allocated by skill set. Train additional support personnel to enable the company to exceed customer expectations.

Results:

Customer service was aligned with customer demands. Service levels and capacity increased. Representatives gained a greater understanding of building long-term customer relationships and securing future business.

Sales Support Systems

Situation:

Increased demand and a market-wide shortage of qualified sales reps: Important but time-consuming quote-building activities performed by a Canadian manufacturer's sales reps are limiting the company's ability to adequately cover the market, resulting in lost sales opportunities and share erosion.

Action:

Design a sales support system to perform quote-building activities for sales reps using less expensive, but available, technical and administrative labor.

Results:

Effective market coverage increased by 20 percent. Sales quote quality and uniformity increased through process standardization. Share erosion was halted.[14]

Information and Technology

Technology and information systems are enablers, giving people the tools they need to make intelligent business decisions in real time. The challenge is to facilitate supply-chain execution in a high-velocity transaction environment. Consultants can help assess information and automation needs to make sure the focus is on quality real-time information rather than quantity and history. Consultants can also work with leading system providers to develop an infrastructure in which business systems and processes can match the speed of the marketplace. Consultants usually offer the following information and technology services (see the sidebar, "Information and Technology Mini Case Studies"):

- Sales Force Automation and Order Management
- Sales Information Systems
- Supply-Chain Planning
- Supply-Chain Execution
- Operating Systems Requirements Design
- Tracking and Measurement Systems
- Technology ROI
- Customer Relationship Management (CRM)[15]

Information and Technology Mini Case Studies

Data Warehousing

Situation:

To control costs without missing sales, a nationwide vending operator wants to know how often to replenish inventory at thousands of individual point-of-purchase locations. The company wants a hands-on tool that helps its managers adjust service frequency as needed on an on-going basis.

Action:

Develop an interactive automated data warehouse that managers use to track key indicators at each location. The desktop program analyzes weekly sales and productivity data, and recommends changes in service frequency when appropriate.

Results:

Guesswork was eliminated with more accurate and useful performance history information by site and route. The company became better equipped to adjust to shifting demand and improved truck utilization and driver resources. Route service productivity increased by 21 percent.

Implementing Technology

Situation:

A multiline wholesaler faces high distribution costs due to poor route efficiency and ineffective customer service strategies.

Action:

Redesign customer service standards based on cost/profit data. Implement new route engineering technology designed to balance workloads, identify appropriate service levels, boost productivity, and reduce distribution costs.

Results:

The company achieved a $4-million improvement in net profits, with a 25-percent improvement in delivery efficiency (volume per route).

Technology ROI

Situation:

A Fortune 500 consumer products company is investigating the acquisition of an advanced remote ordering technology. An anticipated return on investment for the technology is required prior to acquisition.

Action:

Complete a detailed assessment of the current activities associated with order generation. Determine the time associated with these activities and identify the direct costs. Develop direct activity costs to calculate the tangible value of the new technology.

Results:

Significant opportunities to improve the existing system without technology were identified. Process changes were implemented to maximize the existing system prior to the implementation of new technology. The ROI of the new technology is now based on the costs of an optimized system.[16]

So, because e-business is a technological revolution, organizations that formulate and implement merchandising strategies today will have a considerable advantage over their competitors. Organizations that wait to develop e-business merchandising strategies may never meet the success of their predecessors. Within five years, e-business is likely to refer not to a single type of business but to all business. Thus, implementing next-generation e-business merchandising strategies is an invaluable resource for those responsible for *e-merchandising* business practices to gain a competitive advantage.

INTERNET TECHNIQUES

Techniques for using the Internet are documented practically everywhere, from daily newspapers to the thousands of books being published to articles in mainstream magazines. And of course, even more material is available online on the Internet itself as well as the online services. Attempting to reproduce all this information in this chapter would clearly be unreasonable. Instead, a small selection of techniques useful to online merchants and customers is presented here.

Shopping Techniques

Online shopping seems to be breaking down into two categories: commodities and specialty items. In the past, commodities were mostly raw materials that were available with minimal differentiation from any number of different sources. For instance, coal, wheat, or sugar is essentially the same no matter where it comes from, and pricing is usually about the same from any source. There are many more differentiable products that can now be considered commodities, simply because they are available from many different sources and differ only in price from one source to another.

Specialty items, on the other hand, include anything that cannot be bought elsewhere. Specialties could simply be a piece of information or software not sold anywhere else, or special chocolates, or practically anything else sold only in one place.

Buying Commodities Online

Many computer products are sold as commodities: No matter where you buy a Whizzo XT-10 Ethernet card or a Praxiteles 20? color monitor or a copy of Word-O-Rific Writing Wizard 5000 word processing software, the products themselves will be essentially the same, with the same documentation, service, and support. Shopping for name-brand products like these is generally done on the basis of price, delivery, and availability. Many different merchants, both online and offline, are competing for your patronage.

If you are shopping for this type of product, there are certain things to keep in mind:

- Do your research first. Determine the vendors, product numbers, and options you want ahead of time—the quality and detail of online merchants' product descriptions vary widely. Check other sources for pricing, as well, if that is important.
- Low prices are important, but another one of the greatest benefits of shopping online is instant gratification. Find out how products are delivered, and how much shipping and handling will cost.
- Keep track of what you order. Merchants selling hard goods online should send you e-mail confirmations of your order, as well as shipping information. Save your e-mail confirmations, and keep them backed up, so you can verify credit card bills.
- If the product you want has to be special-ordered, consider dealing with a local merchant to avoid additional shipping costs. Overnight delivery of a product that won't be in for two weeks may be an expense you can do without.

Don't be surprised to find prices online consistently lower than prices in magazine or newspaper advertisements, particularly for computer products. Print ads must be submitted well in advance to publications, while World Wide Web sites can reflect the absolutely latest prices.

Finally, the online customer should exercise the same or greater caution in choosing an online trading partner as in choosing a mail or telephone order merchant. Even with the development of SET and other security measures, common sense should be used in picking any trading partner, either online or driving down the street.

Buying Specialty Items Online

Buying commodity items online is much like buying them in person: The customer has many opportunities for comparison shopping, and impulse purchases may not predominate. Purchase of specialty items, however, may be more impulsive. The greater challenge is finding the merchant if there is only one source.

Merchants with unique products can be found by chance, or by looking for them using any of the many Internet catalogs, or by browsing related Internet sites. Word of mouth is another way to locate specialty merchants.

Keeping security issues in mind, as well as local regulations, is about all you need to consider when buying something you want or need online. Logic and common sense should be your guide: Purchases of military secrets, criminal services, and bootleg versions of copyrighted or patented materials should be avoided online as well as in person.

While military secrets and criminal services will usually be readily identifiable (and avoidable), it might be more difficult to determine when intellectual property rights are being violated. If there is any question about ownership of information, you may want to think twice about buying it. Some cases of piracy will be clear-cut: If someone other than the publisher is offering scanned copies of a best-selling book for a fraction of the cover price, that merchant may be a pirate.

Online Selling Techniques

Simply having a Web page is not sufficient for making sales online. Even if it is equipped to take online orders through a payment system like Cyber-Cash, or through a secure World Wide Web server, or both, sales will not automatically follow. There are many issues involved with online marketing, and although this is not a marketing text, there are a few guiding principles that will help the Internet merchant.

Make Your Store Easy to Reach

Every Internet URL is, at least in theory, as easy to retrieve as any other. In practice, however, there are many factors that will affect the accessibility of your Internet store. You should make it as simple as possible for potential customers to reach your Web site. This includes making it simple for them to refer to your store, as well as making it easy to see what you have to offer, and to order products.

The first step in making your store accessible is making sure that potential customers know your store's URL. Include it in your advertising materials, on your company letterhead, on your business cards—anywhere you would include your business telephone number or address.

Another important technique is to get as many links to your Web site as possible. Listing in Internet catalogs like Yahoo!, Lycos, and others is akin to listing in business directories or the Yellow Pages business telephone directory. Look, too, for other Web sites that are relevant to your products, and request reciprocal links. Consider links and ads in special Web sites that may charge for the privilege. Depending on the cost, your product, and the audience these sites can deliver, your investment may be worthwhile.

Once your potential customers have arrived at your Web site, make sure they don't leave right away by providing the best service you can afford. Customer performance will vary depending on many variables over which you have no control, but if your Internet connection is slow, your customers may suffer. Likewise, if you are sharing a Web server with other popular Web pages through an Internet presence provider, your customers may have a hard time getting through.

If you anticipate high demand for access to your Web site, make sure you can handle it. If it takes five minutes to download your page, you'll lose a lot of customers who would rather not wait that long.

Make Your Site Easy to Use

People don't like to wait for Web pages any more than they like waiting for anything else. Make sure you deliver your message fast and concisely up front. For example, if you are selling classical music CDs online and you accept CyberCash only, make sure that is clear up front. Otherwise, customers may spend half an hour browsing your site, find half a dozen CDs they want to buy, and then never return when they realize they can't buy them right away. If you put that information up front, along with a pointer to the CyberCash site, your customers will thank you.

Another common method for reducing waiting time without upgrading your Internet link is to cut down on graphic images, or give customers the option of viewing text-only.

Avoid using too many unnecessarily nested menus. Don't make the customer wade through half a dozen submenus with a few options on each if you can use one big main menu with lots of options all together.

Finally, learn as much as you can about Web site design by browsing other sites, taking courses, and reading books. Observe how successful Web sites succeed, and how unsuccessful Web sites fail.

Make Your Products Easy to Buy

If you plan to sell your products online, make sure that customers can get everything they need to make a purchase. That means considering all the questions a typical customer might have, and providing the answers, which might include the following:

- Product specifications
- Prices
- Delivery information
- Product options
- Complete product description
- How to use the product
- Testimonials from satisfied customers
- References to product reviews and press coverage

Of course, ordering information must be included; this should be as simple as adding a BUY button to the Web page that points at an online order form.

Making online ordering possible is not always desirable. For example, any product that must be customized to the individual customer pretty much requires direct contact. However, if you do not make online ordering available, you should provide some way to initiate a sales contact online. Simply using an automatic e-mail responder is not enough, especially if the response is simply a version of the same information available through the Web site. There should be some way for the potential customer to directly contact a merchant representative with questions about the product. If e-mail is not practical, at least include a telephone number or postal address.

If you do choose to sell online, be sure you accept as many different methods of payment as practical and possible for you. For the near term, this may mean accepting different credit cards online through a secure server, as well as accepting CyberCash or some other payment system (see the sidebar, "American Express Provides Innovative Way to Pay Online: Unique, Random Number Safeguards Customers and Helps Reduce Fraud"). However, as other payment methods like Internet checking and digital currency systems become more common, you will need to accept some of them. Just as important, you should also include telephone and mail-order information for those who prefer to do business that way.

American Express Provides Innovative Way to Pay Online: Unique, Random Number Safeguards Customers and Helps Reduce Fraud

Addressing consumer concerns about online privacy and security, American Express recently announced a new series of products that provide customers with greater choice and protection when browsing and shopping online. The first product, known as Private Payments™, is an industry breakthrough that offers a more secure way to pay online using a random, unique number for each online purchase. Private Payments enables customers to purchase online without transmitting their actual card account numbers over the Internet. Private Payments is now available free of charge to American Express consumers and small-business cardmembers in the United States.

The company has also signed an agreement with and made a minority investment in Privada Inc., a digital privacy infrastructure provider, to deliver a second product that will enable customers to choose how much of their information is shared when they browse any site on the Web. This private browsing product will allow customers to select from settings that range from sharing their full identity to anonymity. This service is now available. Additional offerings in the new suite of American Express products will be announced in the fourth quarter of 2001 and 2002. While the Internet has dramatically eased the way in which consumers research and purchase products, it also has increased concern for protecting privacy and security.

How Private Payments Works

Using Private Payments to shop online is quick and easy. Interested cardmembers can register for the free service. When cardmembers are ready to purchase online, they can access the service by going to the Private Payments home page at http//www.americanexpress.com, or by clicking on the Private Payments icon on their desktop. This launches the service, which then prompts them for username and password, and to select the American Express® Card they want linked to the Private Payments number. A unique Private Payments number with expiration date is then randomly created by American Express. The cardmember transfers this information to the merchant order form to complete the purchase. The cardmember's actual card account number is not sent over the Internet, thus keeping this information secure. The item purchased is charged to the cardmember's selected American Express Card and appears on the monthly billing statement, as usual.

Further safeguarding the online purchase, the Private Payments number is designed to be used for a single purchase and to expire after the merchant authorization process is completed. Upon expiration, the Private Payments number cannot be used again if stolen.

Private Payments should give consumers peace of mind, knowing that their actual card number is not transmitted over the Internet. Merchants benefit from the increased confidence consumers have when shopping online and decreased potential for fraud, since each unique Private Payments number expires within a limited timeframe.[17]

IMPLEMENTING E-COMMERCE DATABASES

Many issues come into play when deciding the best way to implement your e-commerce database on the Web, including: the platform on which your current database was developed, the size of your database, the number of users accessing your data, and security concerns. Databases allow the electronic commerce in interactive marketing and Internet shopping. Web sites will increasingly use integration of back office systems combined with the advanced personalization features provided by database solutions for its customers.

Research findings reveal that 78 percent of Web sites will use databases in 2000. Seventy percent (70%) of the non-database Web sites will evaluate and use databases in 2001.

Businesses now rely on databases to deliver the best electronic commerce Web sites. This means that if the customer is on the telephone with an account representative, sending an e-mail to the company, or updating his or her personalized catalog page, he or she will enjoy the same access to information and same level of service regardless of his or her point of contact with the company. Also, the customer will have a high-level personalization with respect to the look and feel of the site, pricing, customer support, and billing.

Building and Managing Your Databases with SQL Enterprise Manager

Today, most businesses use Microsoft's SQL Enterprise Manager to build, implement, and manage their e-commerce databases. SQL stands for *Structured Query Language.*

Why You Should Use SQL

An SQL server is a high-performance database server that is designed for high traffic and large databases. The technology behind SQL makes it far superior when compared to traditional databases such as Access, Paradox, FoxPro, etc. SQL is faster, more powerful, and very fault tolerant.

How to Access/Transfer Data from an SQL Database

Connecting to an SQL database can be accomplished through many means. You can use an ODBC connection to make applications like MS Access or Visual Interdev directly connect to your SQL database. However, if you want total control over all the aspects of your database, it is recommended that you use SQL Enterprise Manager or a Transact-SQL Client application such as SQL Query.

Making Web Sites that Interact with an SQL Database

How do you make a Web site interact with an SQL database? This can also be accomplished through different technologies. The typical method of doing this is by using scripting languages such as Active Server Pages (ASP) or ColdFusion. These languages have the built-in capability to execute SQL statements that can interact and even modify SQL databases.

Some advanced applications like Visual Interdev and FrontPage 2000 or higher also have the capability to easily create Web pages that interact with SQL databases. Using applications such as these makes things a lot easier for novices or people under time constraints.

How to Get SQL

In order to obtain SQL, you should have an account. Your database technicians (inhouse or outsourced) should be able to set up your SQL account with the necessary parameters. Several pieces of information are required to set up your SQL database account. The technicians should complete a setup request form similar to the one shown in Figure 9.1.[18]

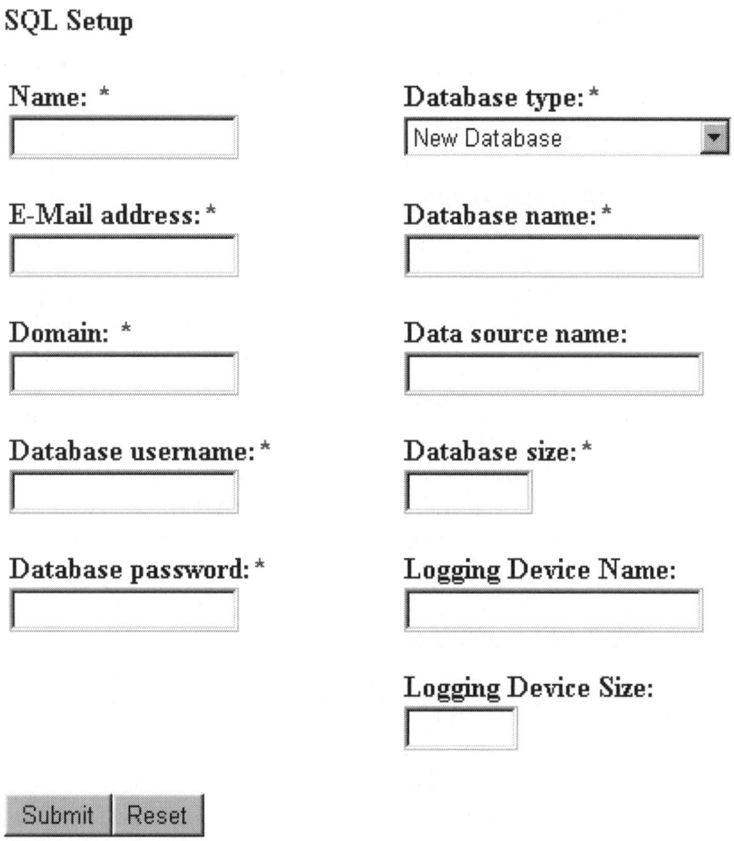

SQL Setup

Name: *	**Database type:** *
[_____]	[New Database ▼]
E-Mail address: *	**Database name:** *
[_____]	[_____]
Domain: *	**Data source name:**
[_____]	[_____]
Database username: *	**Database size:** *
[_____]	[_____]
Database password: *	**Logging Device Name:**
[_____]	[_____]
	Logging Device Size:
	[_____]

[Submit] [Reset]

FIGURE 9.1 Example of an SQL account setup request form.

Once your technicians have completed the database setup, you will be able to access your SQL server account.

Usage Limits on Your SQL Account

Your SQL disk usage will be included in your total allowable disk usage. For example, if you are on an account plan that allocates 100MB of disk usage, and you use 50MB of disk usage on your SQL account, that leaves you 50MB of disk usage for your Web site or other options before going over your account plan.

How to Access SQL

To access the SQL database you can use any database management software, such as Microsoft Access, Visual InterDev, or the SQL Enterprise Manager. If you are using Microsoft Access or Visual InterDev, you will be connecting to the SQL database via an ODBC connection, which requires you to create a Data Source Name on your local computer. To do this, follow these instructions:

1. Go to the ODBC section on your computer and open it. In Windows 95/98/NT or 2000/NT, your ODBC settings can be found in your Administration page.
2. Add either a File DSN or a Machine DSN. It does not make a difference; the decision is up to you.
3. Click the Add button, and then select the SQL server driver. If you do not have this driver, you must get it in order to make a connection to the SQL server. You can get this driver by going to Microsoft's Web site at: http://www.microsoft.com/SQL/downloads/
4. After it displays the information on the DSN you are setting up, it will ask for the server location. In this field, type in the IP address your received in your setup confirmation e-mail. It also asks for a username and password; type in the one you requested on the SQL setup form (see Figure 9.1).
5. Click the Options button. You will see a series of drop-down boxes. Find the box labeled "Database" and click the down arrow. If your ODBC driver is working correctly, you should see a list of databases, and yours will be highlighted.[19]

If you are using SQL Enterprise Manager, you need to follow these instructions:

1. Open the SQL Enterprise Manager.
2. Click "Server", "Register Server".
3. Once the dialog box is open, fill in the fields. In the Server field, type in the username and password you received in your setup confirmation e-mail.
4. Fill in the login information with the username and password that you requested. If you did not request one, enter your FTP username and the original password that was set up for you when you opened your account.

5. Once all the information is entered press the "Register" button—this will make contact with the SQL server. Now that you are connected, you can add tables and manipulate the following information as you wish:

■ Design product, order, and customer databases
■ Update database architectures and products
■ Create product/price tables
■ Prepare SQL queries
■ Import from existing databases[20]

INTERNET TOOLS

In a strict sense, tools are those things that are necessary to create some result: A carpenter would use a hammer and saw to create furniture, and a programmer would use a compiler and a program editor to create software. However, transacting business online is a much more broadly defined pursuit, and the tools you must use cover far wider ground.

The most basic, and most important, tool you can put at your disposal is a connection to the Internet and software to use that connection. A good Web browser, electronic mail client, file transfer software, and the underlying networking software necessary to make it all run are requirements to get at the information available online. With these tools, you will be able to locate information about practically any other Internet tool or technique, including HTML tagging and translation software, secure transaction software, consulting services, World Wide Web server and browser tools and packages, industry organizations, consultants, and vendors of services.

Choosing a Browser

If you can use only one Internet application, a World Wide Web browser is probably the most logical choice. It is the easiest Internet interface to use; it can support other Internet applications, including Telnet, FTP, Gopher, and e-mail; and it is widely implemented on different platforms.

The personal computer browser market is currently dominated by Microsoft with the Internet Explorer, and Netscape Communications with the Netscape Communicator browser. Both products are readily available for download from many different locations—as long as you already are online. You can also purchase Communicator packaged with Internet connectivity software through computer software and hardware retailers.

Other Internet Client Software

Electronic mail has been an essential application for decades, from the time it first became available on mainframes in the 1960s to the present. An electronic mail client should be able to save messages sent and received, allow file attachments, preferably using the MIME standard, and be almost completely intuitive to use.

Organizations may prefer to continue using their existing e-mail client by implementing an Internet gateway to their existing e-mail server. Individuals may wish to purchase a package like Eudora or others. Microsoft includes e-mail client software with its Windows 95/98, 2000 or higher and Windows Plus! products, as well as other Internet applications software (see the next section).

FTP, or the File Transfer Protocol, defines procedures for transfer of files between Internet hosts. This protocol is often invoked when transferring files from World Wide Web sites, but can also be used on its own. While FTP-only sites used to be fairly common, they are becoming less common as more sites move their published data to Web sites, or at least to Web interfaces. FTP may be implemented much like a Windows file manager program, including drag-and-drop file copying. Look for it to be included with complete TCP/IP packages like those from Wollongong, FTP Software, and many others.

Telnet, a remote terminal session application, is less frequently used. It is included with complete TCP/IP packages; Microsoft includes a Telnet implementation with Windows 95/98 and 2000 or higher.

APPLYING WEB COMMERCE TOOLS

Finally, the Web is just the way to take customer interactions and relationships to a new level. Forget about just publishing and informing users—today, we can captivate, enhance, educate, compel, and motivate customers on the Web.

As companies, we are not the only ones with power. Customers are armed with the power of *choice*, and this makes building customer relationships and intimacy even more important in order to differentiate your company from the next—remembering that the next company is but a *click* away.

What follows is a brief, but good summary of what these Web commerce tools are and how they can be applied and used; but, remember, new uses and techniques for building relationships are surfacing all the time.

E-Mail Rules

More people have e-mail than Web access. Mailing lists can be very powerful and cheap. The strength of e-mail is that it is easy to administer, update, and communicate with customers. Its weakness: Many customers can't read HTML e-mail messages that can expand this communication channel (for probably another 12–18 months).

Cookies and Server Databases

Cookies and server databases help customize Web views based on customer preferences, characteristics, selections, surveyed information, etc. These tools maintain information on each customer to determine what to present to him or her on the web. Their strength can be used to better *serve* the customer if integrated with your business strategies. Their weakness: There are privacy concerns with cookies, but companies can be up front if the customer is receiving a strong value.

Push Technology

Push technology can broadcast selected information. Compelling uses for push technology have been limited; and this metaphor wears thin quickly. Its strength: It works well for routine information that varies among groups and when customers/employees are overwhelmed with information. Its weakness: There is no standard here, and the customized information is likely better suited for internal employees as opposed to customers.

Presentations

Presentations can save travel costs, but don't benefit the customer. Several companies like Evoke Communications offer technology to hold *virtual* presentations over the Net while you talk to the customer via a regular telephone or not at all if audio is included. Presentations are dismissed as cost savers, not relationship enhancers.

Browser Control

Finally, browser control is here and features a new level of interaction. New technology allowing representatives to take and give up control of a customer's browser enables new applications in the areas of customer support, troubleshooting, assembly, and basically any interaction that would normally need more than a telephone call. Its strength: a new way of interacting with a customer for specific applications that add value. Its weakness: Customers need another telephone line for voice and it is not quite here yet. For more information on Web commerce building tools, go to the following URL: http://winfiles.cnet.com/apps/98/webauth-commerce.html

END NOTES

[1]Creative Good, Inc. 307 W. 38th St., 17th Floor, New York, NY 10018, 2000.
[2]Ibid.
[3]Ibid.
[4]Ibid.
[5]Zona Research, Inc., 900 Veterans Blvd., Suite 500, Redwood City, CA 94063, 2000.
[6]The Denver Management Group, Inc. Management Consultants, 1777 South Harrison St., Suite 1100, Denver, Colorado 80210, 2000.
[7]Ibid.
[8]Ibid.
[9]Ibid.
[10]Ibid.
[11]Ibid.
[12]Ibid.
[13]Ibid.
[14]Ibid.
[15]Ibid.
[16]Ibid.
[17]American Express Company, 200 Vesey Street, New York, NY 10285, 2000.
[18]JP's High Tech World, Inc., R R 2 Box 406 G, New Wilmington, PA 16142, 2000.
[19]Ibid.
[20]Ibid.

10 Designing and Building E-Commerce Web Sites: Hands-On

"The actual tragedies of life bear no relation to one's preconceived ideas. In the event, one is always bewildered by their simplicity, their grandeur of design, and by that element of the bizarre which seems inherent in them."

—JEAN COCTEAU, FRENCH, FIRST TRUE MULTIMEDIA ARTIST (1889–1963)

The key to e-commerce (particularly on the Web) is to provide compelling content for visitors and to enhance the experience of conducting business online. The quality of a site's content is directly correlated to its success.

What makes Web sites effective? In brief, effective e-commerce sites assume the customer's perspective rather than the company's perspective, providing substantive information of value to the visitor rather than providing the online corporate brochures often referred to as *brochureware*. The site must be easy to use and navigate; if online sales are offered, the process should be as easy as possible for the user. The site should be updated frequently, providing the user with an incentive to return. Because the Web is a two-way communication medium, customers should be able to provide feedback either using online forms or through an e-mail address; the company should then respond to the feedback. The Web is both educational and entertaining; when appropriate, a touch of creativity enhances the interaction, placing communication with the user on a more personal level.

CUSTOMER-DRIVEN DESIGN

When companies launch a Web site, the design focus is often placed on the company and the desire to tell the world about it through a company profile. It is, after all, XYZ Corporation's site, and should explain who XYZ Corporation is. Although seemingly intuitive, this approach neglects to consider the audience of the Web site, customers, and prospective customers. While corporate information should be available from the home page of any e-commerce site, including information for contacting the company offline, the driving design principle behind the Web site must be to provide information wanted or needed by the customer.

So, can the Web replace traditional channels of customer service? It cannot and should not. It can, however, reduce the substantial cost of providing effective customer service. According to the Gartner Group of Stamford, Connecticut, companies worldwide spent an estimated $820 million on help desks and customer support in 2000. Answering repetitive questions is tiresome for customer service representatives (CSRs), not to mention expensive for the employer.

The Web streamlines the ordering process, allowing customers to fill in their own name and address rather than give out this information over the telephone. Web-based forms can replace calls to 800 numbers. At Greyhound, customers who want to charter a bus can fill in online forms at the Web site and then receive an estimate of the cost in a follow-up e-mail message from a CSR.

Partially designed to provide answers to common questions, voice response units (VRUs) at many companies provide callers with a range of options. VRUs have gained in acceptance in the business world, handling about 75 percent of all calls in the banking industry alone.

Recognizing that the Web can answer repetitive questions more effectively than VRUs for those customers connected to the Internet, a variety of companies that have call center software offer a Web interface to the call centers. Using such software, customers who need to speak with a representative can leave messages on the Web by pressing the *Call me* button.

While customer service over the Web can reduce expenses, the Web site should also provide information about a company's products and services. FAQs provide a straightforward approach to asking customers' questions, helping them evaluate whether the product is suitable, and potentially educating customers about some of the technical or little understood benefits of the product in question.

To help decide what value-added information can enhance the corporate Web site, consider the wants or needs of the customer. Customer surveys provide one source of information, but CSRs can also help by informing the site designers of the types of questions normally received from customers.

NAVIGATIONAL EASE

Valuable information, then, is the foundation of Web development. The structure of the Web site, which enables customers to locate that information, is at least as important. The Web is less art than architecture. If a site is not structured so that users can quickly find what they are looking for, it matters little how much valuable information the site contains.

A site's Web pages should contain an intuitive structure. Some sites even include an index, a table of contents that allows users to quickly locate pages of interest. Sites that are difficult to navigate are, not surprisingly, often rejected by users.

While designers tend to construct a site in a tree structure, moving from the home page out to all the branching pages, keep in mind that customers do not always start from the home page. Using search engines such as AltaVista, all pages on the site are indexed. A much-focused search may lead the user to a page eight levels into the site, perhaps to the technical specifications for a product. Because one cannot predict on which page a user will start, it become essential to provide a link to the home page on each page of the site.

Providing links to each major topical area on every page is also effective. By providing links to all major areas of the site, users get an overall feel of the types of information available and may stay longer at the site.

In addition to providing sound structure and easy navigability among pages, include a search engine so users can retrieve information quickly. The larger the site, the more diligent designers must be to structure it in a way that enables customers to quickly locate information.

According to IDC, serious e-commerce Web sites have an average of 40 categories, 12 levels of depth, and perhaps 90,000 stock numbers from which to choose. Navigation that gets customers where they want to go quickly is essential.

STREAMLINING THE SHOPPING PROCESS

The goal of e-commerce is to encourage customers to order products. Surprisingly, the ordering process at many sites can be frustrating, using too many forms to accomplish the task. Given the time it may take each page to load, shopping online can prove to be more time consuming than ordering by telephone. Online ordering systems should make the process of shopping at least as easy as traditional methods.

Some sites with a variety of items allow customers to aggregate purchases in a virtual shopping basket. In this process, sites should estimate the most commonly ordered quantity and default the quantity field to that number rather than require users to type it in. Previous customers should be able to retrieve their customer information rather than retype it, making it easy for customers to conduct repeat business. Usability tests involving novice users can provide valuable insight into flaws in the site's design that may not be apparent to experienced Web users.

Successful sites typically accept payments using a variety of methods, both online and offline. Offering multiple payment methods, including browser-based encryption for handling credit cards, makes purchasing online convenient for shoppers. Providing an option to arrange for payment offline using fax or telephone accommodates customers who prefer not to input credit card numbers on the Internet.

Pages on the Web are far more interactive and graphical today than the flat gray pages that predominated in early 1995. Graphics abound, as do multimedia elements, including streaming audio and video that play in real time when encountered (multimedia that does not stream forces users to wait for large files to download before playing). Small programs written in Sun's Java programming language or Microsoft's ActiveX are embedded in Web pages, providing unlimited interactivity. A hyperlink today may simply bring up another page of text-based information or it might download an application or start a video. Further complicating this scenario are the differences among browsers. An ActiveX control, viewed through a Netscape browser, will simply appear to be a broken link or produce an error message. Various multimedia content types require software viewers.

 Accepting unencrypted credit card numbers at a Web site is inadvisable. It puts the user at risk of having his or her credit card misused. From the vendor's point of view, storing credit card numbers on the site increases the likelihood that hackers will attempt to break into it.

The range of options available requires designers to focus on and be aware of the demographics for their site. For example, sites aimed at independent construction contractors must realize that hardware and software upgrades are often a low priority in this marketplace. Expecting visitors to have more than Windows 2000 and a 28,800 baud modem would be a mistake. Mass-market sites should design to the current mainstream technologies, considering that many users will have slower connections or pay by the minute for connection time. Users will leave if pages take too long to load.

By testing the Web site with a 28,800 modem, designers can see whether pages are too graphical to load quickly. To be effective, clear the browser's cache before testing, or connect from another location. Do not assume that browsers have certain capabilities.

Despite the graphical nature of the Web, text views are important. The best approach is to ensure that the site is visually appealing from text-based browsers such as Lynx (often used by blind users) and from popular graphical browsers with images turned off (an approach often taken by users with low-speed connections). HTML allows users to provide alternative text for each graphic on the page. Because graphic designers often influence how sites appear, few sites offer as clear a representation with graphics turned off as with them on, despite the fact that many serious Web users approach the Web in a nongraphical manner.

GRAPHIC DESIGN

The Web is a graphical medium and requires design work from professionals. Too often, however, artists bring little sensitivity to the technical constraints faced by Web users. Effective e-commerce sites can be created by combining winning designs that make judicious use of graphics with sensitivity to how the design will appear on a variety of browsers.

Various techniques can be used to speed graphics loading. Reducing the number of colors in a graphic makes it load more quickly.

Another factor that designers must consider is that users do not all have the same size window on the Web. Laptop monitors are minuscule compared with oversized graphics workstation screens. Viewing the site from a few different-sized screens can enable the designer to see if common errors have been committed. For example, a page designed on a large screen may have text on the right side of the page cut off when the page is viewed on a narrower display. If a page is created on a small workstation screen and uses vertical bands of color on the left for navigational purposes, the bands may repeat on a larger screen if the page is coded incorrectly.

Even at low speeds, animated graphics interchange formats (GIFs) add interest and liveliness to Web pages. Ice cream company Ben & Jerry's site makes liberal use of animated GIFs to add interest to their pages. Because animated GIFs work by rotating thumbnail images stored in cache, they load quickly and require no special viewer. If a browser does not support animated GIFs, the icons appear as static images.

ADDING MULTIMEDIA CONTENT

Multimedia elements can bolster an e-commerce Web site if these elements are properly aligned with business goals and are appropriate for the demographics of the site's audience. For example, BMW's Web site includes video clips. Although video clips would be far too slow for customers with low-speed connection, BMW's customers are upscale and are likely to have access to the most up-to-date hardware available. Streaming video and audio, animation technologies such as Shockwave, and even three-dimensional (3-D) virtual reality (VR) interfaces, can add depth and interest to a corporate Web site.

MAKING THE WEB SITE INTERACTIVE

Beyond multimedia—the traditional *bells and whistles* of a Web site—are the technologies that add interactive content to make Web pages capable of performing any tasks a normal software program can perform. Sun's Java programming language is one such interactive technology; Microsoft's ActiveX, built on object linking and embedding (OLE) controls is another. The primary benefit of using these interactive technologies is the ability to run programs on the client system, programs that may either have entertainment value (an online game) or perform complex operations such as enabling a customer to conduct banking business, use a spreadsheet, or draw a map.

Java in particular has the advantage of being completely platform independent. For information technology (IT) managers who contend with the maintenance of separate software versions for each platform they support, the idea of writing code once and deploying it everywhere is highly attractive. In addition, these interactive technologies offer promise in e-commerce; rather than sending customers through a cumbersome series of HTML forms, orders can be taken interactively with branches in the program handling various types of orders.

Architecturally, Java and ActiveX differ substantially. Java has its roots in C++, and ActiveX is rooted in Windows programming, OLE, and OLE custom controls (OCX) and draws on the substantial base of Visual Basic programmers. Java is inherently more secure than ActiveX in its design; Java applets, when downloaded and executed over a network, cannot access the user's hard drive or transmit files over the network. ActiveX controls, on the other hand, can do anything a Windows program can do. Although Microsoft's ActiveX is gaining prominence, Java currently dominates in Web-based commerce. Therefore, interactive technology is increasingly being used not to add entertainment value to a site, but to perform business functions.

Interactive Web pages with embedded programs are increasingly becoming commonplace in e-commerce and in the business world at large. As more common platforms run the same code, expect the use of interactivity at Web sites to increase rather than decrease. Having someone on staff who can program in Java or ActiveX will enable companies to extend their use of the Web with these leading-edge technologies.

WRITING FOR THE WEB

While design is prized, information is the most valuable resource on the Web. By structuring the information carefully, writers can effectively create the valuable information needed.

On the home page, text should be kept to a minimum, limited to explaining what various parts of the site offer. Rather than having long documents online, provide links to various sections and keep each page of a reasonable length. When offering white papers or lengthy FAQs for users, provide an option to download them in one piece and read them offline. Busy users and those who pay for connectivity appreciate this convenience.

At times, design teams may include developers and designers, but not writers. In this case, an editor should review the text for the site to suggest improvements and make editorial changes. Even prominent sites have more than their share of editorial errors, perhaps because the publishing process is so easy. Sites using multiple languages should have native speakers check each section, particularly if the translations are computer generated.

Another common problem on the Web is the presence of broken links: hyperlinks that point to nowhere. Broken links can be created by a process as simple as moving or renaming a file. Companies should either use tools that check the links on the site for integrity or test the Web site by hand for quality assurance.

LIGHTEN THE SITE

While business overall tends to be formal, the Web has a lighter side. Many sites benefit from a touch of creativity that personalizes the online experience, making the user feel that there is a person behind the site rather than a machine. In general, the tone of Web sites should be less like a corporate brochure and more like lunch with a customer. While informality and humor may be inappropriate for some industries, generally, Web users appreciate a light touch.

CREATING ONLINE COMMUNITIES

Humor and creativity personalize the Web site, but the Web is capable of even more. Genuine interactivity makes the Web a potential groupware platform, and e-commerce sites can use this to effectively create online communities. Web-based chat groups and discussions called *forums* can move the Web site beyond being a place to review product specifications. Forums can enable discussions among users or with product managers. Sites can have online salespeople respond to queries from users.

Other sites create a sense of community by posting appropriate feedback. Customers are sure to return to see their own writing on the Web site and to show all their associates.

The key, then, is in understanding the needs of the target market and the nature of the information that would be useful to such a market. The Web site should be designed around the information needs of the visitor, not the marketing communications materials the company has on hand. Providing quality information on the Web leads to sales. Health-related sites can sponsor an "ask the doctor feature"; a company selling lawn-mowers could provide information on quality lawn care.

Companies that build comprehensive sites on given topics can take over Web markets entirely. Sites such as these lead to early market saturation. A comprehensive site can provide market domination for the company who creates it.

GARNERING FEEDBACK VIA E-MAIL

Creating an online community is one possibility for e-commerce, but obtaining feedback from users is essential. By responding appropriately to e-mail from customers, companies have an opportunity to cement relationships with these customers. Designate a person capable of appropriately routing e-mail to read the mail. If no e-mail is being received, post questions on the site or solicit contributions. Respond to all e-mail, using templates when necessary, to further the interaction with the customer. E-mail is the response card for the Web; if customers respond with e-mail, they deserve the same follow-up attention that telephone calls and letters to the company receive. How and whether the company responds to e-mail may determine whether the visitor returns.

Whether a result of fear of an overwhelming response or out of ignorance, many companies ignore this (e-mail) powerful means of hearing a customer's response to a Web site. Although marketers would covet the opportunity to look over the shoulder of a customer viewing an advertisement, e-mail's obvious value as a response mechanism is often overlooked. Companies that provide a means for customers to write in with feedback and then handle that feedback appropriately, stand to gain market share and a positive reputation on the Web.

PROVIDING FRESH CONTENT

One of the advantages of the Web is that it can provide the most up-to-date information to customers. Changes in pricing, specials, and even strategies can be reflected on the Web site as they occur. The opportunity for timely information also creates maintenance headaches. Who is responsible for updating the Web site and how often should it be updated?

Some sites use scripts that run automatically to refresh content for each day or week. Other sites rotate content in the same way advertisements are rotated, providing fresh views for readers whenever they enter the site.

Compelling *survival strategies* are key to success on the Web. By focusing on the customer rather than the company, and by using a design that considers users with various levels of connectivity, site builders will be able to create a site that adheres to the needs of their audience.

EFFECTIVE SURVIVAL STRATEGIES FOR ELECTRONIC COMMERCE

Like the recent *real TV* show *Survivor*, survival strategies can take on many forms. In this chapter, the crucial business objectives (building the right team, merchandising, listening to customers, etc.) and several survival strategies for the site itself are described.

Strategy 1: Making the Customer Experience Your Strategy

Before beginning customer experience work, it is important to understand its scope. Customer experience scope is *strategic*: in fact, it's the most strategic issue an e-business can work on. A dotcom's strategy should be directly *based* on the customer experience:

- Senior management should be focused on the customer experience.
- The dotcom's key success metrics should be measuring the customer experience.
- The budget should include funds for improving the customer experience.

Unfortunately, many companies don't see the customer experience as part of their strategy, and instead confuse it with usability, a much more tactical concern. As described in the "Listening "Labs" section later in the chapter, traditional usability focuses on improving the efficiency of certain discrete tasks on a Web site—a useful benefit, to be sure, but it doesn't approach the strategic nature of the customer experience.

The customer experience is the holistic combination of everything that the customer sees, touches, feels, or interacts with on a site. Part of this is certainly the usability —but so are other components: the site's business goals, its merchandising, the wording and messaging on the site, the use of graphics and color, the flow of pages in core processes, the choice of features to offer (or not), and the dotcom's own team and its processes to create and refine the site.

All areas of the dotcom's strategy should come down to one question: Is it good for the customer? Thus, it's essential for dotcoms to view the customer experience as a central, ongoing, *strategic* priority, not a *tactical* concern to be farmed out in a couple of user tests. Only when a dotcom has fully formed its strategy can it begin to address the tactical concerns of the customer experience (like those included later in the chapter under "Survival Tactics").

Why Is Customer Experience So Important?

As the Web has become increasingly complex, more and more new users have gotten online. The Web in 1994, used mainly by computer experts, was simple and fast, containing only text and graphics. Today, for a customer base of new users, the Web serves up a complicated soup of frames, Java, cookies, plug-ins, banners, bookmarks, secure servers, and streaming media.

Clearly, there's a difference between what the Web gives its customers and what they actually want. Customers want simplicity, but the Web offers complexity. Customers want service, but the Web offers technology. Customers want to accomplish their goal, but the Web offers *compelling features*. In each case, the Web doesn't offer the experience that the customer wants. This is the *customer experience gap*: the difference between what customers want and what they get. There is a widening customer experience gap online. *To survive, dotcoms must bridge the customer experience gap.*

How to Value the Customer Experience

Bridging the customer experience gap can lead directly to higher revenues. On an e-commerce site, building a great customer experience makes it quicker and easier for customers to buy, raising the conversion rate. On high-volume e-commerce sites, raising the conversion rate by one tenth of 1 percent can add as much as $20 million in incremental revenues per *month*.

Another way to value the customer experience is by considering the value of a single customer relationship. On the negative side, one bad customer experience can cause a customer to abandon a site permanently. With plenty of competitor sites to visit, customers have little incentive to return to a site that has failed to meet their needs. Even worse, any customer who has a bad experience on a site is likely to tell several other people. An e-business may lose the lifetime value of several customers by providing one bad experience.

On the other hand, providing a great customer experience can generate tremendous value. In addition to the revenue from the customer's purchases, a happy customer also brings free word-of-mouth exposure— bringing even more customers to the site. A good customer experience brings loyal, buying customers who want to bring in more loyal, buying customers.

The following are three steps to take to base your strategy on the customer experience.

Step 1: Identify Your Customers' Goals and Your Goals

Before you can build the right customer experience, you must know who your customers are and what they want. Get clear answers to questions like these:

- Who are our target customers?
- What do customers want from our site? Why would they return after their first visit?
- How do customers want to accomplish their goals on the site? What technology do they use, what features are they familiar with, and how long do they want to spend at our site?

Next, clearly define your site's business plan and marketing goals. Study online competitors, offline competitors (such as competing channels), and any *comparable* dotcoms who are facing similar issues in a different market. Finally, find the common ground between the site's goals and the customers' goals; this reveals the ideal customer experience.

Step 2: Commit the Organization to Building a Great Customer Experience

Give the development team the task of creating the customer experience described in Step 1. To renew the team's focus, and prevent internal politics from driving the process, draw heavily on *objective* data. Solicit customer feedback, run usability tests or listening labs, or bring in outside experts to evaluate the site. If objective resources aren't involved, any development team will tend to develop *tunnel vision* and design the experience for itself.

Step 3: Monitor the Customer Experience

The customer experience is not a one-time event. After the site relaunches with its new customer experience, it's essential to continually monitor and improve the experience. Watch (and respond to) customer e-mail, continue to run listening labs, and occasionally involve outside experts to give objective guidance. After all, the customer experience is never perfect. Building a great customer experience is not an event, but a continuous process toward online success.

The rest of the survival strategies in this chapter show in more detail how to bring about strategic success by focusing on the customer experience.

SURVIVAL STRATEGY 2: BUILDING A CUSTOMER EXPERIENCE TEAM

While it's easy to focus on the customer experience in the short term, many companies find it difficult to maintain that focus over a period of months or years. One way to maintain the momentum of a customer-focused strategy is to create a *customer experience team* within the organization.

A customer experience team is a group of employees, from separate areas of the organization, focused on looking at their company from a customer's perspective.

How to Get Started

It can be difficult to build enthusiasm around starting a new team, but certain events or situations can serve as catalysts, flagging the need for such a team. Here are some possibilities:

- A recent customer survey rated your company or Web site poorly.
- Your Web site has a low conversion rate (a low ratio of buyers to unique visitors).
- Your company is planning a major Web site redesign and you want to make use of the customer's perspective during the redesign.
- Design and development teams (or marketing and IT teams) rarely sit in the same room and discuss customer tradeoffs for design or technology decisions. Both teams are frustrated by the current working relationship.
- Senior management or other decision-makers are noticing that few company decisions are made with customers in mind.
- Competition in your market is heating up.

What Is the Purpose of the Customer Experience Team?

The purpose of creating a customer experience team can be wide open, depending on a company's needs at the time, its history with customer-facing projects and corporate culture. The following is a list of common purposes of a customer experience team:

- Raise the organization's awareness of customers' problems.
- Unite different teams around the customer perspective. Specifically, bring together representatives from distinct business groups

(operations, marketing, IT, customer service) to discuss needs of customers, how the company is meeting them, and how it can improve.

■ Help the whole organization learn that the customer experience is not just one group's responsibility (traditionally marketing). Encourage the whole company, and each employee, to take responsibility for the customer experience.

■ Get the company started on measuring the important success metrics of the site—(the conversion rate of visitors into customers, rather than measuring *hits* or *registrations*). The conversion rate is the single most effective measure of a customer's experience on a site, and hence the overall success or failure of a site.

Who Should Be On the Team?

The customer experience team should discuss the tradeoffs of one decision or another from various perspectives. Therefore, several key roles need to be included on the customer experience team. Many companies will want a larger group than what is outlined here, but this represents a core team:

■ **Technical representative**–Someone with a development background who can explain the implications and tradeoffs of each technology decision to the other (mostly nontechnical) members of the team.

■ **Designer**–An individual who has Web design experience and business acumen, who can function like the technical person, offering a perspective on design tradeoffs and communicating it clearly to the other members of the team.

■ **Web business leader**–A person who can lead the team and has ongoing and direct impact on the site and customer experience. This could be the site manager, or it could be a director or VP-level position of someone in charge of the Web business or e-commerce within the company. Some companies even appoint a *director of Web customer experience* and build a team around that director.

■ **Other functional areas**–Other employees whose work affects the customer experience (both online and offline)—from marketing, operations, etc.

■ **Any major third-party vendors**–Any outside firms that need to understand the customer experience to deliver good work—design and development firms, for instance.

The Customer Experience Team At Work

The scope of the customer experience team's work can vary. Some teams may deal with the entire customer experience offline and online—from offline advertising, to the online transaction on the site, all the way through offline fulfillment. Other teams may choose a smaller scope, choosing (for example) to focus on the redesign of the site. Here are other examples of the projects that customer experience teams can tackle:

- Map all the customer interaction points (offline and online) to identify areas of improvement or excellence anywhere in the customer experience.
- Integrate the online and offline customer experiences. Are the promises of your marketing messages being fulfilled by the experience on the site?
- Conduct customer feedback sessions (listening labs) to gather information on where customers are succeeding and failing on the site.
- Develop customer-centered scenarios of common ways customers might use your site—and then optimize the site for those scenarios.
- Prototype a new ideal site designed specifically with customers in mind.
- Engender a sense of ownership across the company for customer issues through an internal *PR* program.
- Identify customer-oriented, measurable goals that the company can use to incent departments and individuals to focus on and improve the customer experience.
- Make customer feedback regularly available to the whole company.

How to Maintain Momentum?

Cross-functional teams don't always succeed; they often start with some momentum, but dwindle in effectiveness over time. Your team needs to clearly define its purpose and, as time passes, incrementally change the scope as necessary. Be ready to reassess any aspect of the team to keep the team motivated and enthusiastic; this could mean reevaluating who is on the team, how often it meets, the scope of its work, and when its work is done and should disband.

If created and maintained right, an effective customer experience team can substantially improve the experience your customers have when interacting with your company.

SURVIVAL STRATEGY 3: MERCHANDISING ONLINE

The art of merchandising has enjoyed decades of refinement in offline retail. Today, e-commerce retailers have just begun to figure out how to effectively merchandise online. This is an important area of study: A recent Forrester survey reported that 85 percent of e-tailers consider merchandising one of their most important objectives.

One way to think about online merchandising is to compare it to what works best offline: the salesperson. A good salesperson can identify the customer's needs, recommend relevant products, and give advice on how to use the products.

A literal translation of the live salesperson to the Internet, however, usually creates a bad customer experience. By not recognizing the technological constraints of the medium, sites that have tried to emulate the salesperson with *virtual sales assistants* have mostly failed in their merchandising attempts.

An effective merchandising strategy would use the best aspect of the salesperson (understanding the customer's needs) without making a mess of the technology in the process. The site should understand, either intuitively or through direct questioning, what products to suggest (and when) to the customer.

Another Forrester report found that *targeting* is the most important factor of success for online promotions. For perfect targeting, the retailer would have complete information on the specific shopper, including past purchases at other stores, known needs, and even unarticulated desires. Obviously, it's unreasonable for e-tailers to expect to capture that much information about their customers. Without a huge database of information, though, there is still a way e-tailers can merchandise effectively.

For example, in past client work, Creative Good[1] has developed an algorithm that calculates, with relatively limited data, the best products to recommend to each customer. By selecting the most appropriate products, the promotions are then targeted to the right customers, at the right time. It's also much easier to develop occasion-based sales scenarios around the products, once a company has done the work to create the merchandising algorithm. The steps to create the algorithm are as follows (see Chapter 9 for a detailed discussion of these steps):

1. The most important step is to identify those success criteria that will help you make a decision about whether to include a certain product or, in the case of occasion-based promotions, a certain occasion.
2. Check to ensure that you have data to support each decision criterion.
3. Assign each criterion chosen a relative weight in percentage terms.
4. Construct an analytical model that can evaluate each product (or occasion) using the criteria identified.
5. Launch the algorithm.
6. Once the algorithm is running, test its effectiveness by tracking customer usage.

SURVIVAL STRATEGY 4: LISTENING LABS

Core to any survival strategy methodology is the customer input tool known as the *listening lab*. While it is a new approach to generating customer feedback, the listening lab draws from traditional usability testing.

Traditional usability testing is a process of getting face-to-face feedback from customers as they use a Web site (or software). Sessions are usually one on one and directed by a moderator, while observers look on from behind a two-way mirror. Usability tests traditionally involve scoring users' performance (in time and accuracy) in fulfilling a set of predefined tasks.

Any sort of customer tests are important to the development process because they provide *objective* feedback. Test results cut through the subjectivity of developers, whose attachment to the site can make it difficult to adopt the customers' perspective. Even the best developers can't avoid some *tunnel vision* after looking at the same site for several months.

Usability tests, while helpful, are less effective for the Web than they are for the software industry from which they originated. The task-directed nature of usability is much better suited to the hermetically sealed *user interface* of a single software package; likewise, traditional usability does *not* fit well with the holistic, multidimensional, often chaotic experience that the Web serves up to customers.

What Listening Labs Are

While they are based on traditional usability processes, listening labs are less task oriented and more open ended than usability tests. In particular, listening labs are one-on-one sessions in which the *customer* (not the moderator) sets the context. The labs are set up to best recreate the environment at home, where customers would actually use the site (and where there would be no predefined tasks or scripted moderator sitting beside them). Listening labs overcome some key shortcomings of usability and focus groups:

■ Listening labs are non task oriented: Pre-defined tasks neglect what each individual customer wants to do on the site, and often miss a larger strategic finding.

■ They rely less on quantitative measurement: Such scoring of users tends to neglect important qualitative factors such as frustration or enthusiasm.

■ Traditional usability tends to *lock in* users to the defined tasks; in listening labs, customers can give up at any time.

■ Focus groups rely on what customers say, not what they actually do. Labs observe what customers *do*.

■ Moderators control traditional testing; customers control listening labs. This key distinction delivers more accurate and strategic findings.

Who Runs Listening Labs?

Listening labs should be conducted by trained moderators with expertise in the methodology. Moderators must know how to let customers set the context and best simulate the actual experience of using the site.

Setting up the labs requires strategic work beforehand to understand who the target customers are and what the key business objectives are. To best simulate the actual experience, the customers recruited for testing must match the demographic group likely to come to the site.

Who Attends Listening Labs?

To gain most from the labs, it is critical that senior management from the company attend. Customer experience is not limited to marketing or to IT—it is the central driver of a merchant's success online. To truly build a customer-focused business, senior managers need to understand how customers experience their site.

It's not sufficient for senior managers to observe the video or hear the results. Real customer focus (and thus real e-business success) comes from all levels of the client organization (including senior management) seeing first-hand how live customers interact with the site.

Why Listening Labs?

In e-commerce, it is critical to inform both strategic direction and interface decisions with customer feedback. While it is true that customer input is important in all businesses, it is particularly important online because customers *rule the Web*. Switching costs are low and competitors are abundant. The listening lab methodology is designed to identify the most important strategic and interface issues facing online retailers and to begin the cultural change necessary for companies to be successful online.

When to Conduct the Labs?

Listening labs should be held throughout the life of a site. This includes initial testing of the site strategy, continuous testing of prototypes and changes to the site, and ongoing testing as business objectives evolve. Managers need to keep a close watch on how customers are interacting with the site—especially as their customer base grows as more consumers shop online.

The Impact of Listening Labs—One Client's Experience

One major e-tailer recently used listening labs to shape its ongoing customer experience strategy. In the labs, the client found that its customers were enthusiastic about the service but had difficulty using the site. None of the nine tested customers who were new to the site actually completed a purchase, for various and multiple reasons.

After the listening labs, the company's CEO shared that he was shocked to learn how difficult his customers found his site. The CEO concluded from the labs that his business *should be three times bigger than it is today*. Ironically, a task-oriented usability test conducted on the same site declared that the *response from users was very positive*.

Nondirected listening labs helped the e-tailer focus on its conversion rate and understand how customer experience challenges were leaving millions of lost revenue dollars unrealized. The client is in the process of making changes as a result of the labs.

SURVIVAL STRATEGY 5: EFFECTIVE E-MAIL

From newsletters to order confirmations, e-mail is an increasingly important aspect of the customer experience. There is *much* more to say about effective e-mail than can fit into a brief column, but the following tips are a good start. The e-business industry is still so inexperienced about e-mail that even following these basic tips will put any dotcom ahead of most of the industry.

Use a "Hook"

An e-mail must have a good reason for being sent; otherwise, it's better to not send it. The hook of an e-mail is the single thought or message conveyed by that e-mail and should be stated in the first sentence or two.

By containing a hook, the e-mail makes it easy for a customer to understand the point of the e-mail. The customer is more likely to respond if the choice is clear: act or don't act to get the specified benefit. Customers are less likely to act, understand, or otherwise have a good experience if they have to spend time figuring out the point of the e-mail. In other words, do refine the hook to express the idea or message clearly and simply; and, don't rely on jargon or indirect wording to express the hook.

Support the Hook

Just as the hook provides focus for the e-mail, so should the rest of the e-mail refer to the hook for focus. For example, an e-mail telling customers that there is a sale on a particular product line on an e-commerce site should do just that: tell customers about the sale.

This same e-mail should *not* be considered an opportunity to inform customers of every promotion, feature, or tidbit of corporate news. Customers tend to scan e-mails, and if several propositions are presented, even the hook will go unnoticed. In other words, do stick to a single subject in the e-mail; and, don't try to incorporate as many elements as possible.

Be Succinct

Keep the e-mail short. From the subject line to the farewell, the e-mail should offer the reader the most relevant information in as few words as possible.

Customers are busy, and many feel overwhelmed by too much e-mail. Messages that are short and to the point are more likely to be read. When writing e-mail text, try to state the ideas in as few words as possible. Choose words carefully, and don't think that having a lot of space means that you should use it all.

State the Most Important Things First

Customers will start reading an e-mail from the beginning and read the introduction to see if it's worth spending more of their time. Readers tend to pay less and less attention to what is written as they scan more quickly through the rest of the e-mail.

To make sure customers read the most relevant information, *put the most important information (the hook) at the top*, followed by the most important supporting information. Each successive paragraph will receive less and less of the reader's attention and should contain less and less important information. As soon as the hook is well enough supported, end the e-mail. In others words, do provide the customer the most important information at the beginning of the e-mail, and don't *save up* the key information for the middle or end of the e-mail.

Write for Scannability

After absorbing the hook in the opening line of the e-mail, if customers choose to read the rest of the message, they will do so quickly, looking for the most important components. Thus, it's important to make it easy for customers to scan the e-mail. In other words, do use dashes or bullets to express lists of ideas or section headings, and don't require users to read long continuous blocks of text.

Use the Active Voice

The most effective way to communicate a message or idea is to use the active voice. The active voice focuses on the subject rather than how the subject is being acted upon, creating a more powerful image or idea (see the sidebar, "Passive and Active Voices").

Use the Right Tone for Your Audience

E-mail communication tends to be less formal than traditional business and marketing writing. It's important not to be too formal, or too familiar, when e-mailing your customers. The right tone for an e-mail varies, depending on the customer being mailed and the topic of the e-mail. In other words, do feel free to make your e-mail fun and irreverent, *if* this is appropriate for the customer and the moment; and don't be overly casual and risk being disrespectful to your audience with the wrong tone.

 An e-mail apologizing to a customer for poor service should be more formal than the weekly newsletter.

Use Language that Counts

Avoid using words for their own sake. Remember, you don't communicate with your customers just for the sake of communication, but to get across

Passive and Active Voices

The Following are some examples of the active and passive voice:

Passive

We're happy to announce that there are now over 20 new product categories on our site. Best of all, more categories are still being added every day.

Active

We're happy to announce that you can now shop in over 20 new product categories—and we're adding more products every day.

Passive

You've been selected for a special discount on any of the following products!

Active

Buy any of the below products at a special discount:[2]

an idea or proposition. To do this, each word and each sentence must *carry its own weight* and have something to do with the hook. If you can get your idea across in fewer words, do so. In other words, do make sure every sentence provides valuable information; and don't include text just to fill space.

Avoid URLs that Wrap

URLs can behave in peculiar ways when they are so long that they are broken into two lines of text. It's best to avoid *wrapping URLs* entirely. Here are some things you can do:

- If the URL is within your control, reduce its length so that it fits on a single line.
- Instead of listing it in the middle of a paragraph, insert a carriage return before listing the URL so that it starts on a new line.

■ If the URL is so long that it must fit on two lines of text, tell the readers how to put together the composite URL in their browser window.

Wrap Text at 68 Characters Per Line

E-mail applications vary in hundreds of ways, but what they have in common is a basic text width. All applications will correctly display text that is 68 characters or less per line. While this *hard wrap* may sometimes result in excess white space on the right side of the page, it is better than having lines of hard-to-read, distorted text. Most good text editing software contains a feature to wrap text at a certain line length.

Use Only ASCII Characters—Not "Smart Quotes"

Many e-mail readers can't display text other than the standard set of ASCII characters (roughly equal to the characters you can see on a keyboard). An easy way to follow this ASCII-only rule is to type the e-mail newsletter in a plain text editor, *not* in a word processor (like Microsoft Word).

The most common infraction of the ASCII-only rule comes in the use of "*smart quotes*." Notice that the quotation marks in the previous sentence are curved a bit —the left set of quotes (") curve one way, and the right set (") curve the other way. Similarly, the apostrophe (') also curves. All three of these characters are outside the basic ASCII character set and would display as error characters in many e-mail programs. Instead, regular quotes (") and a regular apostrophe (') display correctly in *all* e-mail programs. Microsoft Word defaults to using smart quotes, and text editors default to using e-mail-friendly regular quotes.

Why are there different kinds of quotes at all? Because smart quotes look better on the printed page. E-mail, viewed on low-resolution screens, doesn't benefit much from the aesthetics of curvy quotes, so there's no need to deal with the complexities of smart quotes in e-mail.

So, use a text editor, not a word processor, to write your e-mail newsletters. A good text editor for Microsoft Windows is UltraEdit (http://www.ultraedit.com). Macintosh users are blessed with the excellent BBEdit (http://www.barebones.com—the free version, BBEdit Lite, works well). And Linux users, who hardly have to be told about text editors, can of course choose between emacs and vi.

Thankfully, the main software on the Palm Pilot only uses the basic ASCII set.

*Avoid Excessive Use Of ALL CAPS, ****, and !!!!*

It can be tempting to use these techniques for emphasis or urgency; however, using them in excess can be ineffective. It's best to employ these techniques sparingly. The example in the sidebar, "Employing Urgency Techniques," shows some well-placed emphasis.

Employing Urgency Techniques

_____

In This Issue:

_____

* Messages from our Sponsors

* Top E-Commerce News Headlines

* How to Advertise in this Newsletter

* E-Commerce Times Job Board

_____

* * * * N E W * * * *

Visit the new E-Commerce Times Letters to the Editor page and see what other readers have to say about today's e-commerce issues! http://www.ecommercetimes.com/letters

_____

* * * A D V E R T I S E M E N T * * *

eTranslate GlobalWeb is changing the face of eBusiness through Dynamic Localization. A revolutionary new form of multilingual content development, Dynamic Localization gives companies the ability to deliver perishable content simultaneously to multiple language markets.

http://www.ecommercetimes.com/perl/mod_gotoad.cgi?etranslatenl-1[3]

_____

Space and Spacing

In an e-mail, *white space* is as important as the text in effectively communicating an idea or message. The eye can comfortably take in a limited amount of text at a glance, particularly on a computer screen. Cushioning the text with space helps readers scan the text more easily (see the sidebar, "Using Text and Space"):

- Most paragraphs should not exceed three or four lines of text.
- Use *bullets* liberally to make individual points without writing a whole paragraph.
- Place double spaces between paragraphs and sections.

Using Text and Space

The following is an example of good use of text and space:

——

Thank you for ordering from Amazon.com.

Your purchase information appears below.

To see the latest information about your order, or to make changes to your order, visit:

http://www.amazon.com/your-account

Your Account lets you manage your orders online by giving you the ability to do the following:

* Track the status of this order

* Combine open orders to save on shipping

* Change payment option for this order

* Change shipping option or address

* Cancel unshipped items from this order

You can also reach Your Account by clicking on the link in the top-right corner of any page on our Web site.

If you still need to get in touch with us about your order, send an e-mail message to orders@amazon.com (or just reply to this message).

If you ordered several items to be delivered to the same address, we may send them to you in separate boxes to give you the speediest service. Rest assured, this will not affect your shipping charges.

Thanks for shopping at Amazon.com

— Amazon.com Customer Service

Use Hyphens to Delineate Important Information

Text and space aren't the only way to highlight text. Lines of hyphens or equal signs (=) can also be effective (see the sidebar, "Hyphens and Equal Signs").

Always Offer an Option to Unsubscribe

As explained earlier, e-mails should only be sent when customers have requested information or if there is something noteworthy to tell them. Even with this level of permission, there will still be people who will want to unsubscribe from the e-mail list or newsletter.

Always offer the option to unsubscribe. As an emerging convention, customers can now typically expect to see unsubscribe instructions as the last item at the bottom of the e-mail, following the signature and P.S.

The Three Most Important Pieces of Real Estate

There are three key opportunities to get your message across to your customer. Failing to optimize these three opportunities will likely result in a large number of deleted e-mails.

The subject line, first line of the e-mail, and the P.S. at the end can hold the customer's interest. These three elements get more attention than any other section of an e-mail. If a customer is scanning the e-mail, as most customers do, those three may be the only elements read at all. Now, let's discuss each of the three elements in more detail.

Subject Line

Whether a customer opens an e-mail is affected quite a bit by the subject. If the subject line is relevant or informative enough, customers are more likely to open the e-mail. The subject line offers a very small space in which to make a very large impact. Here are some principles to follow when writing a subject line:

Hyphens and Equal Signs

Consider the following example:

============ The Creative Good Update - 09 Oct 00 ============

By Mark Hurst, President of Creative Good

http://www.creativegood.com

In This Week's Issue:
_____

- Will the Web Be Easy Tomorrow?

- Best Practices Site Launches

- E-Recruiting Launch

- Creative Good Speaks

- Creative Good is Hiring

- Subscription/Contact Info

Will the Web Be Easy Tomorrow?

The Internet will soon become so easy to use, one commentator argues, that today's PC skills will be irrelevant tomorrow.

...4

- An e-mail subject should tell the customer what the e-mail is about in clear, simple language.
- Even if the product or service offered is lighthearted or fun, the subject should not rely on quirky or jargon-filled language to invite the reader in.
- The subject should give some indication of the benefit the customer stands to gain by opening the e-mail.
- One way to write a strong subject line is to use a shortened version of the hook.

First Line of the E-Mail

A bad first line of an e-mail will be the only part of the e-mail the customer reads. However, a strong and informative first line, clearly stating the benefit of reading the full e-mail, will increase the chance that more customers will at least scan most of the message.

Like the subject, the first line of the e-mail should be explicit and contain the hook of the e-mail, including the benefit to the customer. Again, if the first line offers something the reader considers valuable, he or she is likely to continue.

P.S.

After reading the opening line of the e-mail, most customers will scan the remainder of the message. The postscript is a convention most readers will recognize. While the *p.s.* is not an essential element of all e-mail communications, it can be an effective way to highlight a reminder or a particular point of interest.

SURVIVAL STRATEGY 6: IMPROVING SEARCH

Many dotcoms offer thousands of products in hundreds of categories, making it essential to provide customers with a good search feature. Unfortunately, many dotcoms' search features are implemented poorly. This part of the chapter gives a basic road map for how to offer customers a better search experience. Many dotcom searches today give one of these unacceptable experiences:

- Too many results
- Zero results
- Irrelevant results

Too Many Results

Simple search queries tend to return dozens, even hundreds, of results. For example, a search on *fishing* at an outdoor site returned over 700 results.

Zero Results

Many searches return no results at all, sometimes because of trivial mistakes in the search query. For example, one site's search returned no results because the query was plural (*stereos*), and the product was listed in the database only in the singular (*stereo*).

Irrelevant Results

Some searches return results that are not directly related to the intended search, but instead contain one of the search terms somewhere in their database entries. For example, searching for *fish food* at a pet supply site resulted in water filters (on the first of several pages of results).

A good search can avoid these problems by providing results that are *few* and *relevant*. The following describes how the search should work for simple and detailed queries.

Simple Query

Searching on a common, one-word query (*khakis*) should not return excessive results. Ideally, the results page should display the *one* page that is most appropriate for that query.

For example, the customer should be taken directly to the khakis page.

However, if there must be a long list of results, the list should begin with those results most likely to be what the customer wants. For example, if there are 30 kinds of khakis available, the top-selling khakis should be at the top of the results. In particular, searching on a simple query like *fishing* should bring back four types of results:

- The first result should be a link to *the* fishing page. This result would be hard-coded in the search engine to appear upon any query of *fishing* or *fish*.
- The second result, or set of results, would be products whose names *begin* with the entry "fishing" (*fishing rods*).
- The third set of results would be products whose names contain the word *fishing*.
- Finally, the last set of results would be products whose names contain some derivation of *fishing*.

This organization ensures that the most relevant results (those most likely to be the *right* product) are displayed first.

Detailed Query

A multiword query (*mediterranean flower vases*), if it doesn't yield an exact match, should not show the customer empty results. Instead, the search engine should find *parts* of the query that do begin to return results, and then display those.

If a detailed query returns no results, one way to look for results is to progressively abbreviate the query from the left. For example, for *mediterranean flower vases*, the search engine can then try *flower vases*, and then *vases*. This algorithm would work best on dotcoms where detailed search queries tend to be a string of adjectives followed by a noun. Different search strategies, of course, will work better on different dotcoms (depending on the product set, the customer base, and the language the queries are written in).

Keyword Mapping

An easy way to give few and accurate results is a system called *keyword mapping*, a system where popular search queries lead to human-made results pages. To understand how it works, consider how a pet supply site and a toy site could be improved by keyword mapping:

The pet store's Web team would identify *fish food* as a keyword. Any search on *fish food* would take customers to a page containing fish food *only*.

This would be an improvement over a results page also showing filtration systems.

The toy site's development team would identify *tonka* as a keyword. Any search on *tonka* would take customers to the Tonka page, specially created and maintained by the development team, that showed customers a well-designed overview of the Tonka products carried by the site.

This would be an improvement over a page showing a long alphabetical list of every Tonka product.

The secret to keyword mapping is that humans can build better search results than machines can. Search engines can find every product with the word *fish* or *food* somewhere in its description, but that can result in irrelevant products like filters climbing to the top of the results. A human being, on the other hand, can manually construct a much more relevant page of fish food products.

Any online store can implement keyword mapping with a small investment in technology and an ongoing commitment (by people on the team) to improving the search experience. Here's how to implement keyword mapping:

- Using Web site logs, identify the top 10 most popular search queries. For example, on a pet store site, *leash* might be in the top 10. These 10 search queries are now the *keywords*.
- Manually construct a page for each of the 10 keywords. For example, create a page prominently showing the top-selling leashes, followed by a simple list of links to all other leashes.
- Modify the search engine. If any search query is one of the keywords, the Web site must take the customer directly to the manually constructed page, bypassing the standard results page altogether.
- Watch sales increase as customers have a better experience when searching for these 10 popular items.
- Go through this process every month, turning 10 more popular search queries into keywords mapped to specially constructed pages. Consider adding keywords for new products and product classes as they are introduced.

SURVIVAL STRATEGY 7: THE PAGE PARADIGM

There exists one simple rule—the *Page Paradigm*—which describes the online shopping habits of most online shoppers. The idea behind the Page Paradigm is that most customers go page by page through the shopping experience, not thinking too much about pages they've seen previously. Customers concentrate most on the individual page they're on, not on the site as a whole.

The Page Paradigm

On any given page, customers will do one of two things: either click on something that appears to take them closer to their goal, or click the Back button.

Why This Matters

Many online stores concentrate on telling customers where they are in the site, where else they could go, or what other features they could try. Some sites are crowded with navigation bars (*navbars*), toolbars, and other features that are totally irrelevant to the customer. Customers don't care where they are in the overall hierarchy of the site; they only care if they can accomplish their own, personal goal.

Most customers want to achieve one particular goal on a site.

Customers don't want to experience everything on a site. Instead, customers want a simple experience that helps them achieve their primary goal, and doesn't distract or confuse them. This is why a customer's behavior fits the Page Paradigm: Since customers want to achieve a goal, they look to each page to take them closer to the completion of their goal. The Page Paradigm might be restated this way, from the customer's perspective: Does this page take me closer to my goal?

■   YES: Click to go closer to the goal.
■   NO: Click Back to try again on the previous page.

Another important takeaway of the Page Paradigm is that Web pages should not try to accomplish too many goals at once. Focusing a page (and the overall site) on one goal (the goal that customers have) makes it much easier for customers to use the site.

Focus each Web page on one goal, and delete anything that doesn't serve that goal.

The Page Paradigm also shows why *site maps* are irrelevant. Despite all the information architects who say otherwise, customers do not care about site maps. A site map is fun for the development team to look at, and it gives information architects something to do, but it's mostly irrelevant to customers. Customers don't want to spend time learning how to use the site; they just want to accomplish their goal and leave the site as quickly as possible.

A site map is a page that functions as a table of contents for a Web site. Some books on Web design encourage sites to link to a site map from the home page.

The next challenge is to promote the site. Let's now look at the survival tactics of a few dotcom examples.

SURVIVAL TACTICS: DOTCOM EXAMPLES

The following are a few survival tactics, each accompanied with a screenshot of a site that exemplifies the tactic, either executing it well or poorly.

As you read the tactics, keep in mind a few thoughts: First, remember that these are just reviews of small, individual tactics; they are not reviews of the entire site. There are plenty of e-commerce sites that are good overall, but have certain tactics that could be improved; likewise, some of the *good* tactics below are part of sites that could really improve!

Also, notice the evaluation date at the bottom of each column. Sites change quickly, and you might expect (and in many cases, fervently hope) that some sites have changed since the screenshots were captured and evaluations made. In a couple of cases, sites have made the very improvement that was encouraged.

Finally, remember that customer experience is primarily a strategic issue (as previously explained), and tactics become important after the strategy is fully formed.

HOME PAGE

The home page has the unique responsibility of creating a good first impression on the customer. If the experience on the home page is poor in any way, the customer may leave the site forever. Thus, it is important to ensure a good experience: The home page should load quickly, clearly explain the purpose of the site, and speed customers toward their goals. Figure 10.1 shows that Quixtar.com's original home page was not clear enough.[5]

Quixtar.Com: Poor Practice

An effective home page tells customers what site they're on and what they can do there. Quixtar's home page, however, creates a bad customer experience by failing to give visitors such basic information.

Customers must first wait as the flash-enhanced home page slowly loads. When the page finally does load, it hardly helps customers figure out what Quixtar is. Just saying "Welcome" doesn't explain why customers should spend time on the site.

What Quixtar does provide is links to information on becoming a *Quixtar Client,* becoming a *Quixtar Member,* and becoming a *Quixtar-Affiliated Independent Business Owner.* But what's the difference between a client and a member? Quixtar boasts its *Store for More* and *Exclusive* stores, but what kind of stores are these?

What can customers buy there? Clothing? Furniture? Hamsters? The page doesn't say. And what is Quixtar, by the way?

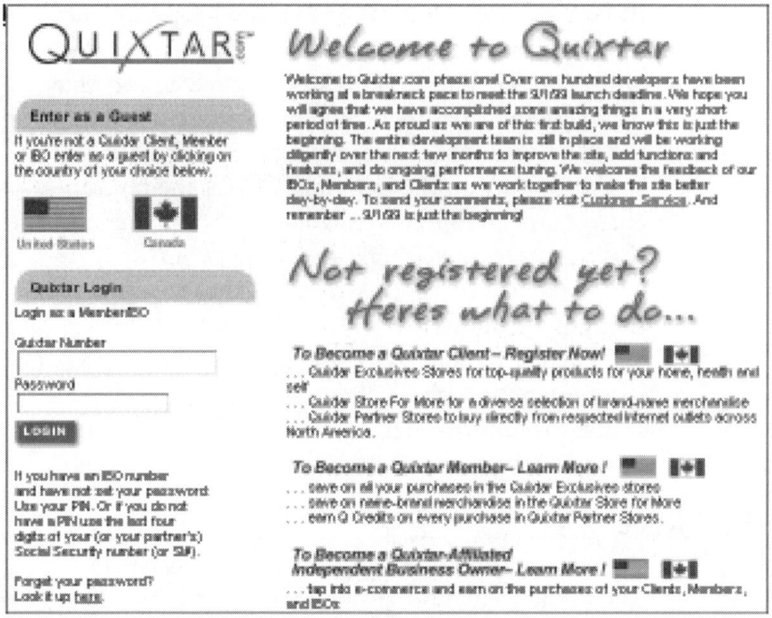

FIGURE 10.1 Quixtar's home page says little about what the site is.

The one thing Quixtar is clear about is perhaps the most irrelevant information to customers: how hard the Web development team has been working. A full paragraph of text at the center top of the page announces that *over 100 developers have accomplished some amazing things* with the site while working at *breakneck pace*. Customers, however, don't care about how great the design team is; they just want to use the site.

Quixtar should improve its home page by clearly stating what the site is, who its affiliated merchants are, and what customers gain by signing up. Quixtar should also remove the irrelevant and excessive praise of its design team. Perhaps then, customers will actually want to join.

Quixtar.Com: Second-Look Evaluation

Seven months later, Quixtar's redesigned home page makes clear to customers that they can shop (see Figure 10.2).[6] When Quixtar first launched in September 1999, it did not clearly communicate why customers should spend time on the site. Its home page did not clearly state what the site is, who Quixtar's affiliated merchants are, and what customers gain by sign-

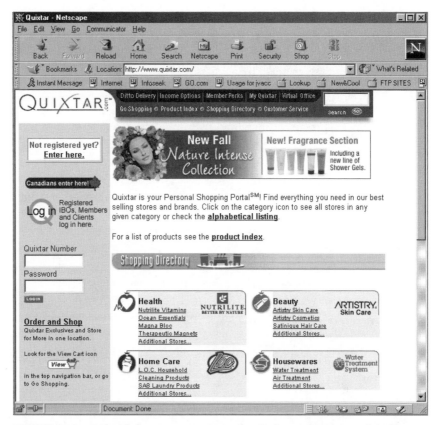

FIGURE 10.2 Quixtar's home page now makes it clear to customers that they can shop.

ing up. The home page created a bad customer experience by failing to give visitors basic information.

Fortunately for customers, Quixtar has redesigned. Its home page states that Quixtar is a *personal shopping portal* along the top of the page. Even if customers do not read this text, it is clear that they can shop from the site. A list of affiliated merchants, broken down by categories, is the main focus of the page. The home page no longer is Flash-enhanced and downloads quickly. With these few changes, Quixtar has created a good customer experience from the moment customers land on the site by giving them information that they need to know.

Despite these changes, Quixtar could further improve its customer experience. Quixtar requires customers to register before entering its partner stores but fails to clearly state what the benefits of signing up are. If it's not easy to see *why* shoppers should register, new customers are likely not to bother. Some customers may thus be likely to abandon Quixtar and go directly to the partner sites.

Swissarmy.Com: Poor Practice

This collection of bad customer experiences hides the fact that you can't actually buy anything here as shown in Figure 10.3.[7] Swiss Army knives and other products are highly functional tools created in the fine tradition of European design. The Swiss Army site, however, is a collection of customer experiences so bad that it all but destroys whatever value the brand has for an online user.

Customers coming to swissarmy.com must first get past a splash screen featuring a large Swiss Army logo. The page may make Swiss Army feel good, but for customers, it's just an extra step toward their goal of getting into the site. The splash page also warns customers that the site is designed for version 4.0 browsers or above. Unfortunately, trying to move on to the home page with Navigator 4.7 (PC) led to a series of 20 JavaScript errors before the browser gave up on loading the page.

Assuming customers get to the home page, they're greeted with a collection of slow-to-load graphic images that don't help them navigate the

FIGURE 10.3   Swiss Army's home page hides the fact that you can't actually buy anything here.

site at all. The bottom frame features a series of nine identical buttons with absolutely no labels. The only way to see where they lead is to put the mouse over one and read the *rollover* description. Surprise: The nondescript buttons are crucial to the navigation of the site—a lousy way to move around a site, but a good memory test.

If customers have the patience to click through several layers of slow-loading graphics and frame-laden pages, they'll eventually find that they can't actually buy anything on swissarmy.com. There is a link that says *Buy Now*, but it loads an order page from REI.com (along with its entire toolbar and a very different user experience), accompanied by the frame with the Swiss Army logo and those nine unlabeled buttons. Next time you're on swissarmy.com, it is suggested that you buy a compass.

Swissarmydepot.Com: Second-Look Evaluation

A year later, Swiss Army has replaced graphic buttons with text links as shown in Figure 10.4.[8] When Swiss Army's site was first reviewed, the splash page was criticized harshly because it warned users about browser versions necessary to view the site; the slow-to-load graphics; and the series of identical, though unlabeled, buttons in the bottom frame. Without labels on these important buttons, Swiss Army made it extremely difficult for customers to navigate the site.

Swiss Army has since redesigned its site as shown in Figure 10.4.[9] The splash page is gone and the unlabeled buttons on the home page have been replaced with clear graphic and text links. The site no longer sends customers to other sites to buy; instead, it shows clearly how to purchase from affiliate Swiss Army sites.

Despite Swiss Army's home-page improvements, customers may still have some trouble with navigation. Shoppers might not realize that the product images at the top of the page (a pocketknife, watch, etc.) lead to product category pages. In addition, Swiss Army makes it difficult for customers to buy the product pictured in the middle of the home page by failing to make that image clickable.

Swiss Army should label the images more clearly so customers don't need to move the cursor over them to see where they lead. Swiss Army should also make the featured product clickable, easily taking customers to the corresponding product page.

FIGURE 10.4 Swiss Army's redesigned site.

REGISTRATION

Sites shouldn't make it difficult for customers to do business with them. If registration is a hassle, a site could lose valuable transactions. What follows are poor and good examples of registration.

Reflect.Com: Poor Practice

Reflect.com takes personalization too far with its forced customer survey as shown in Figure 10.5.[10] Reflect.com, a Procter and Gamble beauty e-commerce Web site, tries hard to create an online beauty experience for customers. Reflect promises to customize its Web site and products for each individual customer, but it takes customization too far by forcing customers through an unnecessarily long personalization process.

Reflect requires customers to take a *new visitors* survey before they are allowed to view a single product. Customers coming to the site for the first time may become frustrated and leave the site because they can't shop immediately.

Those customers who do continue with the survey face questions such as, "If I were a house, I would be . . ." with answer choices ranging from "A beautiful mansion filled with art and the hottest artists" to "A maintenance-free townhouse with an exercise room." Another question asks "what the person closest to me would say I am most likely to dream about."

Reflect's survey might be tolerable if it actually led shoppers to customized products. Unfortunately, it appears that the only purpose of the

FIGURE 10.5 Reflect.com's Web site.

survey is to customize the site's colors and images. Some customers, for example, will view the site with purple flowers while others will see it with yellow ones. To actually customize *products*, shoppers must go through yet another survey when they finally access the site. In all, customers must answer more than 20 survey questions before viewing a single product.

Reflect claims to create the ultimate experience for customers with a personalized Web site and beauty products. Instead, Reflect's lengthy surveys create a bad customer experience.

eBay.Com: Good Practice

eBay provides useful links to help customers learn about auctions as shown in Figure 10.6.[11] Many customers are unfamiliar with the process of online

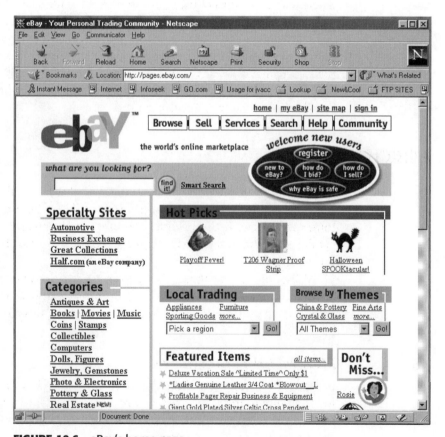

FIGURE 10.6 eBay's home page.

auctions. Customers must register, decide what auction to participate in, and figure out how to bid or sell. eBay makes it easy for customers to learn about online auctions by linking to key questions directly off the site's home page.

eBay presents five straightforward links in the upper-right of the home page. The links *How do I bid? and How do I sell?* inform customers about the various types of auctions and how to take part in them. Another link, *Why eBay is safe*, allows customers to participate in a Feedback Forum where they can participate in an auction tutorial or comment on their buying and selling experiences.

Customers on eBay need not go to a *Help* or *About us* section; the site directly addresses their key concerns on the home page. eBay's links are also more helpful than a lengthy FAQs (frequently asked questions) section that overloads customers with mostly irrelevant information. And eBay wisely places the links in the upper right, leaving the bulk of the home page for actual auctions.

In general, good e-commerce sites should not require explanations of how to shop. Navigation and buying should be intuitive, so that the experience explains itself. Auctions, however, are unfamiliar and thus may need more introduction. By effectively providing this introduction, eBay makes browsers more likely to become bidders.

MERCHANDISING

Displaying and promoting products is a crucial aspect of the customer experience. Even if customers can navigate easily to the products, the customer may leave if the products are not clearly presented (consult the "Online Merchandising" section presented earlier in the chapter for more information).

What follows are three examples of merchandising. The first shows how *not* to display sale items; the second shows a good use of situation-based merchandising; and the third shows a better way to incent impulse buys.

Ninewest.Com: Poor Practice

Ninewest.com makes it difficult for customers to find the price of sale items as shown in Figure 10.7.[12] Ninewest.com offers a wide selection of women's shoes and sandals on its Web site. Unfortunately, poor page design hides the price of sale items.

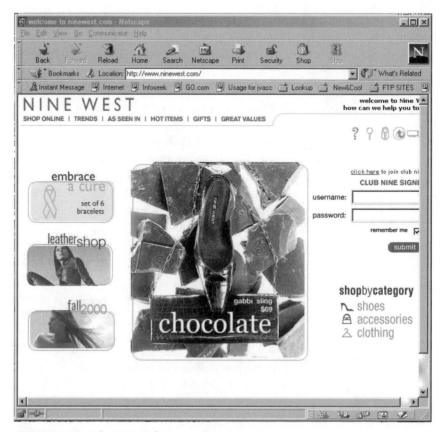

FIGURE 10.7   Nine West's home page.

Ninewest.com's category pages present images of products accompanied by their name and price—unless the item is on sale. A chocolate-colored shoe called *Gabbi Sling*, for example, is shown with a price of $69.00, while a discounted sandal called *Angell* is merely marked *SALE*.

To find the price of sale items on the category page, customers are forced to click each individual product page. Only there can they find the regular price, the discount, and the new price. This adds an extra step to the shopping process, which may prevent customers from investigating discounted items.

If Ninewest.com replaced the word *SALE* with the old price, crossed out, and the new price in red, customers could easily compare items. By forcing customers to look at individual product pages to find the discount price, Ninewest.com may lose impulse buys.

Guess.Com: Good Practice

Guess.com's *GUESS? Collection* merchandising appeals to customers' lifestyle as shown in Figure 10.8.[13] Guess.com, the apparel retailer, creates a good customer experience with its *GUESS? Collection* situational merchandising. The site's appeal to a relevant situation can both help customers find useful products and help Guess communicate the breadth of products the site offers.

Customers on Guess's home page see links to *GUESS? Collection* for men and for women. Clicking on the link *For Her* takes shoppers to a page featuring a variety of items that might be useful for a weekend trip or vacation. The page includes, for example, a jacket, sneakers, and a casual dress. Next to each piece, Guess provides prices and clear text links to the corresponding product page.

FIGURE 10.8 Guess.com's GUESS? Collection page.

Customers may find the *GUESS? Collection* page helpful in suggesting items to buy before a vacation. The page anticipates shoppers' needs (shopping for a getaway) and presents relevant merchandise. By including products from many categories, Guess shows shoppers that they can buy a wide range of items on the site.

Guess could improve the *GUESS? Collection* page by clearly stating which featured items are on sale. Shoppers looking for a good deal might thus be more inclined to buy. The page might also offer discounts to customers who buy multiple *GUESS? Collection* items.

Outpost.Com: Good Practice

A good example of contextual add-ons is shown in Figure 10.9.[14] For decades, supermarket checkout lines have allowed customers to buy items on impulse. This practice has not yet translated well to the Web, since adding buttons to gum and candy would overwhelm the checkout page in a typically small browser window.

Outpost.com, however, offers a more customer-centered way to buy on impulse. The checkout page displays add-on products that are natural companions to the products the customer has already bought.

Here's how it works: On the Shopping Cart page, the items already added are displayed in the large yellow column. Less prominent (so as not to distract the customer), but above the fold, is a purple column containing add-ons that are appropriate to the items in the shopping cart. For example, if the shopping cart contains a PalmPilot, then the PalmPilot MacPac automatically appears in the left-hand column.

This feature is particularly good on *Outpost.com*, a computer good store, since it's often difficult to know what add-ons are necessary for a particular technology — or how to find them. In the PalmPilot example, a Mac user would be happy to find the relevant MacPac link immediately available.

Another good aspect of this feature is the prominence of both *Add It* and *More Info* buttons beneath each add-on. This makes it easy for customers to either make the buying decision immediately or get the information they need to then make the buying decision. The gain for Outpost.com is obvious: By making it easy to buy add-ons, more customers will buy add-ons.

Finally, this chapter has mainly focused on dotcom survival. To give dotcoms' survival a more balanced perspective, this last part of the chapter focuses on other perspectives of dotcom survival.

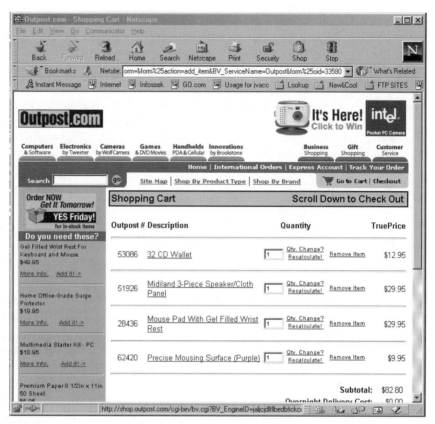

FIGURE 10.9   Outpost's Shopping Cart page.

OTHER PERSPECTIVES

On Wall Street and Main Street, the last five years have brought much sound and fury — and we are only now trying to understand what it signified. Call it the birth of a New Economy or the rise of the dot-com domain, but it's undeniable that business these days is happening in a new world of information, enabled by information technology, and most of us know it as the Web.

It's been fashionable for some time to observe that this new world, with its New Economy, would write itself new rules—that everything we knew about business would now be obsolete. Witness the readiness of New

Economy entrepreneurs to put customers in the back seat of a vehicle designed for a more important race. For years, dotcom CEOs blithely argued that profitability and sometimes even revenues were irrelevant as compared with building traffic and growing their users' numbers. In the same breath, these New World czars downplayed quaint Old Economy notions such as service quality. In the race to a near-mythic liquidity event, concerns about customer satisfaction and loyalty fell by the wayside.

Many today argue that the correction in the NASDAQ of recent months is a wake-up call. Suddenly, dotcom survival requires dotcom profitability. Consequently, online companies are laying off staffs in droves to realize improved gross margins. That might appease Wall Street, but it won't play on Main Street. The reason is simple: Main Street is where dotcom customers live, and, increasingly, they are demanding good, if not great, customer experiences. Dotcom companies will not generate good experiences without recognizing that building customer satisfaction and loyalty requires not short-term cost cutting but aggressive, long-term investment. What the dotcom economy needs is investors who provide not just capital, but patient capital, who believe that staying the course on good experience is the only way to ensure survival.

Remember that there is no business on the Web that cannot be characterized as a service business. Web businesses create value through interactions with customers based on flows of intangibles made of media and information. If physical products flow up and down supply chains as a result of Web interactions, that's fine; however, Web businesses are not product or industrial businesses any more than Wal-Mart is a maker of consumer packaged goods or an industrial distributor.

THREE DIMENSIONS

Service businesses have always realized revenues and profitability based on optimizing three dimensions of customer relationship management. First, they must select customers with whom they can do business profitably. This may sound obvious, but every credit issuer or retail bank and every distributor or industrial supplier does business with customer accounts on which they lose money. Needless to say, this is especially true among Web businesses, where familiar brands such as Buy.com and CDNow routinely sell goods like music CDs at negative gross margins, resulting in the painful reality that every customer relationship is unprofitable.

Second, they must find customers who value their services offered sufficiently not just to browse but to purchase—and not just to purchase but to return frequently to purchase again over time. This means registering not just any users but, in large proportions, those users who exhibit high yields to purchase when they visit a site and high repeat rates after the first purchase. On the Web, where serving customers who browse and those who buy costs roughly the same in fixed resources, maxing out a company's servers with hits from people who merely look and leave does not drive attractive economics.

Finally, they must find customers who will maintain a relationship with a business over time (preferably, for a long time), since longer relationships generate higher customer lifetime values than shorter ones. It's another obvious point, perhaps, but its reality is not often factored into business decisions in real time.

Put these three requirements together (intrinsic customer relationship profitability, high rates of conversion of customer visits to purchase and repeat purchase, and extended duration of relationships over multiple visits), and it's clear why the great companies of the Old Economy's service sector focus on customer satisfaction as a way to drive customer loyalty. Companies do not create vast populations of returning customers unless they can create great customer experiences. Whether it's Nordstrom in retail or Southwest Airlines in air travel, leading service companies generate loyal customers by delivering experiences, each and every time, that meet or exceed customer expectations. Find ways to satisfy or even delight customers, and the benefits are enormous. Scores of academic studies suggest that loyal customers become less price sensitive over time, will refer their friends, spread positive word-of-mouth (or word-of-mouse), and incur lower costs of relationship management than demanding prospects who have never done business with a company before.

So, if you want to survive in a dotcom world, the answer is clear. You may have to cut back somewhere in today's climate, but you can't cut back on good experience. Indeed, entrepreneurs should be investing in it more aggressively than ever before. Get the experience right with your customers (assuming they're the right ones) and the financial results will follow. Get the experience wrong, and you may as well stop raising money, because it will be Game Over. Good experience wins every time. Just wait.

AVOIDING THE SINS OF OMISSION AND GLUTTONY

Companies that seek to drive revenue through the digital channel must remember that being digital does not exempt them from the need to sell. True selling (qualifying, serving, and closing) goes beyond the novelty factor that until recently has been the savior of the online world. Digital buyers know that they have the upper hand in the buyer-seller relationship. They demand a positive, effective experience. The best sites (Dell, Amazon, Schwab) meet this expectation; why do so few others? Companies looking to survive online need to take a good hard look at the causes to understand how to avoid making similar mistakes.

The Internet has created tremendous value for consumers and business buyers alike, yet sellers fail to deliver on its full potential. This error can often be traced to a strategic miscue on the part of the company, but even companies that *get it* can stumble when it comes to translating their strategic vision into an operational reality. They forget that implementing e-selling requires not only a single-minded focus on the end customer, but the discipline to remove barriers that impede a buyer. The two most common sins that lead companies astray from this approach come in the form of omission and gluttony.

Omission

The sin of omission arises when companies do not consider their whole relationship with the customer and all of the points where they can use the online channel. This is often the case with B2B sites and B2C sites built by distributors or manufacturers. In many cases, these companies and their consultants suffer from post-ERP syndrome. As the successor to ERP, practitioners of e-business tend to turn companies inward: they design and build systems that automate internal processes or the needs of functional silos. The customer gets left out or is seen as a secondary consideration. Not surprisingly, these companies often create sites that map product lines rather than customer needs. The result is a system that can actually be less functional than a paper catalog.

Those guilty of omission reads like a who's who of the Internet. Even Sun Microsystems, one of the driving forces behind the online world, has room for improvement. No one would doubt they get the Web. The sheer volume of information, product descriptions, white papers, and tools available to help companies make the transition to the dotcom world demonstrate Sun's enthusiasm for the online channel. Unfortunately, the site seems to reflect the internal organizational structure of the company more than a sensitivity to the needs of buyers. This is not surprising given Sun's early entry to the Web and the rapid expansion of its site.

However, Sun should now consider restructuring its offering around specific customer segments and the activities required to qualify, serve, and close these customers. It could also expand the functionality available to help a buyer or partner make decisions about Sun products. By acting on the answers to the questions *"who is going to be using this site, for what purpose, and in what way,"* Sun could make a quantum leap from a functional site to an outstanding one.

Gluttony

As for the sin of gluttony, it far exceeds that of omission. In this case, companies (and their consultants) are dazzled by the choices available and want it all. They put in a little Shockwave here, some rich media content there, and then top it all off with a flaming logo on the front page. As often as not, these choices are justified by a *brand building* imperative or by the need to create something distinctive. The resulting disaster zone buries the core functions of finding a product, ordering, paying, fulfilling, and serving under an avalanche of gratuitous technology. The most common sinners here are the managers and Internet consultants who allow them to be seduced by the sexiness of technology and the excitement of *brand essence.*

Boo.com is (or rather was) the gluttony poster child, burning through millions to deliver a site that was months behind schedule and hopelessly out of touch with customer needs. The site was created for speeds of 56k and above, and it offered features like an animated Ms. Boo fashion consultant and 360-degree views of shoes. Despite a successful campaign to create awareness, the site's overdose of functionality made purchasing difficult even for those who met the bandwidth requirements. As a company that was clearly obsessed with making a brand statement, Boo.com and their consultants apparently got blinded in a quest to create a distinctive experience. They forgot to ask *"How does this feature serve the customer to help them buy from us?"* or *"How will this decision impact the customer likelihood to buy from Boo.com?"* The result failed to create value for the buyer and hence for Boo.com.

Boo.com is an extreme case and its spectacular implosion makes it an easy target. But, for the many other sites that suffer from gluttony (even to a lesser degree than Boo) as well as those guilty of omission, they too underserve their customers. And in the e-selling world, the failure to deliver value to buyers results in a failure to create value for the company. To avoid the sins of omission and gluttony, companies need to continually wrench their view away from internal priorities and look outward. Organizational priorities and brand-building imperatives cannot take precedence. e-selling demands building a system for the customer and letting their needs and requirements drive every technology and design decision. Go outside of this framework and your site will fail to meet its full potential.

END NOTES

[1] Creative Good, Inc., 307 W. 38th St., 9th Floor, New York, NY 10018, 2000.

[2] Creative Good, Inc., 307 W. 38th St., 9th Floor, New York, NY 10018, 2000.

[3] Ibid.

[4] Ibid.

[5] Ibid.

[6] Quixtar Customer Service, P.O. Box 430, Grand Rapids, MI 49501-0430, 2000.

[7] Ibid.

[8] Swiss Army Depot, 255 Alhambra Circle, Coral Gables, FL 33134, 2000.

[9] Ibid.

[10] Ibid.

[11] Procter & Gamble, 1 Procter & Gamble Plaza, Cincinnati, OH 45202, 2000.

[12] eBay Inc., 2145 Hamilton Avenue, San Jose, CA 95125, 2000.

[13] Nine West, Nine West Plaza, 1129 Westchester Avenue, White Plains, NY 10604, 2000.

[14] GUESS?, Inc., 1444 South Alameda Avenue, Los Angeles, CA 90021, 2000.

[15] Outpost.com, 23 North Main Street, PO Box 636, Kent, CT 06757, 2000.

11 E-Commerce Environments and Future Directions

"Peace, commerce, and honest friendship with all nations—entangling alliances with none."

—THOMAS JEFFERSON

Internet commerce is growing fastest among businesses. It is used for coordination between the purchasing operations of a company and its suppliers; the logistics planners in a company and the transportation companies that warehouse and move its products; the sales organizations and the wholesalers or retailers that sell its products; and the customer service and maintenance operations and the company's final customers.

The cost of installation and maintenance of value-added networks (VANs) put electronic communication out of the reach of many small and medium-sized businesses. For the most part, these businesses relied on the fax and telephone for their business communications. Even larger companies that used electronic data interchange (EDI) often did not realize the full potential savings because many of their business partners did not use it.

The Internet makes electronic commerce affordable for even the smallest home office. Companies of all sizes can now communicate with each other electronically, through the public Internet, networks for company use only (intranets) or for use by a company and its business partners (extranets), and private value-added networks.

Companies are quickly moving to use the expanded opportunities created by the Internet. For instance, Cisco Systems, Dell Computers, and Boeing's spare parts business report almost immediate benefits after putting their ordering and customer service operations on the Internet. They are so convinced of its benefit to their own companies and their customers that they believe most of their business will involve the Internet in the next three to five years.

Although still in an embryonic stage, analysts predict businesses will trade as much as $500 billion annually over the Internet in the next five years. Some believe the volume of Internet commerce will be much higher. As statistically valid sampling data are not yet available, determining the actual growth rate is very difficult to do. Thus, the growth of business-to-business (B2B) electronic commerce is being driven by lower purchasing costs, reductions in inventories, lower cycle times, more efficient and effective customer service, lower sales and marketing costs, and new sales opportunities.

This final chapter does not attempt to size the current market or predict the size of the future market. Instead, it describes the underlying drivers of growth of business-to-business electronic commerce, using specific company and industry examples as illustrations. This chapter also focuses on three specific areas of business-to-business e-commerce: electronic data interchange (EDI), supply-chain management (SCM), and the outlook for electronic commerce. EDI is a relatively well-established technology, typically offered through a service provider, that facilitates the exchange of information about commercial transactions between trading partners. SCM is a more recent incarnation of B2B e-commerce, often incorporating EDI as one component, that enables sharing of in-depth business intelligence between business partners.

BUSINESS-TO-BUSINESS ELECTRONIC COMMERCE

There is a wide range of potential benefits motivating today's enterprises to undertake B2B e-commerce initiatives, including the following:

- **Cost reduction via improved logistics and management**–The opportunities range from basic electronic information delivery to facilitating transactional exchanges of information. Such applications can create tighter links among business partners, improving the efficiency of the various support functions involved in bringing products to market.
- **Improved competitive posture**–Rapid growth, efficient reduction of product time-to-market, and optimization of product distribution channels contribute to a superior competitive position.

- **Improved internal information access**–Quantitative and qualitative improvements to information access for personnel can yield big payoffs for the business. Business areas such as the development of business opportunities and business strategy are particularly rich in this respect.

In the emerging networked economy, established companies are finding that they must adopt B2B e-commerce in order to fend off competition (see the sidebar, "Rewiring the Old Economy with B2B"). Newer, smaller, and/or other-market companies are entering new markets as traditional barriers such as geography fall. Unless existing businesses prepare to meet this competitive challenge, these new players may be better positioned to enhance their supply chains, get to market more quickly, or leverage technology to realize process efficiencies.

Rewiring the Old Economy with B2B

If Hollywood were looking for a place to shoot a remake of The *Andy Griffith Show*, it could do worse than Van Wert, Ohio. It's the kind of town (population: 13,000) where everybody seems to know everybody. The American Legion sponsors pancake and sausage breakfasts, root beer stands do big business, and families go to drive-in movies.

Take a stroll along West Main Street, however, and you can glimpse the next phase of the Internet revolution unfolding. In a factory built in 1953, a company called Aeroquip makes nitty-gritty parts for the likes of John Deere, Caterpillar, and Navistar. For years, the plant was terribly inefficient. When Jan started working there 13 years ago, her job was to help sort hundreds of green, yellow, and white sales slips. Working the night shift, she punched information from the slips into an old computer system. The data didn't even show up until the next day, so there was a 24-hour lag before the company knew what it had sold. The only way the company could tell anything right away was how big their stacks of paper were.

Recently, however, Aeroquip installed an Internet-based, business-to-business (B2B) system in a 120,000-square-foot distribution facility next to its factory. Now customers can use the Internet to see what parts are available or to order up to 300,000 customized products for same-day shipping. It's almost scary how much has changed so fast.

Wired Curlers

Like Aeroquip, a subsidiary of Eaton, mainstream companies across the nation are taking the Internet plunge. The auto industry was one of the first traditional industries to embrace B2B, raising the prospect that more customers will be able to order precisely the features they want. Today, old-line businesses ranging from retailers and insurers to restaurants and even beauty parlors are attempting to exploit B2B methods.

It's amazing how fast the technology is diffusing. How long did it take electricity or the telephone or just-in-time inventory management to diffuse throughout the bulk of the manufacturing sector? This is bigger, and it's happening faster. Indeed, the Gartner Group projects that B2B transactions will soar from $348 billion in 2000 to $3.9 trillion by 2005.

The economic stakes are profound. New gains in productivity could be unleashed, with companies reducing procurement costs by as much as 11 percent, according to a recent study by investment bank Dresdner Kleinwort Benson. If B2B works as advertised, it could help beat back inflation and boost economic growth. Indeed, Goldman, Sachs & Co. estimates that B2B efficiencies alone could bolster annual growth rates in all industrialized nations by a quarter of a percentage point.

The B2B push could also alter the way Wall Street thinks about *old economy* companies. Take Caterpillar. Between its factories and dealers, the heavy-machinery giant has roughly $5 billion in inventory at any given time. Using B2B innovations like its cat.com system, Caterpillar hopes to reduce that inventory by $2 billion within five years, dramatically lowering costs and boosting profits. That, of course, could translate into a higher stock valuation.

To consumers, the technology is largely invisible, but they, too, should benefit from B2B. Shopping online can still be a frustrating experience, for example. The Amazon.coms of the world have launched Web sites selling just about everything, but e-tailers often have trouble procuring goods and delivering them to customers on time. To rectify the situation, Web retailers will have to foster closer ties to the companies that manufacture and distribute products. B2B will help make that happen. Manufacturing is no longer going to be a backwater; it's going to be a key component in making e-business work.

There is a potential B2B payoff for consumers in the offline world, too. For example, restaurants, hotels, and hospitals are increasingly turning to the Internet to order food, shaking up the creaky food-distribution business.

As they strip out costs, they will make more money, but customers also may win. Some of the savings will ultimately flow through to the consumer in terms of better prices.

The Holy Grail

If B2B were a cult, its spiritual leader would be Cisco Systems. It not only makes hardware that allows B2B to work (routers, switches, and the like), but also serves as a model of how companies can best exploit the Internet. Cisco customers can visit its Web site to check out product specs and place their orders. That information is then routed on the Internet through Cisco to its suppliers. A full 76 percent of the orders move directly from the supplier to the customer—Cisco never touches them. Things are built only after they are ordered, so little, if any, inventory is kept in warehouses.

Based on Cisco's success, businesses across the country are beginning to reorganize themselves. It used to be that firms distinguished between their *front-end* contact with customers and their *back-end* ties to suppliers. Their own internal systems were usually quite separate. Now the Holy Grail is to tie all these systems together (with proper safeguards) and make them Internet-based.

Of course, it's much easier to create a company like Cisco when you can build it from scratch. Traditional companies will have to strip out layers of management and transform decades-old practices. Most of them make forecasts (guesses, really) about what customers will buy and then build inventory in anticipation. Do they really have a prayer of creating Cisco-like models? It's not only possible, it's imperative. You have to do it.

Eaton is a diversified, $10 billion-a-year company that makes everything from golf-club grips to engine components. Like other widget makers, it faces rising labor and petroleum-based-material costs, but it cannot afford to raise prices. The only way it can make money is through productivity gains of about 5 percent a year, which B2B technology is making possible.

The fact that so many companies are scrambling to implement B2B strategies has set off a land rush for the companies that sell the necessary software. Oracle has emerged as one of the field's early leaders. It will help General Motors, Ford, and DaimlerChrysler set up an online *exchange* to buy parts. Oracle has also launched an exchange with Sears, which is expected to draw other department store chains, and a similar deal with the $300 billion-a-year convenience store industry.

Among other things, companies will conduct *reverse auctions* on those exchanges. Ford, for example, announces it wants to buy 200,000 seat assemblies of a certain sort. Suppliers then bid for the job. The price moves lower as the competition among suppliers intensifies, and Ford gets its seats more cheaply.

Crowded Field

Altogether, at least 1500 software companies are competing to sell B2B systems, according to AMR Research. The problem is that most have specialized in only one piece of the overall B2B arena, not the entire value chain that links customers, companies, and tiers of suppliers. The upshot has been a flurry of deals as companies try to create coalitions that can sell complete systems. Recently, Dallas-based i2 Technologies, one of the hottest players in *supply-chain* management, spent more than $9 billion to acquire Aspect Development and Supplybase. It was the largest software merger ever. At the same time, IBM has plunked down millions to take stakes in i2 and Ariba, another high flier, which is based in Mountain View, California.

Where will the B2B revolution lead? One clear implication is that suppliers whose goods can be *commoditized*, meaning they are barely distinguishable from those of competitors, are going to face huge downward price pressure. The good news is that if you're a manufacturer, you can get suppliers to compete against each other. However, if you're not the most efficient supplier, this is a serious threat to you.

The surge of corporate spending on B2B will result in new inflationary pressures as vendors are forced to pay more to the specialists who can make the technology work. But over the long haul, the B2B revolution appears likely to offer more choices, faster delivery, and lower prices for most of the goods and services that Americans buy—online or offline. Those are exactly the results that the folks in Van Wert are trying to provide.

Information technology (IT) professionals must bring Internet technology into their business strategies in order to remain competitive. Businesses successful with B2B e-commerce are those that have learned to address several fundamental challenges:

- **Identify/measure quantifiable business objectives**–Businesses must accurately measure the impact an e-business initiative has on a business process in order to ensure that initiatives are delivering on their promises. A common reason for not doing this is a lack of understanding of the relevant technologies and their e-business implications.

- **Define business processes**–To support measurement, business processes must be well defined. Companies should create models of existing processes and interactions, determining the relevant events, time frames, resources, and costs associated with the business process. This model is then used to help streamline and evaluate new electronic processes, and serves as a benchmark for determining ROI.

- **Identify distinct value-propositions of peer value-chain entities**–Each business entity in the value chain must clearly understand the value propositions of each other entity. An e-commerce-enabled application may represent value to one participant but have neutral (or even negative) value to others. Initiatives with such imbalances can erode the business alliance they were intended to support.

- **Align business organizations with IT architecture**–The business must be organized to allow the needs of lines-of-business (LOBs) to be reconciled with the common architectural framework developed by IT. IT may act as a catalyst within the enterprise to organize various LOB initiatives within the scope of an e-business committee. An LOB may also champion e-business initiatives, while the IT group functions as a liaison, ensuring architectural integrity across the LOB initiatives.

- **Understand security issues**–Even the most demanding security considerations can be addressed cost-effectively for the vast majority of businesses. The core security issue is unchanged: Security demands must be accurately identified and matched with appropriate mechanisms.

- **Ensure organizational/operational flexibility**–Business transaction growth, expanded markets, and increased information accessibility can become irresistible change agents. However well organized the business was before deployment of e-business initiatives, the situation will necessarily change as the result of the initiatives. Organizations must preposition themselves (in their structure as well as in execution) to flourish in a significantly more dynamic environment.

INFORMATION TECHNOLOGY LANDSCAPE

Whether the e-business system presents a simple online *virtual storefront*, typically an element of B2C e-commerce, or performs sophisticated business-to-business supply chain management, network professionals face three key issues in designing a network infrastructure to support it:

- **Performance**–An e-business system requires good performance to be successful. In fact, superior performance can serve as a competitive edge as e-business initiatives proliferate. Aggregate performance is a function of speed (bandwidth) and reliability.
- **Security**–Comprehensive security measures are essential to the success of e-business. Four critical areas are required: confidentiality, integrity, authentication/authorization, and nonrepudiation.
- **Manageability**–E-business enables a dramatic increase in both the complexity and scale of a business entity's interaction with others, presenting unprecedented network management challenges.

A successful e-business implementation yields growth in sales volume, orders, and deliveries across additional manufacturers, distribution centers, retail outlets, and other consumers. As the e-business implementation grows and matures, so must the network infrastructure that supports it. The simple Internet connectivity prevalent today must evolve into a fast, reliable, secure, and manageable communications medium between an infinite number of trading partners.

B2B e-commerce comprises two primary areas: electronic data interchange (EDI) and supply-chain management (SCM). The rest of this chapter discusses these two solution areas in depth.

AN EXISTING E-COMMERCE STRUCTURE: ELECTRONIC DATA INTERCHANGE SOLUTIONS

Electronic data interchange (EDI) has traditionally been characterized as a well-defined interaction between two trading partners (see the sidebar, "What Is EDI?"). However, EDI has evolved from strictly mainframe-to-mainframe communication to a multipoint exchange involving a variety of hardware/software platforms, corporate entities, and information. EDI has been widely used for more than a decade, and remains a central dimension of e-commerce.

What Is EDI?

EDI is electronic communications or transactions between businesses via their software applications. Traditionally, EDI has comprised three basic components: a protocol standard, software, and the hardware delivery system. The protocol standard, ASC X.12, UN/EDIFACT, establishes an agreed-upon language for use between multiple partners in the business chain. The software component enforces the protocol standard and processes the exchanged information. The hardware delivery system comprises servers and network components.

EDI has been evolving rapidly in the presence of e-commerce consortiums (such as RosettaNet (http://www.rosettanet.org/), Commerce-Net, Open Buying on the Internet (OBI), and World Wide Web Consortium) and technological developments such as eXtensible Markup Language (XML). This evolution is being spurred by evolution in the business climate and the need to overcome limitations of traditional EDI standards and technologies. XML-based initiatives are leveraging the work embodied in standards such as ASC X.12 that support the needs of the advertising, insurance, education, entertainment, and mortgage banking industries. XML-based initiatives are also targeting these industries and their associated business transactions (such as inquiries, planning, purchasing, acknowledgments, pricing, order status, scheduling, test results, shipping and receiving, invoices, payments, and financial reporting). As XML assumes an enabling position for EDI, vendors will develop and offer bridging technologies to support the integration of new, XML-based and older, ASC X.12–based EDI systems between trading partners.

Depending upon the type of B2B relationship, there are three basic network infrastructure approaches:

- Value-added networks (VANs)
- Internet EDI
- Direct connections[1]

Business Environment

The EDI dimension of e-commerce has grown its roots in top-tier companies by enabling shorter business process cycles and greater accuracy of information exchange between both businesses and customers. In fact, it is estimated that 97 percent of Fortune 1000 companies currently use EDI.

Although very real benefits are available to EDI adopters, costly implementation, maintenance, and transaction fees have historically hindered its acceptance by the vast majority of mid- and lower-tier users. Indeed, (according to Meta Group) only 4 percent of companies outside of the Fortune 1000 with more than five employees currently use EDI. Nevertheless, these smaller sectors feel increasing pressure to invest in and use EDI to better support their larger trading partners. Much like a telephone or a fax machine, the effectiveness of EDI relies on its widespread adoption, and larger companies are beginning to require their partners to be connected.

EDI vendors are working to address and capture the opportunity this represents. Adoption rates are increasing as innovative EDI offerings focus on providing virtually maintenance-free EDI capabilities at a very reasonable price. As costs diminish, penetration within small to medium-sized markets will accelerate further. In addition, enterprise resource planning (ERP) and supply-chain management (SCM) vendors that have targeted small- to medium-scale users have realized the potential advantages of incorporating cost-effective EDI in their product suites.

Business Drivers

The most important business driver for EDI is the opportunity to increase market presence. Because so many companies use EDI today, joining the EDI community enables businesses to broaden growth strategies and engage in meaningful collaboration with new clients from around the world.

Another important business driver for EDI is the opportunity to reduce transaction costs by replacing manual, paper-based processes with electronically automated processes. When used in concert with SCM, EDI streamlines operations by improving on-time shipments, minimizing setup and cycle times, and reducing overall inventory costs. Speed, accuracy, and increased communication are key EDI benefits.

Other common EDI business drivers have been to improve order accuracy and process cycle time for large-dollar-volume purchasing transactions. Furthermore, EDI strategies are not only suitable for securing business objectives associated with large trading partners; they can also be leveraged to improve business process and cycle efficiency with smaller suppliers and customers.

EDI INTEGRATION SOLUTIONS

Now, let's begin the look at EDI solutions by examining a set of logical integration strategies. These logical perspectives address discrete scenarios, independent of physical implementation. Let's then examine physical implementation strategies that are capable of supporting these logical approaches.

Logical EDI Integration Strategies

Three fundamental logical integration strategies support the SCM-driven, business-to-business connection:

- Data integration
- Application integration
- Middleware integration

Data Integration

Tightly integrated business partners share a central data store and a common understanding of structured data. A variant of this strategy may use nonstructured data or document sharing. This enables computer display of paper documents. The data integration strategy offers companies the advantage of inhouse access to trading data, enabling better management of business processes and control over transaction flow. However, it is still essentially a manual process, subject to human error, and the transactions are not mapped to existing business applications. This strategy has traditionally been the mainstay of value-added networks (VANs) (where even the databases can be located inside the VAN premises) or carrier-assisted services.

Application Integration

Business partners access each other's systems using application programming interfaces (APIs). This strategy allows much greater flexibility for supporting a changing business environment. It typically involves a hands-off, application-to-application process, enabling EDI documents (purchase orders, requisitions, invoices, etc.) to update associated business applications (sales tracking systems, inventory management, accounts receivable, general ledger, etc.).

The application integration strategy enables companies to reap the full benefits of EDI implementation: cost savings, improved work processes, easily accessible and better-quality information, and improved customer responsiveness. However, it involves higher cost than the simpler data integration strategy, and development/maintenance costs tend to skyrocket when more than a couple of applications are integrated. Again, VAN- and carrier-centric solutions dominate this landscape.

Middleware Integration

Sophisticated connections between businesses use middleware (for example, message brokers) to facilitate access to business services (such as document translation, data mapping, and ERP APIs) and infrastructure services (such as security, messaging, and transactions). The middleware integration strategy is by far the most robust solution. It stresses a decoupled arrangement between applications, permitting integration between applications on a larger scale. Interface characteristics (whether message-, service-, or component-oriented) tend to be well defined and public.

Few solutions currently offer the types of services demanded by this EDI strategy, or offer a meaningful degree of integrated support across the hardware/software technology spectrum. Current strategies that involve the Internet require the development of additional infrastructure such as globally accessible directory and security schemes and reliable, interoperable transactional middleware. Finally, service quality must be transportable across multiple network infrastructures, placing additional demands on Internet Service Providers (ISPs).

Physical EDI Integration Strategies

This part of the chapter describes three fundamental EDI configurations, upon which any of the three logical relationships can be projected:

- VAN EDI solutions
- Private WAN EDI solutions
- Internet EDI so5lutions (with or without VPN services)

VAN EDI Solutions

The simplest EDI solution is to outsource service delivery by using EDI service providers, or VANs. In this solution, business partners exchange information indirectly through a specialized service provider that maintains a cross-business information host in multiple data formats and supports various access methods. During 2000, startup costs have ranged from $470 to $700, but transaction charges are typically higher.

VAN solutions have traditionally been based on legacy networking protocols such as X.25, X.435, and SNA, and have been offered as part of a unified EDI solution including data and application integration services. Recently, VANs have migrated their infrastructure to modern, open WAN protocols such as Frame Relay and Asynchronous Transfer Mode (ATM) in order to position themselves as specialized service providers rather than one-stop shops. The use of open WAN protocols allows VANs to act as EDI service providers, providing WAN connectivity that can be easily integrated into most enterprise networks as well as data integration, application integration, and middleware integration services that can be either bundled together or used à la carte.

VANs provide a fully outsourced network solution, including such value-added services as network management, service level maintenance, and integration with other EDI services. However, the connectivity provided by the VAN is essentially that of a private WAN between businesses and their trading partners. Because the VAN is providing an outsourced solution, the VAN typically chooses the WAN equipment to be used. Businesses must therefore ensure that their internal WAN devices support a wide array of connectivity, routing, security, and management standards. Table 11.1 summarizes the VAN EDI solution, and Table 11.2 summarizes the private WAN solution.[2]

TABLE 11.1 VAN EDI Solution

Description	Private-line network (including routers at line termination points) managed and operated by an EDI service provider, or VAN; the network can support legacy (X.25, X.435, and SNA) or modern (IP-based Frame Relay, ATM, or leased line) applications, depending on the EDI service provider and customer base.
Cost	High.
Availability	High; available in most areas, although obtaining circuits may be an issue in remote areas.

(continues)

TABLE 11.1 (*Continued*)

Performance	High; low-latency, dedicated network links lead to better performance of interactive applications.
Scalability	Medium; scalability is dependent on the EDI service provider's ability to increase available network bandwidth and connections.
Security	Medium to high, depending on EDI service provider–supported equipment.
Ease of Management	High; being a fully outsourced solution, all management tasks are offloaded to the EDI service provider.

TABLE 11.2 Private WAN EDI Solution

Description	Private-line network managed and operated by user (including routers at line termination points), supporting IP and IP-based applications.
Cost	High, especially internationally.
Availability	High; available in most areas, although obtaining circuits may be an issue in remote areas.
Performance	High; low latency leads to better performance of interactive (Web-based) applications, assuming no additional latency is added by terminating routers.
Scalability	Medium to low; cost of leased-line networks can become prohibitive when scaled to include a large number of nodes or when remote sites are connected by low-speed circuits.
Security	Medium to high, depending on supported equipment; remote access servers introduce a security risk, which can be mitigated through the use of two-factor authentication schemes (Security Dynamics' SecureID).
Ease of Management	Medium to low; routers and remote access servers must be configured and monitored by the user.

Internet EDI Solutions

Internet EDI represents a set of technologies, tools, and services such as virtual private networks (VPNs) that enable EDI transactions to be conducted securely over the Internet. This scenario is an evolution from a VAN configuration in which legacy EDI systems externalize access to the Internet domain. Such configurations are usually based on two-tier architectures, even though they may employ technologies (such as the Web) used in N-tier architectures. Companies often turn to the Internet in the hope of lowering the communication costs of VAN services. Another advantage of this approach is the promise of a consistent, browser-based user interface that can reduce training and integration costs relative to proprietary interfaces.

Virtual Private Networks

Provisioning Quality of Service (QoS) over the Internet involves the creation of extranets VPNs (secure, prioritized WAN connections across public IP infrastructures) between trading partners. A variety of Internet transport providers (such as ISPs, carriers, and VANs) and large end users provide VPN services that securely and preferentially treat EDI traffic. 3Com enables these types of next-generation VPN/extranet offerings by supporting the Internet Engineering Task Force (IETF) IPSec and Layer 2 Tunneling Protocol (L2TP) draft specifications and de facto standards such as the Point-to-Point Tunneling Protocol (PPTP), as well as by providing a complete, end-to-end VPN solution.

VPN connectivity must be secure, minimizing exposure to the corporate LAN but still allowing access to key resources via the Internet. Typically, firewall software is used to protect the corporate LAN, and a separate network (commonly referred to as the *demilitarized zone*, or DMZ) placed between the Internet router and the firewall holds the computers interfacing with the outside world. Table 11.3 summarizes the Internet EDI solution enhanced with VPN services.[3]

Evaluating EDI Options

These three EDI solution options can be evaluated along a number of dimensions. Perhaps the most critical of these are cost, ISP selection, performance, and manageability. The next section discusses these dimensions in more detail, and Table 11.4 summarizes key characteristics of the physical alternatives.

TABLE 11.3   Internet EDI Solution with VPN Services

Description	Use of existing Internet access facilities to connect with private business applications.
Cost	Low; currently, users lacking connectivity can purchase unlimited-usage consumer services (in 2000, prices in the United States started at about $30/month); existing users simply add traffic to their current ISP connections; VPN software products are typically inexpensive.
Availability	High; Internet access is possible virtually anywhere in the world, even if service grades vary dramatically by region (many countries may have only low-speed circuits, back-haul all traffic to the United States, etc.).
Performance	Poor; there are multiple sources of latency (IP services, routers, physical distribution) and multiple sources of outages, with no centralized point-of-contact for problem resolution; some carriers offer SLAs, but scope is invariably limited to carrier premises.
Scalability	Medium to high; IP scales easily from dial-up, through dedicated (56 Kbps, T1, T3, etc.)—and even SONET— connectivity; IP services are connectionless, thus avoiding mesh connectivity problems except in some VPN scenarios (for example, tunneling effectively creates embedded circuits in the IP stream).
Security	Poor; standard IP offers no credible security constructs; VPN products can offer authentication and confidentiality services, but management can become problematic with large numbers of users.
Ease of Management	Poor; realistically, the IT department must bear the full load of user support; decentralized nature makes problem sources difficult to identify; carriers and ISPs keep lean support staffs and resist involvement in problem identification efforts

TABLE 11.4 Key Characteristics of EDI Alternatives

EDI Alternatives	***C***ost	***A***vailability	***P***erformance	***S***calability	***S***ecurity	***M***anagement	***Comments***
VAN Solutions							
Basic Transport Services	H	M	M	M	M	M	Similar to private WAN.
Enhanced Devices	H	H	M	M	H	H	High cost; integration opportunity limited.
Internet Solutions							
Open Internet	M	H	L	H	L	L	Unsuitable for business critical transactions.
VPN Enhanced Internet	M	H	L	M	H	L	Performance issues outweigh cost savings.
Private WAN Solutions							
Leased Lines	H	H	H	M	M	M	High cost, particularly internationally.
Frame Relay	M	M	M	M	M	M	Preferred over leased lines.

N = High

M = Medium

L = Low

Cost

Companies hope to lower the communication costs of VAN services by using the Internet as the transport mechanism. Unfortunately, the Internet does not offer QoS guarantees or value-added security services (such as authentication, confidentiality, and nonrepudiation). Addressing these needs dramatically increases solution costs. For example, in 2000, a $4,000 Web server could increase in cost to $70,000 when one or more of these components were added. Nevertheless, higher-volume transaction environments may still realize per-transaction cost savings from an Internet EDI solution when compared to other solution options.

There are other costs involved in the Internet solution. The enterprise now bears the responsibility for maintaining this environment, troubleshooting failures, and retransmitting data as errors occur. As a result, many companies have found continued value in maintaining their EDI VAN services. Most users will employ private WAN services until ISPs provide credible service-level agreements, quality of service, and corporate-focused offerings. Longer term, the evolution to VPN services will make the Internet the dominant form of EDI-based access. This evolution can be seen in smaller EDI implementations today.

Selecting an ISP

Given their demand for reliability, business consumers are obviously concerned with the suitability of the Internet for business-critical applications. The ISP selection process must assess the candidate's ability to provide the following:

- Physically redundant local loop connections
- A number of high-quality connections to other ISPs at Internet exchange points, metropolitan area exchanges (MAEs), and private peering connections
- A robust internal topology using high-quality components
- Expertise with high-end routing protocols such as BGP-4
- Network management expertise

EDI users will require guaranteed service levels as their systems become increasingly mission critical. They will need QoS policies to ensure that mission-critical applications and users have priority access to the critical systems so that business objectives can be met in a reliable and predictable manner.

Performance

Obtaining a high-speed Internet connection is one of the easiest ways to increase the raw speed of the EDI system. Depending on the application, fractional T1, T1, inverse-multiplexed T1, T3, or higher can be used to ensure that the Internet connection is not the bottleneck.

Load-balancing strategies distribute requests among multiple Web servers and are another way to increase EDI transaction speed. Strategic Web page distribution, round-robin Domain Name Service (DNS) assignment to mirrored servers, or server *clustering* can be used to distribute the transaction load. Regardless of the load-balancing strategy used, an enterprise switch should be employed as the backbone of a Web server farm and between the Web server and corporate application servers. Full-duplex Ethernet, Fast Ethernet, or high-speed (Gigabit Ethernet or ATM) links should be considered.

In addition to speed and scalability increases, Web load balancing also enables increased reliability by protecting against single-server failure and allowing some site/server configuration modifications to be performed without downtime. This can be particularly critical in supporting e-commerce applications.

Administration and Management

The adoption of EDI and a network-centered business model brings new requirements for comprehensive network management and administration. To support mission-critical e-business operations, network management must extend beyond myopic, device-level management to address strategic business issues such as service level management, security, and network availability—including application response time management as well as reliability and redundancy. Such a management environment requires the ability to set and enforce policies to ensure that the network operates in the best interests of the business. Also, in order to ensure that the EDI infrastructure includes adequate server hardware and bandwidth, it is necessary to first identify the amount of network traffic being generated by the EDI solution.

Maintenance and management of service-level agreements (SLAs) with users or vendors allow specific service-level metrics and goals of the EDI solution to be related to the objectives of the business. Service-level management is an interactive process that encompasses defining and implementing policies, collecting and monitoring data, analyzing service levels against the SLA, reporting in real time and over longer intervals to gauge the effectiveness of current policies, and taking action to ensure the stability of services.

Middleware-Specific Configurations

As discussed earlier, middleware plays an important role in implementing sophisticated integration of SCM, ERP, and other enterprise applications. Enterprise-grade middleware messaging products exploit messaging models (see the sidebar "Middleware Messaging Models") to provide organizations with high-quality middleware solutions. Used correctly, these products provide a robust application infrastructure for applications integration, promoting faster IT response to business demands. As the middleware market has matured, integration support with packaged applications (such as SAP's R/3) and core IT components (such as DBMS) has expanded the appeal of middleware, as IT organizations seek to strike a better balance between built and bought functionality. Middleware maturation has also extended downward from the application perspective (leveraging IP Multicast technology), enabling synergy between middleware and networking products. This combination of technological soundness with improving maturity of implementations has brought middleware into the mainstream of IT enterprise solutions.

Middleware Messaging Models

In most cases, synchronous communication with SCM/EDI information servers should be excluded from any implementation that would require transport over wide area networks. Even if the application logic requires a strong level of synchronization in cross-business operations, it should never be implemented by means of synchronous online middleware. Asynchronous communication methods with sufficiently short response times should be used to simulate synchronous cross-business interaction.

By their very nature, asynchronous models are event driven. The event-driven paradigm is a natural and efficient style of computing for many applications, including data warehousing, Internet mirrors, incremental schedulers, just-in-time inventory management, real-time decision support, and data monitoring applications. There are two fundamental asynchronous messaging models: *publish-subscribe* and *request-reply*.

In the publish-subscribe model, a publisher distributes information in response to monitored business events. A subscriber places a standing request for information; whenever the publisher broadcasts information, the subscriber is guaranteed to receive it. Publishing is typically decoupled from subscribing, in that publishers are not aware of the population or identity of subscribers. Communication between the producer and consumer is in one direction only, and is often one to many.

In the request-reply model, a consumer submits a specific request to a producer; the producer computes an individual response and returns it to the consumer. Communications between the producer and consumer flow in both directions. There is no separation between the functions of business event monitoring and event interest/reacting. All entities interested in events within this model must individually monitor for their occurrence by polling observers. A further variant of request-reply is a broadcast request-reply. Here, there are multiple producers known to the consumer, all equally capable of satisfying the request. The consumer broadcasts a request to all known capable producers and accepts the first response.[4]

SUPPLY-CHAIN MANAGEMENT SOLUTIONS

EDI tends to be quite limited in the types of information that can be shared between business partners, and therefore in the extent of e-business integration it can facilitate. Supply chain management (SCM), by contrast, is much broader in scope, allowing the sharing of deep levels of inventory, forecasting, and logistical information to enable business partners to respond quickly and collectively to changing market conditions (see the sidebar, "What Is SCM?"). Companies seeking to maintain or increase competitive advantage are looking for this greater depth of integration with their supply chain partners.

What Is SCM?

SCM is the planning and control of the flow of goods and services, information, and money electronically back and forth through the supply chain. Figure 11.1 illustrates a simple value chain.[5] It shows a basic producer-consumer relationship, with an extension of a supplier to hint at the larger picture. A manufacturer creates a product for a consumer, using a supplier's materials, and exchanges information with both of them.

This simple relationship is repeated on the larger scale of a supply chain as a supplier, in turn, holds the place of the manufacturer in its own value chain. Figure 11.2 illustrates some of the entities that can exist in *real-world* supply chains. Distributors, retailers, and transport providers (such as shipping companies) mediate the value chain between manufacturers and consumers; and all parties simultaneously have concerns of both suppliers and consumers. Because participants play multiple roles in the supply/value/demand chain, supply chain management requires a holistic approach.[6]

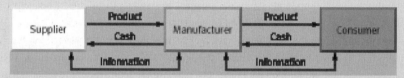

FIGURE 11.1 Simple value chain.

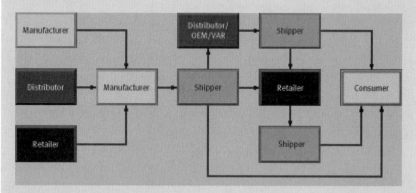

FIGURE 11.2 Supply chain.

Network Implications of SCM

The network infrastructure that connects the supply chain constituents is the glue that holds the SCM system together. Extremely reliable communication channels must be maintained at all times between the SCM application and all data sources and chain participants to ensure data integrity throughout the SCM process. Early implementation efforts involve planning paradigms such as what-if scenarios and constraint-based optimization. These activities often involve planning application packages, including ERP tools, that focus on the integration of disparate business functions.

Over time, each member of the chain learns to recognize those specific SCM events that are critical to it. Corresponding responses or actions are then encoded so that they occur automatically. These interactions, occurring faster and faster, become mission-critical transactions that can place additional performance demands on the supporting network infrastructure.

Network implications increase as supply chains become globalized, with multiple sources of information required to assemble each participant's required view. Figure 11.3 depicts a generalization of an advanced SCM system.[7] Network professionals must carefully examine all aspects of the network infrastructure relative to the supply chain to ensure that both data integrity and associated performance concerns are addressed. Is your SCM application getting data from a legacy mainframe-based order management or ERP system in time to prevent excessive backlog?

Building or campus networks may need to be upgraded to higher-performing legacy system connectivity and/or switched topologies that deliver high-speed IP services. Are your suppliers connected via the Internet? If so, extranets and VPNs that support QoS, security, and manageability are paramount. Is the data valid? Network reliability becomes essential. A successful SCM implementation requires the availability of several key network characteristics, including the following:

- **Interoperability**–SCM requires support for disparate network, application, and database assets. The system must provide heterogeneous connectivity, well-established APIs, and common data representation between constituent organizations.
- **Reliability**–Timely event routing requires fault tolerance and resiliency on the part of networks and servers.
- **Scalability**–A successful SCM implementation yields unprecedented growth in sales volume, orders, and deliveries across

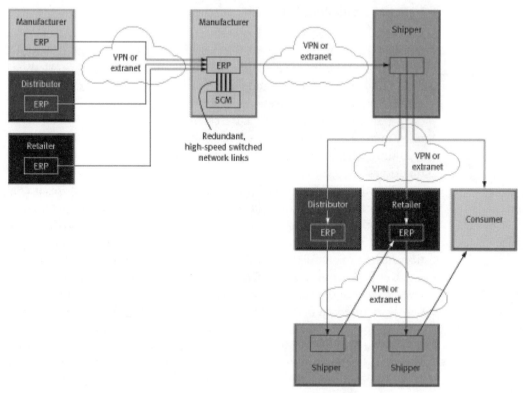

FIGURE 11.3 An advanced SCM system.

additional manufacturers, distribution centers, and retail outlets. At each point, the infrastructure must offer flexibility and scalability to support this growth.

■ **Performance**–Because SCM requires near real-time decision-making, the network must be instrumented with sophisticated QoS mechanisms.

■ **Manageability**–QoS and application performance must be regularly monitored. This requires network monitoring and analysis tools along with the ability to manage traffic flows.

■ **Security**–Increased usage of the Internet for SCM functions requires comprehensive encryption and authentication mechanisms.

SCM Back-End Requirements

SCM applications analyze and process large volumes of data, so the interaction between the application server(s) and the remote database management system (RDBMS) is highly intensive. The supporting network must have high bandwidth availability and very low latency to avoid performance degradation and enable real-time transactions. A dedicated network path is recommended. Today's high-speed network technologies—dedicated Fast Ethernet (shared or switched), Gigabit Ethernet, and ATM—all offer sufficient capacity and control. Figure 11.4 illustrates the key network components.[8]

Connecting applications and RDBMS resources with a wide area link is not recommended because typical WAN latency is too high. If the servers must be located in separate sites, as is usually the case when using a planning product at the plant, high-speed WAN connectivity can be employed to ensure that the SCM applications have timely information and do not negatively impact the performance of other enterprise applications. Inverse multiplexing of T1 and T3 leased lines or high-speed local/metro transport services, such as ATM switching running over high-speed SONET/SDH (Synchronous Optical Networking/Synchronous Digital Hierarchy), can be used to provide this connectivity. Figure 11.5 shows wide area SCM components.[9]

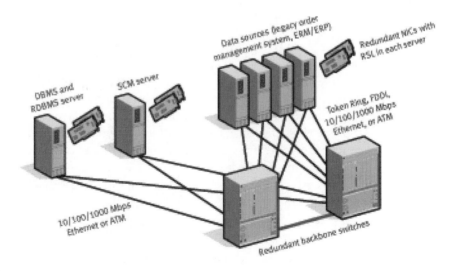

FIGURE 11.4 Campus SCM network.

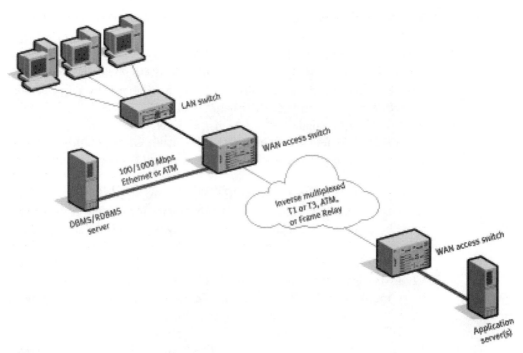

FIGURE 11.5 Wide area SCM infrastructure.

QoS mechanisms should be used to ensure that other application traffic does not negatively impact business-critical SCM transactions. As the supply chain expands, it is critical that network managers actively monitor their networking services.

Finally, as SCM applications become increasingly important to the business, the network supporting SCM applications must be highly reliable. To protect against server link failure, SCM servers can use two or more NICs with Resilient Server Link, a DynamicAccess technology feature that provides a *standby* server-to-switch link in case of a primary connection failure. For added reliability, these servers should be connected to redundant switches in a mesh topology to ensure NIC and switch fault tolerance.

SCM Front-End Requirements

Typically, the SCM application itself has very few clients, since strategic planning is a restricted function in most organizations. However, those clients require near-real-time access to the SCM systems. In the campus or building environment, the best way to provide this access is to upgrade from contentious, shared LAN topologies to dedicated connections by deploying switching. In addition, migrating to dedicated, full-duplex Ethernet or Fast Ethernet desktop connections and corresponding riser/backbone links (such as Fast Ethernet, Gigabit Ethernet, or ATM) significantly increases the bandwidth available to the SCM clients (and throughout the campus). Figure 11.6 illustrates these components.[10]

Careful attention must be paid to the SCM client-to-application server interactions across the wide area, because the bandwidth and latency issues typically associated with WAN connectivity can have a severe impact on application performance. WAN link connection speeds should be at least 56 Kbps. If the interactions are efficient, the challenge becomes to prioritize the traffic appropriately on what are typically costly or bandwidth-constrained links. Numerous QoS alternatives are available, ranging from IP Type of Service (ToS) priority queues in routers, to WAN-link-level bandwidth management, to mapping traffic to specific Frame Relay permanent virtual circuits (PVCs) with associated committed information rates (CIRs).

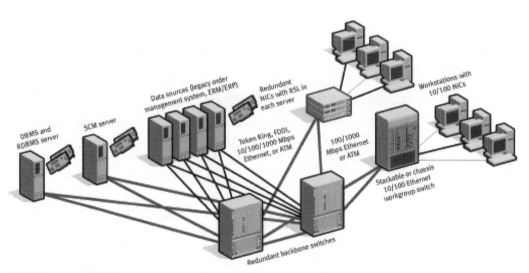

FIGURE 11.6   SCM front-end network.

ADVANCED SCM NETWORKING AND FUTURES

As SCM networking becomes more widely deployed, its functionality will expand in a number of directions.

Continued Expansion of the Value Chain

As the SCM implementation matures, it expands from the organization's internal value chain to the external supplier, distribution channel, and buyer value systems. Initially, large organizations will focus on managing internal supply chains with respect to quasi-independent business units, but this will quickly evolve to address external players. As this occurs, a variety of Internet transport providers (ISPs, carriers, VAN providers) will offer VPN services that preferentially treat SCM-related traffic. By combining QoS and security features in VPNs, these providers will create application-specific extranets between organizations. Figure 11.7 illustrates this type of network configuration.[11]

SCM Network Quality of Service

As described earlier, SCM-originated events may not always be given the necessary priority, either within a constituent organization or between constituent organizations. With the unprecedented growth of multimedia and other high-bandwidth-demand applications, a prioritization scheme will be required that can marshal network resources and, ultimately, consider traffic value.

SCM Network Monitoring and Reporting

In addition to QoS, organizations must have the means to ensure that established levels of service are being delivered. For SCM, this requires very granular network behavior measurement.

SCM Security

Trusted connections are critical for wide-scale business-to-business collaboration. These connections will require increased support for confidentiality (not allowing third parties to see transmitted information), authentication (enabling each party in a transaction to determine with certainty the identity of the other party), and nonrepudiation (ensuring that the parties cannot deny their participation in a transaction).

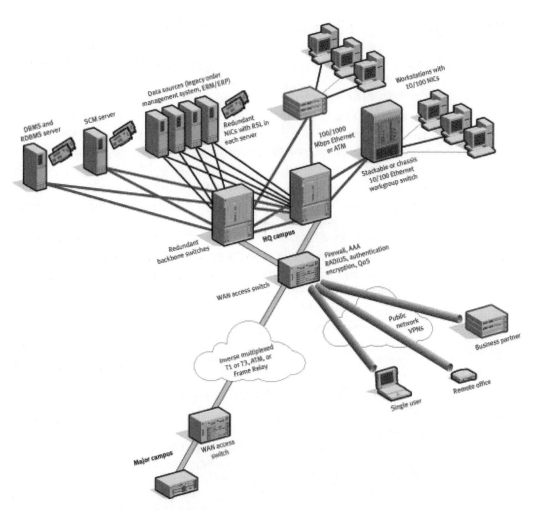

FIGURE 11.7 Expanded SCM with VPN connectivity.

SCM Web Interfaces

Many SCM vendors are adding Web interfaces to their applications. SCM Web interfaces range from basic Hypertext Markup Language (HTML) markups of client screens and reports to sophisticated, next-generation clients based on Java or ActiveX. The key for these vendors is leveraging the intellectual capital and financial resources being invested in Internet-related products. For users, the promise of a relatively consistent set of browser interfaces is much more attractive from a training and evolution standpoint than proprietary interfaces. As SCM applications become increasingly Web savvy, new security and service-level challenges emerge.

Dynamic Trading Networks

As discussed throughout this chapter, accelerated business cycles and channel alignment strategies will transform *closed* supply chain relationships into large, open, dynamic trading networks (DTNs). Competitive forces are driving supply chain integration, including increased trading partner integration as well as interaction with an increasing number of trading partners through electronic process interchange and application-to-application integration. Leading organizations within supply chains are beginning to equip small and medium-sized enterprise trading partners with technology infrastructure, applications, integration, and support services.

As business cycles compress, companies must be able to anticipate and react quickly to customer demands. To improve the effectiveness of their own supply chain (thereby improving competitive abilities versus other supply chains) and realize the substantial benefits of network technologies (such as cost savings, incremental revenue, and effective use of resources), companies will seek opportunities to proffer, or *push*, solutions to smaller trading partners. This will drive standardization across the supply chain and promote adoption of solutions where they otherwise would be financially unfeasible.

These push opportunities will connect smaller companies that were formerly excluded from EDI due to required infrastructure investment and service expense, or small companies where existing IT infrastructure is incompatible with a larger company's existing or proposed systems. Processes involving substantial quantities of paper-based information (such as catalogs and marketing materials) or personnel as data transfer agents (for example, rekeying faxed orders or distributors taking customer order information on paper forms) are also candidates for DTN solutions.

Business processes most appropriate for pushed SCM infrastructure solutions include production procurement (materials required for creation of an organization's primary products), distribution, logistics, order management (entry, tracking, status), and other collaborative inter-organizational processes. Pushed e-commerce solutions may reside within partner organizations, with inter-application communications via secure or open channels, or they may be hosted by third parties such as ISPs or VANs. Indeed, VANs and business transaction brokers will continue to play a significant role in inter-business relationships for the foreseeable future, as trading partner relationships and the management of inter-business transaction/interaction architectures continue to be difficult.

Therefore, business-to-business e-commerce is bringing profound changes in the structure and business practices of organizations and the interactions between business partners. Potential benefits of this inexorable transition include cost reduction, improved competitive position, and enhanced information access both within and between business organizations. Large companies are implementing a variety of technologies and business process models (including EDI and SCM) to harness these benefits while avoiding the pitfalls of the e-commerce economy. Over time, small and medium-sized companies will also be integrated into global dynamic trading networks based on these systems.

Business-to-business e-commerce is also bringing profound changes in how we secure Web sites. With the Internet fundamentally changing the way business is conducted, the opportunity for security breaches within an organization are increasing exponentially.

SECURITY FOR BUSINESS-TO-BUSINESS E-COMMERCE

Businesses that accept transactions via the Web can gain a competitive edge by reaching a worldwide audience, at very low cost. However, the Web poses a unique set of business-to-business security issues that businesses must address at the outset to minimize risk. Customers will submit information via the Web only if they are confident that their personal information, such as credit card numbers, financial data, or medical history, is secure.

According to the recently released Computer Security Institute (CSI) fifth annual Computer Crime and Security Survey, 54 percent of respondents now conduct electronic commerce on their sites, as opposed to 30 percent in 1999. Clearly, unless one has decided to forgo any contact with the American media, you can't have a conversation with even novice technologists without the subject of B2C or B2B electronic commerce coming up. Yet, while everyone seems to be paying a lot of attention to stock prices and market segments, the implementation of e-security (in most large companies) is not keeping pace with the rapid deployment of their Internet, intranet, or extranet sites.

According to IDC, e-security marks a departure from traditional security. In the past, security technologies (both physical and electronic) essentially operated to limit outsiders' access to corporate resources. E-security assumes outsider access and works to encourage and enable that access.

That is, pre-e-business security's main function involved limiting access to corporate data networks to only those individuals who had been previously identified and deemed trustworthy. Today's e-security model invites outside access. It works within an Internet architecture that assumes some degree of "street level access" for all.

Today's e-Security Business Requirements

With the nationwide coverage of recent, high-profile *denial-of-service* attacks, more people are becoming aware of security concerns. However, more advanced security implementations are required as companies get more sophisticated with their enterprise and Web-enabled solutions.

For example, most corporations today have taken adequate steps to implement password protection, antivirus programs, firewalls, and intrusion detection mechanisms. While these are relatively easy security solutions to deploy, with little impact on a company's infrastructure, by themselves they are not enough. Companies are still investing heavily in network-level and system-level security solutions, when the largest returns are to be found in securing higher-level transactions. The decision to implement more advanced security hinges on six primary business requirements:

- Enablement
- Mitigation of Risk
- Cost Reductions
- Regulatory Compliance
- Customer/Partner Requirements
- Competition

Enablement

As organizations race to open up data to customers, suppliers, and employees, greater security mechanisms are required in order to make transactions secure.

Mitigation of Risk

Customers need to acknowledge the value of information assets and determine the level of security required based on that value. The CSI study reported that 85 percent of respondents acknowledged financial losses due to computer breaches—with 53 percent quantifying those losses at a whopping total of $37,869,005,140.

Cost Reductions

The deployment of e-commerce, VPNs, and intranets can provide significant cost savings in information distribution, delivery cycles, employee communications, and overhead. Cost reduction numbers plus the mitigation of risk contribute to justification for bulletproof security measures.

Regulatory Compliance

Some industries, like healthcare and financial services, must also factor in regulatory compliance measures in the overall formula for secure information systems.

Customer/Partner Requirements

The last year has seen the business-to-business craze heighten substantially. Suppliers in every industry, from solid waste to steel to medical and office supplies, are now developing sites to speed procurement, delivery, and cut costs. The new Internet Age is requiring online transactions and VPNs in order to stay competitive.

Competition

Competitive viability is the key to success. Unless organizations step up to the plate in the New Age, they'll be left behind. They'll be equally left behind if key assets are lost to serious computer security breaches.

SECURE WEB SITE ACCESS FOR BUSINESS PARTNERS

A secure Web site can provide your business partners with powerful competitive advantages, including online sales and streamlined application processes for products such as insurance, mortgages, or credit cards. Credit card sales can be especially lucrative: According to independent analysts, cash transactions on the Internet will reach $10 billion by 2001, and $40 billion in 2006. No merchant can afford to ignore a market this large.

When you secure your Web site, you can increase business by reassuring the 86 percent of Web users with concerns about Internet security. You can also improve competitiveness by securely delivering electronic products at no cost, streamlining enrollment, and learning valuable information about your customers.

To succeed in this market, however, you must become fully aware of Internet security threats, take advantage of the technology that overcomes them, and win your customer's confidence. This part of the chapter describes the benefits of e-commerce, and the specific risks you must address to realize the benefits.

Extend Your Reach to More Customers

By offering your product on the Web, your business can gain unique benefits.

Worldwide Presence

The Web represents a new source of customers. Anyone with an Internet connection is a potential customer: More than 60 million people around the world are already using the Internet for business transactions. Your Web storefront is open all the time, and requires no investments in brick and mortar.

Market Share

In a recent study, 86 percent of Web users surveyed reported that a lack of security made them uncomfortable sending credit card numbers over the Internet. The merchants who can win the confidence of these customers will gain their loyalty—and an enormous opportunity for expanding market share.

Cost-Effective Delivery Channel

Many products and services, such as software or information, can be distributed directly to customers via the Web. This saves time for your customers, which increases your competitive appeal. It also increases your profitability by eliminating the shipping and overhead costs associated with order fulfillment.

Streamlined Enrollment

Paper-based enrollment workflows are fraught with delays. Applications for insurance, a mortgage, or a credit card, for example, can be held up in the mail and your mailroom. Once received, the application must be entered into your computer system, a labor-intensive process that can introduce errors. By accepting applications via a secure Web site, you can speed application processing, reduce processing costs, and improve customer service.

Better Marketing through Better Customer Knowledge

Establishing a storefront on the Web positions you for one-to-one marketing—the ability to customize your products and services to individual customers rather than large market segments. The Web facilitates one-to-one marketing by enabling you to capture information about demographics, personal buying habits, and preferences. By analyzing this information, you can target your merchandise and promotions for maximum impact, tailor your Web page to appeal to the specific consumer who is visiting, and conduct effective, tightly focused marketing campaigns.

Ensure the Security of Your Electronic Transactions

In business-to-business transactions, security is based on physical cues. Consumers have come to accept the risks of using credit cards in places like department stores because they can see and touch the merchandise and make judgments about the store. On the Internet, without those physical cues, it is much more difficult to assess the safety of a business. Also, serious security threats have emerged. By becoming aware of the risks of Internet-based transactions, businesses can acquire technology solutions that overcome those risks, such as:

- **Spoofing**–The low cost of Web site creation and ease of copying existing pages makes it all too easy to create illegitimate sites that appear to be published by established organizations. In fact, con artists have illegally obtained credit card numbers by setting up professional-looking storefronts that mimic legitimate businesses.
- **Unauthorized disclosure**–When transaction information is transmitted in the clear, hackers can intercept the transmissions to obtain your customers' sensitive information.
- **Unauthorized action**–A competitor or disgruntled customer can alter your Web site so that it refuses service to potential clients or malfunctions.
- **Data alteration**–The content of a transaction can be intercepted and altered en route, either maliciously or accidentally. Usernames, credit card numbers, and dollar amounts sent *in the clear* are all vulnerable to such alteration.

Thus, with its worldwide reach, the Web is a lucrative distribution channel with unprecedented potential. By setting up an online storefront, businesses can reach the millions of people around the world already using

the Internet for transactions. And, by ensuring the security of online payments, businesses can minimize risk and reach a far larger market: the 86
percent of Internet users who still hesitate to shop online because of security concerns.

Finally, we can't leave a discussion of B2B security without a brief
overview of the Gateway security model in the Java Commerce Client
(JCC).[12] In other words, this part of the chapter describes an extension to
the current Java security model called the *Gateway* and why it was necessary to create it.

GATEWAY SECURITY MODEL

The Gateway security model allows secure applications, such as those used
in B2B electronic commerce, to safely exchange data and interoperate
without compromising each individual application's security. The Gateway
uses digital signatures to enable application programming interfaces (APIs)
to authenticate their caller. JavaSoft is using the Gateway to create a new,
integrated, open platform for financial applications called Java Commerce
Client.[13] The JCC will be the foundation for electronic wallets, point of sale
terminals, electronic merchant servers, and other financial software. The
Gateway model can also be used for access control in many multiple application environments that require trusted interaction between applications
from multiple vendors. These applications include browsers, servers, operating systems, medical systems, and smart cards.

The Java language provides the appropriate technology for deploying
tight integration between applications while maintaining application data
integrity. The JCC builds on Java's inherent extensibility and adds the ability to safely share some information while keeping other information secret. Applications can precisely define the limits of their trust of the data
and behavior that they extend to other applications.

Overview of the Java Security Model

Java is a portable, safe, object-oriented language. The safety properties of
the Java language and the run-time security model of the Java environment, called the *Java Sandbox* security model, provide safeguards that in-
hibit inappropriate activity. The Java application environment has an
extensive application framework that includes a set of common utility
classes, a portable window system, database interfaces, and many other
useful reusable classes that enable programs.

Many Web browsers contain Java implementations. Java-enabled browsers support a unique application type called an *applet*. It is easy for Web page authors to embed applets into Web pages. When the browser loads the Web page, a Java-enabled browser also loads the implementation of the applet into the browser and executes the applet's instructions. Without appropriate safeguards, viruses could use the dynamic loading mechanism to damage the host system. Java's safeguards allow applications from unknown sources to download and execute safely.

Safety Properties of the Java Programming Language

Java is similar to other strongly typed object-oriented languages such as C++. C++ is designed for systems programmers. Unlike C++, Java prohibits certain language loopholes that might damage type safety. System programmers use C++ because it provides them with necessary unsafe features to implement device drivers, memory management systems, and other low-level features. The unsafe features of C++ increase the expressive power and efficiency of the language, but sacrifice reliability and portability. For example, both C++ and its predecessor C have a feature called a *cast*. A cast allows a programmer to write an expression that tells the compiler to treat an integer as a pointer, or treat a pointer to one type as though it were a pointer to another. This feature breaks type safety, but low-level system programmers often need this feature to efficiently implement many systems. In contrast, Java is designed for application programmers and does not allow such unsafe designs.

Isolation Properties of Java

The Java language sacrifices some of C++'s expressive power and efficiency to get greater reliability, safety, and tighter inter-application coupling. There are no unsafe casts in Java. All references to objects conform to the type system of the language. Type safety can never be broken. This allows multiple Java applications to run in the same address space. Java applications running in one address space may actually run faster than those C++ applications that must be run in two address spaces.

The Java virtual machine enforces safety, privacy, and isolation rules. Instead of using address space separation between applications, Java access modes protect unauthorized access and isolate one application from another. The Java type system has explicit visibility declaration rules that define three access modes: *public*, *private*, and *protected*.

The idea behind Java's access comes from C++ access modes. But the underlying object model of C ++ does not enforce access modes. Unlike

Java objects, C++ objects are simply bits in memory. Adroit programmers exploit the memory model of C++ and break the type safety of the language both for good and malicious purposes. For example, to falsely create as an object, a programmer merely sets an array of characters to suitable value and casts it into the object's type.

Unlike C++, a Java object must emerge only from a new operation. The new operation invokes a special method called a *constructor*. The constructor's access mode controls object allocation. The constructor also ensures that the object is initialized to a known value. Thus, if the constructor is not public or protected, another module cannot create the object. Unforgeable objects provide the basis of security in Java.

Another safety loophole of C++ is that pointers may point anywhere in memory, even into the interior of objects. C++ arithmetic pointer operations allow a program to move the target of a pointer to any location in memory. Additionally, there is no bounds checking on arrays or checks against referencing outside the boundaries of an object. This obliterates any of the security properties of C++ access modes.

It is also trivial in C++ to cast an integer into a pointer and access any location in memory. Even the dynamically typed language Smalltalk-80 has a loophole operation called asOop that allows a programmer to transform an integer into an object.

Unlike C++, the Java programming language has no operations that allow pointers to break access mode safety. All accesses to objects are bounds checked. There is no language mechanism for forging an integer into an object reference. Array dereferencing is either statically or dynamically checked. Object dereferencing must occur only in the boundaries of the object. It is not possible in Java to turn an integer value into a pointer.

Using the safety model of the language as a basis, it is now possible to have multiple isolated applications residing in the same address space. The applications may communicate as specified by the type system of the Java language. Java makes it possible to isolate one application from another. Isolation allows Java to have the next tier of security called the Java Sandbox security model.

The Java Sandbox Security Model

The Java Sandbox security model controls dangerous operations such as writing to users' disks or network communication. The Sandbox security model is intended to evoke the notion of putting a child in a sandbox. The child cannot get hurt, nor can he or she wander outside of the sandbox and cause any damage.

The Sandbox security model divides applets into untrusted applets and trusted applets. Untrusted applets may access limited system resources. Trusted applets have greater access to system resources, but still must obey the language safety rules as previously described. Trusted applets are digitally signed. The browser has a list of digital signatures of trust authorities. The Java implementation consults the list at applet load time to determine the correct security manager to use for the applet.

The security manager is an object that is a subclass of class Security Manager. When an applet performs a dangerous system operation, the implementation of the operation consults the applet's security manager. Potentially dangerous operations include opening a file or a network socket, changing a system variable, and setting the security manager. Each method in the security manager either allows the operation or throws a Java language exception to prohibit it. In many browsers, the security manager for untrusted applets limits the effect of applets by denying all dangerous operations. The only exceptions are that an untrusted applet may make a socket connection to the applet's originating network site.

There are untrusted applets and trusted applets, but no partially trusted applets possible. Therefore, the Java Sandbox supports single applets, but it does not support interaction between applets that do not completely trust each other. Since limited trust applets are required for electronic commerce, the new Gateway model was a needed component of the Java Commerce Client (JCC).

Framework and Responsibilities

Many object-oriented practitioners use the term *framework* to mean an *application programming interface*. In this part of the chapter, the term *framework* refers to a set of APIs that impose responsibilities among participating software packages. The JCC defines application responsibilities for merchants and financial institutions. The JCC provides services, such as database services, to merchant and financial institution applications. These layers are depicted in Figure 11.8.[14]

The Merchant Applet Layer uses Java applets to enhance the shopping experience. Applets are an appropriate way to implement short-term customer relationships such as the shopping experience. Example consumer applets are shopping cart applets and content charging applets. Merchant Applet Layer code does not require a long-term customer to merchant relationship. Examples of bank applets include loan questionnaire applets and CD investment selling tool applets.

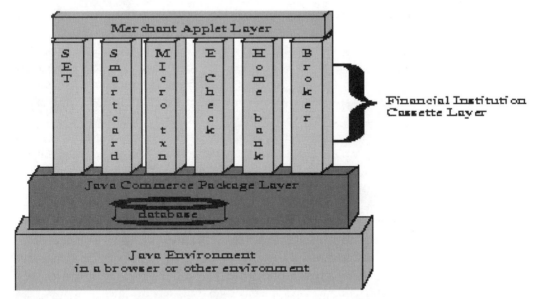

FIGURE 11.8 Simple schema of the JCC.

The Cassette Layer implements long-term customer relationships such as credit cards, home banking, and brokerages. *Cassettes* are a new feature that JCC adds to Java. Similar to applets, cassettes are downloaded from servers to client computers. Unlike applets, which disappear when users quit the browser, cassettes are retained on the customer's system. Cassettes store information in a database provided by the JCC. Cassettes may safely store valuable information such as public key certificates and transaction records since the entire database is encrypted. Cassettes provide long-term customer-to-institution relationships. Examples of cassettes include SET certificates and protocols, home banking, brokerage accounts, financial analysis, and planning software. Cassettes contain code, digital certificates, GIF images, and other resources. Financial institutions will use cassettes to deliver customer service features. Smart-card application developers can put smart-card reader device drivers and application user interfaces in cassettes.

The Java Commerce Package Layer implements the infrastructure needed by the merchant and the cassette layers. Features at this layer include a user interface, an application model, a database, and access to strong cryptography. The Java Environment Layer is the underlying browser or operating system.

The Services in the JCC

Applets and cassettes use several layers of service in the Java commerce package. Figure 11.9 details the layers.[15]

The GUI Services Layer provides a graphical metaphor of a wallet. The wallet depicts credit cards, ATM cards, membership cards, and other commonly found documents. The wallet user interface plays a central function in user interaction. GIF images implement the simplest card. Alternatively, a cassette may use all of Java's user interface components, such as JavaBeans, to create elaborate animations and interfaces. As with all user interfaces, developers should use good taste and discretion to avoid creating excessively elaborate cards.

The Application Services Layer implements common application metaphors. Currently, the Java commerce package supports metaphors most appropriate to purchasing; however, future metaphors will include other financial services. The central classes in this layer are Instrument, Action, and ActionBuilder. There is a one-to-one mapping between

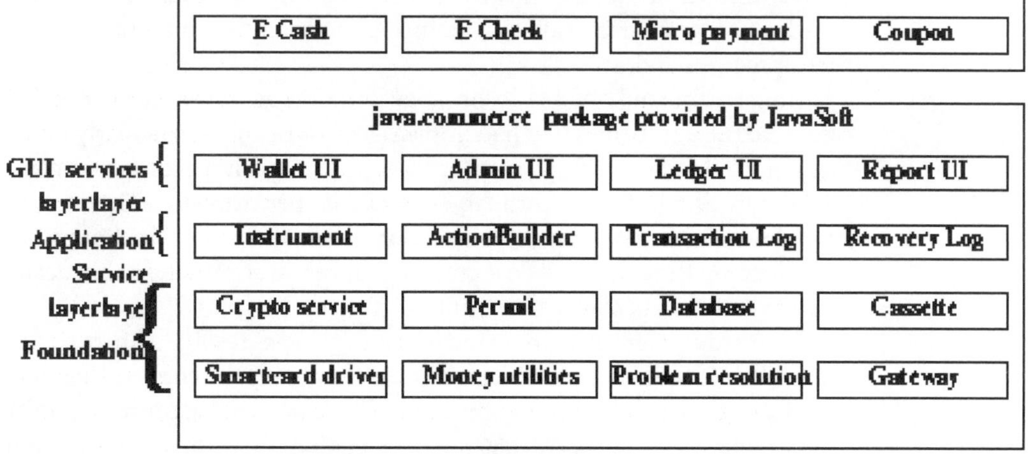

FIGURE 11.9 Detailed schema of packages in the JCC.

Instruments and the card objects. An Action is an individual payment transaction. A MasterCard or Visa SET transaction would be one Action. A coupon redemption is another Action. ActionBuilders assemble actions to create one business transaction. For example, the PurchaseActionBuilder is responsible for understanding the business rules for merchants. Merchants who do not like the PurchaseActionBuilder provided by the JCC may define their own.

The Foundation Service Layer includes the database classes, access to strong cryptography, smart-card device access, and various common utility classes such as Money. The Java commerce database provides a subset of the functionality of a relational database. The database is reliable and uses very little memory and disk resources. Although designed for computers with local or remote disks, the database is pluggable to meet the needs of diskless network computers. Third-party database vendors will create scalable commercial databases to provide software safe deposit box services.

So, what is the outlook for e-commerce? Will the explosion of dotcoms last? Questions still remain about the ability of dotcoms to cut costs. All of this is explored and questions are answered in this part of the chapter.

THE OUTLOOK FOR ELECTRONIC COMMERCE

Dotcoms have tried cutting costs to become profitable, but the strategy isn't working, according to a recent study by Getzler & Co., Inc., a New York-based turnaround firm. Instead, cost cutting has resulted in significantly lower growth rates that could further undermine companies' already depressed valuations.

In a recent study of 324 technology and dotcom firms, Getzler & Co. identified 68 companies that had implemented cost cuts, particularly in the area of sales and marketing. Getzler then studied the impact of these cost-cutting measures on the companies' financial performance. They found that dotcoms are reducing costs in order to become profitable, but rather than helping the company, cost cutting reduces sales growth so drastically that profitability becomes nearly impossible.

The study analyzed first- and second-quarter results of firms with more than $2 million in quarterly sales. On average, the cost-cutting dotcoms grew sales at an annual rate of only 20 percent, yet lost $2.30 for every dollar of revenue. At that rate, even assuming certain costs remain constant, it will take many years for these companies to become profitable—and investors aren't likely to wait that long.

The average growth rate for cost-cutting dotcoms severely lagged the growth rate for firms that increased spending—20 percent annually versus 260 percent annually. A 20-percent growth rate is typical of a healthy traditional firm, not a dotcom that is operating deeply in the red and whose stock price has factored in expectations of several years of very high growth. Amazon.com typified the study's conclusions. The company reduced sales and marketing costs in the second quarter of 2000, but experienced virtually stagnant growth.

Among the 68 cost-cutting firms studied, almost half were e-tailers. The e-tailing sector is facing particularly skeptical investor sentiment, making it increasingly difficult for these firms to attract additional funding. The result has been a wave of belt tightening.

The study also corroborated analysts' souring opinion of the loyalty of dotcom customers. Dotcoms have spent vast sums of money (in many cases, most of their capital) on marketing, reasoning that such expenditures were necessary to build a loyal customer base.

However, if your revenue drops as soon as the dollars stop flowing into marketing programs, you have to question customer loyalty and the wisdom of continuing to invest blindly in extravagant marketing campaigns. The study suggests that dotcoms need to be more prudent about their marketing spending: for example, Internet firms that spent millions on short ads during the Super Bowl. In certain cases, firms spent a significant percentage of their entire annual budget on a single advertisement that generated little customer follow-through or discernible revenue.

The study did identify several exceptions. For example, e-tailers Pets.com and PlanetRx.com have managed to increase sales at a healthy clip while reducing spending on marketing and sales. Clearly these companies are finding more efficient ways to spend their marketing dollars. Multex.com and Priceline.com, despite the latter's recent negative publicity, also proved to be exceptions. Both are relatively close to profitability and both have maintained healthy growth rates while reducing costs.

Aside from these few exceptions, the prospects for dotcom restructuring are slim. It is simply unrealistic to think that a dotcom can effect a traditional turnaround. If that is the case, their viability as economic entities is questionable. The only solution for many such companies may be to merge with other firms.

In view of the preceding discussion, what are the challenges faced by e-commerce? Now, let's focus on the emergence of the digital economy, the promise it contains, and some of the challenges it poses. Some of the challenges are technical, others involve the development of standards, and still others require significant capital investments.

THE CHALLENGES FACED BY E-COMMERCE

The digital revolution is also changing the respective roles of government and the private sector. In the 19th and for much of the 20th centuries, governments played a key role in helping build or actively regulate much of the country's infrastructure. The federal government made extensive land grants to encourage private capital to expand the nation's rail network. Government subsidies were used to stimulate the development of an airline industry. Federal and state dollars combined to build and maintain the interstate highway system. In communications, the government granted a virtual monopoly to a single company and regulated the industry after its breakup. Most power companies have been regulated monopolies at the state or federal level.

The federal government funded and developed early versions of the Internet for national security and research purposes. It will continue to provide funding for research and development on future Internet and high-performance computing technologies. However, most of the capital to build the computing and telecommunications infrastructure is being provided by the private sector.

The pace of technological development and the borderless environment created by the Internet drive a new paradigm for government and private sector responsibilities. Creating the optimal conditions for the new digital economy to flourish requires a new, much less restrictive approach to the setting of rules. For example:

- Governments must allow electronic commerce to grow up in an environment driven by markets, not burdened with extensive regulation, taxation, or censorship. While government actions will not stop the growth of electronic commerce, if they are too intrusive, progress can be substantially impeded.
- Where possible, rules for the Internet and electronic commerce should result from private collection action, not government regulation.
- Governments do have a role to play in supporting the creation of a predictable legal environment globally for doing business on the Internet, but must exercise this role in a non-bureaucratic fashion.
- Greater competition in telecommunications and broadcast industries should be encouraged so that high-bandwidth services are brought to homes and offices around the world, so that the new converged marketplace of broadcast, telephony, and the Internet

operate based on laws of competition and consumer choice rather than those of government regulation.

- There should be no discriminatory taxation against Internet commerce.
- The Internet should function as a seamless global marketplace with no artificial barriers erected by governments.

As with any major societal transformation, the digital economy will foster change and some upheaval. The Industrial Revolution brought great economic and social benefit, but it also brought about massive dislocations of people, increased industrial pollution, unhealthy child labor, and unsafe work environments. Societies were often slow to respond to these negative side effects.

Similarly, the digital economy may bring potential invasions of privacy, easier access by children to pornographic and violent materials and hate speech, more sophisticated and far-reaching criminal activity, and a host of other as yet unknown problems. The private sector and government, working together, must address these problems in ways that make the Internet a safe environment while not impeding its commercial development.

The U.S. Government's "Framework for Global Electronic Commerce," posted on the Internet at http://www.ecommerce.gov, describes a market-driven framework that will stimulate the growth of the digital economy while offering flexible, industry-driven solutions that will effectively address problems that may arise. Steps are now being taken in the United States and around the world to meet these public policy goals.

Perhaps the greatest challenge the United States faces, however, is to put in place the human resource policies necessary for the digital economy. If the trends described in this chapter continue, millions of jobs will likely be created, while millions of others will be lost.

The good news is that the net economic growth anticipated by this digital revolution will likely create more jobs than those that are lost. Further, the jobs created are likely to be higher-skilled and higher-paying than those that will be displaced. However, it is clear that we will face great challenges in preparing the current workforce and future workers to fill the new jobs that will be created. If we do not have a sufficient number of well-educated and trained people to fill these jobs, then the good news can turn to bad. If these public policy issues can be resolved, and electronic commerce is allowed to flourish, the digital economy could accelerate world economic growth well into this century.

So, what is the future of e-commerce? Some industry analysts predict that the future of e-commerce lies in the success of B2B commerce. B2B commerce is predicted to reach $7.4 trillion in 2006.

THE FUTURE OF ELECTRONIC COMMERCE

Jupiter Research recently released a study with pulse-quickening projections about the growth of the business-to-business (B2B) commerce market. Jupiter's prediction that B2B commerce will expand from $336 million in 2000 to $7.4 trillion in 2006, is likely to raise the heart rates of even the most composed IT administrators as they try to figure out how to accommodate such exponential expansion.

What makes the next generation of e-commerce so different is the connection of entire supply chains to the same network, according to the U.S. Business-to-Business Trade Projections study. If you thought you had big integration problems before, now you have to integrate companies within your firewall.

The degree to which business-to-consumer transactions have moved online will pale in comparison to the number of transactions that include companies and their partners, suppliers, and customers. While 26 to 31 percent of business-to-consumer transactions have gone online, 90 percent of business-to-business transactions will be conducted online in seven to nine years.

Jupiter found that the computer and telecommunications markets should become the largest online B2B market in terms of sales, topping $2 trillion by 2006. Four other industries (food and beverage, motor vehicle and parts, industrial equipment and supplies, and construction and real estate) are expected to exceed $600 billion within six years.

Now that we've briefly talked about the future of e-commerce, let's discuss the outlook for the online markets themselves.

THE OUTLOOK FOR ONLINE MARKETS

As explained throughout this chapter and in Chapter 10, "Designing and Building E-Commerce Web Sites: Hands-On," not all dotcoms will survive. With the recent tightening in the market, investors in 2001 and beyond are challenging dotcoms to show some results: higher revenues, more customers, perhaps even a profit. This is tough news for dotcoms that have spent most of their money on expensive advertisements, PR campaigns, or Web sites that look pretty but haven't succeeded. The year 2001 is the last chance for many dotcoms to show some results—or close their doors forever.

However, there is a way for dotcoms to survive. There is still one resource left untapped that can save dotcoms from failure. It's the one resource that historically is most ignored in favor of ads, press, and flashy features—yet it's the one resource that can lead dotcoms to survival. That resource is *customers*.

Customers can provide the revenues needed to attain profitability. Customers can give the word-of-mouth marketing to drive traffic. Customers can give the feedback needed to continually improve the Web site. Customers are a dotcom's *most important* resource.

To survive, dotcoms must turn to their most important resource: customers.

Where does a dotcom connect with its customers? In its customer experience. Everything from the home page, to the shopping and buying process, to the fulfillment of products—the customer experience is the combination of everything the customer sees, clicks, reads, or otherwise interacts with. The customer experience is the key to dotcom survival.

The Maturing of Online Markets

Forrester recently produced a special report on business-to-business online markets stating that e-commerce is going to grow to $650 billion by the year 2002 (see the sidebar, "B2B: Where The Money Is"). Now, Forrester is renowned for creating big hype numbers—so what can we deduce from this?

Online markets are maturing, but much of the business-to-business commerce is still done within small (in terms of participants) buying groups. Similar to Internet advertising revenue numbers, which are grossly overstated due to the practice of *banner swapping*, it is expected that these online markets numbers are also overstated.

The more interesting question raised by Forrester is what trends can we expect in the online markets area? The answer lies in dynamic trading processes.

Dynamic trading results from 24x7 accessibility and the power of Perfect Information. Think stock market—if we all had perfect information, then no one would make money on stocks. As the customer approaches Perfect Information over the Internet, the theory goes that prices should

B2B: Where the Money Is

Still need proof that B2B e-commerce is the place to be? Just ask some of the experts. Industry analysts agree that B2B projects will make up the bulk of tomorrow's digital economy. The B2B boom is also presenting a wealth of opportunities for savvy e-integrators. Among the analysts' findings:

According to a recent study by The Yankee Group in Boston, Massachusetts, there will be $4 trillion in B2B transactions by 2005. Of that, nearly $961 billion will be generated by e-market transactions, according to the firm, which analyzed 50 industries that approximate the total potential U.S. B2B market.

Gartner Group Inc. in Stamford, Connecticut recently estimated that B2B e-commerce will grow at aggressive rates through 2005, causing fundamental changes to the way businesses interact with each other. By 2005, B2B e-commerce will represent 8 percent of the forecasted $216 trillion total global sales transactions.

Finally, Forrester Research Inc. in Cambridge, Massachusetts recently released a study finding that many established companies' EDI processes can't keep up with e-business automation. As a result, companies will have to replace their one-dimensional EDI-based systems with automated decision chains. Ninety percent of the 46 B2B online site managers interviewed still use EDI as their primary trading method and say they plan to transition to a new solution soon.

come down since the buyer better understands the value of each purchase. We aren't quite at the Perfect Information stage yet, but we are getting there and this is where the opportunities arise.

If your company has the opportunity to bring new information—or stated more correctly, a new value proposition—to the customer over the Net, then there may be gold in those hills. A simple act of buying a PC can be transformed on the Net—customers can mix and match components, and compare prices and performance as they go along to help aid in their decision. More information, improved purchasing decisions, and cheaper prices due to lower customer sales costs makes everyone go away happy.

As online markets evolve and mature, they will become more challenging to innovate. In other words, the bottom line here is:

■ Manufacturers are natural winners with online markets—with service companies needing longer to find their *Net Niche.*

■ Virtual Auctions—Buyers win: These will enable real-time auctions with decreased margins and more participants driving prices down as auctioneers make less and full costs are made available. There will be fewer hidden *gems.*

■ Virtual Bidding—Buyers win: Virtual requests for proposals and quotes will invite dramatic price reductions from global competition.

■ Virtual Catalogs—Buyers win: Virtual catalogs will transform the shopping experience. Catalogs that were big with limited selection give way to virtual catalogs that are fast with customized searches driven off huge, dynamically changing databases. Costs saved in reproduction, distribution, and inventory will result in lower prices.

Finally, it's only appropriate here to conclude this chapter and book with a look at the new rules that move beyond e-commerce. E-biz consultants are playing by a new set of rules than traditional companies.

CONCLUSION

Millennia Vision Corp. is one of a new breed of integrators that says it has what it takes to shape the post-*e* economy.[16] Like the companies that built the foundations of Internet commerce, they're confident, seeking out projects and customers that best fit their needs and discarding the ones that don't. They're proud, demanding to be known as strategic players, not just technology enablers. And the new rules they play by are transforming today's market for digital solutions.

When Millennia Vision first gazed out over the emerging e-business landscape, they couldn't help but notice a glaring hole in the way integrators provided solutions. Sure, customers could go to a McKinsey & Co. for strategy consulting, an IBM or Big Five company for ERP and supply-chain integration, and a RazorFish or Scient for Web services, but Millennia didn't see anyone out there with the skills to package it all together.

Wanting to fill that void, Millennia decided to rewrite the rule book and build the strengths internally that could turn them into a full service provider (FSP). That way, the company wouldn't have to partner with other service companies to provide e-solutions.

They saw the opportunity to bring vertical-industry solutions together by wrapping strategy with technology components to provide a fully integrated solution. Since then, Millennia has taken this concept of being an FSP and run with it. This bold move has certainly paid off for the e-integrator, which has since become a partner to several successful dotcoms including AllAdvantage.com, Branders.com, and GoCampus Inc., as well as a strategic e-consultant for traditional industry giants such as Cisco Systems Inc., Hewlett-Packard Co., Sun Microsystems Inc., and Toyota Motor Corp.

What can you learn from these integrators? Let's look at some of the new players and see how they define what they consider the new rules for success. What follows is a compilation of their ideas and strategies.

Should your company follow every single strategy listed? Probably not, because every business has its own unique strengths and weaknesses. However, understanding them all can give you a deeper insight into the minds of those shaping the future of the new economy, and those competing against you. Don't say you weren't warned.

RULE #1: MOVE BEYOND "E"

Is your company still playing digital catch-up—pumping all its money and resources to transition itself into a pure-play e-business solution provider or Web integrator? Chances are, you're setting yourself up to fall behind.

Virtually all leading integrators (from Scient Corp. to Lante Corp. to Sapient Corp.) have already gone to great lengths to establish their own *e-methodologies*. And other companies, such as Viant Corp., are spending millions on new branding and advertising campaigns to get the e-word out to customers. So, isn't it a little late to be playing catch-up?

On the customer side, it's clear that the worlds of brick-and-mortar and dotcom companies are quickly converging around the Internet. With traditional companies building online initiatives to support their existing businesses, dotcoms are finally starting to realize the importance of embracing offline supply-chain, marketing, and call-center processes. Smart integrators have already realized that, as industries ranging from chemical manufacturing to licensed merchandising to interior design increasingly embrace e-business solutions, individual companies are going to be searching for new ways to differentiate themselves, outside of the Web. If you can't show them how to do that, they'll look for someone who can.

What does that mean for you? It's no longer enough to sell e-business as a be-all, end-all solution for your clients.

What happens once everyone out there already has a digital channel and strategy? In this new phase of the marketplace, doing e-commerce is no longer unique on its own.

Instead, companies such as Extraprise and Chicago-based consultant Diamond Technology Partners Inc. teach their customers to leverage Web solutions as a single part of an overall business strategy that may also include integrated click-and-mortar initiatives such as direct mail, point-of-sale systems, and—get ready for this—human contact. By the looks of Extraprise's customer list, which includes such heavyweights as American Express, Great-West Life & Annuity, Hewlett-Packard, and Sun Microsystems, it seems they are having no problems finding companies with similar ideas.

What will differentiate companies is their ability to grow revenue and create customer relationships across all channels, both online and offline. The Internet value chain is one of many channels to the customer, but it can't be the only one.

RULE #2: AVOID CIOS LIKE THE PLAGUE

Once an integrator's best friend, the CIO is no longer the only player on e-integrators' *must-see* lists. Instead, he or she is being joined by a line of business managers and top-level executives. Why? Call it a renewed emphasis on business strategy consulting.

Today's e-business companies are no longer seeking specific technology fixes. Instead, they want end-to-end solutions that can completely transform their business models so they can compete in tomorrow's digital economy. To better serve their needs, e-business architects are expanding their services way beyond technology to incorporate overall business strategy and industry expertise.

With that new focus in mind, why waste time pitching your strengths to a techie who only has IT issues on his or her mind? Instead, go for the ear of the executives and line of business managers who have their hands on the purse strings and are responsible for driving their customers' revenue.

The purchase process for e-business solutions extends from IT departments to corporate executives and management to sales and marketing departments. But the opinions on e-business solutions are far from uniform.

Despite low grades from IT departments on compatibility and maintenance of e-business solutions (.36 and.56, respectively, out of a possible 1), sales, marketing, and corporate executives still gave e-solutions high scores (.77 and .78 and .72, respectively).

In addition The Gartner Group, in a recent report on the state of CIOs, reported that in companies where a CIO has not clearly established an influence on e-business solutions, innovations will be *driven and managed by the emerging power brokers in enterprises* who include business process managers and customer relationship management.

The lesson: The power of CIO input is eroding in many of today's e-businesses. Therefore, it pays to go to the people who oversee spending and can see the overall picture of what the company is doing.

When the last generation of consultants such as Cambridge Technology Partners and Sapient made their marks, they were selling solutions to IT groups and CIOs. However, this new generation of products (our generation) is based much more on a company's revenue generators. Those are the people responsible for the customer relationships and for generating next quarter's numbers.

The strategy is working for smaller companies as well. When dealing with large clients, most dotcoms prefer going directly to the individual business units rather than a CIO. That way, they can feel out the types of business issues they address on a daily basis.

Technology is no longer ancillary to business processes, but is instead a critical gear in part of their economic engine. Certainly, the president or CEO is the right person to talk to at a high level, but a fair amount of traction can also be found at the business unit level—but be careful, you don't want to alienate the CIO either.

If someone isn't involved in the main decision-making, they'll always find reasons why the plan won't work. We never want to forget that the CIO will always be a key player, even though he or she is no longer the lead player.

RULE #3: DON'T GO CHEAP

If you're the head of a New Age consulting outfit, chances are that most of your Web-savvy young guns are playing more strategic roles in your company than you did at their age. So, isn't it time to loosen the purse strings and pay them accordingly?

As an integrator for e-business, you want the best e-business minds out there working for you. The problem is that everybody else does, too. If you're not willing to pay top dollar for top talent, one of your competitors will. And that means the money you may save today will mean nothing tomorrow once your market share is being eaten up by faster, sleeker, and better-equipped companies.

Forget what you made when you were 25—today's kids are worth more than you were. Write bigger checks and give bigger bonuses. And while you're at it, share a piece of the business with your people, even if you're private. You'll attract a higher caliber of talent and build a better workforce.

According to recently released Hot Jobs Report by Menlo Park, California-based consulting services firm RHI Consulting Inc., Internet development professionals have become the hottest commodity. With 23 percent of the technology executives surveyed, skill was listed as the leading growth area in their IT departments.

Amid one of the worst labor shortages ever to hit the IT industry, newcomer Etensity Inc. in Vienna, Virginia, has been having few problems increasing its professional staff. Since its August 1999 debut, the e-consulting company, which serves industries such as entertainment, retail, and education, has been growing by more than 50 new consultants a month, already boasting a team of more than 300 with plans to break 500 by the end of the year. Its secret: Build a strong company culture while remembering to compensate staffers well with salary and benefits.

Etensity's *Hot Wheels* employee incentive program pays up to $400 a month in car expenses for employees who have been with the company a year or more. For those who pass the two-year mark, the company's *Raise the Roof* program will shell out $10,000 toward the purchase of a new home.

Etensity really focuses on building the infrastructure internally that will help them attract the best people in the marketplace and allow them to grow organically. What Etensity is trying to do is show employees that, as they progress in their careers, they are going to help them maintain their quality of life along the way.

E-business consulting firm AppNet Inc. in Bethesda, Maryland has combined attractive benefits and employee programs in its effort to maintain a turnover rate of less than 5 percent among its more than 1200 employees. It's important for them to keep and develop the folks they have, so they strive to maintain a certain type of employee culture and environment.

They offer stock options to every employee and a very attractive benefits package.

RULE #4: DITCH YOUR DOTCOMS

Scared by the demise of Boo.com? Well, you ought to be. If you haven't already heard the news, we'll break it to you: The dotcom revolution is over—at least as you once knew it. The time to hook up with the promising but risky startup ventures has come and gone, according to industry players.

In a recently released study, Forrester Research Inc. predicted that the combination of weak financials, increasing competitive pressures, and investor flight will drive most of today's dotcom retailers out of business by 2001. Want proof? Aside from Boo.com, other high-profile sites have struggled, including CDNow.com, eOutlets.com, and Peapod.com.

And, with so many bad ideas continuing to spread in the form of flimsy Web startups, Wall Street investors have grown skeptical of the dotcom generation. Goldman, Sachs & Co. Internet Index, which includes valuations for 21 different Internet stocks, has fallen significantly recently—from a high of about $785 in early March 2000 to well below $400 for the first week in June 2000. As you can clearly see, these stocks have gone down quite a bit.

Investors are no longer willing to accept grandiose pipe dreams for tomorrow in lieu of profitability today—and neither should you. Focus instead on clients who can pay, not defray.

That's why the most successful Web integration firms are increasingly embracing *Old World* stalwarts—Fortune 1000 firms that have the business experience and deep pockets necessary to pull off a large Web initiative and integrate it with their existing business models. And analysts agree in advising integrators to base less than a quarter of their total Internet services revenue on dotcom clients, with the rest going to established companies.

Millennia Vision has only about 25 percent of its business based on true dotcom clients, with the rest going to established Fortune 1000 and high-growth midmarkets. Of those dotcoms, the company deals almost exclusively with B2B companies, ignoring trendy B2C outfits.

Millennia Vision does very little in B2C right now. Instead, they follow the smart money. They work closely with some venture capital firms and follow someone like Kleiner Perkins. They follow where their money is going and work with those companies.

That's not to say there are no longer any worthy dotcom ventures out there—you just have to dig a little deeper to find them (for more, see Rule #6). The key: Seek out the handful of dotcoms that want their e-business sites fully integrated with offline channels.

RULE #5: CHOOSE YOUR PARTNERS AS YOU WOULD YOUR PARENTS: TWO AND ONLY ONCE

Remember the days when you spent most of your resources sending your staffers to training programs for every single technology platform out there on the off-chance one of your customers would need it? Don't bother.

Today's customers care a lot less about the name on the box and a lot more about whether the solutions you build are fast, reliable, and effective. It's your job to pull the strings to bring all three together.

Smart integrators are picking a handful of vendors whose technology best complements their strengths and are riding them all the way to success. Those who spend time and money making friends with every vendor in every product category are steadily falling behind.

For example, Etensity evaluates what they feel are the best-of-breed technologies in each given area, and then they choose long-term partnerships and train 100 consultants in that platform. The following are some of the companies they count on: Commerce One Inc., Microsoft Corp., MicroStrategy Inc. and XMLSolutions Corp.

Etensity tries not to be totally technology agnostic because they can't be all things to all people. You need to understand where you think the market is going and try to build your strengths in those areas. Being agnostic is a recipe for failure because the industry changes too rapidly.

For some integrators, sticking to this kind of strategy means occasionally passing up work opportunities for the sake of building expertise. A few integrators have made the decision to focus on a handful of reliable Internet technologies when building solutions for its customers.

Lotus Notes or Domino requires a very different set of expertise than what they usually do, so they have chosen not to chase that market. If a project comes up in those areas, Lotus Notes or Domino will simply walk away because it would spread them too thin.

So how do you decide which platforms are the right ones to dig into? A good idea is to stick with the ones you know well, because they'll ultimately give you the best chance for success. Another trick: Why not increase your chance for high margins by focusing on the one or two technologies your competitors aren't leveraging? The reason being—that you can build yourself a profitable niche in the market.

RULE #6: DOMINATE, DON'T DUPLICATE

If your biggest client is an online pet supply company whose main distinguishing feature is that its puppet mascot is a brown dog rather than a white one, then perhaps it's time to find some new customers. Let's face it, right now there are myriad dotcom startups and traditional companies looking for someone with the e-business skills to get their initiatives up and running quickly. And despite the great Web stock shakedown of 2000, chances are that many of them still have enough funding to hire a talented Web developer such as you.

But what happens when the trendy Web site you helped build goes out of business after six months of pitiful revenue? It's not exactly the kind of reference you'd want to put on your client list. That's why it's your job to seek out the projects still out there (whether they're Web startups or Internet projects for traditional companies) that have the unique angle and strong business plan to achieve success. Throw the rest away.

Center 7 Inc., an application service provider based in Lindon, Utah, has been approached by nearly 50 prospective customers since the company was formed in August 1999. However, the ASP has only taken on about five of them as clients.

The reason for such a low customer-engagement rate? Center 7 teams only with businesses that have at least one significant element to distinguish them from the competition.

Center 7 goes with the people they believe can get the money they need and have viable opportunities in the market. Successes include TheGuyStore.com and Idea Exchange.com. Their goal is to be with their customers for years, so they have to have the sense that they will survive.

Differentiating factors may include having a major backer for the project—deep technology requirements that only a large company can develop and maintain, or a significant business partner that can give the initiative an extra boost in the marketplace. In each case, Center 7 got in with the customers before they got their VC money, and so far, four out of the five they chose got their money. The fifth is about to get it. The other 50 or so they passed on didn't get their money and still haven't made it.

They do appear, however, to have got a pretty good track record for picking them.

The good news is that venture capitalists are becoming less eager to pump money into virtually any person with a dot-com dream and an untested business plan. That will ultimately make it easier for companies such as Millennia Vision to choose worthwhile clients by wiping out a good portion of start-ups with bad ideas.

Companies that don't have a clear path to profitability and a sustainable business model aren't going to be funded anymore. Millennia Vision has been focusing on those companies that have excellent funding, and as a result, they have been doing very well.

RULE #7: THINK WORLDLY, ACT GLOBALLY

Many companies think in terms of international expansion, with little regard for completeness. When Atlanta-based iXL Enterprises Inc. expanded internationally, for example, it did so mostly at the behest of existing customers. After proving its worth to Virgin Atlantic, the company picked up a much larger assignment from Virgin Management Ltd. to work on the ambitious Virgin.com megaportal. That, in turn, is what led iXL management to begin building a world-class office near the Piazza and Central Market in London's historic Covent Garden section.

To many who follow e-business, that's a tactical way to build an international business. But is it strategic? Others are beginning to wonder.

A look at some of the numbers reveals that the market is set to explode for global e-commerce. According to research firm International Data Corp., the U.S. portion of Web users worldwide will decline from 43 percent in 1999 to a mere 33 percent in 2003. In addition, the U.S. portion of Internet commerce revenue will decline from 61 percent of the total $130.5 billion in 1999 to less than half, 44 percent, of the $1.6 trillion total in 2003.

As Internet use explodes outside the United States, the newest hot spots for Internet development dollars will include the Asia/Pacific region and Western Europe. The lesson for integrators? Go where the money is.

Inforte Corp., a Chicago-based e-business solution company, is expanding beyond the United States as well. Work done here with Toshiba America Inc., for example, has been leveraged into an assignment in Japan. Similarly, work done in the United States for French communications giant Alcatel has turned into projects in France. But such piecemeal expansion won't make the company a worldwide giant anytime soon. So, they're looking at international expansion differently than before. They are encouraged by the work their people are doing out of homes and apartments overseas, but they are worried about their limited infrastructure over there.

There is this misconception that Europe is 12 to 18 months behind the United States. Really, it's more like six to eight months. People who get there soon are going to be the big winners."

That's thinking worldly, not just globally—and more companies are beginning to do it. Another company that thinks worldly and not just globally is Razorfish. This company has expanded deep into Scandinavia not just with the hopes of finding customers there, but with the hopes of finding world-class development talent as well. The company believes that the Europeans, and the Scandinavians in particular, are a year or more ahead of the United States in terms of wireless capabilities. Even though they are not a Swedish company, college kids in Sweden rate them among the top businesses they'd like to work for. That's worldliness.

RULE #8: A FOOT IN THE DOOR WON'T LEAD TO AN INVITATION TO COME IN

For years, traditional VARs and consultants lived by the belief that doing the small, thankless jobs for a larger client would ultimately open the door to more strategic and more profitable work. Well, chances are it will—for someone else.

There's plenty of good work out there right now, according to today's integrators, so it's time to forget the door and throw that tired notion out the window. If a prospective client doesn't want to let you in as a strategic player, then find someone who will. Keep doing the small jobs, and it's the small jobs they'll keep giving you.

Many of the industry's leading players, such as Lante, Razorfish, and Scient, are increasingly turning away prospective clients without so much as a second thought. Is it because they don't have the resources or skills to do the work? Don't bet on it. It's usually because they think the job (and perhaps more often the customer) is not worthy of their efforts.

The general rule to remember when scouting out work is that, as an e-builder, you're only as good as the solutions you create. So do you want to be known by your clients as a company that can connect pipes, or do you want to be known as a strategic asset that can develop and implement fully integrated e-business initiatives?

Etensity is absolutely going in now and trying to be more of a strategic partner. When client-server dominated the market, you had the Big Five building all of these vertical strategy practices. However, with Internet technology and the range of different applications for things like e-procurement and business intelligence sweeping across all industries, integrators now have a new lever to move up in the ranks and become a strategic partner.

And, remember, the strategic relationships you build today are the ones that will shape you for the future. As Web services space continues to mature and becomes more competitive, there will be a shakeout among consultants. Those who have managed to build a strong vertical expertise and strategic relationships with their customers will now be the ones left standing.

RULE #9: PARTNERING AT YOUR PERIL

Let's say your company can offer clients a soup-to-nuts menu of integration services. Should you still take the piecemeal projects that will ultimately have you partnering with other solution providers? Some Internet architects are starting to wonder.

There's no denying the popularity of partnering for many of today's e-integrators, especially those who are too small or whose resources are too limited to offer clients a full solution. A recent industry survey showed that 60 percent of the integrators surveyed are regular partners with other solution providers.

However, the leaders of some of today's end-to-end strategy firms are starting to give the idea a big thumbs-down. That's because they're spending enormous amounts of money, either through organic growth or through acquisition, positioning themselves as full service providers that can give their customers a complete solution. So, why would they want to bring an outside partner into the fold who can potentially screw everything up?

While making the transition to become a full service provider for e-business, Millennia Vision has shied away from partnering with other solution providers. Now, the only real partnering Millennia Vision does is with executive management agencies, law firms or venture capital companies, and entities that can provide assistance well beyond the boundaries of its end-to-end e-business solutions.

When it comes to the core solution, looking at the business model, the consulting, or the implementation of an e-business infrastructure, Millennia Vision does that completely inhouse. They have a strong belief that it has to be integrated as one solution.

Finally, partnerships among integrators can cause unnecessary headaches by forcing individual companies to learn each other's problem-solving methodologies. Millennia Vision made a significant investment to ensure that they can bring end-to-end skill sets and provide services to their clients, so they don't necessarily have to partner or teach their methodology to someone else. They are open to partnering with technology companies when it makes sense, but on the services side, they try to do the majority of the work ourselves. That allows them to provide quality and speed to their clients.

END NOTES

[1] Ibid.
[2] Ibid.
[3] Ibid.
[4] Ibid.
[5] Ibid.
[6] Ibid.
[7] Ibid.
[8] Ibid.
[9] Ibid.
[10] Ibid.
[11] Sun Microsystems, Inc., 901 San Antonio Road, Palo Alto, CA 94303 USA, 2000.
[12] Ibid.
[13] Ibid.
[14] Ibid.
[15] Millennia Vision Corp., 255 Shoreline Drive, Suite 520, Redwood City, CA 94065, 2000.

A | Internet Glossary and Abbreviations

The Internet has spawned its own vocabulary, mostly consisting of acronyms. Every new technology develops its own jargon. For the uninitiated, *NetSpeak* can be somewhat intimidating. Throughout this book, we tried to make our explanations as *user friendly* as possible. From time to time, however, some Internet terms are included.

This glossary defines those terms and some others you might come across as you explore the exciting commercial opportunities available on the Internet. The interested reader is directed to other texts for more detailed information about the terms presented here, and for more information about other terms not included.

Acquirer–A licensed MasterCard member that has an agreement to process the data relating to a transaction from the merchant.

agent–A system acting on some other system's or individual's behalf. Agents can be used to do comparison shopping, for example.

anonymous FTP–An implementation of the file transfer protocol software that allows users to access files without having accounts on the ftp server.

API–Application Programming Interface; a set of standard routines used to make standard functions available to custom-designed programs.

Application layer–The top layer in the standard Internet Protocol network architecture conceptual model. This is the level at which interaction takes place between the end user and the application.

application–A program providing some network function to end users or systems.

Arpanet–Advanced Research Project Agency Network, originally started by the U.S. Department of Defense, also known initially as DarpaNet. These were the predecessors to the Internet.

ASCII–American Standard Code for Information Interchange; refers to the "standard" alphanumeric character set.

asymmetric cryptography–See **public key cryptography**.

AUP–Acceptable use policy. Often refers to a policy of permitting only non-commercial uses for traffic carried by an Internet service provider subsidized by the U.S. government.

backbone–A special type of internetwork intended specifically to connect other internetworks to the Internet, or used to connect internetworks across wide geographic areas.

bandwidth–The amount of data that can be carried by a communications link in a given time. Usually measured in bits. A typical telephone link is capable of about 28.8 Kbps (thousands of bits per second).

bit–The smallest unit of binary information, represented as either "1" or "0."

bridge–A special-purpose computer that connects two networks of the same type. It reproduces transmissions from one and sends them to the other connected network.

browser–Usually refers to a World Wide Web client program. Browsers are capable of requesting data from Web servers and processing data received in response to these requests.

byte–A basic unit of data, consisting of 8 bits.

card-not-present transaction–A credit card transaction where the merchant receives the credit card number but cannot physically link the card to the purchaser. This includes telephone and mail orders, as well as on-line transactions.

Certificate Authority–A verifier of the relationship between a public key and its associated identifier. A place you can go to get a digital account ID.

CGI–Common Gateway Interface. A specification for creating programs that accept information acquired through World Wide Web pages and pass it on to other programs, or take information from other programs and make it accessible through World Wide Web pages.

CIX–Commercial Internet Exchange. An industry organization for Internet service providers.

cleartext–Text that has not been encrypted.

client–A computer or system that makes requests for some kind type of network service from another computer or system acting as a server.

CommerceNet–One of the first Internet consortiums, set up with partial funding from the U.S. government and the State state of California. Member companies include Apple, IBM, Bank of America, Hewlett-Packard, and many other firms from Silicon Valley and beyond.

Commercial domain–A commercial node or site on the Internet that is controlled by a for-profit entity. It usually has an address that ends in "com" (http://www.mastercard.com), although overseas sites can have an Internet address that ends with a country code, like NL for the Netherlands or UK for the United Kingdom.

cracker–An individual who uses computers for criminal pursuits. This term is not yet in general use, but is current among computer professionals and academicians. See also **hacker**.

cryptanalysis–The study of cryptographic processes with the intent of finding weaknesses sufficient to defeat those processes.

cryptography–The study of mathematical processes useful for keeping data secret by encryption, guaranteeing its provenance, or guaranteeing that its content has not been unchanged.

daemon–A program or process running on a server that listens to the network for requests for its service.

Data Link layer–The bottom layer in the standard Internet Protocol network architecture conceptual model. This is the level at which computers connected to the same physical wire (LAN) communicate with each other.

database–Collection of related pieces of digital information that can be stored and retrieved.

datagram–The basic unit of network transmissions under TCP/IP. A basic unit of network transmission in connectionless services.

decryption–The process of reversing encryption; application of a mathematical process to encrypted data to restore it to its cleartext version.

DES–Data Encryption Standard. A private key encryption standard approved by the United States government for the encryption of data when implemented in hardware. Uses 56-bit encryption and is generally accepted as sufficiently secure when correctly implemented.

DHCP–Dynamic Host Configuration Protocol. A protocol used to automatically configure Internet nodes when they initiate their network connection.

Digital Account ID–An electronic representation of the MasterCard account relationship with its holder.

digital signature–The result of the application of a cryptographic process to the digital document being signed. The signer uses his or her private key (of a public/private key pair) to come up with the signature, which is a sequence of characters. The document can be verified as coming from the signer by using the signer's public key to verify the document.

digital–Information typically represented by a series of 0s and 1s. These representations are often generated by a computer system or chip. It is digital information (0s and 1s) that travels along the Internet.

DNS–Domain Name System. A distributed database system implemented across the Internet for the purpose of linking Internet host names (used by people) with Internet Protocol addresses (used by computers).

download–The retrieving of files from a remote computer to your local hard drive.

EBCDIC–Extended Binary Coded Decimal Interchange Code. This is the data representation standard used by IBM mainframe computers. Most other systems use ASCII representations.

EDI–Electronic Data Interchange. Refers to the exchange of business information, including purchase orders and invoices, between computers used by cooperating companies.

EFT–Electronic funds transfer.

electronic bulletin board–A computer which that offers access to its files by means of telephony from remote computers.

electronic commerce–The conducting of business transactions via remote electronic means.

electronic publishing–The dissemination of information via digital media, such as CD-ROM, computer networks, floppy disks, etc.

Electronic shopping–The use of electronic media by shoppers, such as on-line services, the Internet, or CD- ROM to purchase goods or services.

electronic wallet–Software that stores and provides access to cardholder financial information, including credit card data and digital account ID's.

e-mail–Electronic mail.

encapsulation–The use of headers to "surround" network data for the purpose of handling its proper routing across a network or internetwork. The result is a network transmission unit directed to some destination host, with some unspecified content that will not be accessed until it arrives at its destination.

encryption–A reversible process of modifying cleartext for the purpose of keeping it secret from anyone other than its intended recipient.

Ethernet–A baseband networking medium, initially developed in the 1970s by Robert Metcalfe.

FAQ–A list of frequently asked questions (with answers) pertaining to a mailing list, Usenet newsgroup, product, or activity.

FDDI–Fiber Distributed Data Interface. A network standard for fiber-optic media.

file server–A computer connected to a network and capable of offering other users on that network access to its file system.

finger–A TCP/IP application used for retrieving a list of currently logged-in users on a specific system or for getting information about some specific user of that system.

firewall gateway–A special construct for the prevention of attacks on an organizational internetwork originating from the global Internet. The firewall may include one or more gateways or routers and may comprise separate network segments, as well as software filtering and other mechanisms for protecting corporate network resources.

flame–An extensive admonishment of Internet wrongdoing sent by other Internet users.

FTP–File Transfer Protocol. The set of specifications, or the program itself, for transferring files between two computers on the Internet.

gateway–A special-purpose computer for internetwork connectivity. Often refers to a router (see **entry**). Often refers to a system mediating between protocols, as with e-mail gateways that accept e-mail from the Internet and translate it to the appropriate e-mail protocol on the internal LAN.

gigabit–1 billion bits.

gigabyte–1 billion bytes.

Gopher–A character-based Internet information publishing application, developed at the University of Minnesota.

hacker–A term applied to individuals interested in computers and computing. This term is often used popularly to refer to individuals involved in criminal pursuits such as breaking into computers without proper authorization. Many purists prefer its original meaning, referring to individuals who have deep interest in as well as understanding of computers. See also **cracker.**

handshake–The process of negotiating a connection between two hosts. The initiating host waits for acknowledgment from the destination host, which in turn waits for acknowledgment of its own response.

home page–The opening document of a World Wide Web site. It may also refer to the Web document that an individual user's Web browser points to on start-up.

host–Any device connected to a network that can send or receive requests for network services.

HTML–Hypertext Markup Language. An Internet standard for creating World Wide Web documents, based on the Standard Generalized Markup Language (SGML). Markup languages create plain-text files using tags to set off functional sections of the document, which are interpreted appropriately for display by the document-viewing software.

HTTP–Hypertext Transfer Protocol. An Internet standard defining the interaction between World Wide Web clients and servers.

hyperlink–A digital telephone number of another computer or network location, often represented as a button or highlighted text on a computer screen.

IAB–Internet Architecture Board. Part of the Internet Society, the IAB oversees the IESG and the IETF.

IANA–Internet Assigned Number Authority. A group organized through the Internet Society for maintaining assigned numbers relating to the Internet Protocol suite.

ICMP–Internet Control Message Protocol. A protocol used to exchange reachability and routing information between hosts and routers on the same LAN.

IESG–Internet Engineering Steering Group. A steering committee overseeing the activities of the Internet Engineering Task Force (IETF).

Information SuperHighway–A common idiom that loosely describes a medium that delivers digital information. Some believe that this term will eventually mean the Internet.

Internaut–A combination of the words Internet and astronaut, describing one who explores the Internet.

internet–See **internetwork**.

Internet–The network of networks connecting tens of millions of users around the world.

internetwork–Literally, a network of networks. Any network consisting of two or more discrete networks connected by routers and capable of supporting seamless interoperability between hosts connected to any part of the internetwork.

InterNIC–The Internet Network Information Center. InterNIC administers and assigns Internet domains and network addresses.

interoperability–The ability of disparate computer systems to send and receive requests for network services across disparate networks, seamlessly and transparently to the end user.

IP address–A numerical address assigned to a computer connected to an internetwork that uniquely identifies it on that internetwork.

IP–Internet Protocol. A protocol defining the interaction between hosts communicating across an internetwork.

IPv6–Internet Protocol, version 6. The next revision of the Internet Protocol, to be implemented in the second half of the 1990s. In addition to various new features, IPv6 increases the size of Internet addresses from 32 bits to 128 bits, thus increasing the number of available network and host IP addresses. This is necessary to accommodate continued exponential growth in Internet connectivity.

IPX–Internetwork Packet eXchange. An internetwork protocol used by Novell NetWare and other LAN operating systems.

ISDN–Integrated Services Digital Network. A type of telephone service providing high-speed (128 Kbps and up) and digital services (multiple telephone lines on a single link, conferencing, and many others).

ISOC–The Internet Society. A professional organization supporting Internet standards processes as well as other activities.

issuer–The institution (or its agent) that enters into a contractual agreement with MasterCard and issues MasterCard cards to the cardholders.

Kerberos–A method for securely authenticating users to networked hosts, developed at MIT. Kerberos uses special servers to maintain user passwords and mediate the exchange of session keys between users and hosts.

key–A quantity of data used in cryptographic procedures to encrypt, decrypt, or authenticate other data.

LAN–Local area network. A network of connected computers in the same general area, on a single network cable (or a set of cables that emulate a single wire).

latency–The delay between the transmission of a piece of data and its reception at its destination. Latency is one measure of network connection performance; bandwidth is another. High-latency links will beare very responsive and work well with interactive applications such as terminal emulation even if the transmission rate is low.

MAC–Message Authentication Code. A quantity of data based on the contents of a message, used to confirm that it has been received as transmitted.

MBONE–Multicast Backbone. A special network backbone used to transmit multicasts (including coverage of standards meetings and other content, in real time) over the Internet.

MIME–Multipurpose Internet Mail Extensions. A specification for the linking and transfer of non-text files with Internet e-mail and other IP applications (including Usenet news).

multicast–Transmission of network traffic to some, but not all, hosts connected to the network or internetwork.

multihomed host–A system connected to an internetwork on two or more different individual networks. Routers and gateways are, by definition, multihomed hosts, since they link two or more separate networks.

Net–A shortened term for the Internet.

Netiquette–A combination of the words "net" and "etiquette." A code of behavior for users of the Internet.

NetWare–A commercial network operating system available from Novell Inc. offering network resource services across the IPX network protocol.

network–Any system of interconnected systems. In particular, the system defined by computers connected to the same communications medium in such a way that each can communicate with the other connected computers.

NFS–Network File System. A TCP/IP network protocol developed by Sun MicroSystems, Inc., for sharing resources between connected workstations. Originally implemented mostly on UNIX systems, NFS implementations are now available for most platforms.

NIC–Network information center. An organizational resource devoted to providing information about a network.

NNTP–Network News Transfer Protocol. A TCP/IP protocol defining the exchange of Usenet news between servers and clients.

NOC–Network operations center. An organizational resource devoted to supporting the day-to-day operations of a network.

node–A connection point in a network, usually a computer.
A device connected to a network; more specifically, refers to the network interface itself, so a multihomed host may represent multiple nodes.

nonrepudiation–The ability of the recipient to prove who sent a message based on the contents of the message. The quality can derive from the use of a digital signature on the message, which links the sender to the message.

NOS–Network operating system. A software product that allows hosts on a LAN to share network resources, including disk storage, programs, and peripherals connected to the LAN.

NSF–National Science Foundation. One of the most important organizations involved in development and research in TCP/IP internetworking, NSF funded NSFNET, which ultimately evolved into the Internet backbone.

octet–A term used to refer to an 8-bit byte of data, usually in the context of internetworking.

online (vs. offline)–Communication that takes place in near real time on a computer network.

out of band–Using a medium of exchange different from the primary medium of data exchange. Most commonly refers to the practice of exchanging keys or other sensitive information to be used for network communication by telephone, by hard copy, or in person.

packet switching–A communication method in which data is broken into parts called packets, which are transmitted over diverse routes and then reassembled upon arrival at the receiving end. It is the communication method used on the Internet.

packet–A unit of network transmission; specifically may refer to the unit of data transmitted across a packet-switched network (such as the Internet).

PCT–Private Communication Technology. A protocol specification released by Microsoft in late September 1995, describing mechanisms for secure communication between individuals on the Internet, providing encryption and authentication.

PEM–Privacy Enhanced Mail. An Internet standard defining a protocol for the secure, authenticable, and nonrepudiable transmission of electronic mail.

PGP–Pretty Good Privacy. A freely distributed program implementing public key cryptography for e-mail, and sometimes used for electronic commerce purposes.

Ping–Internet Protocol, Next Generation. Another name for **IPv6.**

ping–Packet Internet Groper. A simple TCP/IP network application in which the originating hosts sends a signal to a destination host to determine whether or not the destination host is reachable through the network.

port–The entry point into a network computer.

PPP–Point to Point Protocol. A protocol defining the connection of a single host to another host over a bidirectional link (such as a telephone line), and connection to network resources.

private key–Of the two keys used for public key cryptography, the one that must be kept secret, so the owner of the key can decrypt messages encrypted with the public key.

protocol–A set of rules defining the behaviors of interacting systems, particularly when applied to rules for the exchange of information between networked systems.

public key cryptography–The cryptographic system in which encryption is done with one key and decryption is done with another.

public key–Of the two keys used for public key cryptography, the one that can be made public, so that senders can encrypt messages.

RFC–Request for Comments. The generic term for Internet standards documents. Originally, researchers and academicians working on specific internetworking projects published their work as RFCs to solicit further comments from others working in the field, as and well as to identify errors and problems.

router–A multihomed host (connected to at least two networks) that is able to forward network traffic from one connected network to another.

RSA–An encryption method using a pair of keys—one public, one private.

secret key–A key that must be kept secret. The term is sometimes used to refer to the private key in asymmetric cryptography (public key cryptography), but more properly refers to a shared secret between parties who use the same key to encrypt and decrypt messages.

server–Any computer connected to a network that offers services to other connected systems on the network.

S-HTTP–Secure Hypertext Transfer Protocol. A protocol that defines security additions to the HTTP protocol, developed within the traditional Internet standards process. S-HTTP operates strictly at the application level, adding encryption and authentication to World Wide Web client/server communications.

SLIP–Serial Line Internet Protocol. A method of connecting a single computer to the Internet through a telephone link, SLIP is generally considered less desirable than PPP for this purpose.

SMTP–Simple Mail Transfer Protocol. The set of rules defining the transmission of electronic mail between users.

snail-mail–Traditional paper-based postal service.

sneaker-net–A humorous reference to the lack of a digital local area network (at your office, for example), where people must run back and forth with diskettes between computers.

SNMP–Simple Network Management Protocol. This protocol defines functions used to monitor and manage network resources across internetworks.

SSL–Secure Sockets Layer. A protocol first developed by Netscape and subsequently provided to the rest of the Internet community to add encryption and authentication at the network layer just below the application level.

STT–Secure Transaction Technology. A protocol specification released by Microsoft and Visa International late in September 1995, intended to define the interchange of credit card payment information across public and private networks.

surf–Going from one place to another on an on-line service. The term grew out of the concept of TV channel surfing.

TCP–Transmission Control Protocol. The protocol defining the way in which applications communicate with each other across the Internet. TCP is a reliable protocol, meaning that all transmissions between applications must be acknowledged by the recipient.

TCP/IP–Transmission Control Protocol/Internet Protocol. The description of any network using the Internet protocols, named for the two dominant protocols used on the Internet.

techno savvies–Those people who are typically knowledgeable about high-tech, cutting-edge technologies, including the Internet.

UDP–User Datagram Protocol. A protocol defining a connectionless, unreliable transportTransport-layer service between applications on the Internet.

upload–The sending of files from your local hard drive to another computer over a network.

URL–Uniform Resource Locator. A protocol for defining the exact location of a World Wide Web resource, and for identifying the method of access, the host on which it resides, and the path and filename of the resource.

virtual–Based on digital bits, not atoms. A simulation of a physical concept such as a virtual store located in a virtual shopping mall.

Web browser–Software that is used by PCs which that allows users to access information on the World Wide Web.

Web server–A dedicated computer that delivers interactive text, graphics, digital audio or video over the World Wide Web to Web browser programs.

WWW–World Wide Web. A set of standards originally conceived at the Particle Physics Lab in Switzerland in 1990 which that allow all connected computers to easily communicate with each other through a mouse-based point-and-click interface.

B Electronic Commerce Online Resources

The best resource for information about any aspect of the Internet is the Internet itself. Sometimes the Internet is too good a resource, particularly since there is such a wealth of material online with very little quality control. It seems as if there are thousands of organizations and individuals presenting themselves as "Internet experts," complete with Web pages full of their "articles" and extracts of talks, courses, and seminars. More useful, in general, are the Web sites maintained by mainstream vendors, financial institutions participating in the digital marketplace, and organizations devoted to supporting the Internet and electronic commerce such as the Internet Society and CommerceNet.

The companion CD-ROM to this book includes URLs pointing to scores of different World Wide Web sites relating to electronic commerce. The reader is directed to these sites for the latest information about everything discussed in this book, as well as information that appeared too late to be included. The links on the CD-ROM are described here (as they are on the CD-ROM itself).

The links in this appendix and on the CD-ROM are subject to change without notice!

Other Internet resources include e-mail distribution lists and Usenet newsgroups. Some relevant ones are listed in the last section of this appendix.

Although every effort has been made to ensure accuracy and completeness, the state of the Internet is such that rapid change is inevitable. Neither this nor any other printed guide can hope to be up to date for any substantial length of time. As a result, although most of these links should be accurate and useable, the reader may prefer to search for more up-to-date links directly on the Internet if one of the cited links does not connect to the expected resource.

WORLD WIDE WEB RESOURCES

There are hundreds of thousands of information sources of all types available online, with many of them accessible through the World Wide Web. This section offers links and descriptions of some of those relating to electronic commerce, divided by categories.

ELECTRONIC COMMERCE COMPANIES

These companies make information available online about their products and services, all of which are directly related to electronic commerce. Many of these companies work together in strategic partnerships, licensing arrangements, consortia, and other arrangements. Some of the listed organizations are in the process of acquiring others, while some may have been spun off from other companies. The point is that these URLs should be considered starting points for searches, rather than authoritative addresses.

BroadVision, Inc.

http://www.broadvision.com/OneToOne/SessionMgr/home–page.jsp
Developing software to support foundations for electronic buying and selling.

Cardservice International

http://www.cardsvc.com
Offers credit card services to Internet merchants.

CheckFree Corporation

http://www.checkfree.com/
Provider of electronic payment services.

ClickShop.Com

http://clickshop.com/
Offers electronic shopping cart software called Shopping 770 to be added to electronic-shop Web pages.

CyberCash, Inc.

http://www.cybercash.com/
Provider of payment services for the Internet.

CyberSource

http://www.cybersource.com/
Provides real-time secure credit authorization software to process credit and debit cards.

Cylink Corporation

http://www.cylink.com
A licenser of public key cryptography algorithms.

eB2B.com

http://company.monster.com/eb2b/
Offers the Dynamic Web Ordering System for setting up online storefronts.

eCash Technologies, Inc.

http://www.digicash.com/Default.asp?bhjs=1&bhsw=1024&bhsh=768&bhswi=690&bhshi=539&bhflver=4&bhdir=0&bhje=1
Developers of digital currency systems.

Enterprise Integration Technologies

http://www.eit.com
A Verifone company, sells software and services in support of WWW commerce; was involved in the creation of CommerceNet, as well as the Secure HTTP specification.

Hewlett-Packard

http://welcome.hp.com/country/us/eng/welcome.htm
A leading provider of hardware and software in many vertical markets, including electronic commerce.

Internet Shopping Network

http://www.internet.net
Internet shopping services, offering computer-related products as well as online catalogs, floral arrangements, gifts, and more.

Internet World Media

http://www.iw.com
Publisher and trade-show sponsor with strong Internet orientation; provides much current information on this Web site.

Microsoft Corporation

http://www.microsoft.com
The software giant continues to lead the electronic commerce community.

Mondex USA

http://www.mondexusa.com
The U.S. branch of an international digital currency and smart cards supplier.

Netmarket Group Inc

http://www.netmarket.com
Produces secure Web server package using PGP.

Netscape Communications Inc.

http://home.netscape.com/
The latest information from the Web browser/server publisher.

Peregrine

http://sdweb02.peregrine.com/prgn–corp_ap/pstHomePage.cfm
Peregrine provides Infrastructure Management solutions to organizations that permit them to manage the availability and cost of their technology,

RSA Security

http://www.rsasecurity.com/
A licenser of public key cryptography algorithms.

SPYRUS

http://www.spyrus.com/
SPYRUS' products enable encryption, digital signatures, access control, and metering solutions for corporate IS, WWW/Internet and intranet applications, electronic commerce, and government applications.

Sun Microsystems

http://www.sun.com
Internet pioneer Sun offers network security solutions and many other products.

Surety.com

http://www.surety.com/index-nn.html
Offers "digital notary" services.

Technology Integration Group

http://www.tig.com
Provider of electronic commerce consulting and services.

Verifone

http://www.verifone.com
Leader in transaction automation industry; is acquiring EIT for its electronic commerce division.

VeriSign, Inc.

http://www.verisign.com
A spin-off from RSADSI, VeriSign provides public key certificates to individuals and companies.

FINANCIAL INSTITUTIONS

The number of banks offering some type of service over the Internet, from simple information services to actual banking services, is growing rapidly. The following banks are just a small sample of the large number that are already online; many more will certainly be there by the time you read this.

Bank of America

http://www.bofa.com/
Currently offering information services online.

Bank of Montreal

http://www.bmo.com/
Canadian bank with WWW services.

BankNet Electronic Banking Service

http://orders.mkn.co.uk/bank/
First bank to allow deposits online, in the United Kingdom.

Barclays Bank

http://www.barclays.co.uk/
Major UK bank offers information services online.

Citibank

http://www.citibank.com/
Major bank offering global services; site provides information about services.

KeyBank

http://www.keybank.com/
Major financial services and banking company.

MasterCard International

http://www.mastercard.com
International payment services organization, including credit and debit cards.

Security First Network Bank

http://www.sfnb.com
A pioneer in Internet-based banking.

Visa International

http://www.visa.com
International payment services organization, including credit and debit cards.

Wells Fargo Bank

http://www.wellsfargo.com/
Major bank, offering actual online services as well as information.

GENERAL CATALOG AND NEWS SERVICES

These general catalog services should be the first stop when tracking down new information sources. The interested reader will find some of them invaluable for tracking down the latest and most-updated sites for electronic commerce, as well as other topics. Also included here are some sites that are neither comprehensive nor catalogs, but that are maintained (usually by individuals) to provide pointers specifically to topics related to online commerce.

All-Internet Shopping Directory

http://www.all-internet.com
A directory of sites offering items for sale over the Internet, including e-mail sales.

AltaVista

http://www.altavista.com/
A very robust search engine provided by Digital Computer.

AT&T AnyWho Info: Toll Free

http://anywho.com/tf.html
Searchable toll-free numbers by company, category, and location.

Go.com

http://beta.go.com/
An Internet search service, covering more than just World Wide Web sites, including Usenet news searches and commercial/premium databases.

Lycos

http://www.lycos.com/
One of the most comprehensive Internet catalog sites.

The NandO Times

http://www2.nando.net
An online, 24-hour Internet "newspaper."

TIME.com

http://www.time.com/time/index.html
TIME.com is the daily online component of *TIME* magazine. TIME.com is updated several times a day with analysis of the day's news, plus photo essays, polls, message boards and chats, and features like Innovators of the 21st Century, Arts & Culture Sampler, and Campaign 2000.

WebCrawler

http://www.webcrawler.com/
Another Internet catalog site, operated by America Online.

Yahoo!

http://www.yahoo.com/
One of the most popular Internet catalog sites.

Yahoo/Electronic Commerce

http://dir.yahoo.com/Business_and_Economy/Electronic_Commerce/
Links to hundreds of sites relating to electronic commerce, online sales, marketing, electronic currencies, and online transactions.

ONLINE COMMERCE ORGANIZATIONS

Trade and industry groups are an important set of resources for any industry, but particularly for a new industry.

CommerceNet

http://www.commerce.net
CommerceNet is a global non-profit organization that has been evolving to meet the needs of companies doing electronic commerce.

Data Interchange Standards Association

http://www.disa.org
A standards body for Electronic Data Interchange (EDI).

Electronic Commerce Resource Center

http://www.ecrc.ctc.com/
A U.S. government-supported resource center for promoting the use of electronic commerce technologies by industry.

Financial Services Technology Consortium (FSTC)

http://www.fstc.org/
A non-profit consortium of financial services companies and academic and research organizations working toward the goal of enhancing the competitiveness of the U.S. financial services industry.

World Wide Web Consortium

http://www.w3.org/Consortium/
Consortium dedicated to development of the World Wide Web.

ONLINE MARKETING, BUYING, AND SELLING

There are literally thousands of electronic malls on the Internet. This list is hardly comprehensive, but gives pointers to a few of the more interesting Web pages devoted to buying and selling, as well as some of the more typical digital malls. For a more complete and current listing of digital malls, check one of the Internet search engines.

Amazon.com

http://www.amazon.com
A major online bookseller.

America Online

http://www.aol.com
The online service provides numerous opportunities for shopping using their own software interface, as well as linking members out to the Internet for Web-based shopping.

CompuServe

http://www.compuserve.com/compuserve/default.asp
In addition to their online service, CompuServe offers private network applications for their customers looking for ways to transact business in a "closed-circuit" environment.

TechSavvy.com

http://www.techsavvy.com/
A powerful technical Web site that helps you identify suppliers, locate critical information, and order worldwide standards, military specifications, millions of parts, and hard-to-find historical data.

Internet Shopping Network

http://www.isn.com
Online shopping for electronics and other products.

SPECIFICATIONS AND STANDARDS

One of the most important reasons why the Internet is moving so rapidly to become a medium for commercial transactions is that it is a system with open standards. Here is a place to look for the open standards being proposed and developed by some of the participants in the electronic commerce marketplace.

Secure Electronic Transaction Protocol (SET)

http://www.mastercard.com/shoponline/set/

COMMERCENET

CommerceNet is a global non-profit organization that has been evolving to meet the needs of companies doing electronic commerce since 1994. This community of influential e-commerce decision-makers is over 700 strong, with a focus on business-to-business e-commerce worldwide. CommerceNet is uniquely poised to talk about e-commerce and to actively work in collaboration with industry executives, academia, entrepreneurs, and investors to promote and advance e-commerce globally. CommerceNet is the source of information, education, research, and inspiration for the unfolding e-commerce marketplace.

CommerceNet Charter

The CommerceNet charter includes the following goals:

- *Advise* CommerceNet members of current/upcoming regulatory and legislative activities, in the International, Federal, and State arenas, that will impede or enhance the growth of Internet commerce.
- *Develop* recommended CommerceNet positions, working in conjunction with appropriate CommerceNet resources (task forces, members, staff, etc.).
- *External voice:* Through proactive advocacy and educational efforts, communicate CommerceNet's positions to appropriate government entities.
- *Cooperate* with other advocacy organizations to amplify CommerceNet's positions, when appropriate.

The entire enterprise is oriented toward the goal of making electronic commerce a superior alternative to paper-based commerce.

CommerceNet Participation

Participation in CommerceNet can take the form of full corporate member, for large organizations; however, this option may cost $40,000 per year. Associate memberships are available for as little as $6,000 annually for smaller businesses (those with less than $20 million in annual revenue).

For those who do not need or wish to participate as members of the CommerceNet consortium, subscriptions are available for $500 annually, with a $360 initiation fee. Subscribers are entitled to inclusion in CommerceNet directories and Internet software and information packages, among other benefits. Subscribers may also purchase Internet host services from third-party Internet service providers at special rates.

What CommerceNet Offers

CommerceNet offers a forum for industry leaders to discuss issues and deploy pilot applications, and from these to define standards and best business practices for using the Internet for electronic commerce. Through these efforts, CommerceNet will help this emerging industry evolve to common standards and practices so that users will see a seamless web of resources. Participating companies get additional assistance from CommerceNet, including the following:

- Provides research on emerging e-commerce business and technology trends and developments
- Offers networking opportunities with the key players in the market
- Advocates consistent and appropriate public policy
- Demonstrates and pilots projects to validate new models and concepts
- Creates new business opportunities through promotion and partnerships providing mentoring opportunities with established leaders in electronic commerce
- Promotes a framework that encompasses interoperability among developing electronic commerce standards and applications
- Expands a company's activities throughout the world by engaging local and regional organizations to establish regionally based programs

■ Focuses on the support and expansion of a worldwide sponsorship that includes both end users and suppliers of technology

Another key benefit comes from CommerceNet's influence on government and standards organizations. For example, CommerceNet is consulted by various organizations (including the White House) to represent the business and industry perspective of electronic commerce. This is your company's opportunity to help define the next-generation electronic commerce and to ensure a consistent voice in the industry for its use and expansion.

C   Guide to the CD-ROM

The companion CD-ROM to this book includes everything you need to get started with Internet commerce.

- The complete text of the Secure Electronic Transaction (SET) protocol in MS Word and PDF formats
- The Adobe Acrobat Reader software for both Windows 3.1 and Windows 95
- The Microsoft Internet Explorer browser software

Use of Adobe Acrobat Reader versions should be restricted to the appropriate operating systems. More current versions of Adobe Acrobat Reader are available through the Internet.

- The CyberCash digital cash electronic payment system that works with your Internet browser
- Links and pointers to scores of different electronic commerce, digital currency, and online transaction sites and Internet resources

URLs (links) are subject to change without notice!

This appendix describes how to install and use these materials.

If you already have Internet connectivity and a World Wide Web browser, it may not be necessary to install the Microsoft Internet Explorer software. Please skip to the last sections to read about accessing the World Wide Web links document and protocol specification documents using your existing software.

If you already have Internet connectivity and a World Wide Web browser, but do not have a CyberCash digital wallet, skip to the second section to read about installing the CyberCash client to work with your existing Web browser.

MICROSOFT INTERNET EXPLORER

Microsoft Internet Explorer software for both Windows 3.1 and Windows 95 users is provided in case your current Internet browser software does not support SSL and the related security features discussed in previous chapters. As the size of these files continues to grow, so that downloading them takes even more time, this software is provided to get you going quickly.

This section is offered to help you locate the software on the CD and begin the installation process. The installation wizards are complete and self-explanatory, with context-sensitive help.

WIN 3.1

To install the Microsoft Internet Explorer for Windows 3.1, use File Manager to locate and execute the file d:\MSIE\WIN31\DLFUL30F.EXE.

You may wish to visit the Microsoft Web site for the latest information on Microsoft Internet Explorer for Windows 3.1 at

http://www.microsoft.com

WIN 95

To install the Microsoft Internet Explorer for Windows 95, use Windows Explorer to locate and execute the file d:\MSIE\WIN31\DLFUL30F.EXE.

You may wish to visit the Microsoft Web site for the latest information on Microsoft Internet Explorer for Windows 95 at

http://www.microsoft.com/

Attempting to install Microsoft Internet Explorer for Windows 95 on Windows 98 or above may cause instability to your system, and running MSIE302M95.exe initiates a warning to that effect as shown here: "This program may not run correctly on Windows 98 because of enhanced operating system features. For

information about obtaining an updated version, or help regarding workarounds for known issues, click Details. If after reviewing the help topic you still want to continue, click Run Program."

ACROBAT READER

As mentioned earlier, the SET documentation is included on the CD in two formats: Microsoft Word version 6.0/7.0 and PDF format.

In case you do not have easy access to a word processor, we have included Adobe Acrobat Reader 3.0, which can be used to review the PDF versions of the SET documentation.

Adobe Acrobat Reader 3.0 automatically installs a plug-in that allows it to work with Netscape Navigator 2.0 or 3.0, and an ActiveX control that allows it to work with Microsoft Internet Explorer 3.0 or greater. This reader does not have an expiration date.

For Netscape Navigator 4.0 and above, please refer to the Adobe Web site at: http://www.adobe.com/prodindex/acrobat/readstep.html

SOFTWARE VERSIONS

Adobe Acrobat Reader software versions for Windows 3.1 and Windows 95 are included separately.

WIN 95

On the CD provided with the book, you will find the file ar32e30.exe in the d:\acrobat\win95\ subdirectory. Before running the program, it is important to close any Web browsers you may have running. You can use the Windows file manager to locate and run the program. Simply double-click on the file d:\acrobat\win95\ar32e30.exe. The installation program will provide complete installation information as the installation process proceeds.

If there is a failure at any point during the installation of Acrobat Reader 3.0, the installer performs a complete uninstall. For this reason, it is important not to close the installer application by using its close box in the upper right corner of the background window after clicking the "Thank

You" dialog box that appears at the end of the installation. If you wait for a second or two, the installer will automatically close the background windows after the installation is complete.

The installation procedure will ask you to read and accept the Electronic End-User License Agreement.

Minimum Hardware Requirements

- i386, i486, Pentium, or Pentium Pro processor-based personal computer
- Microsoft Windows 95, or Windows NT 3.51 or later
- 8MB of RAM (16MB for Windows NT) for Acrobat Reader
- 10MB of available hard-disk space

Recommended Hardware Requirements

- Pentium processor-based personal computer
- Windows 95
- 16MB of RAM
- 10MB of available hard-disk space

WINDOWS 3.1 AND 3.11

On the CD provided with this book, you will find the file ar16e30.exe in the d:\acrobat\win31\ subdirectory. Before running the program, it is important to close any Web browsers you may have running. You can use the Windows file manager to locate and run the program. Simply double-click on the file d:\acrobat\win95\ar16e30.exe. The installation program will provide complete installation information as the installation process proceeds.

If there is a failure at any point during the installation of Acrobat Reader 3.0, the installer performs a complete uninstall. For this reason, it is important not to close the installer application by using its close box in the upper right corner of the background window after clicking the "Thank You" dialog box that appears at the end of the installation. If you wait for a second or two, the installer will automatically close the background windows after the installation is complete.

The installation procedure will ask you to read and accept the Electronic End-User License Agreement.

Minimum Hardware Requirements

- i386, i486, Pentium, or Pentium Pro processor-based personal computer
- Microsoft Windows 3.1 or Windows 3.11 or later
- 8MB of RAM for Acrobat Reader
- 5MB of available hard-disk space

Recommended Hardware Requirements

- Pentium processor-based personal computer
- Microsoft Windows 3.1 or Windows 3.11 or later
- 12MB of available hard-disk space

CYBERCASH DIGITAL WALLET

The companion CD also includes the CyberCash digital wallet software. Using either your Windows Explorer or File Manager, you can install CyberCash by executing d:\CYB_CASH\WINCYBER.EXE.

CyberCash software requires at least an 80386 25-MHz PC running Windows 3.1 or higher or Windows 95. It also requires at least 2MB of free hard-drive space and 4MB of RAM.

This version of the CyberCash software includes the CyberCoin features that will allow you to use your software to make micropayments (i.e., less than $10).

We take a very thorough look at the installation process in Chapter 6, "Electronic Payment Systems."

You can also check the CyberCash Web site at http://www. cybercash.com/ for the latest information on CyberCash and the wallet software.

WORLD WIDE WEB LINKS DOCUMENT

The CD-ROM includes a special file containing links to the World Wide Web resources referenced in Appendix B, "Electronic Commerce Online

Resources." If you already have World Wide Web connectivity, you can go directly to any of these sites by opening this file with your Web browser program. To do so, put the CD-ROM in your CD-ROM drive, start your Web browser, and point the browser to the following URL:

file:d:///commerce/links.htm

Once loaded, you should be able to click on any of the links to reach the referenced electronic commerce Web pages.

The Internet is a rapidly evolving environment, and although every effort has been made to ensure that the URLs included in this book and CD-ROM are accurate and current, some will undoubtedly change over time. In the event that a listed site is not accessible, the reader is urged to search for it using an Internet search site or some other mechanism.

SET PROTOCOL DOCUMENTS

The CD-ROM also includes the documents detailing the Secure Electronic Transaction (SET) protocol published in June of 1997.

The SET documents are organized into three books:

Book 1	Business Description	Contains background information and processing flows for SET. Intended as a primer on software that both interfaces with payment systems and uses public-key cryptography.
Book 2	Programmer's Guide	Contains the technical specifications for the SET protocol. Primarily intended for use by software vendors who intend to create cardholder and merchant software.
Book 3	Formal Protocol Definition	Contains the formal protocol definition for SET. Primarily intended for use by: • Cryptographers analyzing security

- Writers producing programming guides
- System programmers developing cryptographic and messaging primitives.

Standards and specifications are updated and upgraded regularly to reflect changes and improvements. These documents, as well as many others, are available online through links defined in the World Wide Web links document described earlier. If in doubt, please refer to the online versions of these documents rather than the versions included on this CD-ROM.

SET files have been published in two document formats: Microsoft Word (d:\set\word) and PDF (Adobe Portable Document Format) (d:\set\pdf) based on the format in which they were prepared.

MICROSOFT WORD FILES

If you are using a word processing program that can view a Word 6.0 file, start your word processor, and open files in the d:\set\word subdirectory on the CD-ROM.

The Word version of the SET documents is spread over several Word files. All the files for each book are contained in a single directory for each book.

Book 1 is contained in the directory d:\set\word\book_1, which contains the following files:

ReadMe.txt	Set_Bk1.DOC
SEC41.DOC	SEC42.DOC
SEC43.DOC	SEC44.DOC
SEC45.DOC	SEC46.DOC

Book 2 is contained in the directory d:\set\word\book_2, which contains the following files:

ReadMe.txt	Part1.DOC
Part2.DOC	Part3.DOC
Appendix.DOC	

Only one file contains Book 3; it is found in **d:\set\word\book_3**:

SET_BK3.DOC

PDF FILES

If you do not have access to a word processing program that can view a Word 6.0 file, you can use the Adobe Acrobat Reader software discussed earlier.

Once the reader is installed, run the Acrobat program. Use the File and Open commands to open files in the d:\set\pdf subdirectory of the CD-ROM.

The PDF version of the SET documents is contained in three files.

- To view Book 1, select d:\set\pdf\set_bk1.pdf
- To view Book 2, select d:\set\pdf\set_bk2.pdf
- To view Book 3, select d:\set\pdf\set_bk3.pdf

DISCLAIMER!

The information contained in this appendix and CD-ROM is provided on an as-is basis. Software and system requirement recommendations contained herein can be followed at your own risk. Charles River Media and the author bear no responsibility whatsoever for any damage resulting from use of the software and system requirement recommendations contained in this appendix or CD-ROM. Nothing in this appendix or CD-ROM should be viewed as a commitment by Charles River Media and the author to release or maintain any product, version, feature, or performance level at any time.

D Electronic Data Interchange Transaction Codes

M uch of the information contained in a transaction set is the same as the data found in business documents used in paper-based systems. A transaction set is a specific type of business data exchanged between parties using EDI. It consists of the specific data that comprises a business document, such as a purchase order or an invoice.

ANSI X12 transaction sets can be grouped together by business functionality. Examples of these groups are Engineering and Management, Manufacturing, Quality and Safety, Transportation, Finance and Insurance, Warehousing, and Purchasing. Each of these groups contains transaction sets that support a similar business function. For example, the Purchasing group transactions consist of Requests for Quotation, Purchase Orders, Purchase Order Acknowledgments, Purchase Order Changes, and Material Dispositions. As a more specific example, the X12 standard for a purchase order is called the 850 transaction set. Additionally, each transaction has a unique standard designation. For example, the X12 standard designation for the 850 purchase order transaction set is X12.1. Table D.1 lists all of the EDI ANSI X12 transaction set codes.

TABLE D.1 X12 Transaction Set Index

Transaction Code	Transaction Type
104	Air Shipment Information
110	Air Freight Details and Invoice
125	Multilevel Railcar Load Details
126	Vehicle Application Advice
127	Vehicle Baying Order

(continued)

TABLE D.1 *(continued)*

Transaction Code	Transaction Type
128	Dealer Information
129	Vehicle Carrier Rate Update
130	Student Educational Record (Transcript)
131	Student Educational Record (Transcript) Acknowledgment
135	Student Loan Application
139	Student Loan Guarantee Result
140	Product Registration
141	Product Service Claim Response
142	Product Service Claim
143	Product Service Notification
144	Student Loan Transfer and Status Verification
146	Request for Student Educational Record (Transcript)
147	Response to Request for Student Educational Record (Transcript)
148	Report of Injury or Illness
151	Electronic Filing of Tax Return Data Acknowledgment
152	Statistical Government Information
154	Uniform Commercial Code Filing
161	Train Sheet
170	Revenue Receipts Statement
180	Return Merchandise Authorization and Notification
186	Laboratory Reporting
190	Student Enrollment Verification
196	Contractor Cost Data Reporting
204	Motor Carrier Shipment Information
210	Motor Carrier Freight Details and Invoice
213	Motor Carrier Shipment Status Inquiry
214	Transportation Carrier Shipment Status Message
217	Motor Carrier Loading and Route Guide
218	Motor Carrier Tariff Information
250	Purchase Order Shipment Management Document
251	Pricing Support

TABLE D.1 *(continued)*

Transaction Code	Transaction Type
260	Application for Mortgage Insurance Benefits
263	Residential Mortgage Insurance Application Response
264	Mortgage Loan Default Status
270	Health Care Eligibility/Benefit Inquiry
271	Health Care Eligibility/Benefit Information
272	Property and Casualty Loss Notification
276	Health Care Claim Status Request
277	Health Care Claim Status Notification
290	Cooperative Advertising Agreements
300	Reservation (Booking Request) (Ocean)
301	Confirmation (Ocean)
303	Booking Cancellation (Ocean)
304	Shipping Instructions
309	U.S. Customs Manifest
310	Freight Receipt and Invoice (Ocean)
311	Canadian Customs Information
312	Arrival Notice (Ocean)
313	Shipment Status Inquiry (Ocean)
315	Status Details (Ocean)
317	Delivery/Pickup Order
319	Terminal Information
322	Terminal Operations Activity (Ocean)
323	Vessel Schedule and Itinerary (Ocean)
324	Vessel Stow Plan (Ocean)
325	Consolidation of Goods In Container
326	Consignment Summary List
350	U.S. Customs Release Information
352	U.S. Customs Carrier General Order Status
353	U.S. Customs Events Advisory Details
354	U.S. Customs Automated Manifest Archive Status
355	U.S. Customs Manifest Acceptance/Rejection

(continues)

TABLE D.1 *(continued)*

Transaction Code	Transaction Type
356	Permit to Transfer Request
361	Carrier Interchange Agreement (Ocean)
404	Rail Carrier Shipment Information
410	Rail Carrier Freight Details and Invoice
414	Rail Carrier Settlements
417	Rail Carrier Waybill Interchange
418	Rail Advance Interchange Consist
419	Advance Car Disposition
420	Car Handling Information
421	Estimated Time of Arrival and Car Scheduling
422	Shipper's Car Order
425	Rail Waybill Request
426	Rail Revenue Waybill
429	Railroad Retirement Activity
431	Railroad Station Master File
440	Shipment Weights
466	Rate Request
468	Rate Docket Journal Log
485	Rate-making Action
490	Rate Group Definition
492	Miscellaneous Rates
494	Scale Rate Table
511	Requisition
517	Material Obligation Validation
527	Material Due—In and Receipt
536	Logistics Reassignment
561	Contract Abstract
567	Contract Completion Status
568	Contract Payment Management Report
601	Shipper's Export Declaration
602	Transportation Services Tender
622	Intermodal Ramp Activity

TABLE D.1 (*continued*)

Transaction Code	Transaction Type
805	Contract Pricing Proposal
806	Project Schedule Reporting
810	Invoice
811	Consolidated Service Invoice/Statement
812	Credit/Debit Adjustment
813	Electronic Filing of Tax Return Data
815	Cryptographic Service Message
816	Organizational Relationships
818	Commission Sales Report
819	Operating Expense Statement
820	Payment Order/Remittance Advice
821	Financial Information Reporting
822	Customer Account Analysis
823	Lockbox
824	Application Advice
826	Tax Information Reporting
827	Financial Return Notice
828	Debit Authorization
829	Payment Cancellation Request
830	Planning Schedule with Release Capability
831	Application Control Totals
832	Price/Sales Catalog
833	Residential Mortgage Credit Report Order
834	Benefit Enrollment and Maintenance
835	Health Care Claim Payment/Advice
836	Contract Award
837	Health Care Claim
838	Trading Partner Profile
839	Project Cost Reporting
840	Request for Quotation
841	Specifications/Technical Information

(*continues*)

TABLE D.1 *(continued)*

Transaction Code	Transaction Type
842	Nonconformance Report
843	Response to Request for Quotation
844	Product Transfer Account Adjustment
845	Price Authorization Acknowledgment/Status
846	Inventory Inquiry/Advice
847	Material Claim
848	Material Safety Data Sheet
849	Response to Product Transfer Account Adjustment
850	Purchase Order
851	Asset Schedule
852	Product Activity Data
853	Routing and Carrier Instruction
854	Shipment Delivery Discrepancy Information
855	Purchase Order Acknowledgment
856	Ship Notice/Manifest
857	Shipment and Billing Notice
858	Shipment Information
859	Freight Invoice
860	Purchase Order Change Request (Buyer Initiated)
861	Receiving Advice/Acceptance Certificate
862	Shipping Schedule
863	Report of Test Results
864	Text Message
865	Purchase Order Change Acknowledgment/Request (Seller Initiated)
866	Production Sequence
867	Product Transfer and Resale Report
868	Electronic Form Structure
869	Order Status Inquiry
870	Order Status Report
872	Residential Mortgage Insurance Application
875	Grocery Products Purchase Order

TABLE D.1 *(continued)*

Transaction Code	Transaction Type
876	Grocery Products Purchase Order Change
878	Product Authorization/Deauthorization
879	Price Change
880	Grocery Products Invoice
882	Direct Store Delivery Summary Information
888	Item Maintenance
889	Promotion Announcement
893	Item Information Request
894	Delivery/Return Base Record
895	Delivery/Return Acknowledgment or Adjustment
896	Product Dimension Maintenance
920	Loss or Damage Claim (General Commodities)
924	Loss or Damage Claim (Motor Vehicle)
925	Claim Tracer
926	Claim Status Report and Tracer Reply
928	Automotive Inspection Detail
940	Warehouse Shipping Order
943	Warehouse Stock Transfer Shipment Advice
944	Warehouse Stock Transfer Receipt Advice
945	Warehouse Shipping Advice
947	Warehouse Inventory Adjustment Advice
980	Functional Group Totals
990	Response to a Load Tender
996	File Transfer
997	Functional Acknowledgment
998	Set Cancellation

E | E-Commerce Conferences

The following is a list of the major e-commerce conferences and trade shows, including contact information regarding upcoming conference dates and locations. The telephone numbers and URLs are subject to change without notice.

2nd Annual eCustomer Intimacy
(887) 423-3111
http://www.icdevents.com

Auto Insurance Online
(800) 882-8684
http://www.iqpc.com

B2B Electronic Publishing
(212) 967-0095
http://www.americanbusinessmedia.com/news/institute.htm

B2B eMarketplaces
(800) 778-1997
http://www.gartner.com

B2B eMarketplaces
(800) 882-8684
http://www.iqpc.com

Beauty & Fashion Online
(800) 882-8684
http://www.iqpc.com

BidCon
(800) 882-8684
http://www.wbresearch.com

Call Center Demo & Conference
(888) 428-3976
http://www.ctexpo.com

Call Center Week
(800) 882-8684
http://www.callcenterweek.com

Chemicals Online
(800) 882-8684
http://www.iqpc.com

Consumer Electronics on the Internet
(800) 882-8684
http://www.iqpc.com

Consumer Online European Forum
(800) 611-1693
http://www.jup.com

Contact
(212) 885-2718
http://www.wbr.co.uk

Converting E-Browsers into E-Buyers
(800) 882-8684
http://www.iqpc.com

Corporate Portals
(800) 767-2755
http://www.dci.com

CRM Demo and Conference
(888) 428-3976
http://www.ctexpo.com

Customer Relationship Management Conference & Exposition
(978) 470-3880
http://www.dci.com

Cyberbranding
(800) 882-8684
http://www.iqpc.com

Cyber-Sabotage!
(800) 882-8684
http://www.iqpc.com

CyberSummit
(510) 649-1100 x20
http://www.globaltouch.com

Digital Kids: Online Kids Forum
(800) 611-1693
http://www.jup.com

Direct Response eMail Marketing Strategies
(800) 882-8684
http://www.iqpc.com

Driving E-Business—1:1 Advice
(781) 792-2669
http://www.gigaweb.com

Dynamic ePricing
(800) 882-8684
http://www.iqpc.com

E-Apparel
(800) 882-8486
http://www.iqpc.com

eB2B Marketplace World
(804) 643-8375
http://www.emarketworld.com

eB2B World Conference & Exhibition
(978) 470-3880
http://www.dci.com

e-Baby
(800) 882-8684
http://www.kidpowerx.com

E-Business for the Aerospace Industry
(44) 0 207 375 7575
http://www.firstconf.com

E-Business in the Construction Industry
(800) 274-0122
http://www.bpinews.com/ebizconstr.html

E-Business Summit
Co-sponsored by *eCommerce Business* magazine
(617) 247-1511
http://www.delphigroup.com

eCommerce and Global Business Forum
(310) 206-5317
http://www.ac.com/ecommerce/ecom_conferences.html

e-Commerce Customer Care
(212) 768-7277
http://www.the-dma.org

E-Commerce for Oil & Gas US
(800) 814 3459
http://www.firstconf.com

E-Commerce for Travel East
(800) 814-3459
http://www.firstconf.com

eConsolidation
(800) 882-8684
http://www.iqpc.com

e-Construction & Contracting
(800) 882-8684
http://www.iqpc.com

eCRM
(800) 882-8684
http://www.iqpc.com

eCustomer Conference and Exposition
(800) 767-2577
http://www.dci.com

e-finance
(800) 777-8774
http://www.efinanceexpo.com

e-Freight World
(800) 882-8684
http://www.iqpc.com

e-Fulfillment
(800) 882-8684
http://www.iqpc.com

eHealth & Fitness
(800) 882-8684
http://www.iqpc.com

e-Insurance
(800) 882-8684
http://www.iqpc.com

Electronic Commerce for Pharmaceuticals
(800) 814 3459
http://www.firstconf.com

Electronic Commerce World
(800) 336-4887
http://www.ecomworld.com

E-Logistics
(44) 0-171-691-3000
http://www.wbr.co.uk

e-Logistics
(800) 882-8684
http://www.iqpc.com

eMediatainment World
(804) 643-8375
http://www.emediatainmentworld.com

eMediatainmentWorld
(310) 473-4147
http://www.emediatainmentworld.com

E-Partnerships & Alliances
(800) 882-8486
http://www.iqpc.com

e-Pets
(800) 882-8684
http://www.iqpc.com

ePurchasing Week
(800) 882-8684
http://www.iqpc.com

eTail Asia
(212) 885-2718
http://www.wbresearch.com

eTail
(44) 0 171 691 3000
http://www.wbr.co.uk

e-Travel & Tourism Canada
(800) 882-8684
http://www.iqpc.com

eTravel World
(804) 643-8375
http://www.etravelworld.com

eVenture World
(804) 643-8375
http://www.eVentureWorld.com

Fall Internet World
(800) 500-1959
http://www.internet.com

Financial Services Forum
(800) 611-1693
http://www.jup.com

Forrester's Finance & Technology Forum
(888) 343-6786
http://www.forrester.com

Global Online Advertising Forum
(800) 611-1693
http://www.jup.com

Global Privacy Summit
(703) 683-5004
http://www.privacycouncil.com

Global Wireless Forum
(800) 611-1693
http://www.jup.com

Home Furnishings Online
(800) 882-8684
http://www.iqpc.com

Industrial Equipment, Supplies & Inventory Online
(800) 882-8684
http://www.iqpc.com

Internet Commerce Conference & Expo
(800) 667-4423
http://www.iceexpo.com

Internet Commerce Forum—Australia
(800) 611-1693
http://www.jup.com

Internet Commerce Forum
(800) 611-1693
http://www.jup.com

Internet Content West
(800) 814-3459
http://www.firstconf.com

Internet Payments
(800) 882-8684
http://www.iqpc.com

Internet Privacy & ePersonalization
(800) 882-8684
http://www.iqpc.com

Internet Telecom Expo
(888) 428-3976
http://www.ctexpo.com

IT for Travel and Tourism Industry Europe
(44) 0 207 375 7575
http://www.firstconf.com/travel

LatinOnline
(212) 885-2718
http://www.wbresearch.com

L-Commerce: The Location Services & GPS Technology Summit
800) 647-7600
http://www.worldresearchgroup.com

Managing Channel Conflict
(800) 882-8684
http://www.iqpc.com

Managing Transaction Strategies in eMarketplaces
(800) 882-8684
http://www.iqpc.com

Marketing to College Students Online and Offline
(800) 882-8684
http://www.iqpc.com

Mastering e-Commerce Fulfillment
(800) 882-8684
http://www.iqpc.com

Mcommerce
800-882-8684
http://www.wbresearch.com

Mindshare: The Jupiter Executive Forum
(800) 611-1693
http://www.jup.com

Net Markets
(800) 882-8684
http://www.iqpc.com

Net.Finance
(800) 882-8684
http://www.wbresearch.com

NetWorld+Interop
(605) 378-1058
http://www.zdevents.com

NRF.com-Retailing and Technology
(310) 230-9040
http://www.nrf.com events

Online Advertising Forum
(800) 611-1693
http://www.jup.com

Online Entertainment & Media
(800) 882-8684
http://www.iqpc.com

Online Financial Services for Latin America
(800) 882-8684
http://www.iqpc.com

Online Market Research & Web-Based Surveys Summit
(800) 882-8684
http://www.iqpc.com

Online Market Research for Product & Concept Testing
(800) 882-8684
http://www.iqpc.com

Online Media & Entertainment
(800) 882-8684
http://www.iqpc.com

Online Retail
(800) 882-8684
http://www.iqpc.com

Online Retailing for Wireless Products & Services
(800) 882-8684
http://www.iqpc.com

Outsourcing E-Business
(800) 882-8684
http://www.iqpc.com

Plug.In: The Jupiter Online Music Forum
(800) 882-8684
http://www.jup.com

Restructuring Training for e-Business
(800) 882-8684
http://www.iqpc.com

Shopping Forum
(800) 611-1693
http://www.jup.com

Strategic Planning for e-Business
(800) 882-8684
http://www.iqpc.com

Supply Web Exchange
(617) 527-4626
http://www.supplywebexchange.com

Teen Power
(800) 882-8684
http://www.iqpc.com

The Best Practices in Online Retail
(800) 882-8684
http://www.iqpc.com

The World Wireless Security & Payment Summit
(800) 882-8684
http://www.iqpc.com

Web Data Mining
(800) 882-8684
http://www.iqpc.com

Web Marketing World
(206) 285-0305
http://www.thunderlizard.com

Web Site Content Management for B2B
(800) 882-8684
http://www.iqpc.com

Web Site Content Management for Pharmaceuticals
(800) 882-8684
http://www.iqpc.com

Web Site Re-Launch
(800) 882-8684
http://www.iqpc.com

Web-Based Customer Service Summit
(800) 882-8684
http://www.iqpc.com

Wireless Computing
(800) 767-2755
http://www.dci.com

Wireless Content Management
(800) 882-8684
http://www.iqpc.com

Wireless Partnership & Alliances Congress
(800) 882-8684
http://www.iqpc.com

x @d:tech New York
(804) 643-8375
http://www.ad-tech.com

x @d-tech
(804) 643-8375
http://www.ad-tech.com

x Customer Relationship Management Conference & Exposition
(800) 767-2755
http://www.dci.com

F PDG Shopping Cart

Included on this CD-ROM is a free, 30-day trial version of PDG Shopping Cart for Microsoft Windows NT and multiple UNIX platforms.

PDG Shopping Cart is PDG Software's core product and serves as a complete e-commerce solution. Some of its most notable features include real-time shipping cost calculation from UPS, easily customizable HTML templates, compatibility with multiple online payment processors, and the ability to sell softgoods (i.e., downloadable products such as computer software, electronic music files, and electronic documents).

ABOUT PDG SOFTWARE

PDG Software, Inc. provides Internet commerce solutions for small to mid-sized companies. Based in the Atlanta area, the company was formed in 1997 and has a growing list of customers in the United States and abroad. Its core product, the PDG Shopping Cart, allows customers to create a customized Internet commerce Web site. The company also offers merchants a 30-day free trial period for its software and has been lauded for its customer-centric focus. PDG Software Inc. is a certified Microsoft [NASDAQ: MSFT] Solutions Provider and a certified Sun Catalyst Developer [NASDAQ: SUNW]. Visit their Web site at http://www.pdgsoft.com.

Other Products from PDG Software

PDG Software offers a full suite of e-commerce solutions in addition to its PDG Shopping Cart application. The PDG product suite includes PDG Shopping Mall, PDG Distributor, PDG Auction, and PDG Commerce. For more information and/or trial downloads, please visit http://www.pdgsoft.com.

Index